The Economics of Criminal Behavior

A Survey of Selected Topics

Second Edition

WRITTEN AND EDITED BY RON LIGGETT
University of Texas at Arlington

cognella® | ACADEMIC PUBLISHING

Bassim Hamadeh, CEO and Publisher
Carrie Montoya, Manager, Revisions and Author Care
Kaela Martin, Project Editor
Abbey Hastings, Associate Production Editor
Jess Estrella, Senior Graphic Designer
Natalie Lakosil, Licensing Manager
Natalie Piccotti, Senior Marketing Manager
Kassie Graves, Director of Acquisitions and Sales
Jamie Giganti, Senior Managing Editor

Printed in the United States of America.

ISBN: 978-1-5165-1298-0 (pbk) / 978-1-5165-1299-7 (br)

cognella® | ACADEMIC PUBLISHING

CONTENTS

ACKNOWLEDGMENTS

There are many reasons to be involved in academia, but certainly a key reason is an individual's appreciation of the learning process and his or her continuous quest for knowledge and understanding. Putting together this textbook has been a significant learning experience. But one's desire for learning must be directed and encouraged, and in this area, I have been aided by several "mentors" during my time at the University of Texas at Arlington. Firstly, I am grateful to Daniel Himarios and Roger Meiners for their consistent and steady leadership in the Economics department; through the years, I have benefitted not only from their economic perspectives, but also from their wise counsel and mentoring.

"Talking shop" with colleagues has also been helpful, and I am particularly appreciative of the stimulating debate offered by Bill Crowder and Mike Ward on areas germane to this publication. Two former senior faculty members, Ryan Amacher and Rick Wilson, likewise served in mentoring roles, and I was enriched by their vast array of knowledge as well as their readiness to sort through my inquisitive streak of questions.[A,B]

Several other current and former colleagues have helped shape my economic world view, so thank you to Craig Depken, Jane Himarios, Kathy Kelly, Courtney LaFountain, Aaron Smallwood, Roger Wehr, Dennis Wilson, and Tim Wunder. I also wish to thank former colleague and instructor Clif Chamberlain for helping spark an interest in economics and for providing me with my first teaching opportunity.

A Professor Rick Wilson is now retired. His enthusiasm in the classroom was renowned on the UT-Arlington campus and, as a teacher, he was truly "one of a kind" in a grand way.

B Dr. Ryan Amacher retired from UT-Arlington in 2013. Sadly, he passed away November 25, 2016 at the age of 71. A book he authored in 2012, *A Baby Boomer's Guide to Their Second Sixties*, is a rather entertaining read on a variety of topics although with an occasional touch of crude humor tossed in. As the title suggests, it is written to offer some utility to those nearing or entering their "second sixties."

Getting any text to print is a huge task and one also worthy of acknowledgement, so thanks to Cognella again for their professionalism. This is an impressive publishing group and one with a bright future. I have been fortunate to have extremely talented editors with Jessica Knott on my first edition and Kaela Martin on this current project. Thank you, both. Likewise, thank you to Carrie Montoya for her patience and encouragement as another new west coast friend as well as Abbey Hastings for carrying this edition down the home stretch. Thank you also to Jess Estrella for her creativity and willingness to work with me on the cover for both editions.

Closer to home, thank you to Tim Liggett for providing proof work for several chapters. Thanks to Kelsey Liggett for her proof work, but mostly for three very clever cartoons. (It's nice to have other graduate degrees in the family!) Also, I remain appreciative to Rachel Goold, Barbara Sellers, and Linda Wilson for their insight and helpful input on the first edition of this text.

Finally, one more special thank you is offered to Dr. Lawrence Ziegler. Dr. Ziegler was the consumate professor and an outstanding teacher and mentor in my early years in the department, and before he died in 1996, he directed and encouraged me to begin teaching a course on the economics of crime.

PREFACE

By Ron Liggett

A local grocery store that I used to frequent employed a pleasant young lady to stand near the front door and greet customers as they came in. Or so it appeared. In reality, her duty was to observe and watch for consumer theft, which could vary from an individual attempting to get out with a 12-pack of beer (either discreetly or at a sprint) to those who tried to conceal items in or under their clothing in stealth-like fashion. Popular items on the theft list—other than beer—were infant formula, shaving accessories, and even packaged meat. The result of all those shenanigans? For the grocery store, higher labor costs to keep the young lady in her security role and lost revenue from the "shrinkage," or theft, of product. And from a different perspective, rumination in an effort to determine the underlying and decisive element that might have motivated the perpetrator. What were they thinking?!

This example is a simple one that, no doubt, is replicated innumerable times every day across the country. But it is representative of a basic scenario involving criminal behavior, resource allocation, and choice. Accordingly, with these and other situations in mind, this textbook was put together for use in a one-semester course dealing with economics and criminal behavior. The course will involve the following:

- The use of economic theory to help explain criminal behavior
- An analysis of the range of relationships that exist between economic conditions and crime
- A study (case and otherwise) of various economic crimes, enforcement issues, and other selected topics.

The approach for the class is to focus on policy issues over technical aspects. In fact, I tell students that the curriculum should not be technically difficult for those with a comprehension of basic economic principles. Additionally, with a wide range of debatable social topics and crimes occurring literally every minute of every day, the opportunity for class discussion is seemingly endless. Consider, for example, the following questions:

- How far will the drug legalization path go? (As this book heads to print, eight states plus the District of Columbia have approved the recreational use of marijuana. At least 28 states have legalized medicinal marijuana.)
- On the topic of drugs, is there a relationship between increased opioid addiction and the labor force participation rate?
- Does capital punishment still serve as a deterrent?
- What can we do about border issues and the corresponding crimes—on both sides?
- Will extending the border wall deter illegal crossings and drug traffic?
- Do violent video games lead to more violent and aggressive behavior?
- Does it make sense to imprison non-violent offenders? (So, how much did we really benefit by imprisoning a Martha Stewart for five months back in 2004?)
- Why did crime drop so significantly in the 1990s and did abortion really contribute to the drop, as suggested by Steven Levitt?
- What about the drop in lead exposure in the environment? Did that have an impact on crime reduction as suggested by some?
- And, if a fatherless home is such a strong indicator of criminal behavior, why don't we speak out more sternly on the topic?

Some of these questions are discussed in the following pages, and some will be left for classroom debate and the corresponding lecture notes that will follow. In the aggregate (the text, classroom discussions, and lecture notes) the information provided should allow for a deeper and better understanding of the relationship between economic theory and some of the various criminal issues we face in our society.

In regards to the education process, 28 years of teaching at the college level has provided exposure to countless ideas, concepts, and, of course, the writings of many wonderful scholars. In addition, years of classroom interaction with students, coupled with the usual discourse among colleagues, has helped shape my own theories about this field and education in general. Accordingly, I have listed here three very basic concepts or goals in the overall education process. Keep these in mind as you study and complete the requirements for this course.

1) **Knowledge Base.** Create and develop a **knowledge base.** Facts, figures, data, ideas—there are times when details do matter. If we are going to present an argument, we need a knowledge base to draw from and to think with. This knowledge base contributes to the development of what is also important, our "frame of reference."[A] A recent Wall Street Journal article offers additional and

A Frame of Reference: a means by which we perceive or evaluate data or ideas, which helps determine how something will be approached or understood.

timely insight on this topic by assessing the intellectual impact caused by our 'obsession' (my word) with the smartphone:

> Now that our phones have made it so easy to gather information online, our brains are likely offloading even more of the work of remembering to technology. If the only thing at stake were memories of trivial facts, that might not matter. But, as the pioneering psychologist and philosopher William James said in an 1892 lecture, "the art of remembering is the art of thinking." Only by encoding information in our biological memory can we weave the rich intellectual associations that form the essence of personal knowledge and give rise to critical and conceptual thinking. No matter how much information swirls around us, the less well-stocked our memory, the less we have to think with.[1]

My assessment is that we must "plant" some specifics in order to think deeply and effectively.

2) **Issue Recognition.** Master the concept of **issue recognition**. What are the most important factors in a given argument? What bears the highest cost or presents the biggest challenge in the acquisition of utility? At a particular point in time, can we determine what is truly significant from an economic and rational approach?

3) **Problem-Solving Skills.** Fundamental to the education process is the development of **problem-solving skills**. If we acquire an adequate knowledge base and understand the most relevant of issues, we are prepared for the next step. That is, to resolve the dilemma, to determine how to overcome the obstruction or conflict. In my opinion, economic analysis is an excellent foundation to be used in the acquisition and development of true problem-solving skills.

In addition to my own writings in this second edition textbook, I have also included journal articles, essays, and other commentary from a variety of sources over a variety of topics. For example, Chapter 6 offers some interesting observations in regards to various enforcement issues in the world of professional sports. Other text materials chronicle specific criminal behavior—such as the white collar pages dealing with the crimes of Bernard Madoff. Those pages could be read much the same as a case study and therefore should increase the reader's knowledge base and frame of reference. Other sections address issues sometimes deemed divisive, yet uniquely tied to economics, such as illegal immigration and profiling. Additionally, there is plenty of coverage related to basic economic theory, including an informative and thoughtful paper by Isaac Ehrlich and some added commentary on economic efficiency. The final selection in the text is a comprehensive look at the decrease in crime from the perspective of Steven Levitt.

As with the first edition, researching content for the book has been invigorating, but also humbling when perusing the depth and abundance of scholars in the field of social science, and it has led me to the following conclusion: Whether it comes from Bastiat, Becker, Friedman, Wilson, or Levitt, or a colleague in my own department—regardless of the year—the ideas still jump off the page and are stimulating and worthy of discussion.

Finally, through an extended involvement in athletics, I have generally found that the best instructors (and coaches), at both the professional and amateur levels, were those who had the ability to keep things simple rather than overly complex. Likewise, my private sector and educational experience tells me the same—simple over complex. Or, to expand on a point I heard from former Dallas Federal Reserve Bank President Bob McTeer, sometimes what you need is a "grasp of the obvious." I am still working to master that trait—but it seems a worthy goal, and certainly one that served Dr. McTeer well.[B]

But back to the subject of simplicity. Several years ago, one of my summer students noted how much she was drawn to a particular economic textbook because "it doesn't read like a stereo repair manual." I took this to be a thoughtful, honest, and profoundly accurate assessment of that particular text. So, as with the first edition, this text is not intended to be anywhere close to a complete and comprehensive compilation of all issues related to the subject of economics and crime. Again, this book carries the title "Selected Topics" and should be used to complement lectures, classroom activities, and other supplemental materials that are necessary for an understanding of the subject. And taking a cue from my previously mentioned student, I have included a few brief and relevant anecdotal comments along the way while attempting to avoid too many similarities to the proverbial "stereo repair manual."

ENDNOTE

1. Carr, Nicholas (2017 Oct 7–8). "How Smartphones Hijack Our Minds." Wall Street Journal. p C2.

B In addition to his 36-year career with the Fed, Dr. McTeer spent two years as chancellor of the Texas A&M University system and has also been a distinguished fellow at the national center for policy analysis in Dallas.

An early look at cost-benefit analysis!

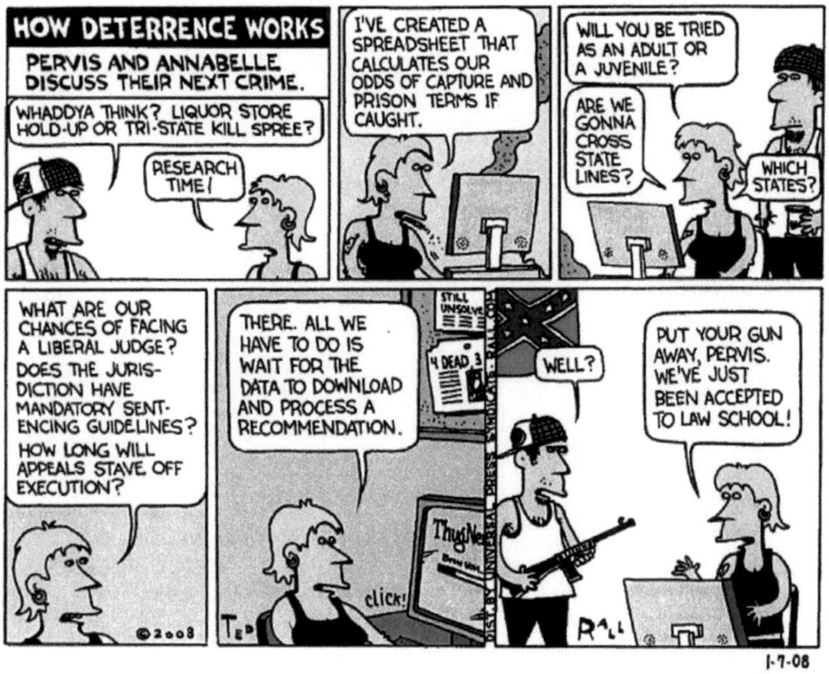

SECTION 1

CHAPTER 1

ECONOMICS, CRIME, AND CAPITALISM

By Ron Liggett

> "Little else is required to carry a state to the highest degree of opulence from the lowest barbarism, but peace, easy taxes and a tolerable administration of justice..." Adam Smith[1]

At times, I have been prone to use the phrase "life is cyclical." In truth, the concept of "cyclical behavior" is widespread through many facets of our existence. In business we see corporations in specific industries that, for a time, become the proverbial "model" for all organizations to follow. For a period in the 1990s, Enron was seen as the quintessential firm—the true capitalist organization, perhaps even impervious to harsh economic conditions. Likewise, professional sports teams frequently follow this pattern after winning a championship. That is, they quickly become the standard or benchmark as other clubs attempt to replicate their behavior; to follow their model. Alas, in both business and sports, we often find that it is only "for a time." The players change, parameters shift, and in the case of Enron, the fallibility of man takes center stage in the form of excessive and criminal behaviors.

We find the concept of cycles to be very much present in studying the economics of crime. The "business cycle," which refers to a nation's fluctuation in economic activity over a period of months or years, is frequently a starting point for researchers and economists focused on presenting a model for analyzing criminal behavior.[A] Additionally, as a nation, we see cyclical flows of behavior that, for a time, may consume discussions over topics of criminality. During the 1992 presidential election, crime prevention was at the forefront of discussion and debate, as the country experienced a significant rise in criminal behavior and the issue seemed to approach "critical mass." Candidates proposed plans to tackle this dilemma; perhaps most prominent was the call by then-presidential candidate Bill Clinton for federal funding to facilitate the addition of 100,000 police officers.[2]

A A more detailed analysis of the economic impact can be found in Chapter 3.

The Clinton proposal would eventually become legislation that not only increased the number of police, but also encouraged the lengthening of prison sentences as well as the expansion of the death penalty.[3] Yet what was a leading issue in 1992—the nation's crime rate—was only remotely a part of most presidential campaigns which have followed. (For the moment, we will exclude terrorism and the attacks on the World Trade Center from the discussion.)[B] And why was such an important issue set aside? Essentially, the cycle of behavior had changed, overall crime rates dropped significantly through the remainder of the 90's, and any talk of "critical mass" was tabled. We will discuss the significant decline in crime rates later, but for now, we will be motivated to analyze basic economic theories, along with the relationship between criminal behavior and the economy.[C]

And, while crimes rates may, in fact, be cyclically "lower," the reality is that criminal behavior most certainly still presents negative consequences for our economy. That is, "crime acts like a tax on the entire economy; it discourages domestic and foreign investments, reduces the competitiveness of firms, and reallocates resources, creating uncertainty and inefficiency."[4] When we begin to look at the overall crime cost in the U.S., including law enforcement, the judicial system, prisons, lost wages, damaged resources, psychological impairment, and other social costs, we arrive at a number approaching, and likely exceeding, $1 trillion annually.[5, 6]

"CLASSIC" ARTICLE

In 1968, Gary Becker published "Crime and Punishment: An Economic Approach." Aside from being labeled the "classic" economic analysis of criminal behavior, Becker's work undoubtedly encouraged economists to do more research in the field of criminal behavior—an area previously reserved for sociologists and other social scientists. Becker took Utility Theory and mathematically explained how the usual economic analysis of choice might be used to explain criminal behavior. That is, a criminal commits an act when the benefits of that act exceed the expected costs. By suggesting that criminals may take a rational approach in their decision making, Becker was proposing, and proving, that the same theories we

B Terrorism has obviously been a key topic for all elections since 2001. For our purposes, we will consider terrorist attacks such as 9/11 to be acts of war. However, from an economic perspective, the Becker-Posner blog (5/29/05) offers some interesting thoughts on the connection between terrorism and poverty and is deserving of scrutiny.

C Following in the "cyclical" pattern, the Clinton crime bill seems to have truly come full circle. In recent years some scholars and activists have attacked parts of the bill. Most particularly, the sections which led to greater incarcerations for low level offenders.

use to explain legitimate behavior were also valid in explaining certain illegitimate activities.[D]

Throughout this book we will use of some of these legitimate theories and analyze behavior accordingly. However, while the economist has found room for theoretical observations in the study of criminal acts, we must note that the influences of other factors—family dynamics, education, and various internal inhibitors still have relevance.[E] Consequently, investigations in this field also include analysis of the sociological fabric that affects behavior in a myriad of ways. Consider one very significant example. Studies have shown that the chance of incarceration doubles with the absence of a father from the home. This incarceration rate holds even when consideration is given to characteristics such as race, family income, and parent education, among others.[7]

The study of any discipline brings its own vocabulary, so as we move forward, let us begin by establishing some basic terminology in addition to reviewing various fundamental principles.

WHAT IS ECONOMICS?

Economics may be defined as a social science that deals with the use of scarce resources to meet unlimited material wants. In other words, it involves studying the allocation of resources and how those resources are used to meet the needs of both the private and public sector. Determining how, when, and where these resources are used involves the concept of choice and the realization that, at certain times, the resources we need may not be available; i.e., they may be scarce. Accordingly, this concept of "scarcity" is considered the economizing problem; one that must be resolved through some type of economic system.

RESOURCES

The study of basic economic principles categorizes resources into two main groups with the first being our **Human Resources**. The typical human resource list includes **labor** and **entrepreneurial ability**. Additionally, we will add a third

D It is worth stating that Becker, seemingly, did not feel that his work was a "novelty" as he referenced the contributions made by Beccaria and Bentham during the 18th and 19th centuries. In regards to his classic article, he would state "...my efforts can be viewed as a resurrection, modernization, and thereby I hope improvement on these much earlier pioneering studies." The Economic Approach to Human Behavior. (1976). p. 79.

E James Q. Wilson, while acknowledging the strengths of the economic approach, nonetheless referenced "character" as a key determinant. further noting "...that man is governed by something more than mere calculation [...] [including] conscience, sympathy, and a sense of justice." Wilson p. 517.

resource in this category, **human capital**. Human capital refers to the knowledge, experience, and specific skills of an individual and should play a prominent role in this field of study. (Or, more simply, the "tools of the mind.") The second group is the **Property Resources**, composed of both **land** and **economic capital**. Land includes real property, water, minerals, etc.—essentially the natural resources that might exist. Economic capital is defined as a manufactured aid to production and includes items such as computers, equipment and tools, etc.

The true characteristic of all resources is that, at some point, they may be scarce. Therefore, decisions must be made to overcome the issue of scarcity. A private firm will make decisions regarding the use of their employees—the labor resource. As a student, you are developing your own human capital and will face your own concept of scarcity as you decide, for example, how much time to devote to studies and how much time to leisure. Jurisdictions—local, state, and federal—will make decisions on how to allocate their crime prevention resources in order to keep crime at some acceptable level.[F]

WHAT IS CRIME?

A very basic and simple definition of **crime** is "any act committed in violation of a law that prohibits it and authorizes punishment for its commission."[8] Essentially, we are talking about an act that society has deemed itself to be better off without. Barron's Law Dictionary offers—"a wrong which the government has determined is injurious to the public and, hence, prosecutable in a criminal proceeding."[9] While crime is further categorized between serious acts called felonies and more minor offenses—misdemeanors—our focus will not necessarily be to distinguish between these two characterizations. Rather, we will attempt to concentrate on evaluating the overall behavior and circumstances of a criminal act and weigh benefits against costs, whether the act involves robbing a convenience store, an act of prostitution, embezzlement, or perhaps running a red light.

CRIME—A DRAG ON ECONOMIC GROWTH

As stated earlier, crime may be considered a tax—more specifically, perhaps a regressive tax. Consider the definition of a regressive tax in its most basic form—a tax that takes a greater percentage of a lower income (from the poor) than of a

F The concept of an "acceptable" level of crime may be difficult to grasp, similar to defining an "acceptable" level of pollution. Yet by virtue of the fact that a crime budget is established, we are acknowledging that some acceptable level does, in fact, exist. We will attempt to quantify later in the book by using Marginal Benefits and Marginal Costs.

higher income (from the wealthy). In regards to crime, the regressive nature lies in the fact that data suggest many of those impacted by criminal behavior are very likely to be the poor and minorities.[10]

The reality is that crime places significant costs on the economy. While most economists readily acknowledge the existence of taxes, inflation, and regulatory obstacles as the key "drags" on economic growth, our analysis will add to this list the element of criminal behavior and the expense incurred from such acts.[11]

"DRAGS" ON ECONOMIC GROWTH

1. Taxes imposed by the government.
2. Regulatory burdens—also imposed by the government.
3. Inflation.
4. Crime and the costs it brings to both business and consumers.

Each of the items listed above may, in some way, curtail the growth and restrict the smooth operation of our free market economy. Yet these four variables are not equal. Consider the following arguments. First, we likely do not enjoy paying taxes and may not favor all regulations. But, we acknowledge that some taxation is necessary to fund certain public goods and some regulation is useful as a part of the legal framework and as a protective measure.[G] The third "drag"—inflation—is similar to stress for an individual. A small portion of stress adds some flavor to life. Likewise, a reasonable level of inflation may signal us that we have expanding and growing markets. However, too much of either and, as my grandfather used to proclaim in his strong Czech accent, "Now you got trouble."

So on closer analysis, we could argue that, to some degree, positive aspects exist in at least three of the so-called drags on economic growth. But for the fourth variable—crime—there is no redeeming quality. Of course this premise would be in sharp contrast to those who might still believe the "broken window fallacy." That is, just as some suggest a broken window triggers expenditures that stimulate economic activity, there are those who might propose that our spending and investment for crime prevention is likewise a fiscal stimulus. I strongly disagree.[H]

G As my Libertarian colleagues would attest, the tendency for government is to overregulate, and the appropriate emphasis here is for "some" regulation.

H We will compare the Broken Window Fallacy vs. the Broken Window Theory during the course. For more background on the Fallacy concept, see the writings of Frederic Bastiat.

ADAM SMITH—CRIME IS INEVITABLE?

From the comments of Adam Smith, we understand that there are certain behaviors of man that can be labeled as predictable and perhaps inevitable—though not acceptable! The lengthy quote below will serve as segue into our discussion of Capitalism. As you read his call for a civil magistrate—and I suggest you read it twice, and slowly—consider the depth of the passage, and his detailed explanations.

> The affluence of the rich excites the indignation of the poor, who are often both driven by want, and prompted by envy, to invade his possessions. It is only under the shelter of the civil magistrate that the owner of that valuable property, which is acquired by the labour of many years, or perhaps of many successive generations, can sleep a single night in security. He is at all times surrounded by unknown enemies, whom, though he never provoked, he can never appease, and from whose injustice he can be protected only by the powerful arm of the civil magistrate continually held up to chastise it. The acquisition of valuable and extensive property, therefore, necessarily requires the establishment of civil government. Where there is no property, or at least none that exceeds the value of two or three days' labour, civil government is not so necessary.[12]

CAPITALISM AND CRIME—THE IMPACT AND OTHER LINKS

In the United States, we enjoy the benefits of a Capitalistic economic system. While we frequently define Capitalism simply as Free Market or Free Enterprise, in this section we will be more in-depth and look at the detailed traits of the system. More specifically, we will concern ourselves with how each trait is impacted or relates to criminal behavior.

To begin, there are six basic characteristics of Capitalism: Limited government, private property, a system of markets and prices, competition, self-interest, and free enterprise.

1. Limited Government. The first characteristic essentially refers to a limited government involvement in the economic system. Whether or not we achieve this goal is sometimes debatable; some want more government, and some want less. I feel it is safe to say that our current political climate parallels a societal trend of (sadly) expecting more government involvement in the economy.

A functioning government will inevitably establish a bureaucratic system or **bureaucracy**.[I] This system generally operates according to the theory of

I A bureaucracy may be defined as an unwieldy administrative system staffed by non-elected officials who generally follow an inflexible routine.

bureaucratic behavior that follows a goal of maximizing its own welfare—sometimes at the expense of those it serves. Accordingly, if more government and bureaucratic intrusion is required, then the capitalistic economy will be less streamlined and therefore less efficient. So, the impact of crime is quite clear. More crime and/or unlawful civil activity = more government and more government regulations—some possibly beneficial, but others likely detrimental. Reflecting on Adam Smith's earlier discussion of the role of the civil magistrate, crime and civil unrest begets...

- Greater police presence.
- More enforcement issues.
- Loss of freedoms (curfews, cameras, etc.).
- Increased regulations (more SEC, FCC, FAA, etc.).

A significant example in the regulation area would be the passage of the Sarbanes-Oxley (SOX) legislation in 2002. The legislation was passed primarily in response to fraudulent reporting of financial statements and the overall corporate debacles of companies such as Enron, WorldCom, and Global Crossing. Many have praised SOX for enhancing investor confidence, instilling a more ethical culture, and reducing fraud.[13] However, others speak of the additional costs involved and also note the decision of more start-up companies to list with stock exchanges in other countries, such as the U.K. in order to avoid SOX regs.[14]

SOX remains a controversial piece of legislation, much like the Patriot Act, which was signed into law in October of 2001. While there may be few similarities between the two in regards to specific regulations, the common thread is that each was passed due to outrageous acts—some financial, and some terroristic. They became law based on a perceived need for enforcement.

To summarize, a capitalistic system needs to maintain Limited Government involvement. Criminal activity, in any measure, defeats this goal (for discussion, see Markets and Prices).

2. Private Property. The existence of private property on our list deserves special mention and if you are taking notes, put an asterisk next to this one—its importance in a free market system is undeniable. In our world of economics, the existence of private property implies the presence of ownership in goods that are both tangible and intangible. This includes consumable and durable goods such as a car, a computer, and any measure of other personal effects and real property items such as a home, a building, land, or minerals like oil and gas. And finally, financial holdings such as stock ownership, and various other intangible or intellectual properties like copyrights, licenses, patents, and trademarks.

A significant and accepted truth is that individuals respond to incentives and we can easily ascertain that the existence of private property provides a foundation for these incentives. Additionally, global research tells us that economic prosperity in respective countries is improved with the presence of secure private property along with the rule of law.[15] [J] Accordingly, while private property is essential, it is also imperative that it be protected. Whether this simply means installing a security system to protect a commercial establishment, enforcing laws against identity theft, or organizing a legal defense for the protection of real property rights, the consensus is clear. As vital as private property is to the success of Capitalism, a lack of property protection in its most basic form cripples this element of the free market system.

INCENTIVES AND PROPERTY—A DIFFERENT PERSPECTIVE

In *Modern Principles: Macroeconomics*, authors and Professors Tyler Cowen and Alex Tabarrok begin the book by analyzing prisoner shipments from Great Britain to Australia in 1787. It is a summary of a somewhat provocative topic: the establishment of penal colonies, which was common at the time. In this case, the authors resourcefully use this subject to help align basic economic theory in dealing with incentives and property rights.

From their book:

> The prisoners were dying of scurvy, typhoid fever, and smallpox, but nothing was killing them more than bad incentives. In 1787, the British government had hired sea captains to ship convicted felons to Australia. Conditions on board the ships were monstrous; some even said the conditions were worse than on slave ships. On one voyage, more than one-third of the men died and the rest arrived beaten, starved, and sick. A first mate remarked cruelly of the convicts, "Let them die and be damned, the owners have [already] been paid for their passage."[16]
>
> The British public had no love for the convicts, but it wasn't prepared to give them a death sentence either. Newspapers editorialized in favor of better conditions, clergy appealed to the captains' sense of humanity, and legislators passed regulations requiring better food and water, light and air, and proper medical care. Yet the death rate remained shockingly high. Nothing appeared to be working until an economist suggested something new.
>
> Can you guess what the economist suggested?
>
> Instead of paying the captains for each prisoner placed on board ship in Great Britain, the economist suggested paying for each prisoner that walked off the ship in Australia. In 1793, the new system was implemented and immediately the survival rate shot up to 99%.[17]

J In addition to Private Property and the Rule of Law, Political Stability is noted as the third item of relevance in the discussion by Miller, et al.

Prior to this period, British prisoners had been regularly shipped to America. However, the War of Independence essentially changed this flow as America refused to accept any more convicts. As the two professors display in this section, economic theory essentially won! While nobody enjoys labeling any human as "property," in this case, realizing that they essentially were a property that only brought payment when healthy (or at least alive) elevated their status for both treatment and survival. An economic lesson to be sure!

In regards to private property, criminal and unscrupulous behaviors imperil the ability of the individual—or the firm—to own, use, or facilitate property in a manner they see fit. Such behavior not only increases costs, it also negatively impacts the value of land and property for both a homeowner and a commercial establishment. As the negative impact continues, both economic and financial investment declines as entrepreneurs and investors seek safer accommodations for their capital. Further, damaged property loses value and may eventually lead to additional erosion in neighborhoods and the marketplace alike.[K]

Consider the following from Milton Friedman. "Privatization is meaningless if you don't have the rule of law. What does it mean to privatize if you do not have security of property, if you can't use property as you want?"[18]

To summarize, we note that allowing for private property ownership and establishing protection of the property and its value through private property rights "is a critical basis of an efficient, productive, and innovative economy."[19]

3. System of Markets and Prices. Our third characteristic of Capitalism serves as the organizing force of the economic system. A system of markets and prices facilitates the flow of goods and services. First, and most importantly, we note that **prices are a signal** (repeat that statement for good measure).[L] And, from the perspectives of economists far and wide, this pricing signal allows for the most efficient use of resources in any economic system. The market—defined as any activity that brings together buyer and seller—is the structure that allows pricing to perform its most important function, i.e., the signal. Without this organizing force (and the aforementioned private property), the "creation of value," which serves to benefit and grow societies and cultures across the globe, would be minimized. Remember, the essence of capitalism is not just a matter of exchanges as an end; it is also about creating value by mobilizing both ingenuity and "human energy."[20]

So what is the impact of crime? The initial answer is that it results in higher equilibrium prices and a decrease in equilibrium quantity for most goods. In the retail world, the use of electronic article surveillance, cameras, security guards (both uniformed and undercover), sensor tags, magnetic strips, locked boxes,

K See Broken Window Theory by Wilson.

L Understanding that "prices are a signal" is one of the most essential concepts in the study of free market economics.

dummy cartons, and other product alarms is incessant. In addition to the man-hours for the security previously mentioned, there are also hours needed for added inventory counts. Go into your local big box store or department store and look at the ceiling. Security cameras abound—more costs. And, while it is easy to see tangible items such as cameras and monitors, we must understand there are also the extensive hours invested for employee background checks, training programs, etc., all in an effort to deter theft and product shrinkage.

Retail theft studies between 2014–16 estimated the overall cost of theft in the U.S. to be between $42–$45 billion. A 2015 global report of retail theft (including employee theft) estimated the overall cost in North America at just over $50 billion, or approximately $379 per year for a family of four.[21] For many families today, this is not an insignificant amount. Likewise, in the world of white collar and financial crime, where the losses can be even higher, the increased use of and need for auditors and regulatory authorities create a similar problem—higher costs or, as previously noted, a crime tax. We could insert any number of other examples in this area, but the relevant point involves pricing changes due to the impact of criminal behavior. As one of my graduate school professors frequently noted, "Change a parameter, shift a curve."

Before ending this section, we should also note that there are additional market influences from criminal behavior. From a positive perspective, we are reminded of another dynamic of economics—that **markets adjust**. And as the demand for protection from unlawful behavior increases, the "market" brings a diverse selection of security products and services to the consumer, regardless of whether the consumer is an individual or the actual employer.

For example, the need for new technology and software development is constant in the world of cybersecurity where "hundreds of millions" of cyberattacks are launched daily around the globe. Literally billions of dollars have been invested by government sectors and private businesses in an effort to fend off these attacks. And, while many attacks focus on large and major corporations, small businesses feel the threat as well.[22] Needless to say, these incessant attacks ensure a continued need for both software and hardware development.

4. Competition. It has been said that the free market system thrives on competition. So where competitive instincts abound, the willingness to use corrupt or unprincipled methods will also exist, and we frequently observe commerce and espionage going hand in hand.

The theft of ideas and internal information has been brought to the forefront in numerous cases and led to the passage of the Economic Espionage Act in 1996. Some cases are as basic as "dumpster diving"—yes, it really happens! In 2008 chocolate makers Mars and Nestlé became involved in a dispute that led to Nestlé's entering "a corporate-spying campaign that would have made the CIA brass proud."[23] Hired operatives searched and removed garbage bags from

dumpsters at Mars' New Jersey offices, even going to the trouble of replacing the bags they took with "fake" garbage so Mars' workers would not notice.[24 M N]

Other scenarios are more complex. For example, in a case dating back to 1993, an ex-General Motors (GM) employee from their Opel division went to work for Volkswagen, and brought seven executives with him along with internal documents and other so-called trade secrets. When the dust had settled, Volkswagen would end up paying millions to GM in settlement.[25]

Many other cases also exist, however the trend towards cybercrimes and hacking has been particularly noteworthy. As mentioned earlier, billions of dollars are spent to contain and diminish these crimes. And, while some entities may see the attacks as somewhat of a nuisance, for others they represent a true espionage encroachment. Information on corporate relationships, intimate trade secrets, details about new products—all of this material is within easy reach of the talented hacker and could be a competitive "game-changer" in the wrong hands.

M As noted in the *NY Post* article by Wilner, spying among chocolate makers is said to be "legendary." (And was even included in the movie "Willy Wonka & the Chocolate Factory.")

N Dumpster diving has been an issue at various Gamestop stores where gamers were known to have found functional product being tossed as garbage. However, with the legality dependent on the physical location and local laws, the practice is risky. To curb the activities, it was reported that the company instituted a policy whereby employees would destroy product before discarding.

"HACKING" AND OUR NATIONAL PASTIME

Believe it or not, even the so-called national pastime in this country—Major League Baseball—has been victim to criminal activity in the cyber world. In 2016, the former scouting director for the St. Louis Cardinals (one of the most successful MLB organizations) was sentenced to 46 months and ordered to pay approximately $279,000 in restitution for what amounted to a cyber-crime. When a Cardinals employee had left the team for a position with the Houston Astros in 2011, the Cardinals scouting director apparently used the ex-employee's known password to gain access to the Astros e-mail system. He then made use of scouting lists, player evaluations, trade notes, and other confidential information. Authorities stated that 118 pages of information was viewed illegally. Is nearly four years behind bars too much punishment for simply taking a look at player information?[26] Obviously the courts didn't think so. In this case, federal law was violated in the form of the Computer Fraud and Abuse Act (CFAA)—a law taken quite seriously these days.[27] Additionally, we know that professional baseball is a form of competitive entertainment and the potential payoff for fielding a quality team is huge. Combine that with the fact that professional franchises now invest millions of dollars in computer software and sabermetrics, and one can understand the potential costs of "non-enforcement."[O]

5. Self-Interest. The fifth characteristic also deserves an asterisk for its significance. Again drawing from Adam Smith, we reference his description of **self-interest** as the "invisible hand," in essence, the driving force in our economic system. It is by self-interest that decisions are made in our pursuits of both consumption and production as we seek to obtain or maximize utility.[P]

And where is the connection to criminal pursuits? From the economists' perspective it is found in the decision-making process of the criminal who makes choices based on the same concept of self-interest. Like the law-abiding citizen, the offenders are also driven by an invisible hand as they seek to maximize their own utility through an assortment of behaviors. Stated simply—criminals choose.

Before leaving the topic of self-interest, we should note that there are those who feel that some components of economic theory are based on a psychological model of man that, at best, is rigid and outdated. So, as we have previously noted, it is not our intent to focus on economic variables alone. There is recognition among economists that humans (i.e., criminals) are motivated by "complex forces." And, in an attempt to better understand certain behaviors—including

O Sabermetrics involves the empirical analysis of baseball statistics and other in-game data and measurements.

P We will define "utility" as a measure of satisfaction or usefulness.

unlawful ones—the inclusion of each and every complex force in every situation simply may not be necessary. So "it is often possible to obtain predictive results based on very simple assumptions about human motivation [...] [and] the fact that there is altruism in the world does not negate the self-interest model (nor) call for a whole new economic theory."[28] From Sir Dennis Robertson, "There exists in every human breast an inevitable state of tension between the aggressive and acquisitive instincts and the instincts of benevolence and self-sacrifice."[29] Complex forces indeed.

6. Free Enterprise. Our study of Capitalism as it pertains to criminal behavior would be incomplete without some mention of the concept of **Free Enterprise**, defined as: The freedom of businesses (and individuals) to organize and operate for profit in a competitive system without interference from government beyond some basic regulations necessary to protect the public. As noted earlier, those looking for a shorter description of Capitalism sometimes find this characteristic to be functional. However, to advance this discussion one step further, we will focus on the key word in our definition—freedom.

Perhaps it is no coincidence that the writing we have referenced multiple times in the last few pages, *The Wealth of Nations* by Adam Smith, was published in the same year as the Declaration of Independence—1776. Both works seek to affirm a most powerful force—freedom. And, the freedom that is described is that which provides a capitalistic system with the basic attribute necessary for the creation of value. To repeat the point made in the third characteristic, Capitalism involves creating value by mobilizing both ingenuity and "human energy."[30] This ingenuity and energy is most capably synergized through freedom of thought and activity. Yet this same ingenuity and energy is restricted, and even harnessed, by controls that surface in two ways. First, the legal controls of excessive governmental regulation as previously mentioned. And second, the controls exercised by a criminal and unscrupulous element that impedes our actions, threatens our personal and financial safety, and in some manner, calls for our own writ of *habeas corpus*.

Consider the following thought related to freedom and crime:

> "Men, in order to engage in productive enterprise and to seek personal fulfillment, must be free, if not perfectly free, from the actions of other men that, intentional or not, violate their persons or property by force or threat of force. From this point of view, crime is NOT (emphasis added) just another social problem like unemployment or slum housing, but attacks the very essence of civilization."[31]

A FINAL THOUGHT ON CAPITALISM

The previous paragraphs outline in detail our system of Capitalism and offer several theoretical observations. As we conclude this section, let us offer a final thought on the subject from a noted scholar in the field of criminal justice—the late Professor James Q. Wilson.[Q]

> "Capitalism led to greater differences in personal income, exposed many workers to difficult jobs, and facilitated the movement of people into noisy, cramped cities. These things may have helped make crime increase. But capitalism also helped bring crime under control. It required a disciplined urban work force and an impartial court system. It substituted the struggle for money for the struggle for power. The late Ernest Gellner defended the morality of capitalism because it permitted ambition—a natural human instinct—to be fulfilled in the attainment of commercial wealth rather than through conquest and brutality."[32]

ENDNOTES

1. Smith, Adam. (1776). As quoted in *Adam Smith: The Man and His Works* by E. G. West. 1969. New Rochelle, NY: Arlington Publishing House, p. 50.
2. Locin, Mitchell. (1992, July 24). "Clinton: Unite in Crime Fight," *Chicago Tribune*, <www.chicagotribune.com>.
3. U.S. Dept. of Justice Fact Sheet, https://www.ncjrs.gov/txtfiles/billfs.txt. Accessed 2016 Sept 2.
4. Detotto, Claudio and Edoardo Otranto. (2010). "Does Crime Affect Economic Growth?" *KYKLOS*, Vol. 63, August 2010, No. 3, pp. 330–345.
5. Cohen, Mark A. (2005). *The Costs of Crime and Justice*. New York: Routledge.
6. Anderson, David. (1999). "The Aggregate Burden of Crime." *Journal of Law and Economics*, Vol. 42, No. 2, (Oct. 1999), pp. 611–642.
7. National Center for Policy Analysis (1999). "No Father, More Crime," *Executive Alert*, Vol. 12, No. 6, November/December, from Harper, Cynthia C. and Sara S. McLanahan, "Father Absence and Youth Incarceration," August 1998, paper presented at the 1998 annual meeting of the American Sociological Association.
8. Wilson, James Q. and Richard J. Herrnstein. (1985). *Crime and Human Nature: The Definitive Study of the Causes of Crime*. New York: Simon & Schuster, p. 22.
9. Gifis, Steven H. (1984). *Law Dictionary*. New York: Barrons, p. 110.

Q Professor Wilson died March 2, 2012 at the age of 80. Among his scores of written contributions, *Crimes & Human Nature: The Definitive Study of the Causes of Crime*, which he co-authored with Richard J. Herrnstein, stands out as an exceptional and exhaustive commentary on the subject of crime.

10. Reynolds, Morgan O. (1985). *Crime by Choice: An Economic Analysis*, Fisher Institute, p. ix.
11. Reynolds, p. 34.
12. Smith, Adam. (1776). *An Inquiry into the Nature and Causes of the Wealth of Nations*. Bk 5, Ch. 1.
13. Farrell, Greg. (2007, July 30). "Sarbanes-Oxley Law Has Been A Pretty Clean Sweep." *USA Today*. <www.usatoday.com>.
14. Piotroski, Joseph D. and Suraj Srinivasan. (2008, January). "Regulation and Bonding: The Sarbanes-Oxley Act and the Flow of International Listings." Available at SSRN: <http://ssrn.com/abstract=956987>.
15. Miller, Roger LeRoy, Daniel K. Benjamin, and Douglass C. North. (2012). *The Economics of Public Issues*, 17th Ed., New Jersey: Pearson.
16. Quoted in Christopher, Emma. 2007. "The slave trade is merciful compared to [this]": Slave traders, convict transportation and the abolitionists. In Christopher, E., C. Pybus, and M. Rediker (eds.), *Many Middle Passages*, Chap. 6, pp. 109–128. Berkeley, CA: University of California Press.
17. Cowen, Tyler and Alex Tabarrok. (2015). *Modern Principles: Macroeconomics*. Worth Publishers, New York, NY. p. 1.
18. Friedman, Milton. (2002). "Economic Freedom Behind the Scenes." Preface to Economic Freedom of the World: 2002 Annual Report, Vancouver, B.C.: Fraser Institute, p. xviii.
19. Bandow, Doug. (2010, Feb 23). "Help the Third World: Protect Property Rights," *American Spectator-Online*.
20. Palmer, Tom G. (2011). *The Morality of Capitalism*, New York: Jameson Books, p. 4.
21. Centre for Retail Research. (2009). "The Global Retail Theft Barometer."
22. Finch, Brian E. (2017, Aug 22). "The Disturbing Inevitability of Cyberattacks." *Wall Street Journal*, p. A15.
23. Wilner, Richard. (2010, April 4). "Corporate Espionage Creates 'Peek' Earnings," *New York Post*, <www.nypost.com>.
24. Wilner.
25. Chan, Michael. (2011, Sept 19). *Bloomberg Businessweek*.
26. Lozano, Juan A. Associated Press. (2016, July 18). "Former Cardinals Exec Sentenced to Prison for Hacking Astros." *Seattle Times*. https://www.seattletimes.com/nation-world/former-cardinals-exec-sentenced-to-jail-for-hacking-astros/
27. McCann, Michael. (2016 July 18). "Breaking Down Chris Correa's Prison Sentence for Hacking Astros." *Sports Illustrated*. https://www.si.com/mlb/2016/07/18/cardinals-chris-correa-hacks-astros-prison-sentence
28. Amacher, Ryan C., Robert D. Tollison, and Thomas D. Willett. (1976). *The Economic Approach to Public Policy*, London: Cornell University Press, pp. 23–24.
29. Robertson, Sir Dennis. (1956). *Economic Commentaries*. London: Staples Press, p. 148.
30. Palmer 4.
31. Reynolds 18.
32. Wilson, James Q. (1999, Aug 17). "Capitalism Cuts Crime." *Wall Street Journal*. A22.

CHAPTER 2

AN INTRODUCTION TO "THE COSTS OF CRIME AND JUSTICE"

By Ron Liggett

The following section consists of fourteen pages from a book written by Mark A. Cohen entitled *The Cost of Crime and Justice*. The section provides a summary of the myriad costs that are part of any criminal activity and behavior. Starting with the tragic events of Columbine High School, the chapter provides a more inquisitive look at both the direct and indirect costs that result from crime.

Anyone who has studied this field would likely attest to the difficulty in trying to quantify all cost aspects of illegal activity. The avenues for discovery are endless. Accordingly, the table which Cohen provides in this chapter allows for a fairly in-depth listing of cost categories.

On the prevention side, the sizeable outlays for law enforcement, the judicial system, and a means of incarceration are fairly obvious. However, what isn't always obvious is the fact that we are always consuming these "crime prevention" categories whether we are sitting in class, shopping, or watching a concert. Sometimes law enforcement activities are behind the scenes, and sometimes they are in clear view; either way, there is a presence, and a system is in place. Without this presence, and the overall judicial system, we would find ourselves in a laissez-faire crime situation.[A] Such a situation would generally result in a higher rate of offenses.

Finally, it is worth repeating that what also may not be obvious are the indirect costs and expenditures which arise from various criminal activity. In this area, and others, the chapter should strengthen one's frame of reference on the topic. And, while the numbers may have changed over the years, the data included should still be suitable to facilitate a better understanding of the economics of crime and the many costs incurred by both victims and the public at large.

A Laissez-faire crime rate can be defined as the crime rate which would exist with zero law enforcement.

THE COSTS OF CRIME AND JUSTICE

By Mark A. Cohen

INTRODUCTION AND OVERVIEW

On April 20, 1999, 17-year-old Dylan Kebold and 18-year-old Eric Harris walked into the Columbine High School in Littleton, Colorado and began a shooting rampage that was heard around the world. This single act of violence resulted in the death of 13 students and teachers, serious injuries to 28 others, and the death of the two gunmen. This tragedy certainly took its worst toll on the victims and their families. Although no amount of money can bring back the individuals whose lives were lost, the amount of money that was lost as a result of this incident was still enormous. There is no doubt that this incident caused the victims and their families to spend a significant amount of money on medical bills, caused them to lose time at work, and imposed other direct costs. Numerous indirect costs were also likely to have been incurred, such as the cost to families who took their children out of public schools and incurred private school tuition, or those who incurred the cost of moving to another school district or city. Charities around the world helped out, with an estimated $6 million being contributed directly to help families of victims (Washington, 1999). The fact that the murder victims will no longer earn a living means that over their expected future lifetime, hundreds of thousands and perhaps millions of dollars in earnings will have been lost. However, the loss to the victims and their families was considerably more than this amount. Any assessment of their loss must account for the tremendous pain, suffering, lost quality of life, and grief they suffered.

Many would argue that no amount of money would be adequate to compensate the victims or their families for this loss. We'll put that issue aside for now and return to it throughout this chapter and this book.

This act of violence affected others beside the families and victims. The impact and resultant costs were felt by thousands of friends, relatives, and neighbors who attended the funerals—perhaps taking time off work. They bought condolence cards and flowers, spent time visiting, brought food to the grieving family, and also suffered a non-trivial amount of grief and fear themselves. An estimated 70,000 people—many of whom traveled from out of town to express their grief—attended a memorial service for the community. Local florists donated 25,000 bouquets for the service as fighter jets flew overhead as a tribute (Serrano and Moehringer, 1999).

Schoolchildren who were not injured—but endured the five-hour ordeal—were traumatized and spent weeks or months with counselors and therapists. School was canceled for more than a week, and resumed half-days at a nearby high school. This tragedy was so massive that mental health providers were inundated with pleas for assistance. One report indicated that three weeks after the tragedy, "demand for care has not abated. One mental health provider in Littleton...said crisis calls have quadrupled and requests for ongoing services have gone up 50 percent. In the metro Denver area, managed care providers are reporting a 40 percent to 100 percent increase in requests for mental health services" (Cart, 1999). The mother of a victim who was left partially paralyzed committed suicide six months after the incident (Anonymous, 1999). For many, the consequences continue to this day.

The city government (and hence taxpayers) was also significantly affected by this act of violence. Police SWAT teams and investigators were needed to respond to this tragedy. Extra police were required to be on duty to help control traffic during the funeral and memorial services. The mayor's time was diverted from more productive activities to responding to reporters' questions and meeting with concerned citizens and the school board. Numerous lawsuits were filed by family members of victims against the city and police for not preventing and/or not adequately responding during the incident. While most of these lawsuits have since been dismissed, they were no doubt costly to the city of Littleton as well as the federal courts that processed them.

The indirect costs of the Columbine High School shooting went far beyond Colorado. Schools around the country reported high absenteeism rates in the days immediately following the incident, as students and parents feared copycat shootings (Samuels, 1999). Interest in home schooling increased dramatically as parents around the country developed a renewed interest in a safe alternative to public schools. In Colorado calls to the state Department of Education reportedly more than doubled following the shooting (Lloyd, 1999). Schools around the country reportedly have undergone expensive remodeling projects to enhance security in response to these shootings (Kass, 1999), have instituted training exercises for police, fire, and school officials, and hired additional security guards and police officers to patrol high schools (Wilgoren, 1999).

Although there has been no accounting of the total "cost" of the Columbine tragedy, it surely cost society hundreds of millions, if not billions, of dollars. Highly publicized cases such as this extreme case of school violence in the U.S. have highlighted the fact that although crime rates have been declining over the past decade, violence is still a significant social problem and the cost to society is no less real. Recent estimates have tallied the annual cost of crime to victims in the U.S. at about $450 billion. Attempts to incorporate other social costs into the equation suggest that the annual cost of crime to society is even larger—perhaps as much as $1 trillion or more. What do these numbers mean and what should they be used for? How does crime compare to other social ills? This book provides a comprehensive review of the theoretical foundations, methodologies employed, and empirical estimates of the cost of crime. It also examines some of the possible uses—and misuses—of crime cost data.

A complete characterization of crime costs can be an important tool in formulating criminal justice policy. Identifying and quantifying costs and consequences of victimization may be helpful both in characterizing the crime problem and in examining ways to address it. Ignoring the non-monetary benefits of crime reduction can lead to a misallocation of resources. For will prevent one additional rape incident. Considering only tangible, out-of-pocket costs, the average rape (or attempted rape) costs $5,100—less than the $20–25,000 annual cost of a prison cell. The bulk of these expenses are medical and mental health care costs to victims. However, if rape's effect on the victim's quality of life is monetized along with other costs imposed on society at large, recent estimates indicate that society would be willing to pay about $237,000 to prevent one rape from occurring—many times greater than the cost of prison. Thus, from society's standpoint, it is worth spending $20,000 to $25,000 in additional prison costs in exchange for at least $237,000 in benefits from one less rape. Put differently, the "cost" to society of one rape is $237,000; hence it is certainly worth more than $25,000 to prevent one rape from occurring.

By allowing analysts to combine statistics on disparate crimes into a single, readily understood metric, monetary valuations of crime costs may be used to help guide resource allocations across crime types. For example, is a police patrol pattern that prevents a rape better than one that prevents three burglaries? One way to answer such a question is to ask residents of the affected area which they prefer through polling or referenda. However, in many instances, policymakers must rely on less direct methods of determining an appropriate choice. In such cases, one would need to have a metric that allows for comparisons between rapes and burglaries. Dollars provide such a metric for this comparison.

WHY DO WE NEED ESTIMATES OF THE "COST OF CRIME"?

To most economists, there is no question that crime costs should be estimated. Economics involves the allocation of scarce resources in society. Criminal justice policy decisions always involve choices between two or more alternatives, each having their own costs and benefits. The enumeration of those costs and benefits puts the various alternatives on a level playing field and can help policymakers make more informed decisions that enhance society's well-being. Of course, if the enumerated costs and benefits are inaccurate, there is a risk that more information can lead to worse decisions. Further, many non-economists would argue that there is neither a moral justification nor adequate empirical basis for placing dollar values on intangible factors such as pain, suffering, and lost quality of life. I will return to these issues later in this chapter. For now, please indulge this economist and "assume" that such intangibles can be measured. I want to highlight three important policy-relevant purposes of measuring costs and benefits:

- comparison of the relative harm caused by type of crime,
- comparison of the aggregate harm from crime with other social ills, and
- benefit-cost analysis of alternative crime control policies.

Martin and Bradley (1964) provide a more detailed discussion of the importance of identifying and quantifying the costs of crime.

RELATIVE HARM BY TYPE OF CRIME

Policymakers are often interested in comparing the harm caused by different types of crime. For example, most advocates of sentencing guidelines rely on victim harm as one component of their sentencing structure. Those who subscribe to a "just deserts" philosophy of punishment combine harm with culpability, whereas those who advocate a utilitarian approach combine harm with detectability and deterrability. Although one can tally up the various harms associated with each type of crime (e.g. value of property stolen, frequency of injuries by type of injury, mental health related injuries), without a common metric such as dollars, it is difficult to objectively compare these harms.

A few non-monetary metrics have been proposed for comparing harms—such as number of days for a victim to recoup the financial loss or the number of life years lost (see e.g. Maltz, 1975). These are primarily designed to overcome the perceived unfairness of valuing harms according to the wealth of the individual being harmed.[1] However, these proposals also suffer from not having a common metric. One is still unable to compare 100 lost workdays to one lost life year, for example.

Absent a common metric to compare harms, the generally accepted approach to rank the severity of crimes has been to survey the public (see Wolfgang *et al.*, 1985; Cullen, Link, and Polanzi, 1982; Rossi *et al*, 1974). These surveys ask respondents to rank the seriousness of various crimes, and result in relatively consistent rankings over time and across populations. An alternative method is to ask respondents what actual prison sentences they believe should be meted out for different crime scenarios (see Rossi and Berk, 1997). However, these studies are based on subjective public perceptions concerning the severity of crimes—which may include misperceptions about the frequency of injuries in typical criminal events. For example, Cohen (1988a) argues that public-perception surveys tend to underestimate the harm associated with violent crimes relative to property crimes. These studies are also generally unable to distinguish between the generic harm associated with an injury and the actual consequences of any particular victimization. This would be particularly important if one were interested in the extent to which the consequences of victimization vary across communities or different segments of the population (e.g. age or sex), for example. Despite these limitations, public-perception surveys have recently been used in a slightly different context—by eliciting the public's willingness to pay for reduced crime. As we will discuss later in this chapter, assessing the public's willingness to pay is conceptually a better approach than many other methods that have been used to measure the monetary value of crime.

AGGREGATE COSTS AND BENEFITS

One of the most common—yet probably least important—reasons for estimating the costs of crime is to tally up the aggregate cost to society. Multi-billion-dollar cost estimates can easily make their way into the popular press and political debate. There are two basic problems with tallying up the costs of crime. First, having been told that crime costs the U.S. $450 billion per year, what are we to do with this information? If we are successful in fully estimating the aggregate cost of crime, we can compare this total cost estimate to that of other social problems (e.g. cancer, auto crashes, homelessness). Whether one agrees that this is a useful exercise or not, various advocacy groups do compare "cost-of-crime" estimates to the cost of other social ills in an effort to affect policy decisions. Unfortunately, misuses of these data occur on both sides of the political debate.

Until recently, most estimates of the cost of crime (including estimates published by the Bureau of Justice Statistics) have significantly underestimated costs. For example, Irwin and Austin (1994) used the "official" government estimates of $19 billion to illustrate that crime is less of a problem than other social ills and to argue against increased prison sentences. A more comprehensive cost study sponsored by the National Institute of Justice reports the annual cost of crime to victims to be $450 billion (Miller, Cohen, and Wiersema, 1996). An article reporting on that study in the *New York Times* quoted a Republican Congressman as saying the report "demonstrates that the cost of building prisons and adding police are justified" (Butterfield, 1996). Despite the rhetoric, neither small nor large "cost-of-crime" numbers demonstrate that the cost of building more prisons is justified or that alternatives to incarceration are better than more prisons!

Even if properly measured,[2] one cannot simply compare aggregate cost estimates of crime with estimates of the cost of other social ills to arrive at policy recommendations for future public spending priorities. Suppose, for example, that the cost of crime in the U.S. was estimated to exceed the cost of auto crashes. This does not necessarily mean that society should increase expenditures on crime prevention relative to prevention of auto crashes. If the costs of "preventing" crimes and auto crashes are factored into the equation, it might be found that society is already spending too much on the former and not enough on the latter. The more relevant question is how much additional reduction in crimes (or auto crashes) we would observe if we spent more on prevention. This can only be answered if we know such things as the deterrent and incapacitative effect of various sanctions, increased police patrols, etc.

Subject to the above caveat, comparing cost estimates of crime with other social ills can provide a basis of comparison on a common metric. For example, a study by Streff *et al.* (1992) estimated that the total cost of traffic crashes in Michigan was about three times as much as the total cost of crime in that state. Although no immediate policy implications should be drawn from this comparison, it does help begin the process of identifying public policy priorities and puts crime into its proper perspective. Over time, it might also be possible to quantify the magnitude of any change in crime rates by comparing costs from year to year.

A second problem with tallying up the costs of crime is that the true cost of crime is more than the sum total of its parts. If there were no robbers or rapists in this world, hitchhiking would probably be a way of life for a huge portion of the population. If violence was totally eliminated from society, organized crime might evaporate (as it depends on the threat of violence for its survival), and the standard of living of many inner city residents would increase as businesses returned to previously abandoned storefronts. These massive changes in social structure could only come about with equally impressive changes in social behavior. Thus any truly aggregate estimates of the cost of crime would need to account for these factors. To date, most estimates of the cost of crime have been done incrementally—for example, what is the cost of one crime given the current level of crime, or what is the value of reducing crime by 10 percent.

BENEFIT-COST ANALYSIS OF CRIME CONTROL POLICIES

Perhaps the most important—and controversial—use of monetary estimates of the cost of crime is to compare the benefits and costs of alternative crime control policies.[3] There is no shortage of crime prevention and crime reduction programs and proposals that would benefit from government funding. However, the government can only fund so many of these programs. One of the benefits of using dollars as a common metric for analyzing criminal justice policy is that society spends dollars to try to prevent crime from occurring in the first place. Society's ability to control criminal behavior and reduce the incidence of victimization is limited by its ability to pay for police, courts, corrections, and prevention programs. In an effort to reduce crime and the severity of its consequences, society has undertaken many criminal justice experiments, including intensive probation, electronic monitoring of offenders, shock incarceration, targeted and community police, spouse arrest programs for domestic violence, etc. As new policies are tested and policy options are considered, one must be able to apply objective evaluation techniques.[4] If two options have identical crime control effects but differing costs, the choice is simple. Unfortunately, few policy alternatives are so easily compared. In a more realistic case where a new policy reduces crime at some additional expense (or crime increases with less expenditures), one of the key questions is whether that reduced (increased) crime is worth its cost. Only by monetizing the cost of crime can one begin to answer that question.

One of the most compelling reasons to monetize the costs and benefits of crime control programs—and to attempt a benefit-cost analysis—is the consequence of not doing so. Whenever a criminal justice or prevention program is adopted or not adopted, society is implicitly conducting a benefit-cost analysis and placing dollar values on crimes. For example, suppose one program costs $1 million and ultimately will prevent 100 burglaries from occurring. Whether made explicit or not, the policymaker adopting that program has determined that it is worth spending at least $10,000 to reduce each burglary ($1 million divided by 100 burglaries). If another $1 million program that was not funded would have prevented 50 serious physical assaults from occurring, the policymaker is implicitly determining that each assault is worth less than $20,000 ($1 million divided by 50). Thus even the policymaker who has ethical concerns about placing dollar values on crime and conducting benefit-cost analysis implicitly makes a value judgment about the monetary value of crime.

HISTORY OF COST-OF-CRIME ESTIMATES

The idea of measuring the monetary costs of crime and the monetary benefits of crime reduction has been around for many years. Estimates of the cost of crime have a long history, dating back as early as the 1931 Wickersham Commission. A review of some of these studies is contained in Gray (1979). Subsequent presidential commissions have been called upon to report on the cost of crime. Many of these reports noted the difficulty and lack of progress over the years in adequately capturing the full costs of crime. However, they also acknowledged the importance of continuing this line of research. These earlier studies tended to report broad aggregates and focus on direct costs such as victim's out-of-pocket costs, the criminal justice system, the cost of private security, and the value of illegal wagers.

TABLE 1.1. THE COSTS OF CRIME—A TYPOLOGY

Cost category	Party who most directly bears cost
I COSTS OF CRIME	
Productivity losses	
1 Lost workdays	
(a) Lost wages for unpaid workdays	Victim
(b) Lost productivity	Society/employer
(c) Temporary labor and training of replacements	Society/employer
2 Lost housework	Victim and family
3 Lost school days	
(a) Forgone wages owing to lack of education	Victim
(b) Forgone non-pecuniary benefits of education	Victim
(c) Forgone social benefits owing to lack of education	Society
Medical and mental health care	
1 Costs not reimbursed by victim family	Victim/victim's family/society
2 Costs reimbursed by insurance	Society
3 Administrative cost: insurance reimbursement	Society
Direct property losses	
1 Losses not reimbursed by insurance	Victim
2 Losses reimbursed by insurance	Society
3 Administrative cost: insurance reimbursement	Society
4 Administrative cost: recovery and processing by police	Society
Indirect costs of victimization	
1 Avoidance behavior	Victim
2 Expenditures on moving, alarms, guard dogs, etc.	Victim
Pain and suffering/quality of life	**Victim**
Loss of affection/enjoyment	**Victim's family**
Death	
1 Lost quality of life	Victim
2 Loss of affection/enjoyment	Victim's family
3 Funeral and burial expenses	Victim's family
4 Psychological injury/treatment	Victim's family
Legal costs associated with tort claims	**Victim/victim's family/third party**
Victim services	
1 Expenses charged to victim	Victim
2 Expenses paid by agency	Society
"Second-generation costs"	
1 Future victims of crime committed by earlier victims	Future victim
2 Future social costs associated with (1)	Society, etc.

II COST OF SOCIETY'S RESPONSE TO CRIME	
Avoidance costs	
1 Avoidance behavior	Potential victim
2 Expenditures on moving, alarms, guard dogs, etc.	Potential victim
Fear of crime	**Potential victim**
Criminal justice system	**Society**
1 Police and investigative costs	Society
2 Prosecutors	Society
3 Courts	Society
4 Legal fees	
(a) public defenders	Society
(b) private legal fees	Offenders
5 Incarceration costs	Society
6 Non-incarcerative sanctions	Society
7 Victim/family time	Victim/family
8 Jury and witness time	Jury/witness
Victim services	
1 Victim service organizations	Society
2 Victim service volunteer time	Volunteers
3 Victim compensation programs	Society/offender
4 Victim/family time	Victim/family
Other non-criminal justice programs	
1 Hot-lines and public service announcements	Society
2 Community treatment programs	Society
3 Private therapy/counseling	Society/offender
Incarcerated offender costs	
1 Lost wages	Offender/family
2 Lost tax revenue and productivity	Society
3 Value of lost freedom	Offender
4 Psychological cost to family/loss of consortium	Family of offender
"Overdeterrence" costs	
1 Innocent individuals accused of offense	Innocent individuals
2 Restriction of legitimate activity	Innocent individuals
3 Actions taken by offenders to avoid detection e.g. kill robbery victims to reduce chance of being caught	Society/offender victim
"Justice" costs	
1 Constitutional protections to avoid false accusations	Society
2 Cost of increasing detection rate to avoid differential punishment	Society
III OFFENDER COSTS	
Opportunity cost of time spent in illegal activity instead of "working"	Society
Resources devoted to illegal activity (e.g. guns)	Offender

Source: Adapted and expanded from Cohen, Miller, and Rossman (1994), Tables 1 and 2.

The National Crime Victim Survey (NCVS), sponsored by the U.S. Bureau of Justice Statistics, is an annual survey of U.S. households that gathers data on the rate of victimization in the U.S. Among the questions asked of victims identified by the survey, are several questions that directly relate to the cost of crime and violence. Victims are asked about medical expenses, lost workdays and property stolen or damaged. From these questions, national estimates of the out-of-pocket costs per criminal offense can be made (Klaus, 1994). Although used by some researchers in the past, the NCVS estimates of the "economic cost of crime" are now widely regarded as inadequate. As discussed further in Chapter 2, the NCVS estimates are known to significantly underestimate even the out-of-pocket costs of crime and do not even begin to examine indirect and intangible costs.

The earlier studies—and the official government surveys—did not go beyond the out-of-pocket "tangible costs" of victimization. Beginning with Thaler (1978), there have been several attempts to include intangible costs. Thaler examined the price of housing in Rochester, N.Y. and inferred homeowners' willingness to pay for reduced crime by estimating property value differences in high- versus low-crime areas. In theory, homeowners are willing to pay to avoid the risk of both the tangible costs and intangible costs of being a crime victim. Various studies have since replicated and improved on these results for different cities and different time spans, with broadly consistent results. A major limitation in these hedonic property value studies of crime is that they have only estimated the cost of a generic index crime (rape, robbery, assault, motor vehicle theft, burglary and larceny combined). Owing to data limitations, previous studies have been unable to disentangle the cost of individual crimes. Bartley (2000) was only somewhat successful in isolating the cost of individual crimes using a much larger data set than previously.

Phillips and Votey (1981) took a different approach by combining estimates of the value of a statistical life with crime seriousness rankings from public surveys. Their approach was the first to attempt to account for the intangible costs of individual crimes, but it still was not able to account for many of those intangible costs. Cohen (1988a, 1988b) and subsequent follow-up studies by Cohen, Miller, and Rossman (1994) and Miller, Cohen, and Wiersema (1996) have taken a different approach to estimating the cost of crime. That approach combines estimates of the direct out-of-pocket costs with intangible losses estimated from a combination of jury awards in personal injury lawsuits and the value of a statistical life. This approach permits researchers to apply cost estimates to individual crime types. However, it is not entirely a market-based approach. Pain and suffering for non-fatal injuries are based on subjective jury awards in similar cases.[5] Although a good argument can be made that the jury award system is a reasonable mechanism to derive social costs, economists would generally prefer to impute dollar values from actual market transactions. That is why the property value approach was so appealing and is still mentioned by most economists as the preferred method of estimating the cost of crime. In Chapter 2 we will examine this methodology and its criticisms in detail. More recently, however, economists have begun to employ a new method, called "contingent valuation," which is also discussed in more detail in Chapter 2.

THE SCOPE OF THIS BOOK AND CRIME COSTS

As we saw with the Columbine High School example, one criminal event can impose numerous types of cost on many different parties. Victims and their families suffer in many ways—medical costs, earnings losses, property damage, lost quality of life, etc. Sometimes those costs are borne by the victims and their families, oftentimes society pays for these costs through insurance premiums or higher taxes.

The economics-of-crime literature has traditionally distinguished between three types of cost (Demmert, 1979: 2–5):

- those caused directly by criminal behavior (i.e. external costs imposed by the offender),
- those costs society incurs in response to crime to deter or prevent future incidents or to exact retribution, and
- those costs incurred by the offender (such as the opportunity cost of the offender's time while either engaging in the offense or being punished, if he or she otherwise could have been employed in productive activity).

Not all of these costs have been quantified. However, it is useful to enumerate all categories of crime, which is done below.

COSTS IMPOSED DIRECTLY AS A RESULT OF CRIME

Table 1.1 (overleaf) summarizes the various costs of crime. Victims incur many direct out-of-pocket expenses such as stolen or damaged property, medical costs, lost wages while away from work, and mental health or other victim-related treatment. Even if medical costs are reimbursed through insurance or employee benefit programs, society bears the cost through higher insurance premiums. Since the provision of insurance requires administrative (overhead) costs, the loss is even higher than the medical cost itself. If the employee receives paid sick leave or workers compensation during the recovery period, the employer bears the cost of the paid wages and the administrative cost of processing the payments. The employer may even have higher expenses owing to lost productivity or the need to hire temporary help or to pay overtime in the interim. Thus the total "out-of-pocket" portion of injury costs is actually higher than the sum of property losses, medical costs, and lost wages.

Although some costs are incurred as a direct result of victimization, other costs are more indirect—yet no less real. For example, victims might take new precautions such as avoiding certain areas of town, incurring longer commute times and/or more expensive means of transportation. These actions are often called "avoidance behavior." Some victims who now feel unsafe in their neighborhoods may incur the expense associated with moving (selling and buying a house, higher rent, moving expenses, etc.). Others might buy new protection devices such as burglar alarms, guard dogs, or defensive weapons.

Another indirect cost often associated with injuries is a temporary or permanent inability to do housework. In some cases, the family of the victim might hire someone to replace all or part of those household services, such as a maid, lawn care service or babysitter. The cost of hiring replacement services is clearly a monetary loss experienced by the family. In other cases, however, family members devote additional time to make up for the inability of the victim to carry out some of these chores. Although little or no monetary loss might be associated with this form of lost housework, one can estimate the monetary value of the replaced housework using economic principles and market wage rates.

Lost schoolwork for a student might also be valued. In the worst cases, a significant amount of school is missed and a victim might be set back a year in school. In other cases, the loss in education might be temporary and be made up through additional hours of work outside the classroom or result in lowered performance on exams. Although valuing these lost school days is difficult, in theory victims lose potential future earnings and the "psychic" value of an education. The potential cost of missed school days goes beyond the victim, as society values an educated population beyond the amount that the average individual would be willing to invest by him/herself.

In addition to the tangible costs incurred by victims (or paid by third parties), many other "intangible" consequences of crime may be quantified in monetary terms. One of the potentially largest intangible costs associated with victim injury is pain and suffering. Although pain and suffering do not involve a monetary loss, they may be monetized for purposes of comparison with other costs. Related to pain and suffering is the potential cost associated with the inability to continue some enjoyable leisure activities. These might be called "quality-of-life" costs. Not surprisingly, these costs are much more difficult to estimate than tangible costs, a subject that we will examine in some detail in chapter 2.

In addition to the victim, the victim's family may incur costs. One cost mentioned earlier is any additional expense incurred or time spent by family members doing chores previously performed by the family member who was injured and is no longer able to do these household chores. Another cost labeled "loss of affection/enjoyment" involves spousal and family activities that the victim can no longer participate in due to the injury.

Costs also arise when injured victims die. In addition to such costs as lost future wages and premature funeral and burial expenses, the value of the life itself is lost. Unlike other victim losses, the victim cannot be compensated for his/her life. However, various techniques are available to place monetary values on the statistical value of life.

In some cases, victims of violent behavior (or their families) may bring a private tort action against the party who injured the victim (or a third party for negligence). These suits involve various legal and court costs—often to third parties and insurance companies.

Finally, we should consider the long-term consequences of violent crime. For example, there is some evidence that victims of child abuse are more likely to become child abusers themselves. To the extent that the causal connection can be made, one should consider the future cost associated with child abuse to be a cost of today's incident.

COST OF SOCIETY'S RESPONSE TO CRIME

In addition to the cost imposed by the offender onto the victim, society's response to victimization involves many different types of cost. These costs are summarized in the second part of Table 1.1. Crime also has an impact on people who are not directly victimized, by increasing the level of fear in potential victims. Although difficult in practice, one can envision placing a dollar value on the level of fear in potential victims. Further, fear of victimization might result in increased prevention expenditures on items such as security systems and defensive firearms. It might also lead to changes in behavior, such as taking fewer walks at night.

The most visible cost associated with preventing future victimization is the criminal justice system. This includes government expenditures for police, prosecutors, public defenders, courts, prisons, and other non-incarcerative sanctions. It also includes private expenditures on criminal defense lawyers, as well as the amount of time spent by victims, juries, and witnesses dealing with the criminal justice system.

Some of society's response to violent behavior falls outside the criminal justice arena, with programs such as community treatment facilities and public service announcements, and prevention programs targeted at high-risk youth. Whether or not they are effective in preventing injuries or in raising the awareness of others to the problem, society spends resources attempting to publicize the problem and to prevent further incidents such as child physical and sexual abuse, drug abuse, juvenile delinquency, and long-term criminal careers.

Not only does violent behavior impose costs on the victim but some costs fall directly on the offender who is apprehended and subject to the criminal justice system. Other costs are borne by the offender's family. For example, if the offender was working prior to incarceration, he/she will suffer from lost wages while in prison. Regardless of whether or not one wants to include the offender's well-being as part of society's interests, those lost wages are a measure of the productivity loss to society. There is also evidence that incarceration will reduce the future earning capacity of many offenders as they have a more difficult time finding quality employment with a felony record. Potentially more costly is the intangible loss to the family—especially children—of the incarcerated offender.

A second potential cost is the value of lost freedom to an incarcerated offender. Beyond the social productivity loss, some would argue that society should consider the impact that prison has on the offender. A related and potentially more troubling cost associated with incarceration of offenders is the risk that the prison experience will increase the propensity of the offender to recidivate. To the extent that this is true, if one were to compare the cost of imprisonment to the cost of probation (for example), any marginal increase in future crimes should be attributed to the cost of imprisonment.

Finally, two often-overlooked categories of cost are "overdeterrence" and "justice" costs. Although these costs are likely to be relatively small in terms of the overall cost of victimization, it is important to enumerate them, since they have significant policy implications.

Overdeterrence costs are collateral consequences of imposing penalties for violent behavior. First, innocent parties who might be accused of committing a crime will take costly actions to avoid such allegations. Second, violent offenders might increase their level of violence in order to reduce the risk of capture.

The cost of "justice" is primarily determined by society's willingness to take costly precautions to ensure innocent individuals are not accused of crimes. Additional "justice" costs are incurred to the extent that society chooses more costly crime control alternatives than would be required if the concern was solely with minimizing the cost for a given level of deterrence.

OFFENDER COSTS

Finally, the last section of Table 1.1 enumerates offender costs. Note that costs imposed upon offenders by a society that wishes to punish, rehabilitate, or otherwise seek justice were included above under the category "society's response to violence." Here we consider costs that are incurred by the offender or society directly as a result of being involved in criminal activity. For example, offenders might spend considerable time and/or resources committing the violent act. Although all of these costs are borne by the offender directly, society would also benefit from their absence. The most obvious cost would be the opportunity cost of the offender's time. That is, if the offender could have been gainfully employed while not engaging in criminal behavior, society is losing that productivity. In addition, one might consider other resource costs that assist the offender in carrying out this behavior—such as expenditures on weapons.

CHAPTER 3

MACROECONOMICS AND THE CRIME RATE

By Ron Liggett

If you happened to read the preface in this book, you will recall my goal of not having the chapters read like a stereo repair manual. However, in full disclosure, parts of this chapter may drift in that direction. My advice? Grab a cup of coffee (or espresso) and plow through; hopefully things will make sense in the end.

Over the years, there has been considerable research and attention paid to the impact of macroeconomic conditions on criminal activity.[A] Conventional thought (and to some degree, common sense) suggests an inverse relationship between the crime rate and economic performance. That is, poor economic performance should lead to more crime as a lack of fruitful employment means a low opportunity cost for those individuals who may lean toward lawlessness. Ample research supports this conventional view, particularly in regards to property crimes such as robbery and burglary. But what about other crimes? Does auto theft follow this pattern? How about the serious non-property crimes like criminal homicide?

Investigating these and other questions brings awareness to several pertinent issues and a variety of opinions on this topic. In fact, we find a few studies that disagree with the conventional thought described above. Of course, this isn't too surprising since we know that economists, and social scientists in general, certainly don't agree on all matters. And while some of these non-conventional studies might muddy the water a bit, they are also helpful in bringing focus to other relevant variables. For example, what is actually the best method of measuring economic performance to facilitate a clear look into criminal behavior? And, what is the preferred aggregation of data? Should we look at national statistics or is state and local information more useful? Through the next few pages, we will sort through some of the dialogue and attempt to form some useful observations.

A Per Philip Cook, there are references to research in this area going back "at least since the mid-19th century."

MEASURING ECONOMIC PERFORMANCE

The measurement of macroeconomic activity can take many shapes. GDP, the unemployment rate, inflation, and median wage rates are all key measures of economic activity. Data on home ownership and home foreclosures are relevant indicators of economic health as well. Additionally, in the aggregate, looking at the overall business cycle is significant as we try to ascertain the impact of economic recessions.

Defining a Recession: Speaking of recessions, while most students understand that the term refers to an economic downturn, it may be useful to reference a more detailed definition. The National Bureau of Economic Research (NBER) notes that a recession may be defined as "a significant decline in economic activity spread across the economy, lasting more than a few months, normally visible in production, employment, real income, and other indicators. A recession begins when the economy reaches a peak of activity and ends when the economy reaches its trough. Between trough and peak, the economy is in an expansion." [B]

As with any economic investigation, it is easy to get bogged down sorting through myriad data. Accordingly, for this chapter (and in keeping with the book title,...*Selected Topics*) we will limit our focus to crime observations related to unemployment, inflation, and the business cycle.

UNEMPLOYMENT AND CRIME

The unemployment rate has generally been seen as a proxy for the overall health of the economy, so it is not surprising that there are an abundance of studies that analyze crime fluctuations based on this rate.[C] In regards to criminal behavior, economic theory suggests that these "crime-prone" individuals, in seeking economic gain, make rational choices between legitimate (legal) acts and illegitimate (criminal) behaviors.[D] And, as legal job opportunities decline, the attractiveness of illegal acts may increase. Under this theory, we would therefore expect to see a positive relationship between the unemployment rate and the crime rate.

B The NBER, and more specifically, the Business Cycle Dating Committee within the organization, work to determine when a recession is deemed to have occurred.

C While the unemployment rate remains an essential variable in the evaluation of economic performance, the idea that it is still the most reliable and accurate gauge of economic health is open to debate. Increases in part-time employment and the "marginally attached" worker likely give us a slightly different message when compared to prior periods.

D This follows in the seminal work done by Becker which is mentioned in Chapter 1. Also, while we generally focus on property crimes in this discussion, white collar/financial misdeeds could also be included in the debate.

(i.e., higher unemployment rate equals higher crime rate, *ceteris paribus*). Going forward we will label the unemployment-crime rate relationship as UC.[E]

Despite what appears as a rather straightforward theory, research in the UC area has sometimes displayed mixed results. Some studies mention a "consensus of doubt" in this area and describe the UC relationship as 'insignificant' or modest at best.[1] Upon closer examination, the hesitancy to fully embrace a positive UC relationship may relate more to the materiality or the strength of the relationship. Additionally, some studies cite a lack of "statistical significance" between the two variables.[F]

Even with the so-called "consensus of doubt" statement, there are ample studies to support a positive UC relationship. But, to be clear, finding a relationship that is both positive *and* statistically significant has, at times, been elusive. For example, in reviewing five specific studies, Steven Levitt noted, "almost all of these studies report a statistically significant but substantively small relationship" between UC. Levitt further affirms a small but positive correlation by suggesting a 1% rise in property crime per 1% increase in the unemployment rate.[2] Other studies have expressed a positive correlation as well, whereby a 1% increase in unemployment leads to a rise in property crimes of approximately 2%.[3]

So, what have we established? A positive relationship? Yes. Statistical significance? Well, not always. But, if we narrow the data down to a smaller scale, (i.e., state/local data vs. national data, or even local vs. state) the UC relationship becomes more pronounced. At the lower levels of aggregation (think *city* crime rates v. *national* rates), the positive/significant associations *increase*.[4] And why wouldn't they? Consider the following comparison: The reduction in crime rates from 1990 to 2000 was quite substantial.[G] So, in comparing these two periods, exactly what unemployment rates should we use? The overall unemployment rate for Chicago in 1990 was approximately 13%. However, census data from that year had neighborhood rates ranging from 3% to 45%! On a national scale, unemployment dipped to 3.9% for the country as a whole in April 2000. However, state rates ranged from 2.2% in Iowa to 6.6% in Alaska. Most obviously, there are material and relevant variances in all of these numbers, so which should we use as our reference? From Levitt, "Simply summarizing the Chicago unemployment rate in 1990 as 13%, or the national unemployment rate in April 2000 as 3.9[%], ignores all of this variation."[5]

E UC is used to represent the unemployment-crime relationship (see Chiricos and Andresen, among others).

F Statistically significant in the sense that the relationship between variables is caused by specific factors rather than simply random chance.

G Substantial indeed! As noted in Chapter 14 (per Levitt), national homicide rates dropped 43%, violent crime fell 34%, and property crime declined by 29% during this timeframe.

A CLEARER PICTURE FROM LOCAL DATA

Arguing for the importance of local data, we would reference 2014 murder statistics, which showed that a mere 2% of U.S. counties accounted for *more than half* of all homicides. The worst 1% of counties (with 19 % of the population) accounted for 37% of murders.[6] Those sentences need to be read again to fully grasp the data. Drilling down within these counties we see more concentration within specific neighborhoods. For example, in 2016, Chicago—with its 77 neighborhoods—had over 800 homicides. However, more than half of these took place in only nine of the 77 neighborhoods![7] With data such as this, it would seem imperative that more policy debate begin at the very local level.

Consider two other points that are relevant in this discussion. First, city sectors and neighborhoods are quite different in many ways. Income levels, family characteristics, race, and education levels may all vary and, when examining crime stats, we observe that these differences matter: "Research has consistently shown that victimization rates are highest for men, adolescents and young adults, African-Americans, those who have never married, and persons who live in central cities."[8] This is important information when analyzing policy options, but unfortunately these specifics can get overlooked. In essence, the national trends from the large-scale aggregation could be such that "national-level data…literally cancel[s] out the substantial differences in unemployment and crime that characterize different sections of cities or [the] cities themselves" making the previously mentioned variables irrelevant.[9]

Second, and perhaps more intricate,

> *…local data (is) better able to capture what can be termed the "milieu effects" of unemployment on a particular area…high unemployment may have a demoralizing impact on a particular neighborhood or section of a city or county that creates a climate of hopelessness or anomie with criminogenic consequences even for those not directly unemployed (e.g., teenagers or others not in the labor force).*[10]

An argument on the preference of less aggregated data is likely best summed up by Levitt:

> *National-level time series data are a crude tool for distinguishing between two alternative behavioral explanations for a link between unemployment and crime. Consequently, inferences drawn from aggregate time series estimates are likely to be misleading.*[11]

So, while UC studies bring forth a variety of views, it remains appropriate to argue the existence of a positive relationship between unemployment and crime.[H]

H While understanding the relevance of employment, we know behaviors don't begin and end with one data point. Therefore, it is worthwhile to mention the so-called "Theft Triangle," which conveys the role of <u>attitude</u>, <u>opportunity</u>, and <u>need</u> in criminal acts.

Additionally, it is not good practice to focus only on national data when looking to implement crime policies. Clearly, "efforts to increase the availability of work can be expected to have... (negative) effects on the value of property crime as an alternative."[12] Translation: Get people to work and we would expect crime rates to go down. A conclusion which both the ardent conservative and the ardent liberal supporter should agree.

FOR INQUIRING MINDS...

Let us add a few comments to the "national data vs. local data" discussion to see if there is an underlying lesson or theme. The demand for national-type policies in all areas of society seems to grow forcefully louder each year. Yes, louder, and perhaps with a shrill tone at times. However, it could be argued that the dependence on so much policy implementation at the national level is a diversion from the core principles of how this country was established. National policies (both economic and political) mean more central control and more bureaucracy.[I] However, centralized policy and authority have their weaknesses, (review Chapter 1 and the limited government characteristic of capitalism) and while there may be a "time and place" for that course of action, there are limits to its effectiveness.[J]

For example, issues such as a federal minimum wage and national education standards have relevance, but should be approached cautiously. In regards to employment, the value of a young person's first "entry-level" job is enormous. Learning to accept authority, to be on time, to handle challenges in the workforce, to deal with customers in commerce (items we sometimes label as "soft skills")—these are all relevant economically; these skills should help to get so-called "at-risk" individuals on a better course. Therefore, if minimum wage hikes squeeze out some of these positions (as sound economic theory suggests it will), we may find that the lack of entry-level and/or low-skilled positions will have significant and profoundly negative consequences. Accordingly, greater policy efficiencies may very well be seen at the local level and therefore should not be overlooked.

I I am reminded of an observation by Milton Friedman as he asks, "Is it really true that political self-interest is nobler somehow than economic self-interest?" (https://www.youtube.com/watch?v=RWsx1X8PV_A)

J This discussion is not meant to deflect the relevance or importance of federal resources that may be necessary during a crisis period such as the terrorist high alerts, or even the hurricane summer of 2017.

INFLATION AND CRIME

When looking at the "macro goals" of an economy, solving the issues of unemployment and inflation usually appear at the top of the list.[K] We have discussed the unemployment segment, so let us now focus on inflation. We all know that the business environment does not enjoy the element of "uncertainty." And, perhaps no topic creates more uncertainty than inflation—particularly unexpected inflation. The uncertainty caused by high and/or unexpected increases in the overall price level is something both real and tangible. And, just as rising prices create uncertainty in legitimate industries, non-legal sectors and their participants must deal with this problem as well.

As noted earlier, there is a plethora of journal articles analyzing the UC relationship. However, the amount of research into the inflation-crime connection is more limited. Nonetheless, some findings are noteworthy. First, we know that real incomes generally decline during a period of rising prices. While this **real income effect** is true for all income earners—both high and low—researchers have noted what may be a more pronounced effect on low-skilled labor.[13] [L] This becomes pertinent when evaluating changes in wage rates for those in the low-skill category with limited income potential and/or opportunity for growth.[M] Further, and of particular importance in our analysis, the initial impact of inflation on the criminal is identical to the impact on law-abiding individuals. Again, real incomes for each group are lowered during a period of rising prices—even for criminals![14]

Second, a problematic relationship can be seen in markets where increases in commodity prices raise the reward for theft.[15] For example, rising prices in certain precious metals have increased the attractiveness of these products to thieves of all types. Consider the market for copper. As global demand has risen from developing nations and other markets, the price of copper has been driven upward.[16] A simple supply/demand graph helps to provide a visual perspective. That is, the change from P1 to P2 is noticed by both private markets *and* thieves!

Thefts of this product at building sites, energy stations, cell towers, and other locations are estimated to cost U.S. businesses more than $1 billion a year.[17] Perhaps even more concerning than the actual dollar figure is the potential

K While the current generation has certainly seen their share of inflated prices in specific areas like education and health services, they have not yet experienced the destructive impact of an inflationary spike in the overall price level, such as that which occurred in the late 1960s and 1970s.

L As referenced by Tang-Lean, Lott notes that a limitation on access to capital markets may push the poor to commit more property crimes as a means "of borrowing against future human capital."

M When discussing low-skilled workers, we are referring to someone who—at this moment—does not possess certain necessary skills that are in line with business demands. Additionally, we might note that there are characteristics other than physical and mental aptitude which negate legitimate job opportunities (i.e., a "poor attitude").

Graph 1. Increase in Demand for Copper

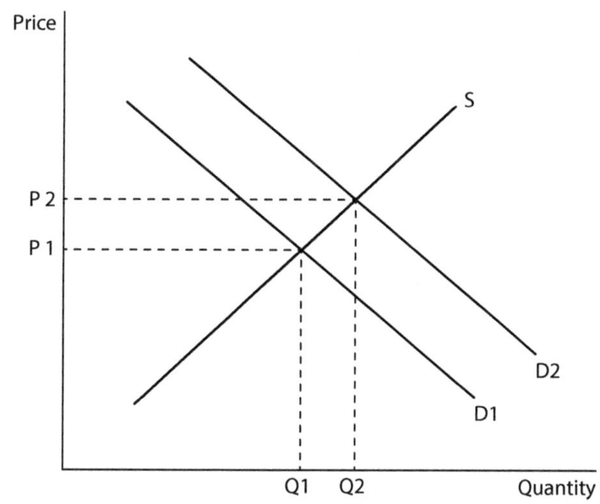

negative impact on the U.S. "critical infrastructure."[N] Again, with much of the pilfering occurring in areas such as telecommunications, railroads, and the electrical and energy markets, there is an infrastructure concern that could negatively impact our overall national security.[18]

When observing the impact of inflation on crime rates, there is definitely a connection. A recent study notes a "stable, positive impact of inflation on all forms of property crime."[19] Even more pronounced is the relationship between crime and "headline inflation" (see definition in footnote) as researchers note "a statistically robust [and], economically significantly link."[20] [O] To summarize, even though the studies are more limited in number, the connection between rising price levels and unlawful behavior should not be glossed over.

N Per the Department of Homeland Security, critical infrastructure includes "assets, systems, and networks...considered so vital to the United States that their incapacitation or destruction would have a debilitating effect on security, national economic security, national public health or safety, or any combination hereof." https://www.dhs.gov/critical-infrastructure-sectors

O "Headline inflation" (as compared with core inflation) measures total inflation and includes measures for items more prone to volatility, such as food and energy prices.

THE BUSINESS CYCLE AND CRIME

To conclude this section, we will look at one more relationship by analyzing movements in crime rates based on business cycle fluctuations. While it might be tempting to look for parallels with the previously discussed section on unemployment, we note that by following expansions, contractions, and the overall cyclical trends, we get a broader and deeper look at the macro relationship with crime. As noted, some social scientists express the relationship between crime and the economy as being "countercyclical" for certain types of street crime.[21] This categorization is particularly noteworthy when looking at changes in crime rate per movements in the business cycle.[P]

As you may recall from Chapter 1, the business cycle refers to a nation's fluctuation in economic activity over a period of time. This fluctuation is sometimes referred to in terms of "peaks and troughs." As the economy expands, it eventually reaches a high-point, or peak performance. After peaking, a downturn in economic activity or contraction eventually occurs which leads to a low-point, or trough.[Q] Using the business cycle as a measure of economic performance is sensible in that the cyclical movements are strongly related to changes in gross domestic product (GDP) as well as unemployment. Likewise, the impact of recessions, as defined earlier in this chapter, can be viewed more clearly by following cyclical trends. Note Graph 2, the typical business cycle graph on the next page.

Many studies have been done in this area, but the one we reference to aid in this discussion comes from Cook and Zarkin. It has direct application for this section as part of the study analyzes behaviors over nine complete business cycles occurring between 1933 and 1981. While this may not be the seminal work done in this area, it remains a study that has held up over time; the work is straightforward and provides clarity to the analysis.[R] In this model, the researchers measured changes in robbery, burglary, homicides and auto theft over the nine business cycles.

What were the general findings from this study? First, both robbery and burglary followed a countercyclical pattern (i.e., more of these crimes occurred during economic downturns).[S] This behavior follows the conventional thought mentioned previously. Second, criminal homicide had little to no statistical relationship to the business cycle ("effectively nil" per

P "Countercyclical" is not a frequently used term, and students sometimes struggle to grasp the concept. We are simply talking about crime rates that move opposite to economic performance. Explaining this trend with explicit graphs of the business cycle may be helpful.

Q Obviously there is no requirement stating that the contraction phase *must* eventually occur. However, this is what is observable over time. As a rough estimate, post WWII expansions have lasted approximately 60 months.

R Good research, like good music, can be timeless if both the model and data are solid.

S This is a finding consistent with the positive UC relationship noted earlier.

Graph 2. Typical Business Cycle

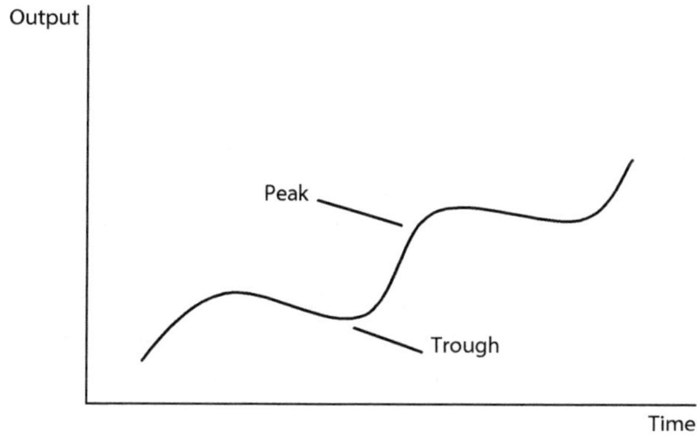

Cook), a finding consistent with other studies.[22] Finally, auto theft differed significantly from the other results and actually showed "procyclical" tendencies. This suggests more vehicle thefts during economic expansion and fewer thefts in the downturn.[23] Why would this occur? Multiple explanations exist. There may be an increased demand for the newer and more attractive vehicle styles, which likely appear during expansions. Alternatively, other scholars (whose studies also confirmed a procyclical relationship) noted the existence of a "guardianship" theory. Under this idea, the unemployed likely make fewer unnecessary trips and spend more time at home, therefore keeping a more watchful eye on their possessions.[24]

Supplementing the Cook and Zarkin work is their listing of specific "linkages," which are part of the study and which are included for your perusal. These linkages have been displayed in other textbooks (including the first edition of this book), and I feel they still serve to enhance discussion in this area. For clarity purposes, I would note that I have amplified each of these with some additional dialogue. For each item in the list, you should note the economic impact—both expansionary and/or contractionary. Further, and more importantly, understanding the impact of economic activity in each of these linkages might help us with an overall and more direct conclusion. That is, with the existence of so many relevant variables, it is simply not possible to have just *one* conclusive statement which explains the impact of macroeconomic fluctuations on *all* crime rates.

RELATING THE BUSINESS CYCLE TO CRIME: RELEVANT LINKAGES [T]

1. **Legitimate opportunities.** The quality and quantity of legitimate employment opportunities are generally procyclical (i.e., stronger economy = more job opportunities). Therefore, the higher unemployment rates and related problems associated with economic recessions may promote crime by lowering the opportunity cost of the time spent in criminal activities and/or prison. On the other hand, higher individual income during strong economic times may create greater "targets" for criminals.
2. **Criminal opportunities.** From another perspective, recessions may also discourage crime by reducing the quality of criminal opportunities—particularly for property crimes. Potential victims, facing hard times themselves, may have a stronger propensity to defend their property against would-be thieves or muggers. Additionally, any demand for stolen merchandise may be lessened during the economic downturn, while potential victims might also carry less cash.
3. **Use of criminogenic commodities.**[U] Intoxication has long been thought to be an important cause of crime, particularly violent crime. If alcohol consumption (and abuse) should increase during good times (normal good theory[V]), then so may the incidence of drunken fights. However, we should also note the obvious in that alcohol consumption is available in bad times as well, since the market for beer and spirits offers a vast array of products at a wide variety of prices.[W] Additionally, the authors noted that handguns might be included in this criminogenic category, and if handgun sales tend to increase during good times, then fights arising from alcohol consumption may become more deadly.
4. **The criminal justice system response to crime.** This is generally driven by tax budgets, although politicians who make budgetary decisions are also influenced by public sentiment. At any rate, reduced tax collections during recessions at the state and local level may result in smaller budgets for police and courts and therefore a reduction in the criminal justice system's ability to contain crime.[25]

T Note the countercyclical and/or procyclical behavior in each item. The content is primarily from the Cook and Zarkin study; however, I have amplified the summaries with some of additional dialogue.

U Essentially the authors are referring to drugs and alcohol, although, as noted, guns could be a component as well.

V A "normal" good is one in which an increase in income leads to an increase in demand.

W However, if alcohol consumption declines during a recession (as some researchers, including Cook, declare), we would then expect less criminal behavior from this product.

CONCLUDING THOUGHT

Even without one overall definitive statement to lean on, some interesting and useful relationships remain in the discussion of macroeconomic performance and criminal behavior. When the data is stratified to specific crimes, with restricted aggregation, we do begin to see more certain and reliable connections. Accordingly, what might be called a 'micro' examination of macroeconomic performance may very well assist in formulating helpful public policy in this area.

ENDNOTES

1. Chiricos, Theodore G. (1987). "Rates of Crime and Unemployment: An Analysis of Aggregate Research Evidence." *Social Problems*, Vol. 34, No. 2, (Apr 1987), p. 188.
2. Levitt, Steven D. (2004). "Understanding Why Crime Fell in the 1990s: Four Factors that Explain the Decline and Six that Do Not." *Journal of Economic Perspectives*, Vol 18, No. 1, Winter 2004, p. 170.
3. Cook, P.J. and G.A. Zarkin. (1985). "Crime and the Business Cycle." *Journal of Legal Studies*, Vol. 14, No. 1, (Jan 1985), pp. 115–128.
4. Chiricos 195
5. Levitt, Steven D. "Alternative Strategies for Identifying the Link Between Unemployment and Crime." *Journal of Quantitative Criminology*, Vol. 17, No. 4, Dec 2001, p. 379.
6. Crime Prevention Research Center (April 2017). Retrieved from https://crimeresearch.org/2017/04/number-murders-county-54-us-counties-2014-zero-murders-69-1-murder/. Accessed 2017 Aug 14.
7. http://heyjackass.com/category/2016-stats/. Accessed 2017 Nov 30. (This is a strangely named website frequently cited for Chicago crime data).
8. Cohen, Lawrence E. and Marcus K. Felson. "Routine Activity Theory," *Encyclopedia of Criminological Theory*, 2010, Sage Publications, p 188. Retrieved from https://study.sagepub.com/system/files/Cohen,_Lawrence_E.,_and_Marcus_K._Felson_-_Routine_Activity_Theory.pdf. Accessed 2017 Sept 7.
9. Chiricos
10. Chiricos
11. Levitt, "Alternative Strategies...", 377
12. Chiricos 203
13. Devine, J.A., Sheley, J.F. & M.D. Smith. "Macroeconomic and Social-Control Policy Influences on Crime-rates Changes, 1948–1985." *American Sociological Review*, vol 53, pp. 407–420. As quoted in Tang, Chor Foon and Hooi Hooi Lean. "Will Inflation Increase Crime Rate? New Evidence from Bounds and Modified Wald Tests." Global Crime, Vol. 8, No. 4, Nov 2007, p. 313.

14. Nunley, John M., Michael L. Stern, Richard A. Seals and Joachim Zietz. "The Impact of Inflation on Property Crime." *Contemporary Economic Policy*. Vol. 34, No. 3, July 2016, p. 496.
15. Nunley 496
16. Federal Bureau of Investigations. Copper Thefts Threaten U.S. Critical Infrastructure. Retrieved from https://www.fbi.gov/stats-services/publications/copper-thefts. Accessed 2017 Aug 14.
17. Koba, Mark (2013). "Stopping Copper Theft Becomes Big-Time Business." CNBC. 2013 Aug 12. http://www.cnbc.com/id/100946683. Accessed 2017 Oct 23.
18. Federal Bureau of Investigations. Copper Thefts.
19. Nunley 496
20. Nunley 494
21. Cook and Zarkin 115
22. Levitt, "Understanding Why Crime Fell…" 170
23. Cook and Zarkin 123, 126
24. Yearwood, Douglas L and Gerry Koinis. "Revisiting Property Crime and Economic Conditions: An Exploratory Study to Identify Predictive Indicators Beyond Unemployment Rates." *The Social Science Journal*. Vol 48. 2011. p. 155.
25. Cook and Zarkin 117.

CHAPTER 4

AN INTRODUCTION TO "PROFILES IN COURAGE"

By Ron Liggett

9/11, WTC, AIRPORTS, AND THE BELTWAY SNIPERS

Profiling is a way of life in the process of apprehending criminals. We draw conclusions based on the data available in regards to criminals and their acts. Again—the importance of data gathering! So perhaps the next question is what part of the data should be used? Sex? Height? Weight? Age? Gun ownership? Race? Prior violations? Immigration status? Education level?

Some forget that the initial World Trade Center attack occurred in 1993. On February 26, "a nitrourea bomb, in excess of 1,000 pounds, with hydrogen cylinders to add impact, was detonated in the now-infamous yellow Ryder Econoline van on the B-2 level of the parking garage, causing massive destruction that spanned seven levels."[1] The blast killed six people, injured 1,000, and caused an estimated $500 million in damage.[2] Should this first strike have led to more action by government, under the assumption that the terrorists had not finished the job? And, should there have been more steps to profile and prevent further attacks? Or were the impending 9/11 terrorist attacks of 2001 so "outside the box" that even with profiling, mainstream intelligence was not able to see them coming?[A]

Again, profiling is part of the process in apprehension <u>and</u> prevention. Consider the situation of the disgruntled employee who morphs into what has become disturbingly common—the "workplace killer." Multiple characteristics exist in many of these settings that can be used as a predictor. In noting 20+ possible characteristics, Dr. Martin Blinder suggests an employee (or prospective worker) exhibiting 10 or more should be cause for concern.[3] A few of these traits are listed below.

A In hindsight, having viewed the 1996 film entitled "Executive Decision," starring Kurt Russell and Steven Seagal, the 9/11 attacks hardly seem implausible.

- Profoundly narcissistic, exhibiting strong sense of entitlement
- Sour attitude
- Repeatedly offended by "slights"
- Controlling and demanding
- They make ominous or cryptic comments
- History of drug/alcohol use, and others...

So the suggestion is that there exists the possibility of recognizing traits of such an employee at early stages, perhaps even pre-hire. But no system of hiring and overall scrutiny is without flaws. And the same can be said for airline boarding procedures and terrorist attacks. The process is simply imperfect.

Consider another situation where profiling played somewhat of a different role—the Beltway Sniper attacks of 2002. Beginning October 2 and ending with the capture of two predators on October 24, the DC/Maryland area was terrorized by sniper shootings that killed 10 people and injured three. Initial profiles were incorrect. "We were looking for a white van with white people, and we ended up with a blue car with black people," said D.C. Police Chief Charles Ramsey. Sadly he also noted a frustrating fact—the killer's blue car actually "had attracted police attention at least 10 times during the critical period."[4] Retired ATF employee Michael Bouchard noted that the "biggest hindrance" in the case was the perceived presence of a white van. Despite having to overcome many obstacles, law enforcement was eventually able to work leads and track down the two killers.[B] [5]

The short reading that follows is entitled "Profiles in Courage" and appeared in the op-ed section of the *Wall Street Journal* shortly after the 9/11 attacks. The article provides an opportunity for examination and discussion of two realities that are pertinent to this topic. First, as noted above, law enforcement does create a "profile" to assist in their focus on apprehension (and prevention). Secondly, scarcity exists and choices must be made in the allocation of resources. So, where should the focus be? Do you check the 80-year-old grandmother as extensively as you check the 20-year-old from a known terrorist-sponsoring country? Certainly there are those who feel that each and every individual should be evaluated exactly the same when boarding a plane. But is this good economics?

In reading this section, consider the following concepts:

- Allocation of resources and the issue of scarcity.
- Problem-solving skills.
- Profiling as a component of the problem-solving mechanism.

B John Allen Muhammad was executed on November 10, 2009 in Virginia. Lee Boyd Malvo was sentenced in 2006 to six life sentences. He confessed to four additional murders that had occurred earlier in 2002.

QUESTIONS

1. How would you describe the issue of resource allocation in regards to this article? (That is, what are the areas of concern?)
2. Evaluate the following statement. "Each and every traveler should be treated and evaluated exactly the same in regards to the boarding process on all flights." Does this statement stand up to economic analysis? Why, or why not?
3. What were three economic consequences of the 9/11 attacks?
4. The "Beltway Sniper" events of 2002 lasted for 23 paralyzing days with the initial profile unfortunately off target. What types of costs were experienced during this period?

ENDNOTES

1. U.S. Fire Administration/Technical Report Series. "The World Trade Center Bombing: Report and Analysis." New York. USFA-TR-076/February 1993. <http://www.usfa.fema.gov/downloads/pdf/publications/tr-076.pdf>. 2012 Nov 29.
2. Hirschkorn, Phil. (2003, Feb 26). "New York Remembers 1993 WTC Victims." CNN News. 2012 Nov 29. <www.cnn.com>.
3. Blinder, Martin. (1997, Feb 10). "Manager's Journal: Profile of a Workplace Killer." *Wall Street Journal*. A 18:3.
4. Bothe, Elsbeth. (2002, Dec 15). "Facing the Beltway Snipers, Profilers Were Dead Wrong." *The Baltimore Sun*. 2012 Nov 19.
5. <http://www.clarkprosecutor.org/html/death/US/muhammad1181.htm>. 2012 Nov 19.

PROFILES IN COURAGE

By James Q. Wilson and Heather R. Higgins

These days, it seems every evening's news leads with another story of consternation by somebody over the use of "racial profiling." But before the country is carried away with slogans, we ought to spend a little time being honest about the question. That means recognizing that most profiling is not racial, that some profiling (even when it involves race) is essential under some circumstances, and that it would be impossible for law enforcement to do its job without taking into account the observable features of people.

Young men are vastly more likely to commit crimes than are young women or older men. When the police scan the streets looking for people to question, should they stop men and women, old and young at equal rates? Black men are six to eight times more likely to commit violent crimes than are white men. When the police patrol the streets trying to prevent crime, should they stop white and black men at the same rate?

Notice, please, that we say "stop," not "arrest." The police have a right to question citizens, but they only have a right to arrest them if they have evidence they have committed a crime. It would be manifestly wrong to arrest or issue so much as a traffic ticket to a person simply because of his age, sex, or race. "Driving While Black" (or while young or male) is not an offense with which anyone should be charged.

We do not doubt that pedestrians or motorists have been stopped because of their race, but we suspect that if someone did a decent study of police behavior (instead of relying on the complaints of politicians and activists) they would discover that in most cases (if unhappily, not in all of them), there were more cues leading to the stop than just sex or race.

Consider the case of the Street Crimes Unit in the New York Police Department. This group, while much maligned, took thousands of guns off the street, helping drive down that city's murder rate. It did so by stopping and patting down people on the street. Heather Mac Donald reported that the unit frisked 45,000 people during a two-year period, leading to 9,500 arrests and the seizure of 2,500 illegal guns.

Getting one gun off the street for every 18 stops is a pretty good outcome, considering that those not carrying guns, or doing something otherwise illegal, were merely inconvenienced for a few minutes. No doubt some people regarded the stop as worse than an inconvenience and no doubt some stops may have been hard to justify. But the hassle factor has to be evaluated in the light of the great gains: 2,500 fewer dangerous weapons in dangerous hands.

Now, in the aftermath of Sept. 11 the task of law enforcement has been taken to a different level. It must figure out how to prevent a tiny fraction of the millions of people who use our airports from carrying knives, guns, and bombs onto airliners. For people working airport security stations, the risks to society of their failure are vastly greater than for the Street Crimes Unit.

In just a few seconds, a screener must decide whether to pat down a person who is hurrying to a plane. Trained properly, these screeners must be able to notice some bits of behavior or body language that may be a tip-off—a nervous, hurried manner, perhaps, or dodgy eyes or a guilty look. But not all terrorists are basket cases. And for many of those serving as the country's final line of defense against terrorism in the skies, physical features may be all they have to go on. As Professor Peter H. Schuck of Yale Law School recently pointed out, the screeners have no choice but to rely on stereotypes to make a reasonable judgment.

So, stereotypes. The word has come to connote any irrational prejudice. But stereotypes are not in fact any different from the fleeting impressions and judgments we all use to govern our daily lives. We are cautious about people who have a rough appearance or speak in an erratic manner just as we are drawn to people who are attractive and well-spoken. And while those instincts of avoidance or attraction are not always reliable, indulging ourselves with the luxury of waiting for conclusive evidence would mean either meeting no one, or everyone.

As Mr. Schuck says, a stereotype is halfway between an error and a fact. We should try to use it cautiously.

When James Wilson's wife, Roberta, recently went flying, she was picked out at the boarding gate by American Airlines for a complete search. She is the least threatening person one could image—five feet tall, blonde hair, older than she would like to be, and with a beatific expression on her face. She was picked, the airline agent said, "at random."

When Heather Higgins went to Reagan National Airport, Delta Airlines selected 15 passengers for complete searches. Though all terrorists involved in Sept. 11 were young Middle Eastern males, Delta picked three elderly men (one an Asian), six Caucasian women, including one with two children, and two

Hispanic women. Yet in the line of 70 or so passengers, there were six individuals who were not only Middle Eastern but young, male, and traveling alone. Not one of them was checked. When asked, Delta said the only searches they would do were at random.

By contrast, when a male Secret Service agent armed with a gun left on his airplane seat his bag and some books, apparently written in Arabic, the flight attendants became alarmed. The pilot reviewed the man's paperwork and found it incomplete. When asked to fill out a new form, the agent became anxious and then hostile. As Christopher Caldwell has pointed out in *The Weekly Standard*, had the agent been named John Smith instead of Walied Shater, there would have been no incident. But Mr. Shater and the Council on American Islamic Relations claimed he was the victim of ethnic profiling.

Mrs. Wilson and Mrs. Higgins get searched, and they pass it off. But a Near Eastern male carrying a gun and claiming he was going to see the president on the basis of incomplete forms starts complaining about profiling?

This is nonsense. Doing only random searches and not questioning an armed Middle Eastern male can only be justified if your only goal is to avoid the charge of "profiling." If your goal instead is to prevent somebody from carrying a shoe bomb or box cutters onto an airplane, then the search should not be random but deliberate, using all available facts to form a useful, if not entirely reliable, stereotype.

Of course, to do that exposes the airline to charges of "profiling." And indeed it is profiling. But it is not a profile based exclusively or even chiefly on race, but on hints—that is, useful stereotypes—supplied by judgments made by rational people. Unfortunately, political leaders and civil rights activists have so polarized the discussion of profiling that an entirely defensible screening policy is now regarded as a threat to our fundamental liberties and is replaced by an irrational screening policy that threatens our safety.

The more we study terrorists, the more we will learn about them and the better our screening profiles—our stereotypes—will become. If we apply that knowledge, fewer innocent people will face any burden and more real terrorists will be caught. We will overcome slogans about "racial profiling" and instead become a bit safer.

*Mr. Wilson is the author of "Moral Judgment" (Basic Books, 1997). Mrs. Higgins is the vice president of the Independent Women's Forum. (See related letters: "Letters to the Editor: Our Terrorist Grandad, and Other Tales"—*WSJ *Jan. 17, 2002.)*

SECTION 2

CHAPTER 5

AN INTRODUCTION TO "CRIME, PUNISHMENT, AND THE MARKET FOR OFFENSES"

By Ron Liggett

INTRODUCTION TO THE EHRLICH MODEL

One of the most informative parts of this text is the following chapter from Isaac Ehrlich titled "Crime, Punishment, and the Market for Offenses." In this selection, Ehrlich essentially builds upon some of the earlier work by Bentham, Becker, and others, to provide an expanded market model. Where Becker focused on offenders and law enforcement in his equilibrium example, Ehrlich has added two other parties: (1) consumers and patrons of illicit goods and services and (2) potential victims.

The market model offered in this chapter is still tightly related to how individuals respond to incentives, thus keeping with standard economic theories on behavior. In regards to an "optimal crime policy," Ehrlich addresses both positive and negative incentives and some of the debate that exists in that area.

As a 1996 journal publication, the data is not current, nor should it be the main focus. However, in scrutinizing the article, one sees many intellectual contributions being made on a variety of topics. All of these are applicable to a market model for criminal behavior. In addition to these items, some of the more relevant topics include the following:

- The existence of an "overall" equilibrium quantity of crime, noted as q^*
- The concept of a "tax" on crime
- The easy "replacement" of certain criminals (essentially an elasticity discussion)
- The topic of "fines"
- An interesting graphical representation of the market model
- References to a "crimes of passion" model

For a simple study of economics, the article may seem a little technical in relation to other discussions in the book. Therefore, a careful reading of this section may be a protracted endeavor. My suggestion is to read slowly, make notes in the margins, and focus on some of the topics mentioned above.

CRIME, PUNISHMENT, AND THE MARKET FOR OFFENSES

By Isaac Ehrlich

The persistence of illegal activity throughout human history and some of its apparent regularities have long attracted the attention of economists. For example, Adam Smith (1776 [1937], p. 670) observed that crime and the demand for protection from crime are both motivated by the accumulation of property. William Paley (1785 [1822]) presented a penetrating analysis of factors responsible for differences in the actual magnitudes of probability and severity of sanctions for different crimes. Jeremy Bentham, the father of utilitarianism, focused considerable attention on the calculus of both offenders' behavior and the optimal response by the legal authorities.

It was not until the late 1960s, however, that economists reconnected with the subject, using modern economic analysis.[A] In this paper I shall focus on two of the main themes that characterize the literature on crime in the last three decades. The first is the evolution of a "market model" that offers a comprehensive framework for studying the problem. Like the classical approach, the model builds on the assumption that offenders, as members of the human race, respond to incentives. Of course, not every single offender does so. But willful engagement in even the most reprehensible violations of legal and moral codes does not preclude an ability to make self-serving choices, and this has been the justification for applying economic analysis to all illegal activities, from speeding and tax evasion to murder. Indeed, the distinguishing feature of the major contributions by economists has

A The seminal paper is Becker (1968). Other works that led the resurgence of the interest in crime include Fleisher (1966), Tullock (1967), Rottenberg (1968) and the papers by Ehrlich, Landes, Posner and Stigler collected in Landes and Becker (1974).

Isaac Ehrlich, "Crime, Punishment, and the Market for Offenses," *Journal of Economic Perspectives*, vol. 10, no. 1, pp. 43-67.

been the attempt to explain the various aspects of crime through the tools of optimization and equilibrium analysis, rather than by reliance on deterministic social and environmental factors that are independent of the human will. At least in the economic literature, there has been little controversy concerning this approach.

The second theme concerns a more controversial issue: what constitutes an optimal crime control policy. The economic paradigm recognizes two sets of incentives that motivate potential or actual offenders: negative and positive. Negative incentives are those that deter and otherwise prevent would-be and actual offenders from entering or actively pursuing illegitimate activity: the probability and severity of punishment, and the type of punishment to be imposed. Positive incentives are those that induce participation in legitimate alternatives to crime: legitimate employment and earning opportunities, rehabilitation programs and a lower disparity in the distribution of income in society. The controversy that has emerged in the literature—subtle in some cases, explicit in others—concerns the relative efficacy and desirability of negative versus positive incentives and thus the appropriate policy inferences to be drawn. I shall try to evaluate some basic points of contention in this controversy.

As a starting point, it may be useful to look at some background data concerning the problem of crime. Consider Tables 1 and 2. The crime rate figures in Table 1, as well as the growing number of offenders in prisons shown in Table 2, imply that crime has been a growth industry in the United States over the last few decades.[B] At the same time, Table 1 also shows that both the probability and severity of punishment for specific crimes have generally been falling over the last three decades. A lower percentage of offenses known to the police is resulting in an arrest; the probability of imprisonment is smaller; and the time served in prison is shorter. The growth in the prison population, substantial as it is, has not kept up with the even larger growth in criminal behavior.

THE MARKET FOR OFFENSES

What I call the "market model" of crime is based on five key assumptions which are typical of economic theory in general. First, offenders, potential victims, buyers of illegal goods and services, and law enforcement authorities all behave in accordance with the rules of optimizing behavior. Second, they generally form expectations about relative legitimate and illegitimate opportunities, including severity and

B The crime rates in Table 1 are those reported by the Uniform Crime Reports of the FBI, which are based on complaints of crime by victims. A puzzling issue is that the trends of some of the FBI-reported crime categories appear to be quite different from those reported by the National Crime Victimization Studies (NCVS), which are based on statistical surveys of the incidence of victimization. The two sets of data cannot be compared over the entire period covered by Table 1, however, because the NCVS series are not available before 1973.

TABLE 1. CRIME AND LAW ENFORCEMENT INDICATORS FOR INDEX CRIMES[A], 1960 AND 1991

	Murder and Non-negligent Manslaughter	Forcible Rape	Robbery	Aggravated Assault	Burglary	Larceny	Auto Theft	All Index Crimes
[b]Crime Rate (per 100,000)								
1960	5.1	9.6	60.1	86.1	508.6	1034.7	183.0	1887.2
1991	9.8	42.3	272.7	433.3	1251.8	3228.5	658.9	5897.3
[c]Median (Mean) Time Served in State Prisons Before First Release, in Months								
1960	52.0[b]	30.0[c]	33.9	19.5	20.4	16.7	18.9	NA
	(121.4)	(44.8)	(42.4)	(25.0)	(24.6)	(19.8)	(21.3)	(28.4)
1991	68.0	44.0	27.0	15.0	15.0	9.0	11.0	17.1
	(84.0)	(56.0)	(40.0)	(22.0)	(22.0)	(14.0)	(14.0)	(24.1)
[d]Percentage of Offenses Known to Police Cleared by Arrest								
1960	92.3	72.5	38.5	75.8	29.5	20.1	25.7	30.8
1991	67.2	51.8	24.3	56.5	13.5	20.3	13.9	21.3
[e]Probability of Imprisonment (State Prisons)								
1960	39.8C	22.7	8.4	3.0	2.4	2.2	2.1	2.8
1991	28.4	5.2	3.6	1.7	1.0	0.2	0.4	0.8

Notes:

[a]Index crimes include the seven categories listed below, as defined in the Uniform Crime Report.

[b] 1960 median time is for homicide, including negligent manslaughter.

[c] 1960 median time is for all sex offenses.

[d] Percentage of those entering state prisons relative to offenses known.

[e] 1960 probability is for homicide, including negligent manslaughter.

Sources (by row): Sourcebook of Criminal Justice Statistics, 1992, Table 3.122. Data are based on revised Uniform Crime Reports. Characteristics of State Prisoners, 1960, Table Al, and R3. National Corrections Reporting Program, 1991, Table 2.3. Uniform Crime Reports 1960 and 1991. Uniform Crime Reports 1961 and 1991, Characteristics of State Prisoners, 1960, National Corrections Reporting Program, 1991.

TABLE 2. PRISONERS IN STATE AND FEDERAL INSTITUTIONS

	1979	1986	1991
Total Prisoners in State and Federal Institutions	301,470	522,084	789,347
Total Prisoners in State Institutions	274,564	450,416	711,643
Percentage of Index Crime Offenders	73.8	68.3	56.6
Percentage of Drug Offenders	6.4	8.6	21.3

Sources: Bureau of Justice Statistics, *Sourcebook of Criminal Justice Statistics*, 1992, Table 6.58 and 6.70. U.S. Department of Justice, Bureau of Justice Statistics Bulletin, "Prisons and Prisoners," 1982.

certainty of punishment, based on available information, so that subjective expectations and objective opportunities can be linked. Third, there is a stable distribution of preferences for crime, as well as for safety from crime, in the population. Fourth, since crime is an external diseconomy by definition, and public law enforcement is a prime example of a nonexclusionary public good, the objective of law enforcement is generally presumed to be maximization of social welfare. Fifth, aggregation conditions concerning the behavior of all relevant parties assure well-defined equilibria. These assumptions lead to an equilibrium model of crime.

By the "market" for offenses, I do not mean necessarily a physical setting where illegitimate transactions are contracted, but the more abstract notion of a Walrasian market in which the aggregate behavior of suppliers and demanders is coordinated and made mutually consistent through adjustments in relevant prices. In Becker (1968), equilibrium is achieved just through the interaction between offenders and law enforcers. In reality, other parties are involved as well: consumers or patrons of illicit goods and services in specific crimes, and potential victims. These parties determine the direct or derived demand for specific illegitimate activities. Public intervention "taxes" the incidence of crime through its interaction with both the supply and demand sides of the market.[C]

THE SUPPLY OF OFFENSES

A person's decision to participate in illegal activity i can be viewed as motivated by the costs and gains from such activity. These include the expected illegitimate

C The following analysis extends Ehrlich (1981), in which the concept of the market is introduced and applied. For related analyses and illustrations, see Van den Haag (1975, ch. 5), Balkin and McDonald (1981) and Cook (1986).

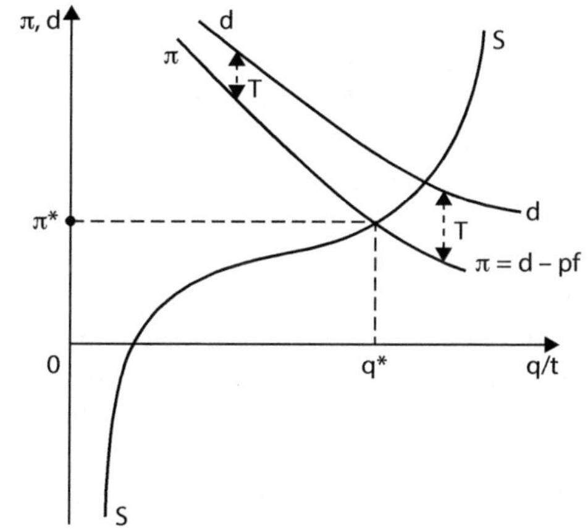

Figure 1. The Market for Offenses

payoff (loot) per offense, w_i; the direct costs incurred by offenders in acquiring the loot (including the costs of self-protection to escape punishment), c_i; the wage rate in an alternative legitimate activity, the probability of apprehension and conviction, p_i; the prospective penalty if convicted, f_i; and finally one's taste (or distaste) for crime—a combination of moral values, proclivity for violence, and preference for risk. For analytical simplicity, assume that offenders pursue only a single criminal or legitimate activity.

A straightforward combination of these components into an overall expected net return per offense, π_i, might read that this is equal to expected gross payoff—direct costs incurred in acquiring the loot—foregone wages from legitimate activity—(probability of conviction) X (prospective penalty if convicted).[D] For crimes that do not involve any material gain, the net return is negative; it can be viewed as the price of crime to the offender.

This formulation includes two additional simplifying assumptions. One is that potential offenders are risk neutral; the other is that "distaste for crime" can be measured as a constant, compensating expected net return that an individual requires to enter a criminal activity. In other words, the net payoff must exceed some threshold level before an individual decides to engage in crime. Given these conditions, the individual supply of offenses will be a function of the personal (expected) net return from crime.

This way of thinking about an individual's decision to participate in crime offers some powerful insights about the aggregate flow of offenses. For example,

D For those who prefer notation to words, this condition would be $\pi_i = w_l - c_i - \omega_i - pf_i$.

imagine that potential offenders faced identical legitimate and illegitimate opportunities. The shape of the market supply-of-offenses schedule would then be determined by the distribution of ethical values in the population as reflected by the different thresholds. These would dictate the *minimal* net returns that different individuals would require before entering a criminal activity. If the distribution were bell-shaped, the supply of offenses per capita, or the crime rate q_i, would be an increasing function of the *actual* net return per offense, as illustrated by the inflected and upward-sloping schedule *SS* in Figure 1.[E]

Herein lies the first lesson to be derived from the economic approach to crime: even if individual supply-of-offenses functions were completely inelastic with respect to variations in net returns above their critical threshold levels, so that active offenders would not react to either positive or negative incentives above these levels, it is still true that the market supply curve would be generally elastic. This is because changes in the actual net return from crime would make the latter exceed or fall below the threshold level of marginal offenders, thus inducing the latter to enter into or exit from criminal activity.

More realistically, one can extend this supply analysis to allow for varying legitimate market wages for different persons, but assume a stable distribution of these wages about the mean wage. In this case, the market supply curve should be interpreted as a function of the *average* net return per offense, and its shape would depend on the joint probability distribution of individuals' taste for crime and their legitimate wages.[F] Similarly, the analysis could allow for differences in individuals' perceptions of their probability of apprehension and punishment about its expected value—say, the current average probability.[G]

It is plausible to assume that community wealth, which is a major determinant of the gross payoff in crimes involving material gain, is exogenous to the model. Similarly, the distribution of legitimate wages may be largely exogenous, because it is determined in the economy-wide labor market of which the criminal sector is a small segment. However, the direct cost of crime to the offender, the probability of conviction and the penalty if convicted are affected by private and public actions to achieve protection from crime, and thus are endogenous to the model. The next two subsections consider the latter activities.

E That is, $q_i = S(\pi_i)$, with $S'(\pi_i) \geq 0$.

F In the case of "crimes of passion" with no material payoff, where the net reward from crime is therefore negative $\pi_i = c_i - \omega_i - p_i f_i$, the supply-of-offenses function would have to be drawn entirely within the southeast quadrant of Figure 1. But the general proposition concerning aggregate supply behavior applies here as well: an increase in the price of crime—a reduction in π, toward a greater negative value—would lower its quantity supplied.

G A process of expectation formation by individuals concerning these probabilities is postulated by Sah (1991).

PRIVATE PROTECTION AND THE DEMAND SIDE OF THE MARKET

There is literally a direct demand for activities defined as crime in the case of illegal goods and services, including stolen goods, which are purchased by willing consumers. But even in the case of violations of persons and property, there is a derived demand for crime, or a tolerance of crime, that is inversely related to the demand for private protection. Individuals desire protection from crime, but protection comes at a cost. Potential victims can purchase insurance policies, or they can affect both the probability of becoming victims and the extent of their loss if victimized by employing a myriad of safety measures ranging from locks, burglar alarm systems and safety deposit boxes, to paying higher rents for living in safe neighborhoods or hiring private guards—a combination of self-insurance and self-protection (Ehrlich and Becker, 1972).

Because protection is costly, its optimal amount would be set at a level where its marginal costs and benefits are in balance. An expected-loss minimizing solution can be shown to imply that the optimal expenditure, e^*_i, would be directly related to the perceived risk of victimization, v_i, and the prospective private loss from crime, L_i. The intuitive reasoning is that individuals are expected to increase or lower their "defenses" against the threat of victimization in some proportion to its expected severity. A factor of proportionality, a, which we take to be a constant, reflects the productivity of self-protective efforts in increasing the offender's direct cost of crime, c_i, as well as the latter's discouraging effect on the probability of victimization.[H] Assuming rational expectations on the part of potential victims, the average perceived risk of victimization, $v(e^*_i)$, for the representative person is the same as the crime rate in the population, q_i. We can thus conceptualize a direct demand-for-protection schedule as an increasing and concave function of the crime rate.

How do we get from the direct demand for protection to the derived-demand-for-offenses schedule—*dd* in Figure 1? The latter schedule shows why a given crime rate, or risk of victimization, is "demanded" (tolerated) by potential victims as an indirect consequence of what they are willing to spend to reduce their risk of victimization.[I] Higher expenditures on protection raise the time and effort offenders must spend on acquiring the potential loot from their victims, c_i. Any increase in the latter, in turn, means a reduction in the differential "gross" return per offense over the direct and opportunity cost incurred by the offender (the loss of a legitimate wage), in the absence of any sanctions, d_i.[J] The bottom line is that a higher crime rate, or risk of victimization, q_i, induces greater efforts at self-protection by potential victims, which in turn reduce the

H An algebraic formulation of this condition would read $e_i^* = a_i v(e_i^*) L(e_i^*)$, where a_i, denotes the sum of the elasticities of v and L with respect to e.

I That is, the demand law can be described by $d_i = D(q_i)$, with $D'(q_i) \leq 0$.

J The algebraic formulation would be $d(e_i) = w(_i) - \mathrm{w}(_i) - c(e_i)$.

differential gain to offenders, d_i. Hence the downward-sloping shape of the derived-demand curve *dd*.[K]

PUBLIC ENFORCEMENT

Since crime is, by definition, an externality, and the maintenance of law and order is essentially a public good, the economic literature has focused mainly on the determination of optimal means of law enforcement and crime control, rather than the basic rationale for public rather than private enforcement of laws.[L] Three main issues have been at stake. One is the absolute and relative magnitudes of probability versus severity of punishment; for example, is it more productive to have many convictions with relatively smaller punishments or fewer convictions with relatively longer punishments? Should sanctions be applied uniformly, or adjusted by the severity of the offense and the prior record of the offender? A second issue is which penalties are more efficient: monetary fines, imprisonment, or probation, restitution and other "intermediate punishments." The third issue focuses on the relative usefulness of deterring would-be offenders as opposed to the incapacitation and/or rehabilitation of known offenders.

The approach economists have taken toward these choices has generally been based on a "public interest" criterion: the law enforcement authority seeks to maximize social welfare by minimizing the losses from crime, including the costs of law enforcement and crime control. The specification of the relevant social welfare function, however, involves normative as well as positive considerations.

We shall return to the welfare criteria issue, but for the sake of a simple closure, assume that the enforcement objective is to minimize the per capita social cost of crime through an optimal expected sanction, $T_i = p_i f_i$, which combines the probability of arrest and conviction and the penalty if convicted. This sanction must be produced at some positive cost of enforcement, $E(p_i f_i, q_i)$, subject to due process constraints.[M]

K Another reason for the downward-sloping shape of the derived demand for offenses are potential scale diseconomies at the market level. Because criminal targets are available in limited quantities in any given geographical (market) area, offenders would tend to select at any point in time the targets that yield the highest potential return per time spent. Thus, if the number of offenders increases in a given area due to factors unrelated to the available stock of criminal targets, the marginal offenses would be associated with less-remunerating targets.

L For thoughts about the role of privately provided law enforcement, see Landes and Posner (1975) and Friedman (1984).

M The function $E(pf, q)$ incorporates both the direct costs of law enforcement and the indirect costs of punishing offenders. The production function of law enforcement activity implicit in the former cost component recognizes the crowding effect which a higher volume of offenses may exert on the probability and even severity of punishment at a given

The optimal public expenditures on law enforcement and the resulting expected sanction, or "tax" on crime, T_i, are determined in roughly the same way optimal private protection was determined—that is, by balancing marginal costs of enforcement with marginal benefits of crime prevention. But there is one important difference. Private crime prevention considers only the potential private costs of crime. Public enforcement, in contrast, is a monopolized state activity, and is therefore determined in view of its marginal efficacy in reducing the equilibrium crime rate and social loss from crime. Moreover, since public enforcement is applied to all criminal activities, any interactions among markets for different crime categories (because of substitutability and complementarity among specific offenses) or across different geographical areas (because of spillover effects in crime control) must also be accounted for in arriving at an optimal enforcement strategy.[N]

The marginal reduction in the equilibrium amount of crime depends not just on the productivity of law enforcement in raising the expected sanction and the latter's effect on the supply of offenses, but also on the elasticity of the private demand schedule, or on possible shifts in the supply schedule resulting from incapacitative sanctions or rehabilitative programs (effects discussed later in this paper). As a starting point, however, it is simpler to abstract from incapacitation and rehabilitation, and focus instead on the case of sanctions that serve only to deter potential criminals. In this case, the supply and (derived) demand schedules already discussed are independent of the public "tax schedule" on crime.

Given the relevant market parameters, the optimal expected punishment $p_i f_i$ can be shown to be a generally increasing function of the crime rate (Ehrlich and Gibbons, 1977).[O] It is shown as the implicit "tax" schedule TT in Figure 1, which accounts for the vertical distance between the private demand schedule dd and the net return (or "after-tax") schedule, $\pi\pi$.[P]

---

enforcement budget (Becker, 1968; Ehrlich, 1973), but since budgets are assumed to be determined optimally, this crowding effect is internalized in setting optimal values of p and f.

N The internalization of relevant external effects for each crime and across crime categories produces a set of propositions concerning the optimal magnitudes of probability and severity of punishment—most notably that the severity of expected sanctions must "fit the crime"—that are generally consistent with their ranking in Table 1 (Becker, 1968; Stigler, 1970). For additional insights concerning optimal magnitudes of probability and severity of sanctions under more general social welfare functions see, for example, Polinsky and Shavell (1979) and Ehrlich (1982).

O That is, $p_i f_i = T(q_i, \psi)$, with $T'(q_i) \geq 0$, where ψ is a vector summarizing the relevant market parameters.

P This illustration ignores possible complementarities in production between public and private protective activities. Thus, as long as punishment involves a purely deterring sanction, both the supply and demand schedules in Figure 1 are independent of the public "tax schedule."

MARKET EQUILIBRIUM

The supply of crime, together with the demand for private and public protection from crime, as shown in Figure 1, form the basic components of the market for specific offenses. This market will be in equilibrium when the quantity of crime, if in Figure 1, is such that neither criminals (looking at the net expected return from crime), private individuals (looking at their risk and costs of victimization), nor government (looking at the relevant social welfare function) find it necessary to adjust their behavior and alter the prevailing net return or price associated with crime.

This "market setting" has important implications concerning the themes of this paper. The model implies (as does Durkheim, 1958) that crime is a "normal" social fact which is assured of historical survival at some positive level regardless of the prevailing economic, political or social system. Crime persists in this model because the interplay between private supply and demand forces and the social costs of enforcement imply that some level of crime will remain socially optimal—that is, tolerable. Similarly, recidivism by known offenders is also an implication of the model rather than an exception to it, because offenders are expected to discount the actual risks of apprehension and punishment in deciding to participate in crime. Private self-protection and public law enforcement set a "price," or "tax," on criminal activity by reducing the marginal net return to the offender. The existence of equilibria in the market for offenses suggests that these prices are effective, at least on the margin.

Of course, this conclusion does not mean that social, political or demographic conditions are irrelevant. Instead, these factors are captured by the components of the expected returns from illegitimate and legitimate pursuits, as determined by both supply and demand forces. Extensions of the model under dynamic conditions seek to explain the role of the family, education, life-cycle factors and social interactions in determining legitimate and illegitimate opportunities, and thus the dynamic stability of supply and demand schedules in specific markets.[Q]

This model can account for apparent secular trends in crime without resorting to assumptions about changes in "taste" for criminality. Economic growth and real asset accumulation raise the potential payoff to the offender (w_i) in many criminal activities. If the distribution of legitimate earning opportunities and private and public protection efforts remain constant, then the rise in wealth or affluence would shift upward the derived-demand schedule *dd*, and thus the net-demand schedule $\pi\pi$, along the supply schedule *SS* in Figure 1, resulting in more crime.[R] Supreme Court rulings on the scope of offenders' rights to due

Q For some current work along these lines, see Glaeser, Sacerdote and Scheinkman (1995) and Ehrlich and Lui (1995). Also see Ehrlich (1975b).

R Higher wealth may also increase private and public protection against crime, as observed by Adam Smith, but even if all the components of the net return per offense rise by the same proportion as w_i, its absolute value, π_i, would also rise by the same proportion, process exert a largely exogenous influence on the productivity of law enforcement efforts, regardless of the basic merit of these rulings as safeguards for civil and human rights. Changes in Court decisions or sentencing guidelines over time shift the implicit tax schedule TT, and thus the net return schedule $\pi\pi$ in Figure 1. They partly explain the observed trends in measures of the probability of arrest, conviction and punishment, as well as in the equilibrium flow of offenses. Similar considerations on both the demand and supply side of the market for offenses can explain acute differences in actual crime rates across poor and affluent neighborhoods without resorting to the possibility of multiple equilibria in the market for offenses.[5]

LIMITS ON THE POWER OF POSITIVE AND NEGATIVE INCENTIVES

LIMITING SUPPLY AND DEMAND RESPONSES

In the simple market model of the preceding section, equal changes in negative and positive incentives produce the same change in the expected net return from crime, and therefore the same absolute deterrent effect on the marginal offender. This conclusion does not follow, however, once we allow for nonneutral attitudes toward risk. It can be shown that a one percent increase in the probability of punishment will have a greater deterrent effect than a one percent increase in the severity of punishment on the decision to enter an illegal activity if the marginal offender is a risk preferrer, while the opposite is the case for a risk avoider (Becker, 1968).

If offenders engage in crime on a part-time basis, however, as is the case empirically (U.S. Department of Justice, 1991; Reuter et al., 1990), there is a theoretical possibility that negative and positive incentives would be ineffective at the individual level because of conflicting income and substitution effects. For example, if offenders prefer risk, then the loss of potential income caused by a higher average penalty per offense, by itself, may induce them to shift the allocation of their working time toward more crime; at a lower income position a risk preferrer is more willing to gamble the cost of punishment for the chance to obtain a higher criminal return (Ehrlich, 1974). This kind of ambiguity applies more generally to

leading to more crimes involving material gains. Even murder may increase as a result (despite the expected increase in private demand for self protection and life saving), since this crime is often committed as a byproduct of robbery and other felonies. Indeed, the proportion of all murders where victims and offenders are unrelated persons (as opposed to those involving family members, friends and acquaintances) has increased drastically from 23 percent in 1960 to 53 percent in 1991, according to the Uniform Crime Report.

5 Analyses leading to multiple equilibria—for example, Freeman, Grogger and Sonstelie (1995)—typically assume, however, that both private and public expenditures on crime control are exogenously determined constants.

the effects of negative incentives if time spent in illegal pursuits were an inferior good (Block and Heineke, 1975). But however important these ambiguities may be at the individual level, they are likely to disappear at the market level because changes in illegitimate incentives do not generate income effects for marginal entrants.

More important, the market framework implies that it is not enough to look only at aggregate supply or demand reactions to changes in incentives. In analyzing the equilibrium quantity and price in the market for a particular good, it makes a considerable difference whether supply is shifting for a good that is inelastically or elastically demanded. Similarly, in the market for offenses, the equilibrium level of crime will depend on interactions between supply and demand forces. Take, for example, the effect of exogenous changes in "general" incentives, such as increases in probability and severity of fines or increases in the average legitimate wage. Such changes would lower the net return from crime, and thus the net demand curve $\pi\pi$ in Figure 1. But the effect on the equilibrium volume of crime would now depend on the shape of both the supply of offenses and the derived demand for crime schedules, which are dictated by reactions of offenders, potential victims, and law enforcers to changes in incentives.

General incentives, such as monetary fines and legitimate market wages, operate on the population at large, including active offenders. The importance of distinguishing individual from market-level responses becomes even greater in relation to the effects of "specific incentives," such as incapacitative penalties and rehabilitation programs, which are targeted on convicted offenders. The efficacy of such specific incentives in preventing crime is constrained by the fraction of offenders who are apprehended and punished and their actual period of confinement in the case of incapacitative penalties, and by the even smaller fraction of released offenders who will remain rehabilitated over their labor careers, in the case of rehabilitative programs.

The successful removal of incarcerated or rehabilitated offenders from the illegitimate market causes a leftward shift in the supply-of-offenses schedule, but the effect on the equilibrium volume of offenses is now *inversely* related to the elasticity of the aggregate supply curve. The reason is that "removed" offenders can be replaced by either new entrants or an intensified illegal activity on the part of active offenders. Suppose, for example, that the market supply of illicit drugs were infinitely elastic. The mere removal of some active drug dealers from the marketplace, or an occasional drug bust, would then cause no change in transactions, if the demand schedule remained intact.

It is plausible that certain types of offenders are more easily replaced than others. For example, sellers of illegal goods and services are probably replaced more easily than those who commit violent crime. The effectiveness of incapacitation or rehabilitation for sellers of illegal goods and services, therefore, would be highly limited, but such programs could be more efficacious for perpetrators of violent crimes.

Incapacitative penalties, such as imprisonment, cause both a deterrent effect on those at large and an incapacitative effect on those imprisoned. Rehabilitation programs, in contrast, even if entirely successful in eliminating recidivism by released offenders, do not exert a deterrent effect. Indeed, the training or work subsidy implicit in successful job-oriented programs has a potential counter-deterrent effect as it reduces the prospective penalty costs for would-be offenders. Incapacitation and imprisonment without any attention to rehabilitation, however, could increase the odds of recidivism by released offenders because of the informal training for illegitimate activities they receive from associating with other convicts.

The general theme that is emerging here is that while specific incentives may be effective at the level of individual offenders, the market model points to significant limitations of their potential efficacy in reducing the aggregate flow of many crimes. By the same token, even if general incentives have a weak effect at the individual level, they may be efficacious at the market level because of the impact they have on the entry and exit of marginal offenders.[T]

LIMITS IMPOSED BY OPTIMAL ENFORCEMENT POLICIES

If the objective of public law enforcement is to maximize social income—that is, to minimize the aggregate (or per capita) social loss from crime—it follows that law enforcement must be effective on the margin. The reason is that probability and severity of punishment entail positive marginal costs, which would be optimal to incur only if probability and severity of punishment effected a marginal reduction in crime. If higher sanctions increase only the indirect social cost of punishment, but not the direct cost of arresting and convicting offenders, the aggregate loss-minimizing criterion also requires that the absolute elasticity of offenses with respect to the probability of punishment exceed that with respect to its severity (Becker, 1968). The reason is that the costlier it is on the margin to increase the means of enforcement, the larger must be its marginal benefit, as indicated by its marginal deterrent and preventive effect.[U] But this restriction does not necessarily hold if the aim of law enforcement is to maximize a social welfare function that incorporates a concern for distributive outcomes of law enforcement in addition to income maximization, as discussed further in the penultimate section of this paper.

T For evidence on the efficacy of rehabilitation at the individual offenders' level, see Cook (1975); Lipton, Martinson and Wilks (1975); Rossi, Berk and Lenihan (1980) and Piehl (1994). Estimates of the incapacitative effect of imprisonment are provided in Ehrlich (1981) and Levitt (1995b).

U The elasticities must also be less than unity in this case because otherwise law enforcement will lower not just the frequency of offenses, but even the number of convicted offenders and will thus not be costly on the margin.

Perhaps the sharpest restriction on the efficacy of law enforcement instruments, which is an outcome of optimal choices by both offenders and law enforcers, is the prediction that the absolute elasticity of crime with respect to the probability of apprehension will exceed that with respect to the conditional probability of conviction given apprehension, and that the latter would exceed the elasticity with respect to the conditional probability of a more severe punishment given conviction (Ehrlich, 1975a). The rationale on the supply side is that the more general the event leading to undesirable consequences for the offender, the greater is the deterrent effect associated with its probability. Optimal enforcement justifies this same result because raising the probability of apprehension, for example, requires not just raising the costs of apprehending offenders, but also the costs of convicting and punishing them in later stages of the enforcement process. The deterrent effects of these probabilities must then have the same ranking as their relative costs.

ESTIMATES OF THE EFFECTS OF POSITIVE AND NEGATIVE INCENTIVES

The empirical literature concerning the effects of positive and negative incentives on crime is voluminous; for example, see the surveys by Palmer (1977), Pyle (1983), Freeman (1983) and Cameron (1988). Taken as a whole, these studies offer a mountain of evidence consistent with the hypothesis that both negative and positive incentives have a deterrent effect on crime. The evidence comes from studies using alternative crime reports; different crime categories and population groups; different countries, states, cities and even city tracts (Thaler, 1977); time series, cross-section and panel data; and both aggregate and individual samples. Moreover, a number of studies find evidence consistent not just with the model's implications concerning the direction of effects of deterrence variables, but also with the latter's relative magnitudes, as predicted by the elasticity conditions above. While most of the evidence is derived from regression estimates of supply-of-offenses functions, corroborating results are obtained from comparisons of "market" returns associated with alternative illegitimate activities, which differ in the degree of punishment risk they impose on offenders (Viscusi, 1986).

This evidence is important to followers of the market model because the model may be used to study alternative crime control policies only if incentives do indeed matter. By contrast, if pure deterrence were estimated to be weak relative to, say, the force of incapacitation, then locking up convicted offenders would appear to be the only option available for effective law enforcement.

Yet it would be premature to view the supportive empirical evidence as conclusive. My main concern is not that a minority of studies fail to find a deterrent effect of either negative or positive incentives: this is predictable on probabilistic grounds alone, even when the same econometric models are being implemented. But while the qualitative results obtained from most studies are similar, the quantitative estimates vary. Such differences may be attributable, in part, to the use of data from different levels of aggregation: for example, the effect of employment opportunities on crime across cities may be quite different from their effects across states, or for the nation as a whole over time, because of different spillover effects across markets, or because cross-sectional (as opposed to cyclical) variations in employment opportunities reflect shifts in supply as well as demand conditions in the labor market. Also, as noted earlier, even if individual data produced estimates of inelastic supply-of-offenses schedules, the aggregate schedule could still be quite elastic.

More troublesome is that differences in econometric estimates may be the result of incomplete, or even inconsistent, specification of the market model, which are exacerbated by the intrinsic limitations of crime statistics. The following sections explore some of the common issues that arise in attempting to implement the market model, as well as their bearing on the second theme of the paper: the role of negative and positive incentives.

SPECIFICATION

Since the empirical evidence developed in the literature on crime and deterrence comes mainly from regression analyses of statistical data, or "uncontrolled experiments," a meaningful estimation of the hypothesized incentive effects requires careful econometric specification of the model being tested. The task involves not just the specification of the supply-of-offenses function, but at least an implicit specification of the complete market model, because of the simultaneous relationship between crime and law enforcement. As the market model indicates, supply responses to changes in alternative incentives can be identified econometrically only if changes in these incentives come about as a result of shifts in demand schedules, such as *dd* or $\pi\pi$ in Figure 1, while variables controlling the location of the supply schedule are held constant.

The problem has been recognized from the outset. The standard specification in many studies of aggregate data (for example, Ehrlich, 1973; Carr-Hill and Stern, 1973; Phillips and Votey, 1975) has been a three-part econometric structure: 1) supply-of-offenses functions relating specific crime rates to measures, or proxies, of each of the law enforcement products and legitimate and illegitimate wage variables discussed earlier; 2) production functions relating the same law enforcement products to resources expanded in their production and factors affecting resource productivity, including the crime rate itself; and 3) expenditure functions, relating enforcement outlays to the crime rate, measures of per capita (social) losses from crime and underlying political constraints that may cause public expenditures to adjust to their desired level with some lag.

Typically missing from this specification, however, are indicators of derived-demand functions—that is, measures of self-protection by potential victims—which affect the differential payoffs per offense.[V] The absence of private-protection variables implies that what has been estimated empirically are relationships between equilibrium crime rates and indicators of incentives that reflect the elasticities of both supply and demand functions. These estimated responses are the relevant ones from a policy perspective, since law enforcement does not control private protection efforts. Also, their relative magnitudes need not be affected because all are subject to the same demand-side adjustment. However, the absolute levels of the estimated responses may understate the pure supply elasticities associated with all incentives.

Also, a complete specification of supply functions for specific crime categories requires the introduction of probability and severity of sanctions for both the estimated categories and interrelated crimes, or a joint estimation of interrelated crime categories using seemingly unrelated estimation procedures. For example, violent crimes may have the attributes of complementary activities—some murders are committed in the course of a robbery—whereas burglary and larceny may be substitutes. Some studies report both complementarity and substitutability across specific offense categories (Ehrlich, 1977; Levitt, 1995b).

Ideally, the functional specification of relevant structural equations should be derived from the underlying objective functions of the participants in the market model. This task has so far proved elusive, especially in connection with supply-of-offenses functions. But typical assumptions concerning the structure of reporting errors in aggregate data and the hypothesized effects of measures of costs and rewards to crime point toward the use of a logarithmic specification, which also permits direct estimation of supply elasticities. These considerations generally receive support from standard tests for optimal functional specifications (Ehrlich, 1977; Layson, 1983). Studies using less efficient specifications in analyzing aggregate data are therefore less likely to confirm the existence of deterrent effects.

ERRORS OF MEASUREMENT

The FBI's commonly used Uniform Crime Reports (UCR) data on crime are subject to notorious underreporting errors, largely because reporting a crime is costly to the victim. Moreover, some measures of the probability of punishment are computed as ratios of the number of convictions or prison commitments to the volume of reported offenses. Errors of measurement in the latter may impart a negative bias to regression estimates of the deterrent effect of the probability measure and also bias the estimated effects of other explanatory variable that are correlated with it (Ehrlich, 1974, pp. 127–30).

V Interesting exceptions are Vandaele's (1978) estimation of a partial market system for auto theft, Bartel's (1975) and Clotfelter's (1977) studies of the demand for private protection, and Goldberg and Nold's (1980) analysis of crime reporting as self-protection by victims.

There are, however, standard approaches for dealing with these problems. As an approximation, reporting errors are likely to be proportional to the true crime rate, so the logarithms of the reported crime figures and probability measures can be thought of as proxies for the true variables. Another standard remedy for potential biases from random reporting errors involves using instrumental variables to estimate a "predicted" probability measure that is in principle free of such errors. A more direct approach involves modeling the economics of reporting on the part of victims and integrating it in the econometric model to distinguish reported from "true" crime rates.

Yet another approach is to test the model against alternative sources of crime data, such as National Crime Victimization Surveys (NCVS) and vital statistics data (in connection with homicide). UCR and NCVS data give quite different pictures of the time trend of specific offenses, especially violent crimes, although recently the differences have narrowed. Deterrent effects of private and/or public protection measures are confirmed in these studies as well (Goldberg and Nold, 1980; Ehrlich, 1977).

Measurement errors in reported crime may not operate in one direction only: victims may be more likely to report a crime when the probability or severity of punishment is higher or if they receive compensation. In regressions using reported crime rates, therefore, measures of criminal sanctions may also be subject to a positive spurious correlation with crime rates. In a study relevant to this point, Levitt (1994) finds the net effect on reporting errors of both police presence and the standard measure of probability of arrest to be rather small and statistically insignificant

SELECTING EMPIRICAL COUNTERPARTS OF THEORETICAL CONSTRUCTS

It can be difficult to measure the theoretical variables of the market model with readily available data. For example, punishment is never quantified in terms of its cost to the offender. Even if time served in prison by currently released offenders is a good predictor of time to be served by current convicts, the discounted present value of the future cost of imprisonment is not proportionally related to its length.

Similar problems affect the measurement of positive incentives for avoiding crime, like the level of legitimate earnings and employment opportunities. For example, using time series variations in the rates of unemployment and labor force participation to measure such opportunities captures mainly cyclical fluctuations in labor-demand conditions, unlike their cross-sectional counterparts, which are influenced by labor supply decisions as well. It is not surprising that time series measures prove to have a weaker link with crime than do cross-sectional measures at a point in time.

Some studies may use average legitimate earnings in the population as a measure of positive incentives, but not only may this average correlate poorly with the legitimate earnings of active offenders and marginal entrants, it is usually strongly correlated with median community income, or wealth, which is a proxy for illegitimate earning opportunities. One remedy has been to introduce both median income and the percentage of families below one-half of the median income to account for the disparity between illegitimate and legitimate earnings of actual and potential offenders. Both variables have been found to produce sizable and statistically significant effects on the incidence of property crimes, and even on the incidence of murder, partly because murder can be a byproduct of robbery (Ehrlich, 1973, 1977).

An alternative remedy involves the use of individual data where information is available on arrests and convictions per months free, legitimate earnings, the fractions of past arrests resulting in conviction, and the severity of past sentences. Indeed, studies based on such data, with some exceptions, provide a more direct support for the deterrent effect of both legitimate earnings and the conditional probability and severity of punishment (Witte, 1980; Myers, 1983; Trumbull, 1989; Grogger, 1991; Tauchen, Dryden and Griesinger, 1994).

One problem with studies employing individual data to estimate supply functions is the use of a person's incidence of arrest or conviction during the sample period as a measure of that person's crime rate. But arrests are a product of the individual-specific crime rate and concurrent probability of arrest. The past probability of being convicted or the severity of the imposed punishment can be expected to affect (in different degrees) both the person's crime rate and probability of arrest in subsequent periods, as the offender's identity is exposed to both potential victims and law enforcement agents. The estimated deterrent effects of certainty and severity of punishment (and for similar reasons that of legitimate earnings) do not provide, therefore, direct estimates of the elasticities of individual crime rates with respect to the chance of being arrested or the length of sentence. Nor can this approach produce conclusive inferences about the relative efficacy of certainty vs. severity of punishment.

IDENTIFICATION RESTRICTIONS

The most serious econometric challenge has been to assure that the estimated relationship between crime rates and measures of law enforcement reflect the causal effect of the latter on the former, rather than vice versa. In terms of the market model, the econometric structure must contain some exogenous or predetermined variables that are included in the demand function for law enforcement or in the production functions of law enforcement measures, but are excluded from the supply-of-offenses function. Changes in these exogenous variables will shift the implicit "tax" and net-demand schedules in Figure 1 and allow us to identify the shape of the supply-of-offenses schedule.

Data concerning such exogenous or predetermined variables that are excluded from the supply function are hard to come by. Some proxies used in a number of studies on specific crimes include past levels of total expenditure on police and courts, past crime rates and measures of urbanization and population density, which constrain the productivity of resources spent on law enforcement. In many studies, severity of punishment is measured by using the length of time served by those released from state prisons; since this figure tended to be constant over previous decades, it has been treated as a predetermined variable. The results of studies using such identification restrictions tend to confirm the existence of discouraging effects on crime of both positive and negative incentives (Ehrlich, 1973, 1975a; Carr-Hill and Stern, 1973; Phillips and Votey, 1975; Wolpin, 1978a).

These identification restrictions are subject to potential weaknesses.[W] In particular, crime rates may be serially correlated, and some demographic variables used to identify the supply-of-offenses function may also affect the supply functions themselves. But serial correlation can be accounted for in time series regressions, and identification restrictions are testable. With some exceptions, studies pursuing the relevant statistical tests and using the estimation techniques justified by these tests have actually found strong statistical support for the impact of positive and negative incentives (Layson, 1983, 1985; Ehrlich and Brower, 1987).

Some studies introduce per capita expenditures on law enforcement activity as a direct determinant of the structural supply of offenses, in lieu of measures of probability and even severity of punishment, even though the earlier analysis of public decision making indicates that such expenditures are likely to be simultaneously determined by, and positively associated with, the crime rate. Without pursuing the proper identification restrictions, it is no wonder that some of these studies find a weak association between, say, expenditures on police and crime.

A promising approach toward the identification problem is to quantify political or institutional (judicial) factors that affect either law enforcement budgets or the "rules of the game" that influence the productivity of enforcement efforts in determining the probabilities of apprehension and conviction. Since law enforcement budgets are determined by elected officials at the state and local levels, they may be subject to electoral cycles. Election dates and Supreme Court rulings are unlikely to be affected by concurrent crime rates. Their impact on enforcement spending and productivity can therefore be used to identify the relevant supply responses. Recent studies that use such institutional and political factors have found new support for the hypothesis that law enforcement instruments do discourage crime (Ehrlich and Brower, 1987; Levitt, 1995a).[X] Studies of individual

W See the critiques in Blumstein, Cohen and Nagin (1978). These critiques focus exclusively on potential negative biases in the estimates of deterrent effects because of the crowding effects exerted by high crime rates on both probability and severity of imprisonment (see note 10), although biases are likely in the opposite direction as well because of optimal enforcement.

X Alternative identification procedures, based on time series techniques, have been pursued by Phillips and Ray (1982) in their analysis of murder. They too find support for the deterrence hypothesis, including the deterrent effect of capital punishment.

data that combine individual and area statistics on law enforcement expenditures reach similar conclusions (Tauchen, Dryden and Griesinger, 1994).

SEPARATING DETERRENCE FROM INCAPACITATION

Perhaps the most unique econometric challenge has been to separate the pure deterrent effect from the incapacitation effect inherent in imprisonment. Separation of the two effects is critical for establishing the validity of the market model.

A decomposition of the total effect of imprisonment on crime into deterrent and incapacitative components can be achieved by using sample data to provide estimates of the maximum possible effect of incapacitation, based on theoretical considerations, and then comparing these to regression estimates of the actual effect of imprisonment, based on the same sample (Ehrlich, 1981). An alternative decomposition method has been used by Levitt (1995b), based on identifying a pure substitution effect of the probability of arrest for one crime on the incidence of a "substitute" crime. Both studies conclude that deterrence constitutes the dominant effect of criminal sanctions.

Some studies have attempted to assess the deterrent effects of criminal sanctions directly, by studying the impact of monetary fines which in principle, can exert only a pure deterrent effect. Use of monetary fines in felony crimes has been highly restricted in the United States, but some evidence consistent with a deterrent effect of fines on specific property crimes has been derived using United Kingdom data (Wolpin, 1978a). Evidence on the deterrent effect of monetary fines has also been inferred from U.S. data concerning antitrust violations (Block, Nold and Sidak, 1981).

INFERENCES ABOUT POSITIVE AND NEGATIVE INCENTIVES

Freeman (1983) observes that most econometric studies using both aggregate or individual data find negative deterrent effects of both probability and severity of criminal sanctions, but that the estimated deterrent effects of positive incentives, such as employment and legitimate earnings measures, are weaker by comparison. This should not be interpreted to suggest that positive incentives are unimportant.

Since positive and negative incentives are generally correlated, consistent estimates of the separate effects of either set of incentives cannot be obtained without accounting for the influence of both. Yet many studies focusing on positive incentives—using such variables as unemployment, labor force participation, income or earnings measures and demographic variables—have completely ignored measures of the probability and severity of punishment. Freeman (1983) reports that 70 percent of the studies of positive incentives he had surveyed are subject to this omission. Similarly, some studies focusing on the role of criminal sanctions omit measures of positive incentives. Others include only estimates of probability of arrests but not of the (conditional) probability of punishment or its actual severity.[Y] As noted earlier, some studies that have attempted a more complete implementation of supply-of-offenses functions find statistically significant deterrent effects associated with proxies of both positive and negative incentives.

The present evidence does not allow one to conclude that positive incentives are either less or more potent than negative ones. The effects of positive incentives that concern the general population can be expected to differ from those applying to marginal offenders, and the effects of rehabilitation and employment-incentive programs that are targeted at imprisoned or ex-offenders are expected to have substantially different impacts at the individual, relative to the aggregate-market level. Some of the ambiguous effects of unemployment and legitimate earnings indicators can be ascribed to the incentive measures used rather than to the pure effect of incentives. Also, the elasticities of crime rates with respect to (general) positive and negative incentives are not comparable, even if the two had the same absolute (pure) deterrent effects on individual would-be offenders, as the simplified model underlying Figure 1 suggests.

The empirical evidence seems more consistent in connection with the deterrent effects of the probability of apprehension relative to the conditional probability of conviction or the conditional probability of a larger punishment, as implied by the sharp elasticity conditions discussed earlier (Ehrlich, 1975a, 1977; Wolpin, 1978a). As expected, efforts at apprehending and convicting offenders are found to be a stronger deterrent to crime than efforts at achieving a specific sentence. Also, many studies find that increasing the risk of imprisonment for most crime categories has a significantly larger deterrent effect in elasticity terms than increasing the length of imprisonment, especially for violent crimes, and that the magnitudes of the elasticities is less than one. The evidence is consistent with Becker's (1968) proposition about the ranking of these elasticities, which was based on a social cost minimizing enforcement strategy. I cannot yet conclude, however, that severity of punishment has a substantially weaker effect than its certainty.

On a theoretical level, others have developed models where the latter elasticity condition need not hold (see note 14). These broader models imply that the marginal cost of raising the severity of punishment might exceed that of raising the probability of punishment. Higher penalties may also raise the direct cost of prosecuting and convicting offenders because they induce greater self-protection by offenders. In both cases, optimal law enforcement implies that in equilibrium,

---

Y Such omissions are common especially in the early sociological literature on deterrence (for example, Sellin, 1959, 1967). Leamer (1983) and McMannus (1985) propose to sort out the merits of incorporating either set of incentives in the supply-of-offenses function through "extreme bounds analysis," which assigns no weight to systematic theoretical considerations. They claim that results are sensitive to researchers' prior beliefs, but their tests have been shown to rely on vacuous test statistics (McAleer, Pagan and Volker, 1985; Ehrlich and Liu, 1995).

the marginal preventive effect of severity of punishment in elasticity terms might even exceed that of its certainty.

There is also a problem with measuring severity of punishment empirically. In some of the studies reporting smaller elasticities of crime with respect to severity of punishment, severity is measured in terms of the length of sentence rendered, rather than the actual time served (for example, Grogger, 1991). As noted earlier, even measuring severity by the actual time served fails to discount its future cost, and thus treats, say, a 10-year term as twice as costly as a five-year term. This bias worsens for crimes with longer imprisonment terms.

Perhaps the single most debated issue in the literature on crime has been the deterrent effect of capital punishment. As argued at the outset, the economic approach to crime is expected to apply to all illegitimate activities, including murder and other "crimes of passion," regardless of whether these entail any material benefits. Violent offenders can still be expected to respond to an increase in the threat of punishment imposed on violent behavior, especially when the potential sanction is capital punishment. Influential studies by sociologists have concluded that capital punishment was not a deterrent to murder (Sellin, 1959, 1967), but these studies did not account for the effects of the complete set of "prices" expected to affect behavior on the margin—the probability of apprehension and conviction, the conditional probability that the death penalty be actually imposed, the severity of the alternative punishment of imprisonment and other relevant incentives. Since murder is also the best-reported crime, the results of testing the deterrence hypothesis in connection with this crime can provide inferences about the validity of the market model in general. There is now corroborating evidence from several studies using independent time series and cross-section data from the United States, Canada and the United Kingdom that is consistent with the hypothesis that punishment in general, and capital punishment specifically, have a deterrent effect on murder (Ehrlich 1975a, 1977; Layson, 1983, 1985; Wolpin, 1978b; Phillips and Ray, 1982).

The econometric issues raised in the debate about the validity of these findings are the same as those already discussed above.[Z] What may be worth stressing is that, as predicted, in all studies supporting the deterrence hypothesis, the conditional risk of execution, while having a significant deterrent effect, has the least impact on the incidence of murder relative to equal percentage changes in apprehension, conviction or punishment risks, and that the alternative, and most frequently used sanction for murder—the length of imprisonment—also exerts a statistically significant discouraging effect on murder. Lower levels of wealth, income inequality and unemployment (in time series studies) have also been found to deter the incidence of murder.

Z For example, see the critiques and studies by Blumstein, Cohen and Nagin (1978), Avio (1979), Hoenack and Weiler (1980), and the responses by Ehrlich and Mark (1977), Ehrlich and Brower (1987) and Layson (1985).

SOME POLICY IMPLICATIONS

The relative desirability of specific means of crime control cannot be determined just by their relative efficacy; it also depends on their relative social costs and on the welfare criteria invoked as a justification for public law enforcement.

For example, if the welfare objective is to maximize social income, then the social cost of purely deterring sanctions, such as fines, would be close to zero, because as transfer payments, fines are free of the deadweight costs associated with imprisonment, house arrests, probation and other intermediate punishments. An optimal enforcement strategy may then involve raising such fines to their maximal feasible level (consistent with a convict's wealth constraint) while lowering the probability of apprehension and conviction to its minimal level (Becker, 1968). Even under this (narrow) efficiency criterion, however, it would be optimal to use imprisonment and intermediate punishments along with fines for those crime categories where the added incapacitation value of imprisonment justifies its added costs.

The enforcement strategy would be different if the social welfare function were broadened to include distributional objectives as well. These include, for example, a preference for promoting equality of individuals under the law, reducing the legal error of convicting the innocent, or lowering the corollary prospect of letting the guilty go free. For example, since the probability of apprehension and punishment is substantially less than one, penalties are in fact applied through a lottery system. Offenders who are caught and punished are subjected to ex post discrimination under the law because they "pay" not just for their own crime, but also for offenders who get away with crime. The degree of such discrimination rises as the penalty becomes more severe, or if the probability of punishment is very low. Such concerns help explain why severity of punishment is often traded on the margin for a higher probability of apprehension and conviction. It also helps explain why the justice system introduces numerous safeguards to protect the rights of the accused, and why the opposition to capital punishment tends to increase when the penalty is applied infrequently and capriciously (Ehrlich, 1982).

Incorporating concerns for equality and legal error in the social welfare function raises not just the marginal social cost of severity of punishment, but that of any strategy of enforcement (as long as the probability of being arrested and punished for a crime is low) relative to its cost under the narrower efficiency criterion. The implication is that more crime would be tolerated as a result of a tradeoff between equity and efficiency in enforcement—a tradeoff typical of social choice in general.

This analysis is applicable to crime control strategies concerning the use of positive incentives as well. The market model implies that a lower disparity in the distribution of earning opportunities in legitimate markets will deter offenders on the margin, by reducing their differential gains from criminal activity. This provides a justification for public policies aimed at equalizing educational and employment opportunities partly as means of reducing crime. However, since these policies, unlike conventional law enforcement, cannot be targeted specifically at actual or potential offenders, they may entail relatively high social costs as means of crime control.

The positive implications of the market model and some corroborating empirical evidence concerning the relative efficacy of deterrence vs. incapacitation and rehabilitation, as discussed earlier in this paper, suggest a direction of reform of the criminal justice system through greater reliance on general incentives and purely deterring sanctions. Forcing offenders to pay fines through work-release programs (including direct restitution to their victims) may in many cases be as effective a means of crime prevention as the more costly incapacitating penalties or rehabilitative programs—especially in the case of many theft crimes or transactions in illicit goods and services. Thus, the dramatic growth in the proportion of those imprisoned for drug offenses, shown earlier in Table 2, appears to be inconsistent with this implication of optimal enforcement.

CONCLUSION

The market model of crime is still a work in progress. Data limitations have so far precluded a complete implementation of its relevant structure, and the model itself is evolving. But the existing literature on the whole lends strong support to the basic premises of the model.

A common confusion about the deterrence hypothesis is that it applies only to negative incentives, while positive incentives may hold a greater promise for "solving" the crime problem. Another often-heard claim is that we don't need to know more about punishment because punishment does not eliminate crime. Both claims are wrong. The deterrence hypothesis and its logical extension—the market model—rely on the *marginal* efficacy of *both* positive and negative incentives and on the interaction between market demand and supply forces, to explain the observed variability in the frequency of offenses across space and time. The empirical evidence is consistent with the hypothesis that punishment and other general incentives exert a deterrent effect on offenders. This suggests, for example, that there is no need to rely exclusively on harsh or incapacitating sanctions to achieve efficient crime control. A better understanding of what does works, however, calls for more, rather than less, research into the general deterrence hypothesis and the market model based on it.

I wish to thank Chaya Ehrlich and the editors of the journal, especially Timothy Taylor, for valuable editorial assistance and suggestions. I have also benefitted from comments by Gary Becker, Richard Posner, Govind Hariharan and Zhiqiang Liu. Shao-Chi Chang and Jianguo Zhong have provided valuable assistance.

Isaac Ehrlich is Melvin H. Baker Professor of American Enterprise and Leading Professor of Economics, State University of New York at Buffalo, Buffalo, New York.

REFERENCES

Avio, Kenneth, "Capital Punishment in Canada: A Time-Series Analysis of the Deterrence Hypothesis," *Canadian Journal of Economics*, November 1979, *12:4*, 647–76.

Balkin, Steven, and John F. McDonald, "The Market of Street Crime: An Economic Analysis of Victim-Offender Interaction," *Journal of Urban Economics*, November 1981, *10:3*, 390–405.

Bartel, Ann, "An Analysis of Firm Demand for Protection Against Crime," *Journal of Legal Studies*, June 1975, 4:2, 445–78.

Becker, Gary, "Crime and Punishment: An Economic Approach" *Journal of Political Economy*, 1968, 76:2, 169–217.

Becker, Gary, and William Landes, *Essays in the Economics of Crime and Punishment*. New York: Columbia University Press, 1974.

Block, Michael, and John Heineke, "A Labor Theoretical Analysis of Criminal Choice," *American Economic Review*, June 1975, 65:3, 314–25.

Block, Michael, Frederick Nold, and Joseph Sidak, "The Deterrent Effect of Antitrust Enforcement," *Journal of Political Economy*, 1981, *89:3*, 429–45.

Blumstein, Alfred, Jacqueline Cohen, and Daniel Nagin, *Deterrence and Incapacitation: Estimating the Effects of Criminal Sanctions on Crime Rates*. Washington, D.C.: National Academy of Science, 1978.

Cameron, Samuel, "The Economics of Crime and Deterrence: A Survey of Theory and Evidence," *Kyklos*, 1988, *41:2*, 301–23.

Carr-Hill, R. A., and Nicholas Stern, "An Econometric Model of Supply and Control of Recorded Offenses in England and Wales," *Journal of Public Economics*, November 1973, 2, 289–318.

Clotfelter, Charles, "Public Service, Private Substitutes and the Demand for Protection Against Crime," *American Economic Review*, December 1977, 67:5, 867–77.

Cook, Philip, "The Correctional Carrot: Better Jobs for Parolees," *Policy Analysis*, Winter 1975, 1, 12–51.

Cook, Philip, "The Supply and Demand of Criminal Opportunities." In Tonry, Michael, and Morris Norval, eds., *Crime and Justice: An Annual Review of Research*. Vol. 7, Chicago: University of Chicago Press, 1986, pp. 1–28.

Durkheim, Emile, *The Rules of Sociological Methods*. 8th ed., New York: Free Press, 1958.

Ehrlich, Isaac, "Participation in Illegitimate Activities: A Theoretical and Empirical Investigation," *Journal of Political Economy*, 1973, *81:3*, 521–65.

Ehrlich, Isaac, "Participation in Illegitimate Activities: An Economic Analysis." In Becker, Gary, and William Landes, eds., *The Economics of Crime And Punishment*. New York: Columbia University Press, 1974, pp. 68–134.

Ehrlich, Isaac, "The Deterrent Effect of Capital Punishment: A Question of Life and Death," *American Economic Review*, June 1975a, 65:3, 397417.

Ehrlich, Isaac, "On the Relation Between Education and Crime." In Juster, F. T., ed., *Education, Income and Human Behavior*. New York: McGraw-Hill, 1975b, pp. 313–37.

Ehrlich, Isaac, "Capital Punishment and Deterrence: Some Further Thoughts and Additional Evidence," *Journal Political Economy*, 1977, 85:4, 741–88.

Ehrlich, Isaac, "On the Usefulness of Controlling Individuals: An Economic Analysis of Rehabilitation, Incapacitation and Deterrence," *American Economic Review*, June 1981, 72:3, 307–22.

Ehrlich, Isaac, "The Optimum Enforcement of Laws and the Concept of Justice: A Positive Analysis," *International Review of Law & Economics*.June 1982, 2, 3–27.

Ehrlich, Isaac, and Gary Becker, "Market Insurance, Self-Insurance and Self-Protection," *Journal of Political Economy*, 1972, *80:4*, 623–48.

Ehrlich, Isaac, and George Brower, "On the Issue of Causality in the Economic Model of Crime and Law Enforcement: Some Theoretical Considerations and Experimental Evidence," *American Economic Review*, May 1987, 77:2, 99110.

Ehrlich, Isaac, and Joel Gibbons, "On the Measurement of Deterrent Effect of Capital Punishment and the Theory of Deterrence," *Journal of Legal Studies*, *January* 1977, 6:1, 35–50.

Ehrlich Isaac, and Zhiqiang Liu, "Extreme Bounds Analysis and the Deterrence Hypothesis—Where is the Con?," mimeo, 1995.

Ehrlich, Isaac, and Francis Lui, "Corruption and Economic Growth," mimeo, State University of New York at Buffalo, 1995.

Ehrlich, Isaac, and Randall Mark, "Fear of Deterrence: A Critical Evaluation of the 'Report of the Panel on Research on Deterrent and Incapacitation Effects,'" *Journal of Legal Studies*, June 1977, 6:2, 293–316.

Fleisher, Belton, *The Economics of Delinquency*. Chicago: Quadrangle, 1966.

Freeman, Richard, "Crime and Unemployment." In Wilson, J. Q., *Crime and Public Policy*. San Francisco: Institute for Contemporary Studies, 1983, pp. 89–106.

Freeman, Scott, Jeffrey Grogger, and Jon Sonstelie, "The Spatial Concentration of Crime," mimeo, 1995.

Friedman, David, "Efficient Institutions for the Private Enforcement of Law" *Journal of Legal Studies*, June 1984, 23:2, 379–97.

Glaeser, Edward, Bruce Sacerdote, and Jose Scheinkman, "Crime and Social Interaction," mimeo, 1995.

Goldberg, Itzhak, and Frederick Nold, "Does Reporting Deter Burglary?—An Empirical Analysis of Risk and Return in Crime," *Review of Economics and Statistics*, August 1980, *62*, 424–31.

Grogger, Jeffrey, "Certainty Versus Severity of Punishment," *Economic Inquiry*, April 1991, *29*, 297–309.

Hoenack, Stephen, and William Weiler, "A Structural Model of Murder Behavior and the Criminal Justice System," *American Economic Review*, June 1980, *70*:3, 327–41.

Landes, William, and Richard Posner, "The Private Enforcement of Law," *Journal of Legal Studies*, January 1975, *4*:*1*, 1–46.

Layson, Stephen, "Homicide and Deterrence: Another View of the Canadian Time-Series Evidence," *Canadian Journal of Economics*, February 1983, 26:1, 52–73.

Layson, Stephen, "Homicide and Deterrence: A Reexamination of the United States Time-Series Evidence," *Southern Economic Journal*, July 1985, *52*, 68–89.

Learner, Edward, "Let's Take the Con Out of Econometrics," *American Economic Review*, March 1983, *73*, 31–43.

Levitt, Steven, "Reporting Behavior of Crime Victims and the Size of the Police Force: Implications for Studies of Police Effectiveness Using Reported Crime Data," mimeo, Harvard University, 1994.

Levitt, Steven, "Using Electoral Cycles in Police Hiring to Estimate the Effect of Police on Crime." NBER Working Paper Series No. 4991, 1995a.

Levitt, Steven, "How Do Increased Arrest Rates Appear to Reduce Crime: Deterrence, Incapacitation, or Measurement Error?," mimeo, Harvard University, 1995b.

Lipton, D., R. Martinson, and J. Wilks, *The Effectiveness of Correctional Treatments: A Survey of Treatment Evaluation Studies*. New York: Praeger, 1975.

McAleer, Michael, Adrian Pagan, and Paul A. Volker, "What Will Take the Con Out of Econometrics?," *American Economic Review*, June 1985, *75*, 293–307.

McManus, Walter, "Estimates of the Deterrent Effect of Capital Punishment: The Importance of the Researcher's Prior Beliefs," *Journal of Political Economy*, April 1985, *93*, 417–25.

Myers, Samuel, "Estimating the Economic Model of Crime: Employment Versus Punishment Effects," *Quarterly Journal of Economics*, February 1983, *98*, 157–66.

Paley, William, *The Principles of Moral and Political Philosophy*. 1785. Reprint, London: T. Davidson, Whitefriars, 1822.

Palmer, John, "Economic Analysis of the Deterrent Effect of Punishment: A Review," *Journal of Research in Crime and Delinquency*, January 1977, *14*:1, 4–21.

Phillips, Llad, and Subhash Ray, "Evidence on the Identification and Causality Dispute about the Death Penalty." In *Applied Time Series Analysis*. Amsterdam: North-Holland, 1982, pp. 313–40.

Phillips, Llad, and Harold Votey, "Crime Control in California," *Journal of Legal Studies*, June 1975, *4:2*, 327–49.

Piehl, Anne, "Learning While Doing Time," mimeo, Working Paper Series R94–25, Kennedy School, Harvard University, 1994.

Polinsky, Mitchell, and Steven Shavell, "The Optimal Tradeoff Between the Probability and Magnitude of Fines," *American Economic Review*, December 1979, *69:5*, 880–91.

Pyle, David, *The Economics of Crime and Law Enforcement*. London: Macmillan, 1983.

Reuter, Peter, Robert MacCoun, and Patrick Murphy, "Money from Crime: A Study of the Economics of Drug Dealing in Washington, D.C.," reviewed by Henry Miller, *Contemporary Drug Problems*, Winter 1990, *18A*, 713–6.

Rossi, Peter, Richard Berk, and Kenneth Lenihan, *Money, Work, and Crime: Experimental Evidence*. New York: Academic Press, 1980.

Rottenberg, Simon, "The Clandestine Distribution of Heroin, Its Discovery and Suppression," *Journal of Political Economy*, 1968, 76:1, 78–90.

Sah, Raaj, "Social Osmosis and Patterns of Crime," *Journal of Political Economy*, 1991, *99:6*, 1272–95.

Sellin, Thorsten, *The Death Penalty*. Philadelphia: American Law Institute, 1959.

Sellin, Thorsten, *Capital Punishment*. New York: Harper 8c Row, 1967.

Smith Adam, *The Wealth of Nations*. 1776. Reprint, New York: Random House, 1937.

Stigler, George, "The Optimum Enforcement of Laws," *Journal of Political Economy*, 1970, *78:3*, 526–36.

Tauchen, Helen, Ann Dryden, and Harriet Griesinger, "Criminal Deterrence: Revisiting the Issue with a Birth Cohort," *Review of Economics and Statistics*, August 1994, 76:3, 399–412.

Thaler, Richard, "An Econometric Analysis of Property Crime: An Interaction Between Police and Criminals," *Journal of Public Economics*, August 1977, *8*, 37–51.

Trumbull, William, "Estimation of the Economic Model of Crime Using Aggregate and Individual Level Data," *Southern Economic Journal*, October 1989, 56, 423–39.

Tullock, Gordon, "The Welfare Costs of Tariffs, Monopolies, and Theft," *Economic Inquiry*, June 1967, 5, 224–32.

U.S. Department of Justice, Bureau of Justice Statistics, *National Corrections Reporting Program* Washington, D.C.: U.S. Department of Justice, 1991.

U.S. Department of Justice, Bureau of Justice Statistics, *Sourcebook of Criminal Justice Statistics*. Washington, DC.: U.S. Department of Justice, 1992.

U.S. Department of Justice, Federal Bureau of Investigation, *Uniform Crime Reports*. Washington, D.C.: U.S. Department of Justice, 1960,1961, and 1991.

U.S. Department of Justice, Federal Bureau of Prisons, *Characteristics of State Prisoners*. Washington, D.C.: U.S. Department of Justice, 1960.

Vandaele, Walter, "An Econometric Model of Auto Theft in the United States." In Heineke, J. M., ed., *Economic Models of Criminal Behavior*. New York: North-Holland, 1978, pp. 303–90.

Van den Haag, Ernest, *Punishing Criminals*. New York: Free Press, 1975.

Viscusi, Kip, "The Risks and Rewards of Criminal Activity: A Comprehensive Test of Criminal Deterrence," *Journal of Labor Economics*, 1986, *4*:3, 317–40.

Witte, Ann Dryden, "Estimating the Economic Model of Crime with Individual Data," *Quarterly Journal of Economics*, February 1980, *94*, 57–84.

Wolpin, Kenneth, "An Economic Analysis of Crime and Punishment in England and Wales," *Journal of Political Economy*, 1978a, *86*:5, 815–40.

Wolpin, Kenneth, "Capital Punishment and Homicide in England: A Summary of Results," *American Economic Review*, May 1978b, *68*:2, 422–27.

CHAPTER 6

SELECTIVE ENFORCEMENT—AN ESSAY ON ATHLETICS, THEFT, AND CHEATING

By Ron Liggett

The world of athletics and competitive sports can offer an interesting laboratory for behaviors of various types as well as an analysis of costs in certain situations. Consider the sport of basketball and the various rules and infractions enforced by referees. Having spent some time coaching the sport at the high school level, I have had the opportunity to inquire as to specific fouls called by the referee during competitive games. Accordingly, on multiple occasions I have received the following response as to why an obvious foul or infraction was not called: "Coach, we're letting them play tonight." Translation—certain violations, which generally would be enforced with the respective punishment of foul shots or perhaps a possession violation, are being ignored. Result—the rules of the game and the costs facing the players have been altered—at least temporarily.

This same type of observation may also appear at higher levels, college and beyond, where TV commentators excitedly and positively proclaim how "the officials are really letting them play." Additionally, the observation might focus on the marginal aspects of a particular violation. For example, in a recent NBA contest, star player Dwight Howard, then a member of the Los Angeles Lakers, was called for his sixth foul in the final minutes of the game, resulting in his removal from the contest.[1] The commentator was quick to observe that while there was definitely a violation, the foul itself was generally not the type of violation worthy of being the "sixth" and disqualifying foul. The suggestion being that requirements for a disqualifying foul should somehow be different from early violations and therefore higher at the margin. (One wonders if this line of reasoning would apply to all players or only to the so-called star performer.)

DECISIONS AT THE MARGIN

This conversation is really more than an analysis of fouls in a basketball game. Rather it's an introduction to an economic principle which recognizes that rational individuals generally make decisions "at the margin." That is, they look at the incremental benefits and costs of a particular decision. In this basketball scenario, the 6th foul had a high marginal cost by virtue of the fact that it caused the player to be removed from the game. In fact, having acquired a 5th foul, the player's behavior could be expected to change slightly, and a coach might hold that player out of the game for a time in an effort to save him until a more opportune moment in the contest. But, should the 6th foul be defined any differently? Or worse, enforced differently?

Granted, many diehard fans no doubt approve of a "letting them play" philosophy, provided, of course, that the ignored violations do not impede the play of their favorite team. With that being said, we dutifully note that we are philosophizing in the area of normative economics, with the realization that such subjective behavior by officials is both possible and perhaps even welcomed by some fans.

AS THE GAME IS PLAYED—BASKETBALL AND HOCKEY

The reasoning noted above allows us to understand that the costs have changed in our competitive environment and the participant behavior will likely change as well. As our respective officials begin to call fewer and fewer violations, player intensity in the area of fouls will likely increase (this is particularly consequential at the outset of a contest where expectations are initially established). Such intensity (behavior), now effectively encouraged by lack of enforcement, may result in the contest evolving into something beyond a spirited sporting event and officials may conceivably even "lose" control of the contest by calling too few violations.

Multiple studies have been done on the impact of the number of officials in sports such as basketball and hockey.[A] But while my earlier anecdote involved basketball, a study done on the impact of the National Hockey League (NHL) adding a second on-ice referee also provides relevance to this discussion. By employing the additional law enforcer (referee) in the 1998–2000 seasons, fighting among players (which is common in the NHL) was deterred. In fact, major on-ice infractions (felony crimes) were reduced more significantly than minor infractions (misdemeanor crimes). The suggestion is that the detection of petty offenses may invoke a calming effect and help prevent hostilities escalating to the point of violence.[2] Additionally, the study noted another interesting point in that the inequality of team production had a positive influence on the amount of violent

A R. E. McCormick and R. D. Tollison (1984) found that the inclusion of a third college basketball official actually led to an overall reduction in the number of called fouls in a post-season tournament, suggesting that the additional referee served as a deterrent and players sought more productive (non-criminal) behavior. (See "Crime on the Court," *Journal of Political Economy*.)

criminal activity.[3] Stated simply, low-quality teams sometimes resort to more aggressive behavior.

While basketball is not prone to the same levels of fighting as seen in the NHL, ignoring violations would still likely decrease any possible calming effect that the officials might have been able to provide. And if we can assume from the study that a lower quality team is more apt to compete in a "rough" manner, then game costs really have been changed, particularly in a sport such as basketball. Therefore, when the official (enforcer) makes a conscious effort to ignore specific violations, he has invoked both explicit and implicit costs on a team or player and changed the dynamics of the contest. Additionally, he has also introduced inefficiencies and uncertainties into the game that may evolve into added negative externalities for other teams who are impacted by the win-loss outcome.[B]

But our analysis into expectations and costs as they relate to these normative consequences of selective enforcement should not be limited strictly to an "enforcer" in the form of an official or referee. Frequently, the expectations are imposed and/or ignored internally within an organization, or company, as they determine what costs are to be absorbed.

A BASEBALL PERSPECTIVE ON SELECTIVE ENFORCEMENT

During the 2012 Major League Baseball (MLB) season, there was an interleague contest between the Washington Nationals and the Tampa Bay Rays that was being played in Tampa. During this game, the Nationals suspected that Tampa Bay pitcher Joel Peralta might be attempting to pitch with a foreign substance on his glove, and therefore, Washington manager Davey Johnson asked the umpires to investigate. Accordingly, after finding that Peralta did, in fact, have pine tar on his baseball glove (MLB rules prohibit a player applying a foreign substance of any kind to the ball), he was ejected from the game, and given an 8-game suspension by MLB. The accusation that Peralta was thought to have been "doctoring" the ball is not unusual. Baseball has a long history of pitchers attempting to use some type of substance—saliva, Vaseline, pine tar, etc.—in an effort to get better movement on the pitch, making the ball more difficult to hit.

But in lieu of Tampa Bay manager Joe Maddon's irritation over what transpired with his pitcher that night, and his pointed post-game comments, let us look at the internal dynamics. During the 2010 season, Peralta had played for the opponent that night—the Washington Nationals. So, one can assume that

B A negative externality is defined as the harmful effects which spillover onto a party that is involved in a specific transaction. For example, those who must breathe second hand cigarette smoke are experiencing a negative externality.

through some mechanism, manager Johnson had reason to believe that Peralta was a user of pine tar.[C]

The question on whether or not the pine tar use was a true violation is a slam-dunk case per MLB Rule #8. Yet it is not a rule that umpires frequently enforce, which might be a part of manager Maddon's discontent, as heard after the game: "To single out Joel Peralta tonight and make him look like a bad guy or villain of any kind, that's what upsets me, that this is all going to lay on Joel and I don't like that at all... Insider trading, man. It's bush. It's bogus," Maddon stated.[4]

Translation—the Ray's pitcher breaks a rule and is caught, and for some reason, Maddon's focus is turned in the direction of the Nationals and their manager for bringing this to the umpires' attention as if they have done something unethical or unsportsmanlike. Perhaps this is simply the "letting them play" philosophy from another angle.

Interestingly, some hitters have also taken a "look the other way" and a "let them play" philosophy to certain aspects of the rule. For example, in a 2014 game against the Boston Red Sox, New York Yankees pitcher Michael Pineda was caught with pine tar applied to his neck. Again, using the tacky substance for a better grip while pitching. And, like Peralta, he too was ejected from the game and also served a 10-game suspension. However, after the game, the famed Red Sox slugger David Ortiz noted, "Everybody uses pine tar in the league. It's not a big deal." Teammate Dustin Pedroia, also a prominent player in the league echoed similar sentiments.[5] Truly professional baseball has some interesting participants.

PROTECTING HIS MONEY

Speaking of interesting players, Dominican born Rico Carty was an outstanding hitter who led the National League in batting in 1970 with a .366 average. According to baseball author Jim Bouton, "Carty could make controversy with the best of them" in his interactions with baseball managers and teammates. However, he was also colorful. "He proudly called himself the 'Beeg Boy' in a heavy Spanish accent. Carty also had an interesting personal habit" which Bouton noted in his groundbreaking baseball book *Ball Four*. Carty had such little trust in either banks or the clubhouse valuables box that he stuffed his money into his game-worn uniform pants. According to Bouton, the big lump seen during baseball games in Carty's back pocket was his wallet![6]

C It should be noted that Johnson did not manage the team in 2010 when Peralta played there, so cries of hypocrisy toward Johnson should likely fall on deaf ears as it relates to the manager's position—he had not actually coached Peralta during the previous season.

ONE MORE POINT IN THE WORLD OF BASEBALL

After referencing a violation where the pitcher is accused of "doctoring" the baseball, it would be quite remiss—or dare I say even negligent—not to provide some mention of the major crisis in MLB over the last 15–20 years in dealing with steroids and other so-called performance enhancing drugs (PEDs). Most certainly, the pitcher has not been the only player on the field looking for an advantage. And while some pitchers have also been positively linked to the use of steroids, or other enhancements, it is my contention (and one held by others) that the overwhelming benefit from PED use in the baseball world has been experienced by hitters.

From 1996 to 2007, many batting records were simply obliterated. For example, having an individual batter hit 50 home runs in one season has always been recognized as a significant achievement, occurring rarely. In the first roughly 100 years of MLB, ending in 1995, this distinctive number was reached by hitters only 19 times. But, in the 12-year period referenced here (1996–2007), we saw players reach the fifty-home run plateau a total of 20 times![7] This is not meant as an indictment of all those who did actually hit 50 home runs, but merely a statistical representation to suggest something strange was going on in our nation's pastime.[D]

There are those who feel MLB, in the period following the 1994 strike season, perhaps looked the other way as the ball began to soar out of the park, and the fans returned to the game in record numbers. That is, they "let them play." Home runs are a source of entertainment at the park, and in the eyes of some, "the more the merrier."

Ultimately some introspection by MLB occurred (perhaps partially spurred by the threat of congressional investigation), and the idea of "letting them play" was no longer an option. The Mitchell report analyzing the use of steroids and enhancements was released in December 2007 and accordingly, the pressure to clean up the game in this area became stronger and a more strict system of testing for steroids and other enhancements was introduced.

Players continue to test the system however, including some prominent ones. For example, during the 2012 season, San Francisco Giant outfielder Melky Cabrera, who was leading the National League in hitting at the time with a batting average of .346, was suspended for 50 games during the last part of the year after testing positive for testosterone.[8] [E] Cabrera certainly isn't alone, and the lengthy list of suspended players continues to grow as MLB seems to be taking

D Of course an economist might also be prone to inquire on the true marginal differences of hitting 49 home runs vs. 50!

E There are actually several positive points related to this story. First, with the Giants reaching the playoffs, they still refused to reinstate Cabrera even as his 50 games of suspension came to an end during their playoff run. Secondly, Cabrera himself formally petitioned the National League that he be declared ineligible for the title of batting champion even

PED use seriously. A list of more recent suspensions levied against some rather prominent players follows (keep in mind this is only a partial list). Most of those on the list are strong offensive players with the power to regularly hit home runs (the popularity of the "long ball"—aka, a home run—is noted in the previous paragraphs). One, Mejia, is actually a pitcher and, as noted, he has received the proverbial "3-strikes and you are out" ruling.

Miguel Tejada – Kansas City – 8/7/2013 – 105 games
Alex Rodriguez – New York Yankees – 8/5/2013 – 211 games
Nelson Cruz – Texas Rangers – 8/5/2013 – 50 games
Jhonny Peralta – St. Louis Cardinals – 8/5/2013 – 50 games
Ryan Braun – Milwaukee Brewers – 7/22/2013 – 65 games
Jenrry Mejia – New York Mets – 2/2/2016 – Permanently Banned
Marlon Byrd – Cleveland Indians – 6/1/2016 – 162 games[9]
Dee Gordon – Miami Marlins – 4/26/2016 – 80 games[10]
Starling Marte – Pittsburgh Pirates – 4/18/2017 – 80 games[11]

As a monetary measurement, we would note that this list alone amounts to more than $50 million in lost wages to the players! Although about half of this amount is attributed to Alex Rodriguez' $25 Million annual salary, the explicit cost to all the players is still significant.

However, it is worth mentioning that even players coming off of suspensions have been rewarded with lucrative free agent contacts, so the risk-reward issue may still make sense for some. From the players noted above, Cabrera, Cruz and Peralta all signed multi-year contracts after their suspensions. And for those just starting a big contract such as Dee Gordon, even though the 80-game suspension may have cost him around $1.6 million in lost wages, roughly $48 million still remained on his 5-year, $50 million agreement with the Marlins.[12]

Finally, let us note that the lost wages are only part of the economic story. When a suspension does occur, there are implicit costs as the MLB clubs deal with the loss of what may be an extremely valuable component to their team. Many of these players are not easily or readily replaced. It is worth noting that even with the apparent increase in suspensions, for 2016 the number of MLB players testing positive is only in the one percent range for the approximately 860 major league players on rosters and/or disabled lists.[13]

YMCA TOWELS AND STUY HIGH

A *Wall Street Journal* story several years ago revealed the dilemma of a New Jersey YMCA struggling with the issue of towels being stolen from their workout

---

though his .346 average proved to be the highest mark this season. Finally, Cabrera, upon reinstatement, has continued as a productive MLB player.

facilities. Amazingly, the location in Montclair was losing, on average, about 50 towels a day! Annual costs were estimated at almost $50,000. What to do about the confiscation? Certainly options exist to prevent this from occurring. The location considered increasing the workout fees, or increasing and expanding the identification and check-in steps while using scanning devices. More drastically, the facility even considered removing all towels—an option that did not sit well with users of the gym.

But what is most enlightening and of particular interest for this section is the attitude expressed by some of those guilty of the heist. From a blogger—"Should I feel bad about stealing those tiny white towels from the gym?" And, from a YMCA member, "I've got some of their towels right now sitting on my laundry shelf. It's predominantly inadvertent and it really is the cost of doing business."[14] Obviously the bar has been lowered in regards to behavior at the local YMCA, at least for a few.

But how does that compare to high school students cheating at Stuyvesant High School in Manhattan? Unfortunately it would seem that "lowering the bar" has found its way to a younger generation as well. In June of 2012, 71 juniors were caught in a cheating web on a state Regents exam. The students were texting answers to each other. But, the overall attitude was not much different than with the theft of towels. For example, to some students the memorizing of a table was seen as a "waste of time," therefore, using cheat notes was deemed to be more efficient.[F] The rationalizing continued in another way. Cheating to provide the answers to a friend was justified, by declaring, "...I have your back, you have mine."[15]

In studying this topic, there is no naïveté in thinking that cheating does not occur among students, or that we never behave improperly. On the contrary, there is clear understanding of what I call the fallacies of man. We are all imperfect. However, what is most disconcerting about stories such as these are the attempts at justifying the specific behavior. While behaviorists would note that such attempts at justification are not uncommon among "criminals," I would somehow prefer to think that the bar is a little higher for these particular students and YMCA members.[G]

F While striving for "efficiency" is at the heart of many economic theories, I am struggling to recall the chapter where cheating, when efficient, gets a "thumbs up."

G We will discuss later how such behavior might multiply. But, can we compare this to a "dumbing down" of academic standards, or in the case of competitive sports, "playing down to your competition?" Is it simply a matter of taking the "low road" with fewer perceived behavioral costs? Maybe that doesn't hit the spot, but the reality is that the participants in these situations are lowering the expectations on behavior. Sadly, things sometimes spiral downhill quickly after that.

SELECTIVE ENFORCEMENT IN FOOTBALL—ONE EXAMPLE

In this discussion on selective enforcement, we have looked at a variety of topics related to major U.S. sports with the exception of football. So, let us complete the conversation and address one specific area of interest as it relates to the National Football League (NFL).

One of the most potentially exciting plays in football is the long pass thrown as the last play of the game when a team is behind. The play is called a "Hail Mary" pass and the overall odds of achieving a score on the play are generally slim. However, even though the play is one of desperation, the anticipation as the ball comes floating down towards a group of players can be stimulating. In this situation, the quarterback is usually throwing the ball into the end zone where several offensive and defensive players will be leaping for the ball. With the offensive receivers and the defensive players jockeying for position (in what possibly could be described as an airborne scrum) the quarterback hopes that his receiver will somehow come down with the ball.[A]

Rewind back to September 24, 2012, when the Green Bay Packers were playing the Seattle Seahawks in Seattle. This particular Sunday was not only the third week of the season, but it was also the third week of regular season games officiated by replacement referees. The replacement refs were substituting for the regular officials who had opted to go on strike. Trailing 12–7 as the clock wound down, the Seahawks would resort to the Hail Mary pass on the last play of the game. When their receiver was ruled to have possession of the football, the result was a touchdown on the play and a win for Seattle.

However, replays would suggest that the call may have been faulty for multiple reasons. First, a Packer defensive player had also come down with the ball and, by many accounts the correct call should have been an interception for Green Bay—game over and the Packers win. But secondly, and more pertinent to our discussion, the Seattle receiver who was credited with the catch, Golden Tate, had clearly pushed a Packer defender away from the ball as it was coming down in what was an obvious case of offensive pass interference. This too would have ended the game with a Packer victory. However, no interference was called.

MISSED INTERFERENCE CALL

So, was the missed interference call simply an issue of inexperienced replacement officials? Or was this an instance of selective enforcement where certain plays are called differently? Perhaps there is some argument for the latter. A Sports Illustrated report cited the NFL network in stating that, over the previous five years, there were 87 Hail Mary end-of-game situations with no offensive

A This is a simplified description of what goes on with the play. Ultimately the interaction of players can be more complex and therefore, from a referee's perspective, perhaps more difficult to interpret.

pass interference being called![1] Eighty-seven such congested and swarming plays without such a call is possible, but a little hard to fathom. Perhaps the comment of the replacement referee at the center of the storm, Lance Easley, sheds some light on the situation. "It's like basketball," says Easley. "If there's a final shot (and) everybody's at the rim, there ain't going to be a whistle. You can see it, but philosophically, do you call it? No. The biggest, toughest guy wins."[2] Selective enforcement at its best!

One more comment on the play. Certainly the win–loss record for each team has economic consequences. However, in the Vegas world of gambling, the outcome of the game was more quantified. Since the masses had overwhelmingly bet on Green Bay winning the game, the monetary shift among bettors which was caused by this one particular play was estimated at $200 Million![3] The result seemed so outrageous to some that a Las Vegas casino actually offered refunds to certain gamblers who were impacted by the officials' call on the last play.[4]

ENDNOTES

1. Reiter, Ben. (2012 Dec 24). "This Photo Tells A Story: (but Not the One You Think)." Sports Illustrated. <www.sportsillustrated.cnn.com>. Accessed 2013 Dec 1.
2. Reiter.
3. Rovell, Darren. (2012 Sept 24). "$150M-$250M in MNF bets shifted." <www.espn.go.com>. Accessed 2013 Dec 2.
4. Ritter, Ben. (2012 Sept 26). "Seahawks-Packers Gambling Refunds: Vegas Casino To Offer Bettors Money Back." <www.huffingtonpost.com>. Accessed 2013 Dec 2.

SUMMARY

In many ways, the basis of economic analysis can be found in the study of the "choices" which are made continuously by all individuals. Certainly each topic analyzed in this chapter presented an evaluation of choice in some form or another. Choices among athletes—whether to use enhancements in violation of league rules. Choices among YMCA members—whether to take (steal) towels which don't belong to them. Choices among students—whether to cheat on an exam.

In considering how or why individuals made their certain choices, let us close this chapter (and essay) with a quote from economist Peter Boettke:

> In deciding courses of action, one must choose; that is, one must pursue one path and not others. The focus on alternatives in choices leads to one of the defining concepts of the economic way of thinking: opportunity costs.[16]

QUESTIONS

1. Assume that MLB had opted <u>not</u> to enforce rules restricting the use of performance enhancements. What are the pros/cons of MLB of taking this action?
2. In the case of athletes using performance enhancements, what steps could MLB (or any other organization) take to reduce the likelihood of such "drug" use?
3. What does economic theory offer in regards to explaining behavior at the YMCA and Stuyvesant High?

ENDNOTES

1. Dallas Mavericks at Los Angeles Lakers. (2012 Oct 30).
2. Wilson, Dennis P. (2005). "Additional Law Enforcement as a Deterrent to Criminal Behavior: Empirical Evidence from the National Hockey League." *The Journal of Socio-Economics*. 34 (2005) 319–330. p. 329.
3. Wilson.
4. Boeck, Scott. (2012 June 20). "Rays Reliever Joel Peralta Ejected for Pine Tar in Glove." *USA Today*. <www.usatoday.com>. 2012 Nov 30.
5. http://www.nj.com/yankees/index.ssf/2014/04/david_ortiz_dustin_pedroia_say_they_dont_care_if_yankees_michael_pineda_used_pine_tar.html. Accessed 9/2/2016.
6. http://www.hardballtimes.com/card-corner-rico-carty/. Accessed 2016 Aug 15.
7. <http://www.baseball-reference.com/leaders/HR_top_ten.shtml>. 2012 Oct 18.

8. Shaikin, Bill. (2012 Oct 16). "Giants Don't Recognize Melky Cabrera." *LA Times*. <http://articles.latimes.com/2012/oct/16/sports/la-sp-1016-giants-cardinals-notes-20121016>. 2012 Oct 18.
9. Brown, Maury. (2016 Jun 2). "Marlon Byrd, And a List of Every Major PED Suspension in MLB History. *Forbes*. http://www.forbes.com/sites/maurybrown/2016/06/02/marlon-byrd-and-a-list-of-every-major-ped-suspension-in-mlb-history/#56e15e1c592e.
10. Corcoran, Cliff. (2016 Apr 29). "Gordon's PED Suspension Proves We Know Nothing About Steroid Users." *Sports Illustrated*. http://www.si.com/mlb/2016/04/29/dee-gordon-marlins-ped-steroids-suspension.
11. http://m.mlb.com/news/article/225044864/pirates-starling-marte-suspended-80-games/. Accessed 2017 Aug 24.
12. Jaffe, Jay. (2016 May 5). "Explaining MLB's Recent Wave of PED Bans, And What League Can Do." *Sports Illustrated*. http://www.si.com/mlb/2016/05/05/ped-suspensions-steroids-dee-gordon-turinabol
13. Ibid.
14. Reddy, Sumathi. (2012 Apr 23). "I Visited the YMCA and All I Got Was This Ugly Towel." *Wall Street Journal*. 2012 Oct 18.
15. Yee, Vivian. (2012 Sept 25). "Stuyvesant Students Describe the How and Why of Cheating." *NY Times*. <www.nytimes.com>. 2012 Oct 18.
16. Boettke, Peter J. Austrian School of Economics. The Concise Encyclopedia of Economics. Proposition 4. http://www.econlib.org/library/Enc/AustrianSchoolofEconomics.html. Accessed 2017 Aug 26.
17. Kelling, George L. and James Q. Wilson. (1982 Mar). "Broken Windows: The Police and Neighborhood Safety." *Atlantic Magazine*. <http://www.theatlantic.com/magazine/archive/1982/03/broken-windows/304465/>. 2012 Nov 30.

CHAPTER 7

ECONOMIC THEORY AND "BROKEN WINDOWS"

By Ron Liggett

What are the societal and economic implications of a broken window? Is there something profound that can be learned? Can anything good come out of a destructive act whether intentional or not? In this chapter we take a look at two theories first promulgated years ago. One, the Broken Window Fallacy dates back to an essay written by French economist Frederic Bastiat in 1850. The second, simply entitled Broken Window Theory, comes from a 1982 academic report by James Q. Wilson and George Kelling. Both are straightforward, yet classic theories of behavior with strong economic implications. And, both are deserving of more attention as multiple communities in the U.S. deal with renewed periods of rioting (and destruction) while sorting through some of the perceived effects of what is known as broken window policing.

BROKEN WINDOW FALLACY

So, as we previously inquired, does anything good come out of the broken window? Well, for some, there might be a silver lining in that the simple repair of the window yields economic activity and commerce. Under this theory, if we assume that a store window was intentionally broken by vandals, we might not be so miffed at their unruly behavior if we determined that a spending multiplier had been initiated, driven by the dollars needed for the repair. Most certainly the dollars being spent for the damages would have an extended life as they flow through the economic business cycle. Of course this example is on a very small scale. I mean, how much of a difference can a $325 expenditure for a window repair really make? But, what about something larger? As a probing Econ question, what if the expenditure in question is now $325 <u>million</u> from a so-called government stimulus package? Before we get ahead of ourselves with too much Macro theory, let's go back to Bastiat and the simple broken window.

The original 1850 essay was known as "That Which is Seen, and That Which is Not Seen." In the words of Bastiat, a broken shop window does cause "money to circulate, and...the encouragement of industry..."[1] Hence that which is "seen." But what about the unseen? How would the $325 have been spent otherwise? Or, would it have been spent at all? We generally attribute the quote, "A penny saved is a penny earned" to Benjamin Franklin and proclaim it as a virtue of being thrifty. However, in economic circles we sometimes note that "a penny saved is a penny *not* spent," and therefore it remains outside what is known as the economic circular flow.[A B] The point here is not to get bogged down in a discussion of pennies, but to acknowledge that spending is most certainly relevant, and therefore the benefits to commerce are real and measurable.

Returning to "that which is *not* seen," we note that what certainly *is* real is the destruction of property (perhaps even property that cannot be replaced). And, along with the destruction, we are likely assured of implicit costs such as finding a repairman, taking care of any temporary arrangements in the damaged facility, and ensuring the repairs are completed satisfactorily. Explicitly, the shop owner has been deprived of the $325, which could have been used on other expenditures—most likely expenditures that would have brought him greater utility (*ceteris paribus*) than a broken window. Hence the broken window fallacy describes an event that is really not a matter of economic stimulus. Rather, it is about destruction and a transfer of spending toward something which, again, likely brings less utility.

A MACROECONOMIC VIEW OF BROKEN WINDOWS

What about the broken window fallacy on a larger scale? Let us briefly expand the discussion to consider the overall economy where government expenditures are made, not to repair property that has been destroyed, but rather to stimulate a sagging economy.[C] Stated differently, the basic intent of a federal government stimulus, as we hear in political circles, is to improve macroeconomic conditions, and, of course, to ***create jobs***.[D] However, whatever the expenditure being made in this analysis, some type of funding

A This is somewhat simplified as bank savings will likely, in some form, flow into the economy through loans made by the financial institution. However, there is no guarantee this will occur since the transaction requires *both* a willingness to lend *and* a willingness to borrow.

B The economic circular flow is a concept noting the movement of goods, services, and dollars from consumer/households to the producer/firms.

C Destroyed property most certainly would be part of the discussion if we were considering government expenditures that occurred after the 9/11 attacks.

D The importance of employment is obvious and, as former president Ronald Reagan and others suggested, the **best social program is a job**. However, the hubris of many (generally through Congress) is required. Consider the words of economist Walter Williams: "Congress has no resources of its very own. Moreover, there's no Santa Claus or tooth fairy who gives it resources...the only way Congress can give one American dollar is to first... confiscate that dollar from some other American through the tax code."[2]

Now, do not let the harshness of the word "confiscate" distract you from the question at hand. Our first question on the "unseen" was, How else could the dollars have been spent? Williams's focus here is essentially the same, but he extends the analysis to emphasize another important matter: Where does the money come from?

Well, aside from the previously mentioned taxation, there is a second means of funding such a program—borrowing funds internally from U.S. sources or externally from foreign investors. However, the end result is still much the same. Since there are limited dollars in the loanable funds market (the money has to come from somewhere) the government essentially competes with the private sector (you, I, perhaps our employer) for the borrowed funds.[E] Additionally, taxpayers service the debt and, when it becomes due, taxpayers are again on the hook for repayment of the loans.[F]

RIOTS AND THE BROKEN WINDOW FALLACY

Let us return to the original point: the economic impact of a broken window or other types of destruction and vandalism. Unfortunately, the U.S. has recently seen destructive events in the form of riots in cities like Baltimore, Maryland; Milwaukee, Wisconsin; and Ferguson, Missouri. Such riots are certainly not new in this country and, to a lesser degree, echo other major (and more serious) rioting events such as Chicago and Detroit in the 1960s, Miami in 1980, and Los Angeles in 1992, to name a few. While the impetus behind the riots is most certainly worthy of analysis, our focus in this section is on the economic theory and impact of the action itself as it relates to the broken window fallacy.

By definition, an actual "riot" involves a violent disturbing of the peace by a crowd that has, to some degree, assembled. Of course, the simple gathering of a crowd itself is not an incipient riot just because it assembles as a group, even if

---

politicians proudly proclaiming "their" ability to create jobs requires added emphasis in the text above.

E While a discussion of the harmful effects of printing money might be entertaining, we'll keep that discussion off the table for now. A curious reader might investigate the recent QE programs of the Federal Reserve System.

F As an aside, the ramifications of the near $20 trillion of debt currently owed by the federal government would be worthy of its own chapter in another economics course. Between 2009 and 2016, our federal national debt nearly doubled!

that group has similar or predisposing demographic traits. Nor can the causes of a riot always be explained simply by observing certain social conditions, such as poverty or racism. As noted by Haddock and Polsby, such "conditions are with us all the time, yet riots are episodic."[3] Additionally, the authors suggest a further complexity in these events by noting that many such actions, be it soccer riots in Europe, or the "civil meltdowns" in the home cities of professional sport champions in the U.S., are actually sparked by *good* news rather than "social injustice or existential anomie."[4] To be sure, cities now make elaborate preparations in order to handle both adverse events and those that are seen as celebratory.[5]

Accordingly, whether the riotous action is driven by social hardship, perceived bigotry, or is simply a celebration that has become "hooliganized," the end result, as suggested by Bastiat, is that destruction of property is simply *not* a stimulus. Rather succinctly, he notes that "[s]ociety loses the value of things which are uselessly destroyed." And further, "[t]o break, to spoil, to waste, is not to encourage national labor..."[6] Moreover, in the case of severe riots—such as those of Detroit and LA—the economic consequences may be so negative and substantial that they take years to overcome![7]

This slow recovery is frequently compounded as many businesses opt to leave the area, resulting in higher unemployment for the community. As businesses leave, not only are jobs lost, but sales and other use taxes also decline. Estimates from the 1992 LA riots suggested a loss of approximately $3.8 billion in taxable sales during the 10 years following the riots.[8] Further, as some stores close their doors—including chain stores—the cost of consumer goods and daily necessities for the local citizen inevitably increases as fewer stores remain

Graph 1. Increase in Equilibrium Prices as Local Businesses and Retailers Close Down Following Rioting and Other Disruptive Behaviors

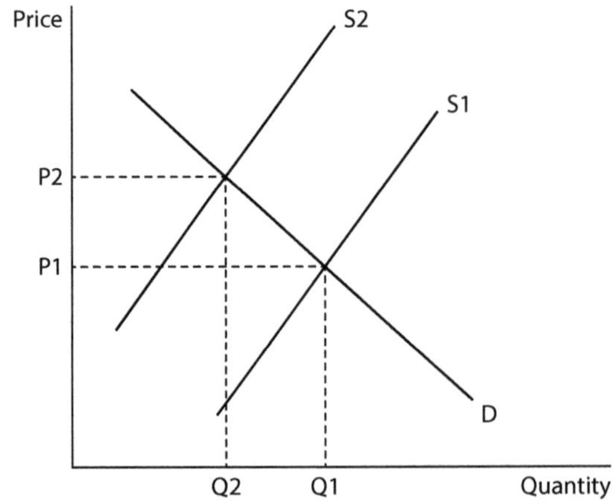

behind. (See the leftward shift of the supply curve to S2 in Graph 1.) It is worth nothing that, by some measures, the LA Riots were the costliest in history. Over 50 deaths occurred during this time with property damages estimated at over $1 billion![9]

In regard to taxes, a negative impact can also be seen when property values in these damaged areas fall, further depleting property tax revenues for local jurisdictions. Additionally, any decline in value in these neighborhoods also limits the accumulation of wealth, which should come from owning a residence—an accumulation on which many homeowners depend over the course of a lifetime.[G]

LOST TAXES AND COMMERCE—ONE EXAMPLE

The city of Baltimore experienced some short-term effects with lost tax revenue and commerce in response to disturbances occurring in April 2015. Following several days of rioting stirred by claims of police brutality in the death of an arrested man, the city's major league baseball team—the Baltimore Orioles—had to make some difficult decisions. While in the midst of a series of home games, the Orioles were forced to postpone and then move games that were originally scheduled for Baltimore. The one game actually played in Baltimore during this home stand was moved from an evening start to a day game, with *zero* fans in attendance. Why no fans? The game was "closed" to the public for safety concerns. While it's doubtful that the Oriole fans were interested in rioting, the city sought to keep crowd activity and public transportation to a minimum to further quell any possible unrest and allow the police force to be on full alert should any disruptions occur in other parts of the city. For the Orioles, the revenue impact was noticeable, if not overwhelmingly so. The estimated lost revenue from ticket sales, concessions, and parking was approximately $1.3 million per game.[10 H]

While this only had a short-term impact in regards to the world of baseball, the long-term impact of racially charged riots in cities such as Detroit in 1967 were immense. Following those riots, the number of looted and burned-out buildings (and formerly thriving businesses), which were never rebuilt, numbered in the hundreds.[11]

Stated in economic terms, "rioting (simply) makes things worse."[12] And, to again quote Bastiat, "destruction is not profit."[13]

G A related discussion on this topic can be found in work by Collins and Margo, "The Economic Aftermath of the 1960s Riots in American Cities: Evidence From Property Values"—Vanderbilt University and NBER, Dec 2005.

H From an economic perspective, this does not include the lost wages and earnings for vendors and other workers at the Orioles ballpark, not to mention the *millions* of dollars lost from stores and shops that were damaged and vandalized in other parts of the city.

SUMMARY BYTES

Bastiat, broken window fallacy, dollars must come from somewhere, that which is unseen.

BROKEN WINDOW THEORY

This uncomplicated theory, which could be described as profound or controversial, depending on your persuasion, generally dates back to a 1982 article published by professors James Q. Wilson and George L. Kelling entitled simply, "Broken Windows." Primarily focusing on police involvement in keeping neighborhoods safe, the article also addresses the impact of various forms of disorder and how they influence criminal acts and societal behavior in general. More specifically, by managing and reducing disorderly behavior in public spaces, the opportunities for crime are diminished. Stated another way, "order breeds more order."[14]

Citing experiments from 1969 (among other data), Kelling and Wilson noted that where disarray exists in the community, there also exists an increased chance of criminal acts in the neighborhood. The consequences of having "untended" property is a rather swift permeation of the idea that "no one cares," and therefore normal restraints on behavior may be set aside. This has become known as the broken window theory. From this theory, we see that the communal disarray, existing in the form of an unrepaired broken window, transcends to multiple broken windows. Or, for example, graffiti left in place likely leads to more graffiti.[15]

Normally, when an offender or other such character decides to exhibit what we could label as rogue, criminal, or unwanted acts of mischief, he or she faces certain costs. These include the expectations as to how the behavior will be seen. That is, how will society and those in charge of establishing our specific rules respond? In this case, if the broken window remains, another one likely follows. More random acts of destruction continue, unchecked, without costs to the criminal. Disorderliness and disarray soon evolves into a rundown neighborhood where the opportunistic criminal may expand his behavior. In the worst case, the world of "street crime" displays more muggings, robberies, and assaults. On a less violent end, businesses in these areas see customers avoiding these sections of the city.[16]

We mentioned the 1969 experiment cited by Kelling and Wilson. This test, put together by Philip Zimbardo of Stanford, involved vehicles left unattended in two distinct locations—one in the Bronx, NY and one in Palo Alto, CA. With the hood up and no license plates attached, the cars were left to appear in some form of mechanical distress and, at least temporarily, abandoned. While the initial patterns of behavior were slightly different (the Bronx vehicle was vandalized within minutes, while the one in Palo Alto took about a week), in the end, the actions were similar. The cars, in one place or the other, were vandalized, stripped, turned over, and essentially destroyed. No one enforced or protected the area (i.e., it appeared that "no one cared." Hence their suggestion "that untended behavior also leads to the breakdown of community controls."[17]

A more recent experiment took place in the Netherlands in 2008 and further supported this theory. The experiment involved deliberately establishing settings where low-level crimes could be viewed—acts such as littering, graffiti, trespassing, theft, etc. Of the many observations, the most striking result found that individuals, when confronted with a condition of disorder, were twice as likely to steal. In summary, as with Kelling and Wilson, the researchers again found "that one example of disorder, like graffiti or littering, can indeed encourage another, like stealing."[18]

Over the years this theory has garnered attention in ebbs and flows, with the city of New York being in the forefront of many of the discussions. Facing serious crime issues in the 1980s and 90s, the city began to incorporate a broken window-type theory in their policing efforts. The result? Significant drops in crime soon appeared. For example, 1,927 murders in 1993—a rate of 26.5 per 100 thousand people—had fallen to 335 murders in 2016, or about 4 per 100 thousand.[19] Likewise, a crime index calculation of seven serious crimes fell markedly, with the overall New York crime index falling more than 20 percent lower than that for the nation as a whole.[20] Were drops such as these due *solely* to the broken window theory of policing? Not likely. However, for the true believers, this style of policing was seen as pivotal in reducing unwanted behavior. Kelling and New York police chief William J. Bratton stated:

> Left unchecked, street corners can degenerate into criminogenic environments. The bullies take over. They drink alcohol and take drugs openly, make excessive noise, intimidate and shake down honest citizens, engage in scams and criminal enterprises—and, worst of all, fight with one another, often with firearms. Conditions like these drove up shootings in New York City to 5,269 per year in 1993.[21]

However, moving into 2017, there is some concern that what many see as an "effective" crime-fighting theory may be pushed aside. For example, in New York, the city council has "downgraded the severity" of several offenses such as public drunkenness and public urination.[22]

As an additional area of application (and concern), consider the issue of illegal immigration as it relates to the broken window theory. If low-level crimes of disorder—as noted in this section—encourage more serious crime due to the fact that criminals assume no one cares about the law breaking, then what does that suggest for our nation's non-enforcement of its immigration laws? Most particularly, how does this play out in the big cities that have adapted "sanctuary" policies for so-called illegal aliens?[23] Does such non-enforcement suggest more crime is to come? While sanctuary supporters frequently proclaim a lower crime rate exists among the cities with sanctuary policies, other reports suggest differently.

No doubt, any such illegal behavior is rarely benign and therefore it should be addressed for what it is regardless of the outcome: an increase in economic costs due to violation of the rule of law.

In reality, the economic costs of *not* enforcing low-level criminal acts are very real. The behaviors continue or worsen and, in the case of real and commercial property, tax values are reduced and social status declines. But, the lesson isn't that the enforcement needs to be severe or harsh. As noted by Kelling and Wilson, a policeman simply walking a "neighborhood beat" can make a difference in the perceived well-being of an area's inhabitants.[24] No doubt the perception in those neighborhoods is that someone is paying attention, someone is willing to enforce, and someone does "care."

SUMMARY BYTES

Kelling, Wilson, broken window theory, 1969, 1982, untended property, graffiti, unchecked behaviors multiply, the Netherlands.

ENDNOTES

1. Bastiat, Frederic. http://bastiat.org/en/twisatwins.html. Accessed 2014 Nov 7.
2. Williams, Walter. http://www.creators.com/conservative/walter-williams/is-there-a-way-out.html. Accessed 2014 Nov 7.
3. Haddock, David D. and Daniel D. Polsby. (1994) "Understanding Riots." *Cato Journal.* Vol. 14, No. 1, (Spring/Summer. 1999), pp. 147–157.
4. Haddock and Polsby
5. Meredith, Robyn. (1997 July 23). "5 Days in 1967 Still Shake Detroit." *New York Times.* http://www.nytimes.com/1997/07/23/us/5-days-in-1967-still-shake-detroit.html?pagewanted=all. Accessed 2016 Sept 3.
6. Bastiat, Frederic. (1850). "The Bastiat Collection." Ludwig von Mises Institute. 2nd Ed, p. 4, copyright 2007.
7. Meredith
8. Pianin, Eric. (2015 April 29). "Riots Could Leave Baltimore's Economy Reeling for Years." *The Fiscal Times.* http://www.thefiscaltimes.com/2015/04/29/Riots-Could-Leave-Baltimore-s-Economy-Reeling-Years. Accessed 2016 Sept 3.
9. https://www.britannica.com/event/Los-Angeles-Riots-of-1992. Accessed 2017 Aug 10.
10. Huddleston, Jr., Tom. (2015 April 29). "Even with fans shut out, Baltimore Orioles don't stand to lose too much money." *Fortune.* http://fortune.com/2015/04/29/baltimore-orioles-empty-stadium-revenue/. Accessed 2016 Sept 3.
11. Meredith

12. *The Economist*. (2015 May 2). "Why Rioting Makes Things Worse." http://www.economist.com/news/united-states/21650158-angry-youths-burn-their-own-neighbourhood-why-rioting-makes-things-worse. Accessed 2016 Sept 3.
13. Bastiat
14. Kelling, G. & Bratton, W. Why we need broken windows policing. In *The City Journal*. Retrieved from https://www.city-journal.org/html/why-we-need-broken-windows-policing-13696.html. Accessed 2017 Aug 9.
15. Kelling, George L. and James Q. Wilson. (1982 Mar). "Broken Windows—The Police and Neighborhood Safety." *Atlantic Magazine*. http://www.theatlantic.com/magazine/archive/1982/03/broken-windows/304465/ Accessed 2012 Nov 30.
16. Wilson, Tom. (2015 July 10). "20 Years of Cleaning Up NYC Pissed Away." *New York Post*. http://nypost.com/2015/07/10/apparently-its-now-ok-to-pee-on-the-streets-of-new-york-city/. Accessed 2017 July 10.
17. Kelling and Wilson
18. *The Economist*. "Criminology: Can the can." http://www.economist.com/node/12630201. Accessed 2014 Nov 8.
19. http://www.nyc.gov/html/nypd/downloads/pdf/crime_statistics/cs-en-us-city.pdf. Accessed 2017 Aug 9.
20. http://www.city-data.com/crime/crime-New-York-New-York.html. Accessed 2017 August 9.
21. https://www.city-journal.org/html/why-we-need-broken-windows-policing-13696.html. Accessed 2017 Aug 10.
22. http://www.foxnews.com/us/2017/06/14/new-york-city-eases-severity-laws-against-public-urination-drunkenness.html. Accessed 2017 Aug 9.
23. Magnet, Myron. (2008 Feb 8). "Immigration Reversals." *Manhattan Institute For Policy Research*. http://www.manhattan-institute.org/html/miarticle.htm?id=7611#.VF8WMclTCBI. Accessed 2014 Nov 8.
24. Kelling and Wilson

CHAPTER 8

ILLEGAL IMMIGRATION—AN INTRODUCTION

By Ron Liggett

This section contains copious amounts of dialogue and pages on the various topics related to the Southern border and the illegal flows of immigration and drugs. It is an important topic in regards to the Economics of Crime in every possible way and one that bears interest for me individually and to border-state inhabitants overall.

As a youngster in the 60s, we lived for two years in the border town of Laredo, Texas. It was an interesting time and one where I developed a fondness for the Mexican culture, the people, and of course, the cuisine. We took frequent trips across the border into Nuevo Laredo for shopping and food and our travels over the Rio Grande were enjoyable. Certainly times have changed on that part of the border and sadly, much of it has not been positive, as the Laredo area, labeled the "Gateway" into Mexico, struggles with tremendous violence, U.S. travel warnings, and in some years, even a disbanded police force. We will address some aspects of the violence in the section of the text dealing with drug markets.

There are two main contributions in this section. The first part includes an overview as well as commentary on specific points of concern in conjunction with economic theory. The second part offers a Cato Institute publication by Edward Alden entitled "Immigration and Border Control." Some of the views from the two pieces may be contrasting and others may be similar, although hopefully not to the point of redundancy. However, as I frequently note to students, when certain points are repeated, it likely means they are relevant.

While there are distinct views on the topic, my opinion in regards to immigration flows is that some type of "process" is necessary to regulate movement into a country and that, in essence, a border has meaning. This is not unlike how we live and treat our own home environment. It is doubtful that many of us left our home, apartment, or dorm unlocked when we left this morning. Nor were we inclined, for example, to leave a note on the door inviting anyone who happens by our residence to simply "Come in and make yourself at home." Yet we would still likely consider our overall attitude as charitable or egalitarian rather than snobbish; a fact generally borne out by contributions millions of Americans make every day, both locally and globally.

However, the idea of a more stringent process and enhanced controls do not appeal to all. Those on the left, some libertarian thinkers, certainly the Mexican government, and the *Wall Street Journal* op-ed page are apt to "slap down" most proposals for enhancement of border controls. Undoubtedly these groups have specific interests in mind as they promote certain agendas and goals. For some, it is a philosophy that a borderless world is righteous and will eventually lead to some type of economic and social utopia (see inset discussion on open borders). For others, the lure of profits from inexpensive labor is no doubt influential in their thinking. And certainly the economic importance of competitive wages is obvious, but the impact on native workers is also highly relevant.

The positive effect from an increased supply of workers (whether legal or illegal) looks attractive, at least graphically. In a simple supply and demand graph of the labor market, an increase in supply pushes certain wage rates downward (Graph 1).[A] Carrying this a step further, in a short-run macro setting, lower-priced inputs—such as labor—contribute to a rightward shift of the SRAS curve and suggest a corresponding growth in GDP (Graph 2). Additionally, an increase in the quantity of labor resources does have long-run implications as seen in a Production Possibilities Curve (PPC) analysis. The outward shift of the PPC curve suggests increases in both consumption and growth over time (Graph 3). One more positive aspect for the economy from the immigrant labor flows (whether authorized or not) is the proven mobility of the workers. This particular workforce readily moves over sectors and beyond border states to contribute flexibility into the economy.

However, while these graphs suggest positive movements, there are other relevant issues to be considered. A quote by libertarian Ron Paul rings true in referencing an additional economic concern—the issue of welfare benefits.[B]

> "Make no mistake, Americans are happy to welcome immigrants who follow our immigration laws and seek a better life here. America is far more welcoming and tolerant of newcomers than virtually any nation on earth. But our modern welfare state creates pervasive incentives for immigrants, incentives that cloud the issue of why people chose to come here."[1]

A An argument can be made that the demand curve will also shift right due to economic growth, but this does not occur until the capital markets adjust. As capital becomes more productive, higher incomes accrue to the owners of capital and the workers most negatively impacted are likely to be natives without a high school degree.

B While technically, only U.S. 'citizens' are eligible for welfare programs, birthright citizenship allows for various benefits to flow thru to households based on the status of children. Therefore, low-income households, headed by illegal immigrants do receive benefits through a variety of safety net programs. Additionally, data shows that forged documents, such as social security numbers, also exist and therefore may make programs available to non-citizens.

Graph 1. Impact of an Increase in Illegal Immigration in Certain Labor Markets Labor from Immigration (Legal or Illegal)

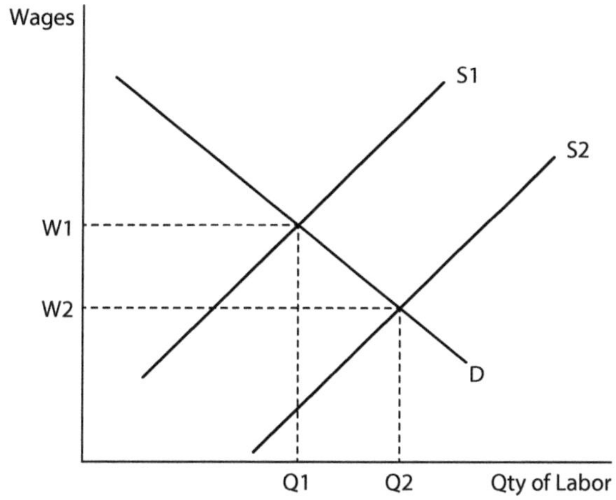

Graph 2. Impact of Lower Input Costs (Due to Illegal Immigration)

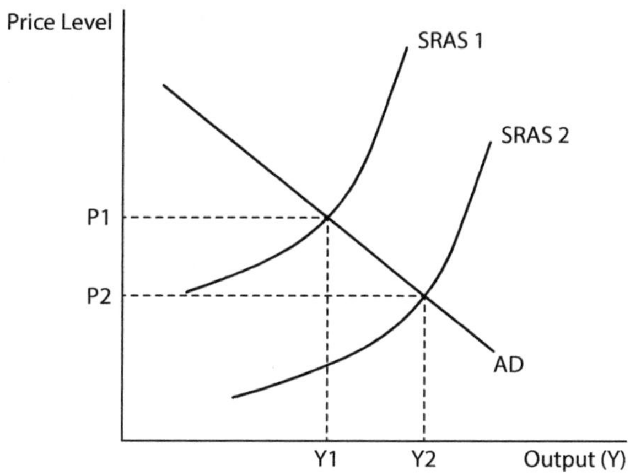

Before closing this introduction, let us ask a currently relevant, probing, and controversial question—Where does a border wall fit into the equation? And, even if we assume this is a good idea, would it actually get built? These are difficult questions. Again, politicians are famous for talking ad nauseam about various policies and issues without ever acting on them. Additionally, there are certainly groups heartily opposed to any border barrier. Many of those would rather fight to remove all obstacles as their perspective aligns with the idea

Graph 3. PPC Increase—Additional Resources

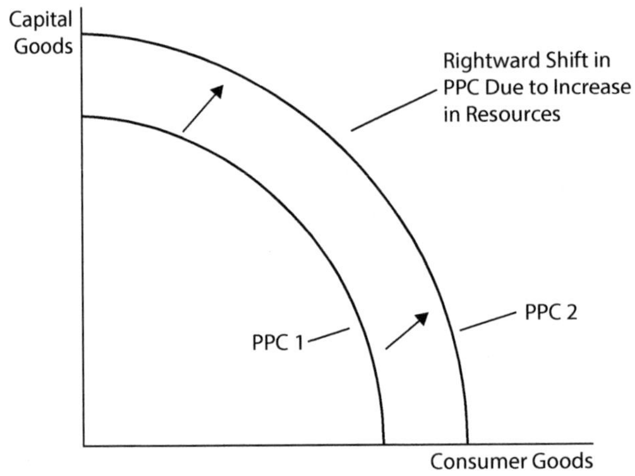

that removing any border barriers is, again, a "righteous" act. After all, what right do we have to restrict an individual from coming to this land which we, as Americans, did not occupy in the first place? And, isn't America just a land of immigrants? In fact, aren't we all immigrants?

Well, the answer to the last question is likely no. If you were born in the United States, in almost every circumstance, you are deemed to be a citizen, and not an immigrant. But, we will leave the remainder of that discussion for another day. However, before we sign off completely, there is a point worth noting. Some economists might feel that topics such as illegal immigration are better left to sociologists and perhaps political scientists. I would strongly disagree and simply refer back to what Gary Becker did, not only with *Economics of Crime* in 1968, but also with his consistent overall work in matters related to human behavior. Economists are trained in problem-solving skills and schooled in the type of rational thought that contributes to and also complements the work of other social scientists.

ENDNOTE

1. Paul, Ron. (2006 Oct 3). "Rethinking Birthright Citizenship." https://www.lewrockwell.com/2006/10/ron-paul/birthright-citizenship/. Accessed 2017 Nov 30.

ILLEGAL IMMIGRATION

AN OVERVIEW OF VARIOUS TOPICS AND CONCERNS

By Ron Liggett

Few social policy topics cover the range of issues that we find in the illegal immigration debate. Economics, politics, and social and criminal concerns are all at the forefront of any in-depth analysis of this subject. In this section, we will focus primarily on the illegal movement across the southern border of the United States. There, the flow of individuals moving north has been continuous, the stream of illicit drugs relentless, and the costs involved significant enough to be worthy of much dialogue and analysis.

Let us begin by issuing the following statement—opposing illegal immigration is NOT analogous to being anti-immigrant. On the contrary, in the study of labor and immigration flows, one can easily document the spirit and desire for liberty that has helped to make this a great nation. Further, an attempt to address the issues created by unauthorized immigration flows should not be viewed as an assault on illegal immigrants individually. With the understanding that both the U.S. and Mexico have significant economic interests in this matter, we must also understand that to solve a problem, one has to be able to discuss and analyze a situation factually, completely, and, as we will note later, hopefully devoid of emotion.

Speaking of emotions, they run high in border-states on both sides of this argument, with additional trepidation caused by geo-political aspects that exist on both sides of the border. And, for anyone who was observant, the presidential election of 2016 raised the temperature even higher with one candidate calling for completion of the wall along the southern border, and one candidate hinting at amnesty in some form. For this election, one could argue that American voters again pushed back against an amnesty centered platform.

But, as noted, the emotions are not limited to the U.S. side. Suggestions of a "wall," or of more immigration restrictions on the U.S. side, have consistently been met with testiness from Mexican authorities proclaiming that further immigration restrictions by the U.S. are not in Mexico's best interest.[1]

Similarly loud protests were heard in 2010 as Arizona proposed state law SB 1070. In that scenario, Mexico actually joined in U.S. lawsuits that were filed against Arizona arguing on behalf of their own interests as well as their citizens' rights.[2] And, from an economic perspective, there is a point to be made. Mexico has a specific interest in ensuring that there is no reduction in the billions of dollars in "remittances" that are sent back to their country by Mexican workers on the U.S. side of the border. These remittances flowing out of the U.S. provide a significant contribution to the Mexican economy and reached a record $27 billion in 2016, surpassing oil and tourism as a source of foreign currency for their nation.[3] That statement may be worth repeating for emphasis—more remittances than oil revenue! In fact, according to World Bank data, remittances to Mexico have exceeded $20 billion for more than ten years.[4] Again, the country has a strong national and economic interest in keeping the flow of remittances in place.

In this analysis we should also take a concerted look at what influences the large-scale flow of illegal immigration, most particularly from Mexico.[A] To be clear, our focus on Mexico (and Central America as well) is a geographical issue. But, it is also an issue readily derived from an analysis of the overall immigration numbers in addition to the immense drug trafficking made easier by a somewhat 'porous border.'

In regards to human traffic, consider that from 2005–2010, approximately 90% of illegal apprehensions, a total of 4,383,247, were from Mexico. While annual flows have slowed since that period, a high amount of illegal trafficking still exists with over one-million apprehensions occurring from 2013–2015.[5] Additionally, in 2016, of the 28,010 non-U.S. citizens in federal prisons, 85.4% were categorized as being in the country illegally, and 74% were from Mexico.[6] Using 2014 average costs of $30,619 per inmate, the incarceration expense for the 74% alone is nearly $635 million per year.[7] Surprisingly, at the state level these numbers are not always easy to get as many states do not post specific and detailed data. Nonetheless, the argument is that better control of illegal crossings could (and should) result in less crime (and lower prison costs).

While the details of drug trafficking are covered in other chapters, we would note that, for the U.S., Mexico continues to be the largest foreign supplier of both marijuana and methamphetamine. Additionally, the country is heavily involved as a transshipment location for cocaine coming from South America.[8] And, if that wasn't enough, federal authorities have estimated that 70% of the dangerous synthetic drug fentanyl is now being smuggled across the border as well.[9] (The fentanyl issue is particularly alarming and is also discussed in the chapter on drug markets.)

The movement of illegal flows across the southern border can be treacherous in regards to the harsh climate and terrain. The trek is also dangerous due to the

A Much concern also exists from illegal flows of MS-13 gang members—many from El Salvador.

human factor as human 'smuggling' may intermix with both human 'traffickers' and drug traffickers.[B] While the distinction between trafficking and smuggling is noted in the footnote below, it is also worth mentioning that the smuggling "service" itself can take many forms when "coyotes" are employed for their service.[C] While there may be some altruistic principles in play, special agents in this area are clear to state that human smuggling should not be confused with "Robin Hood [type] do-gooders helping people make a living. It's a money-making operation and [can be] extremely violent."[10] Immigration surveys support this fact as well.

A BORDER WALL?

Back to our question about a border wall. The topic is one that is currently relevant, probing, and controversial in almost all aspects. In reality, approximately 30% of the southern border already has some 'barrier' in place. While some may question the benefits and the cost of a wall, it would have a measurable impact on illegal immigration across the border. And, while there is no illusion that drug and gun trafficking would halt, the costs to continue these practices would increase as well. Of course, markets do find a way and "traffickers" will seek to adjust (again we reference "willing buyer–willing seller" principles), but if the goal is to reduce traffic flows, barriers are effective.

Not all agree with this assessment however. A perspective supported by many politicians mirrors the following statement from Janet Napolitano. While Governor of Arizona in 2005 she commented, "You show me a 50-foot wall, and I'll show you a 51-foot ladder at the border."[11] Others, including Arizona Senator John McCain have echoed the ladder illustration. While the point is well made, such a statement is more symbolic than realistic. (I've lugged a 16-foot ladder around the house and it's not an effortless task.) Nonetheless, writing off such a plan outright doesn't make sense either. The wall project is a challenge, to be sure, and the cost is significant. But, we are also discussing expenditures which are a capital outlay; not the same, for example, as a yearly outflow for non-durable goods.

Consider another perspective. In a recent interview, a long-term veteran of the Border Patrol, Roy Villarreal, noted the following, "I have 32 years of being a border patrol agent, here in San Diego, in Texas, and in Arizona. Every place where we have erected tactical infrastructure, apprehensions have gone down."[12] In economic terms the simple translation is that a structure, as referenced by Villarreal, increases the costs of crossing the border and reduces traffic.

B In regards to human movement, while trafficking and smuggling are sometimes used interchangeably, there is a legal difference between "trafficking" and "smuggling." Trafficking involves exploitation and forced labor or sex activities through some type of exploitation, etc., while smuggling involves moving or transporting someone as part of a service. To be clear, both are still considered as crimes.

C "Coyote" is the term used for a person who smuggles humans across the U.S. border with Mexico.

On the monetary side, the costs paid to the coyote can vary widely depending on the distance and "services" provided with payments frequently made in stages. For example, on the high end, an initial payment of $1,200 may be followed up by an additional $8,000 at the destination!13 For our purposes, using "ballpark" figures of roughly $3,500-$4,000 per person helps provide some substance to this discussion. However, this may also lead to another question. With low per-capita income in many Latin American countries, how is this affordable for one individual, much less a family of 3–4? Here, DHS provides some insight in noting that "alternative forms of payment" are being reported whereby individuals may also smuggle drugs or other illegal items, promise to pay debts through future work, or depend on payments from other family members.[14]

So, for those illegal crossings that are not drug related, the pull from the U.S. side of the border is fairly straightforward: jobs, a social safety net, and in many ways, a better life. Per capita GDP in the U.S. for 2016 was estimated at $57,466; in Mexico, approximately, $8,201.[15] For countries further south—Honduras, El Salvador, Guatemala—the numbers are much lower ranging from near $2,300 to just over $4,000.[16] Yet, when this subject is brought up for debate, inevitably the focus comes back to the U.S. and what is NOT being done to accommodate the illegal immigration flows. My contention is that an equally (and likely more) relevant issue would be to ask what is Mexico doing, via economic and public policies, to encourage their citizens to stay? Why does the country continue to lose able and steady workers?[D] Of course there are ebbs and flows in the immigration movement and some data suggests a significant slowdown following the U.S. "Great Recession" of 2008, however, as noted earlier, the number of apprehensions is a very real and tangible dilemma.

IMPACT OF LABOR FLOWS

The most significant resource for any nation should be its labor force and the corresponding human capital. Overwhelmingly, what we observe coming to the U.S. from Mexico is an influx of workers, many with low formal education level, but with a variety of skills, and most importantly, a strong work ethic. This is a significant economic resource that has implications in our labor market. Those implications have not gone unnoticed by both American capitalists and politicians. Consider the following quote from former President Barrack Obama in his book entitled "*The Audacity of Hope: Thoughts on Reclaiming the American Dream:*"

> "[T]here's no denying that many blacks share the same anxieties as many whites about the wave of illegal immigration flooding our

D Multiple reasons exist, but as we will note later, certainly one reason is the continuous and extreme violence in Mexico perpetuated by drug trafficking.

> Southern border. The number of immigrants added to the labor force every year is of a magnitude not seen in this country for over a century. If this huge influx of mostly low-skill workers provides some benefits to the economy as a whole it also threatens to depress further the wages of blue-collar Americans and put strains on an already overburdened safety net."[17]

Some might be surprised to see these comments attributed to President Obama and would have surmised the statement as something more in common with a Donald Trump ideology. However, these are candid thoughts and reflect basic economic theory rather than political talking points.

In another view, Harvard economist George Borjas has noted that flows of low-skilled immigrant labor—which would include unauthorized entries—increase returns to the capitalists in particular.[18] He expands on this by addressing what he describes as an "immigration surplus," which occurs out of the reduction in wages of natives who compete with immigrant labor. It is this immigration surplus that accrues to capitalists and business owners. More specifically, Borjas notes that a "10 percent increase in the size of an education/age group due to the entry of immigrants (both legal and illegal) reduces the wage of native-born men in that group by 3.7 percent." Further, he cites that the labor increase from illegal immigrants provides a redistribution effect, reducing the wages of native workers by an estimated $99 to $118 billion a year, while generating a gain for businesses and other users of immigrants of $107 to $128 billion."[19] While certainly those consumers who might make use of the labor benefit from being able to employ more affordable services (i.e., home services, lawn care, construction, etc.) again, it is those businesses and owners of capital that benefit most from the cheaper worker.

OPEN BORDERS AND THE IMAGINE GAME—"A LENNON UTOPIA"

On occasion I have students who desire to debate the idea of open borders. While the topic is not a new one, there have been some interesting ideas in this area floating around cyberspace and on the pages of various publications. One, from economist Alex Tabarrok, suggests a world with completely open borders. Tabarrok states, "The argument for open borders is both economic and moral. All people should be free to move about the earth, uncaged by the arbitrary lines known as borders." He even goes a bit further in labeling open borders, as it relates to the movement of people and labor, as "the world's greatest economic opportunity."[1]

So, the proposal that there would be no borders of any kind is an interesting one. Taking the next logical step, I suppose we would have little need for individual sovereign nations either as we essentially exist in one large homogenous mass. I mean, how hard could it be to harmonize the "rule of law" in such a way as to keep 6–7 billion people happy? Of course, the most important aspect to this theory is that individuals, as economic resources, could simply move about the planet in any way they prefer, again, leading (supposedly) to the world's greatest economic opportunity. Okay, it does sound a little surreal, but it might be functional if individuals actually were some type of homogeneous robots. But, before I simply chirp, "Beam me up, Scotty," let's embrace a little diversity of ideas and get an assessment from an expert in immigration economics, Dr. George Borjas.

Professor Borjas offers a different perspective on such open border ideas and even has a unique name for the proposal—a "Lennon Utopia." The name is in reference to the "iconic" John Lennon song *Imagine* where the Beatle suggests we imagine there are no countries. In analyzing what he refers to as the "*Imagine* game," Borjas acknowledges the usefulness of economic models while also realizing their limitations. There are distinctions between high-skilled and low-skilled workers, and in such an open borders plan, there are productivity spillovers that cannot be ignored. "The spillovers arise from the key distinction between the migration of robotic workers and the migration of people, the actual human beings who work, consume, pray, procreate, vote, fight, and so on."[2] He suggests that such a plan, made without understanding the impact, etc., is seemingly "irresponsible."[A] Further, he states that "it could even turn out to be a misguided attempt at do-gooding with devastating consequences."[3]

There is, no doubt, much more to express in this area and Borjas himself analyzes the idea in more detail in his book *We Wanted Workers*. For undergrads reading this section, I can envision healthy class discussions and debate on the topic.

ENDNOTES

1. Tabarrok, Alex. (2015 Oct 10). "The Case for Getting Rid of Borders Completely." *The Atlantic* https://www.theatlantic.com/business/archive/2015/10/get-rid-borders-completely/409501/. Accessed 2017 Aug 26.
2. Borjas, George J. (2016). *We Wanted Workers: Unraveling the Immigration Narrative*. W.W. Norton & Co. New York, NY. p 45.
3. Borjas 49.

A I agree with Borjas in his concerns, but my reply is shorter. In response to the statement that this could be "the world's greatest economic opportunity," I'll borrow a phrase frequently used by Col. Sherman T. Potter years ago on the M*A*S*H TV series, "Horse hockey!" (If you're not sure what that means, look it up.)

FOOD FOR THOUGHT—LAW OF UNINTENDED CONSEQUENCES

As an aside on this topic, consider for a moment the law of unintended consequences. We understand that a somewhat relaxed policy and attitude regarding unauthorized entries contributed to the existence of widespread cheap labor, particularly in the area of home construction. The corresponding question is, to what extent, if any, did the availability of low-cost labor contribute in the channeling of capital—incorrectly, I might suggest—into the housing markets? We know there were multiple contributors to the now-infamous housing bubble and corresponding "mortgage meltdown," with one being the relatively easy money policy by the Federal Reserve that drove financial capital flows. But, to expand the bubble, there was a need for economic capital and a labor resource to facilitate use of the available financing. Again, food for thought…

So we return to the question at hand—the mass labor flows. And dare we evaluate the effectiveness of fines and penalties placed on U.S. firms in their hiring practices? Certainly those American companies who knowingly violate labor laws are a part of this criminal equation, as they keep the demand high. While Congress has enacted an E-Verify system to electronically confirm immigration status before hiring workers, not all states make use of the process.

But again, what is happening in Mexico? Why are the opportunities so lacking that this durable workforce is compelled to take such great risks to head north? Of course, one part of the equation would be the intense drug violence which has, at times, seemingly overwhelmed various areas of the country. From 2014–16, more than 53,000 homicides took place.[20] Between 2006–2011, it was estimated that more than 60,000 people were killed in Mexico.[21] (Included in this number were 20 Mexican mayors!)[E]

And, while some will argue that there are worse homicide rates in the Americas, the true violence and targeting of specific individuals is chilling. For example, 43 students were murdered in 2014 in a bizarre and heinous case where actual police involvement was speculated.[22] Earlier this year a local newspaper from Cuidad Juarez completely shut down operations with a key reason for this abrupt halt to distribution being the murder of one of their leading journalists.[23] This death brought the murder number for journalists to more than 100 since the year 2000! [24]

And, speaking of unintended consequences, if drug violence is partially to blame for a lack of legitimate opportunity, then we must also look at, and analyze,

---

E In November 2012, Maria Santos Gorrostieta, a PhD and former mayor of Tiquicheo, who had pledged to stand up to the drug cartels and their violence, was murdered. Gorrostieta had survived multiple attempts on her life and seven gunshot wounds before she was finally abducted and brutally killed. Alas, other prominent individuals have met the same fate.

the role of the U.S. as a major consumer of drugs originating in Mexico.[F] Our appetite for illicit drugs contributes to violence and instability in Mexico and we therefore pick up the social costs for many of those "driven" across the border by such violence.

Finally, in regards to violence, a homicide rate that nearly tripled between 2007 and 2011 has only slowly subsided. And, in reality, the violent trend is not only in Mexico, but also in Honduras, El Salvador, and other Latin American countries. A research report from the University of San Diego noted some grave observations:

> Contemporary Latin America has some of the highest rates of criminal violence in the world, in many cases matching or exceeding the levels of violence seen during the civil conflicts that plagued the region decades ago. What is different today about violence in Latin America is that rather than fighting and dying for revolutionary ideologies, the region's young men are fighting and dying for little more than a fistful of dollars. Indeed, some reports in recent years suggest that paid gunmen and assassins working on behalf of organized crime groups earn as little as a few hundred dollars a month… [There is now] violence and conflict in Latin America on a scale and with a savagery that is perhaps even more horrific because there is no cause or deeper meaning.[25]

Aside from the issue of violence, there is also the matter of employment and wages. Accordingly, it is worth mentioning that while manufacturing jobs, particularly those created by NAFTA, have been rather easy to find, the associated wages have been lacking. Some workers deem the wages as "non-livable" as Mexico competes with the same global pressures faced by other countries in regards to compensation. Nonetheless, when "half the country remains poor" and the rule of law is challenged continuously, the attractiveness of the U.S. becomes more real.[26]

Economics, politics, social concerns, criminal behavior—all told, an investigation of illegal immigration, in some respects, represents the ultimate collision between each of these disciplines and leads to a synergy of analysis and thought.

SOME BACKGROUND

In 1986, President Ronald Reagan signed into law the Immigration Reform and Control Act. While providing amnesty to over 3 million U.S. residents who were here illegally, the act also introduced the I-9 program as a means of verifying the

F A study of 17 countries, published in *ScienceDaily*, July 2008, reported the U.S. as the highest consumer of both cocaine and cannabis.

legality of workers. However, despite an initial drop in apprehensions at the border, the legislation did not resolve the illegal immigration problem. In fact, as we entered the 1990s and the early part of this century, the pace of illegal trafficking, as gauged by the number of apprehensions, reverted to the same unprecedented levels we saw leading up to the 1986 legislation.[27]

It should be noted that while a true, scientific measurement of illegal flows is difficult, the U.S. Border Patrol had previously estimated that for every apprehension, there were likely three or four successful illegal entries. Some speculate the ratio is even higher. As noted later in this chapter, Alden has suggested that a "best guess" would be an arrest rate of "between 40 and 60 percent." Additional academic studies have suggested a 30–50% range of apprehension.[28] Considering these specific percentages, the idea that Border Patrol might apprehend 50–60% of the illegal crossings seems optimistic. This leaves us with the lower end of the percentages and something in the neighborhood of 2–3 illegal entries per apprehension.[G] Homeland Security, which had previously declared the relationship as "unknown," have increased their analysis and continue to evaluate statistically in an effort to determine more accurately how many individuals successfully enter the U.S. illegally.

In regards to the original verification legislation (the I-9 program), there has been a continuing effort to amend and enhance this program with an initiative toward an electronic verification program. Additionally, as noted by Alden, the size of the Border Patrol has increased and miles of fencing have been built. When these points are combined with a declining and stagnant U.S. economy, it is not surprising that apprehensions of illegal immigrants in 2010 dropped to their lowest level since 1972.[29]

However, even with using 2010 as an example, if we do approximate two or three entries for each apprehension, we are still looking at the possibility that more than one million illegal entries occurred in that year, or roughly the population of two Texas cities—Austin and Arlington—combined! The costs to enter the U.S. remain high, yet, one must conclude that economic principles remain at work. That is, the durable and resilient market principle of "willing buyer–willing seller" is prominent as employers are agreeable in hiring illegal, undocumented, or falsely documented workers, while on the other side of the equation, the labor supply remains relatively elastic.

Further legislative action on this matter has been difficult, as both political and economic concerns sway the discussion. With a two-party political system, there are certainly differing perspectives and views on this topic. Cynically, one might summarize the topic under a heading of "Voters and Cheap Labor." (See cartoon—could it be that simple?) From a humanitarian perspective, the story could be titled as "Compassion" for those seeking a better life. Putting these differing views aside, there is no disagreement on the fact that a simple solution

G There are groups which strongly denounce these numbers as being extremely low.

is difficult to find. And, as our legislators again search for the proverbial (and politically correct) "comprehensive reform" for this difficult issue, the costs to society and victims continue to increase and the plot thickens.[H]

H Ask a group of students if they favor "comprehensive" final exams, and the answer is a resounding "No." Maybe they know something we don't. From politicians, we see a regulatory stubbornness whereby only comprehensive immigration reform AND comprehensive health care is acceptable. What political folly! Sometimes "less is more" and focusing on a few specifics may breed more efficiency as opposed to growing the bureaucracy, i.e., a 2,700 page minimally read health care bill in 2010, as an example.

FOCUS ON ARIZONA AND A REVIEW OF SB 1070

"Arizona, take off your rainbow shades.
Arizona, have another look at the world... my, my."[30]

The words sung by Mark Lindsay over 40 years ago did not refer to the state of Arizona but rather to a hypothetical hippie girlfriend of the same name.[31] But, no doubt the state of Arizona, in the last few years, did exactly what these lyrics suggest. The "shades" came off and the state opted to take an extensive look at the world in which they had found themselves.

TUCSON CORRIDOR/SECTOR

The "world" of Arizona includes an area of the state known as the Tucson Corridor (or Sector) which, at times, has been the most active and popular entry point for illegal immigration flows in the country. Overall, the state was facing unique illegal immigration issues which most of the country does not have to deal with. Further, they felt that the federal government, which is essentially charged with protecting the sovereign borders of the country, was not adequately addressing the issue—Arizona wanted more to be done. Accordingly, in an attempt to curtail and combat this problem, the state put into law SB 1070—officially known as "Support Our Law Enforcement and Safe Neighborhoods Act." While this legislation has left the front pages and faded from memory for many, the elements and discussion surrounding this legislation are worthy of review.

SB 1070 was controversial, to be sure, and opposition to SB 1070 was immediate and intense, suggesting the bill was primarily motivated by racism. Another argument took a more disparaging posture by declaring that the underlying reason for designating unauthorized immigrants as state criminals was to aid privately owned prisons in Arizona such as Corrections Corporation of America (CCA). These private, or "for-profit," prisons contract with authorities at the local, state, and federal level to house inmates. However, the cynical view referenced here suggests that the sole mission of the law was to generate profits for the private companies.[32] [I]

Yet from an Arizonian perspective, the congestion seen in this sector has been undeniable and clearly evident in the data. From 1999 through 2011, just over 4.8 million apprehensions occurred in the Tucson Corridor alone.[33] This number represents an astounding 37.5% of U.S. arrests in a state with only about 2% of our nation's population. Contributing to the high flows in this area were increased crackdowns in the El Paso and San Diego sectors. So with illegals facing

---

I CCA is the largest private correction system in the U.S. with more than 80,000 inmates spread over 60 facilities throughout the country. Privately-run prisons have been in use for decades with varying degrees of success.

higher costs in those two sectors, the Tucson Corridor became more widely used. With the increased traffic flows came... an increase in overall criminal behavior. An Arizona college professor has estimated that one third of the Arizona prison population are themselves felons from Mexico.[34] Additionally, an estimated 17% of those apprehended at the border were found to already have a criminal record in the United States.[35] A *Washington Times* story documented some of the overall concerns in regards to both human and drug trafficking.

> The federal government has posted signs along a major interstate highway in Arizona, more than 100 miles north of the U.S.–Mexico border, warning travelers the area is unsafe because of drug and alien smugglers, and a local sheriff says Mexican drug cartels now control some parts of the state.
>
> The signs were posted by the Bureau of Land Management (BLM) along a 60-mile stretch of Interstate 8 between Casa Grande and Gila Bend, a major east-west corridor linking Tucson and Phoenix with San Diego.
>
> They warn travelers that they are entering an "active drug and human smuggling area" and they may encounter "armed criminals and smuggling vehicles traveling at high rates of speed." Beginning less than 50 miles south of Phoenix, the signs encourage travelers to "use public lands north of Interstate 8" and to call 911 if they "see suspicious activity."
>
> Pinal County Sheriff Paul Babeu, whose county lies at the center of major drug and alien smuggling routes to Phoenix and cities east and west, attests to the violence. He said his deputies are outmanned and outgunned by drug traffickers in the rough-hewn desert stretches of his own county.
>
> "Mexican drug cartels literally do control parts of Arizona," he said. "They literally have scouts on the high points in the mountains and in the hills and they literally control movement. They have radios, they have optics, they have night-vision goggles as good as anything law enforcement has.
>
> "This is going on here in Arizona," he said. "This is 70 to 80 miles from the border—30 miles from the fifth-largest city in the United States."
>
> He said he asked the Obama administration for 3,000 National Guard soldiers to patrol the border, but what he got were 15 signs.
>
> Arizona Gov. Jan Brewer condemned what she called the federal government's "continued failure to secure our international border," saying the lack of security has resulted in important natural recreational areas in her state being declared too dangerous to visit.[36]

In regards to SB 1070, while the legislation continues to be viewed by many as controversial and racist, the reality is that the main components of SB 1070 closely mirror federal laws, specifically 8 U.S.C.—Sec. 1304(e). "What the Arizona law does is make a state crime out of something that already is...a federal crime."[37]

Two specific areas were at the heart of the conflict, which ultimately was challenged in front of the Supreme Court of the United States in June 2012. One was the requirement that illegal aliens have specific papers, as outlined in 1304(e). While derogatorily referred to as the "Papers Please" law, the legislation merely reflects the same requirement that was already present in the federal statutes. Per the federal statues:

> 8 U.S.C. 1304(e). ***Every alien, eighteen years of age and over, shall at all times carry with him and have in his personal possession any certificate of alien registration or alien registration receipt card issued to him*** pursuant to subsection (d) of this section. Any alien who fails to comply with the provisions of this subsection shall be guilty of a misdemeanor and shall upon conviction for each offense be fined not to exceed $100 or be imprisoned not more than thirty days, or both.

This part of the statute was struck down by the Supreme Court. So, while the "papers please" requirement still exists under federal law, there is no state violation for noncompliance.[J]

The second main component was upheld by the Court. Section 2(B) of the act requires state officers to make a "reasonable attempt...to determine the immigration status" of any person they stop, detain, or arrest on some other legitimate basis if "reasonable suspicion exists that the person is an alien and is unlawfully present in the United States."[38] The law also provides that "[any] person who is arrested shall have the person's immigration status determined before the person is released."[39] These checks would be performed by contacting U.S. Immigration and Customs Enforcement (ICE), which keeps a database of immigration records.[40]

Essentially what this means is illegal immigrants can still look for and work in Arizona without penalty, Arizona cannot punish these same individuals with state penalties for breaking federal immigration laws, and police cannot use "reasonable suspicion" to justify asking about legal status but *can* ask about legal status *after* a crime has been committed (speeding, burglary, rape, etc.).[41]

J Thinking out loud—one wonders why it was so derogatory for the state to put a law in place and attempt to enforce something that was already a federal statute. Wouldn't this line of reasoning suggest that USC 1304(e) is a "papers please" statute as well and worthy of similar condemnation?

WHAT DO THE NUMBERS SAY?

The issue of illegal immigration has no doubt been economically challenging for Arizona (and all border states) as they deal with the costs arising from enforcement and justice issues, the provision of social benefits to non-citizens, and education. Some estimates, such as those put forth by Federation for American Immigration Reform (FAIR) suggest the dollar cost, net of any tax revenues, at approximately $2.4 billion annually.[42] But, these numbers may be as controversial as the debate over population figures. Groups such as the Immigration Policy Center take an opposing view, discounting the FAIR numbers completely, and note that "immigrants are a net benefit to states." However, it is important to mention that the FAIR estimates are calculated based only on illegal immigration.

Nonetheless, passage of the legislation also included its own set of costs. Aside from the additional dollars needed to train police personnel, there have been the legal costs of court challenges. The economics of the act for Arizona were also painful in other ways as some states, such as California, boycotted the Grand Canyon State, and conventions and various events were canceled due to perceptions surrounding the legislation.[43] There was even discussion on whether or not the Major League Baseball All-Star game, scheduled to be played in Arizona in the summer of 2010, might be moved in further response to SB 1070. However, the game went on as scheduled.

An interesting perspective is provided by Florida Senator Marco Rubio, who himself is the son of immigrant parents who fled Cuba in the 1950s. He is cautious to note the distinction between Arizona and other states, while also addressing the question of selective enforcement.

> Both sides oversimplify immigration. On the one hand, there's the real human element here. These are folks that come to this country in search of a better life. Many are desperate. They're doing what many of us would do if we found ourselves in that position. On the other hand, we have to have immigration laws, and they have to be enforced. We can't be the only country in the world that doesn't enforce its immigration laws... The important thing, when I talk about enforcing our laws, is we can't have this attitude that, well, I understand that they broke the law, but now that they're here we've got to look the other way. We have millions of people waiting to come here legally. What do I tell them when they come looking for help to expedite the process? Do I tell them to enter illegally because it's quicker and cheaper?[44]

In life we find many teachable moments. Volatile emotions surround the topic of illegal immigration and no doubt the rancor that followed the passage of SB 1070 is, and continues to be, one of those teachable moments. In regards to emotion and our general topic, we again note that taking an anti-illegal-immigration stance is not the same as being "anti-immigrant." Further, education itself, and most particularly, the study of economics, should enhance both one's problem-solving skills and one's ability for what I call "issue recognition" in this area.[K]

SUMMARY

One may reasonably concur that much of the outcry over SB 1070 failed to consider the uniqueness of Arizona's situation as well as the fact that the legislation was essentially a mirror of federal guidelines that were already a matter of law. Had Arizona really overstepped its bounds? And, had all those who opposed the legislation actually read the law? At a House judiciary hearing, we watched then United States Attorney General Eric Holder comment on the bill with various criticisms and concerns, only to then admit in the session that he had not actually read the proposed legislation.[45]

In a radio discussion, I heard a philosophy PhD student from California Berkeley proclaim about the racism evident in U.S. policy. "If Americans are so concerned about illegal immigration, how come they don't pay as much attention to the northern border with Canada?" he inquired, suggesting that our policy was tied directly to skin color. The response to this is quite simple. Look at the data, as the numbers speak for themselves. Canadians are clearly not illegally migrating across the U.S. border in mass quantities.

Speaking of Canadian policy, at a 2011 conference on global immigration, I listened to a diverse set of researchers and social scientists discuss the various problems and aspects of immigration, legal and illegal. U.S. policies were discussed as were policies from other parts of the world. Canada was highly praised for their open-arm policy and their yearning for diversity. But there are a couple of points to be made in this discussion. First, through geography alone, Canadians do not face the illegal immigration flows that the U.S. faces.[L] And second, the economic "point system" used by Canada arguably discriminates against those with low education levels and poor language proficiencies. But is this discrimination, or economic choice?[M] The current U.S. administration has likewise begun the process of proposing a "point system" somewhat similar to Canada. It will be truly interesting to how, and if, this process unfolds.

As a science of choice, economics and the accompanying reasoning that is part of its study should bring about useful skills for decision making and problem solving. To repeat, it requires careful consideration of the relevant data, and a

K See Preface for more comments on three facets of education.

L One might be challenged to find another country that faces the same unauthorized migration challenges that the U.S. does.

M Speaking at the conference, Dr. George Borjas (perhaps a bit jokingly) noted that for those attempting to enter Canada without sufficient education (such as no high school diploma), the Canadians would likely suggest that they instead try the U.S. since our standards are lower.

thorough overall examination of the issue—devoid of emotion. Even though current trends suggest fewer border crossings presently occurring, the historical data is relevant. As previously cited, for the Tucson sector of Arizona alone, 4.8 million apprehensions over a 13-year period and more than $2 billion net outlay per year cannot be ignored.[46, 47] However, if we set this data aside and allow emotions to rule the day, the accompanying "noise" simply drowns out any possibility of reasonable and rational thought.

ENDNOTES

1. Moore, Mark. (2017 Feb 22). "Mexico 'will not accept' Trump's new immigration ban." *New York Post.* http://nypost.com/2017/02/22/mexico-pushes-back-against-new-us-immigration-plan/.
2. Fox News. (2010 June 23). "Mexico Joins Suit against Arizona's Immigration Law, Citing 'Grave Concerns.'" <www.foxnews.com>. Accessed 2012 Nov 30.
3. Harrup, Anthony. (2017 Aug 27). "Remittances to Mexico Hit Record $27 Billion in 2016." *Wall Street Journal.* https://www.wsj.com/articles/remittances-to-mexico-hit-record-27-billion-in-2016-1485978810.
4. http://assets.pewresearch.org/wp-content/uploads/sites/7/2013/11/PH-remittances-11-2013-2-01.png. Accessed 2017 Nov 3.
5. Homeland Security. Yearbook 2015. Aliens Apprehended by Region and Country of Nationality: Fiscal Years 2013 to 2015. Table 34. https://www.dhs.gov/immigration-statistics/yearbook/2015/table34. Accessed 2017 Aug 27.
6. United States Sentencing Commission. https://www.ussc.gov/sites/default/files/pdf/research-and-publications/quick-facts/Quick_Facts_No. N-Citizens_FY16.pdf. Accessed 2017 Sept 2.
7. https://www.federalregister.gov/documents/2015/03/09/2015-05437/annual-determination-of-average-cost-of-incarceration. Accessed 2017 Oct 19.
8. Central Intelligence Agency. *The World Factbook.* https://www.cia.gov/library/publications/the-world-factbook/fields/2086.html. Accessed 2017 Sept 2.
9. Carr, Will. (2017 Aug 10). "Mexican Drug Cartels Taking Over Fentanyl Market, Fueling a Rise in Overdose Deaths." *Fox News.* http://www.foxnews.com/us/2017/08/10/mexican-drug-cartels-taking-over-fentanyl-market-fueling-rise-in-overdose-deaths.html.
10. Gazzar, Brenda. (2005 Sept). "Mexican 'Coyote' Smuggles Immigrants into the U.S." *Banderas News.* http://banderasnews.com/0509/eded-coyote.htm. Accessed 2017 Nov 2.
11. Greenhouse, Linda. (2011 Jan 23). "Legacy of a Fence." *The New York Times.* http://query.nytimes.com/gst/fullpage.html?res=9E02E5DE1331F930A15752C0A9679D8B63
12. Villarreal, Roy. (2017 Oct 26). U.S. Border Patrol. Interview on Fox News, "Happening Now."

13. Homeland Security. (2017 Sept). "Efforts by DHS to Estimate Southwest Border Security Between Ports of Entry." Office of Immigration Statistics. https://www.dhs.gov/sites/default/files/publications/17_0914_estimates-of-border-security.pdf
14. Homeland Security p. 15.
15. The World Bank. http://data.worldbank.org/indicator/NY.GDP.PCAP.CD. Accessed 2017 Aug 27.
16. World Bank.
17. Obama, Barack. (2006). *The Audacity of Hope: Thoughts on Reclaiming the American Dream.*
18. *The Economist.* (2007 Oct 4). "Counting the Cash—Less Money Is Being Sent Home by Migrants ..." <www.theeconomist.com>. Accessed 2012 Nov 30.
19. Borjas, George J. (2013 April). "Immigration and the American Worker—A Review of the Academic Literature." *Center for Immigration Studies.* Page number https://cis.org/Report/Immigration-and-American-Worker
20. Linthicum, Kate. (2017 Aug 30). "More and More People Are Being Murdered in Mexico—and Once More Drug Cartels Are to Blame." *Los Angeles Times.* http://www.latimes.com/world/mexico-americas/la-fg-mexico-murders-20170301-story.html.
21. Sapp, Lesley. (2011 July). "Apprehensions by the U.S. Border Patrol 2005–2010." Department of Homeland Security Fact Sheet.
22. Archibold, Randal C. (2014 Oct 6). "43 Missing Students, a Mass Grave and a Suspect: Mexico's Police." *New York Times.* https://www.nytimes.com/2014/10/07/world/americas/43-missing-students-a-mass-grave-and-a-suspect-mexicos-police-.html.
23. Mele, Christopher and Sandra E. Garcia. (2017 April 3). "Mexican Newspaper Shuts Down, Saying It is Too Dangerous to Continue." *New York Times.* https://www.nytimes.com/2017/04/03/world/americas/el-norte-closes-mexican-newspaper.html.
24. Ahmed, Azam. (2017 Apr 29). "In Mexico, It's Easy to Kill a Journalist." *New York Times.* https://www.nytimes.com/2017/04/29/world/americas/veracruz-mexico-reporters-killed.html.
25. Heinle, Kimberly, Cory Molzahn, and David A. Shirk. (2015 April). "Drug Violence in Mexico—Data and Analysis through 2014." University of San Diego-Justice in Mexico Project, p. 2.
26. Althaus, Dudley. (2017 Aug 30.) "Mexico's Stubbornly Low Pay Emerges as Target in Nafta Talks." *Wall Street Journal*, p. A16.
27. The World Bank. GDP Per Capita (Current US $). World Bank Indicators. Accessed 2012 Dec 1.
28. Homeland Security p. 4
29. Borjas, George. (1999). *Heaven's Door.* Princeton University Press. New Jersey. p. 67.

30. Fox News. (2012 Nov 28). "Mexican Mayor Maria Santos Gorrostieta Killed by Gunmen Was Defiant to the End." <www.latino.foxnews.com>. Accessed 2012 Nov 30.
31. Sapp.
32. Sapp.
33. Sapp.
34. "Arizona" written by Kenny Young, recorded by Mark Lindsay in 1969.
35. Eddy, Chuck. (1997). *The Accidental Evolution of Rock 'n' Roll.* Da Capo Press. ISBN 0-306-80741-6.
36. James, Tom. (2012 June 27). "Arizona Deserves Better Than SB1070 and ALEC." <www.dailykos.com>. Accessed 2012 Oct 15.
37. U.S. Border Patrol. <www.cbp.gov>. Accessed 2012 Dec 10. <http://www.cbp.gov/linkhandler/cgov/border_security/border_patrol/usbp_statistics/99_10_fy_stats.ctt/99_11_fy_stats.pdf>.
38. Lovell, Terry J. Patriot Network TV Commentary. Posted 8/14/2010. <http://therealrevo.com/blog/?p=30637>. Accessed 2012 Dec 2.
39. Banks, Leo W. (2010 Apr 29). "The Krentz Bonfire—Will the Murder of a Respected Cochise County Rancher Change Anything On Our Border." Tucson Weekly. <www.tucsonweekly.com>. Accessed 2012 Dec 2.
40. Seper, Jerry and Matthew Cella. (2010 Aug 31). "Signs in Arizona Warn of Smuggler Dangers." *The Washington Times.* <www.washingtontimes.com>. Accessed 2012 Dec 2.
41. Will, George. (2010 Apr 25). *ABC This Week.* Panel discussion.
42. West. (2012). Arizona Revised Statute Ann. Sec. 11-1051(B).
43. West.
44. Pavlich, Katie. (2012 June 25). "Decision Reached on Arizona's SB1070." <www.townhall.com>. Accessed 2012 Oct 15.
45. Pavlich.
46. Martin, Jack and Eric A. Ruark. (2010 July). "The Fiscal Burden of Illegal Immigration on United States Taxpayers." FAIR. Washington, D.C: Fair Horizon Press. Revised 2011 Feb.
47. Nintzel, Jim. (2010 May 10). "SB 1070 Fallout: Two Tucson Conventions Cancelled." <www.tucsonweekly.com>. Blog Posting. Accessed 2012 Dec 2.
48. Rubio, Marco. (2012). "Interview with Charlie Rose." *Bloomberg Businessweek,* July 2–July 8, 2012, p. 26.
49. Holder, Eric. (2010 May 13). "Ted Poe Grills Eric Holder—SB 1070." House Judiciary Testimony. <http://www.youtube.com/watch?v=Jr2HCDODPRI>. Accessed 2012 Dec 2.
50. U.S. Border Patrol. <www.cbp.gov>. Accessed 2012 Dec 10.
51. Martin p. 4.

IMMIGRATION AND BORDER CONTROL

By Edward Alden

For the past two decades the United States, a country with a strong tradition of limited government, has been pursuing a widely popular initiative that requires one of the most ambitious expansions of government power in modern history: securing the nation's borders against illegal immigration. Congress and successive administrations—both Democratic and Republican—have increased the size of the Border Patrol from fewer than 3,000 agents to more than 21,000, built nearly 700 miles of fencing along the southern border with Mexico, and deployed pilotless drones, sensor cameras, and other expensive technologies aimed at preventing illegal crossings at the land borders. The government has overhauled the visa system to require interviews for all new visa applicants and instituted extensive background checks for many of those wishing to come to the United States to study, travel, visit family, or do business. It now requires secure documents—a passport or the equivalent—for all travel to and from the United States by citizens and noncitizens. And border officers take fingerprints and run other screening measures on all travelers coming to this country by air in order to identify criminals, terrorists, or others deemed to pose a threat to the United States.

The goal is to create a border control system that ensures that only those legally permitted by the government to enter the territory of the United States will be able to do so, and that they will leave the country when required. The ambition of such an undertaking is little appreciated. For most of its history, the United States had only the loosest sort of border controls. Scrutiny of most visa applicants was cursory; few checks were done on incoming airline passengers; and

Edward Alden, "Immigration and Border Control," *Cato Journal*, vol. 32, no. 1, pp. 107-124.

it was possible to walk freely across almost any portion of the more than 7,500 miles of land borders with Mexico or Canada (Alden 2008).

That began to change gradually in the 1980s with the increase in illegal immigration from Mexico, and then more rapidly in the early 1990s following a political outcry from U.S. border states, especially California. The border control effort was greatly accelerated after the 9/11 attacks, becoming the primary mission of the new Department of Homeland Security (DHS) created in 2003. Yet some two decades along, border control remains a work in progress. Most Americans remain unconvinced that border security is improving; a Rasmussen poll taken in May 2011 found that two-thirds of the public believe the border with Mexico is not secure. While budget constraints will slow the extraordinarily rapid growth of border enforcement, the Obama administration and Congress are determined to continue tightening border control and further reducing illegal entries.

An in-depth stocktaking of the costs and benefits of this effort to date is long overdue. But at least three interim conclusions can be reached.

First, the U.S. borders are far harder to cross illegally than at any time in American history, and the number of people entering illegally has dropped sharply. Evading border enforcement has become more difficult, more expensive, and more uncertain than ever before. But border control will always remain imperfect; it is not possible for the United States to create a perfectly secure border, and that should not be the goal.

Second, more people still wish to come to the United States—even in a weak economy with high unemployment—than are permitted by current legal immigration and work visa quotas. One consequence is an expanding organized crime problem in which increasingly sophisticated criminal networks earn high returns for helping illegal immigrants enter the United States. This has contributed to a growing sense of insecurity along the borders even as illegal entry has become more difficult. The only way to remedy this is through legal programs that hew more closely to labor market demand.

Third, increased border control efforts have not just discouraged illegal border crossers, but legal travelers as well. Tourism, business travel, crossings at the land borders, and other legal entries into the United States have all been flat or falling over the past decade. Skilled immigrants have been discouraged and sought out more hospitable countries. The economic costs of these declines have never been measured in any comprehensive way, but they are certainly large.

The questions for Congress and the Obama administration in the near future ought to be these: What are the goals of border control? How much is enough? How much can we afford? How can the economic costs of tighter border enforcement best be mitigated? How can better legal immigration and temporary work programs help to reduce further the illegal migration problem? Unfortunately, in the current political environment such questions are not being asked. Instead, Congress and the administration continue to be focused on the elusive goal of creating a perfectly secure border through enforcement measures alone.

A BRIEF HISTORY OF U.S. BORDER CONTROL

Immigration has been the forgotten stepchild of the second era of globalization. The United States over the past half century consciously and deliberately freed up trade in goods, lifted controls on capital and investment, and urged and pressured other countries to do the same. Its immigration policy, however—the third leg of freer movement of people to accompany the freer movement of goods and capital—developed largely by accident. Legal immigration levels rose sharply beginning in the late 1970s, largely as an unanticipated consequence of the Immigration and Nationality Act of 1965 that allowed permanent residents and naturalized citizens to petition for family members to join them. The Immigration Act of 1990 added larger quotas as well for skilled immigrants with no family ties. The United States also tacitly accepted high levels of illegal immigration, whether Mexicans and Central Americans coming across the southwest land border or Chinese, Pakistanis, and Filipinos arriving by air and overstaying tourist or student visas. While there was constant grumbling about the problem of unauthorized immigration, especially from the border states, the pressure to do something about the problem was outweighed by economic interests that opposed the sort of the heavy-handed government intervention that would be required to gain greater control. The landmark 1986 Immigration Reform and Control Act (IRCA), which continues to loom over the immigration debate today, coupled legalization for nearly 3 million unauthorized immigrants with a largely unmet promise of better border security and workplace enforcement to discourage additional illegal immigration.

The result of this non-policy and non-enforcement of existing laws was a system that worked rather well from an economic perspective. Many young Mexican or Central American men would come on a seasonal or temporary basis to fill jobs in agriculture, tourism, construction, and other sectors. The numbers would rise in a strong economy and fall in a weaker one, responding effectively to U.S. economic cycles. And given the few legal options available for low-skilled workers, as Gordon Hanson has written, illegal immigration was "the most viable means of entering the country" (Hanson 2007: 14). The few interventions by Congress were generally positive, such as the creation in 1990 of the H1-B visa to permit some of the increasing number of skilled foreign students at U.S. universities to remain and work in the United States.

But the arrangement could not survive two external shocks. The first was the surge in illegal immigration, driven primarily by a demographic bulge of young people in Mexico, successive Mexican economic crises in the 1980s and 1990s that slowed economic growth and limited job opportunities at home, and the restructuring triggered by the North American Free Trade Agreement (NAFTA), especially in the Mexican agriculture sector. Attempted illegal entries, as measured by the number of Border Patrol apprehensions, grew from negligible levels in the 1960s to more than 1 million annually during the 1980s and close to 2 million annually by the end of the 1990s.[A] Illegal migration went from being a nuisance problem to a major issue of public security and state welfare in the border states of California and Texas (and only later in Arizona). The first big buildup of armed agents at the southern border, with Operation Gatekeeper in San Diego and Operation Hold the Line in El Paso, fundamentally changed the economic dynamics of the border. As border crossing became more difficult and expensive, more migrants opted to settle in the United States, often bringing spouses and children with them (Durand, Malone, and Massey 2003). That put pressure on local schools, hospitals, and other social services. And with the option of returning home foreclosed, increasing numbers of illegal migrants began to follow work opportunities away from the border to states like Iowa, Georgia, and North Carolina that had previously seen few immigrants. The total number of illegal migrants resident in the United States swelled to roughly 12 million by 2007 (Passel and Cohn 2011).

The second big shock was 9/11. All 19 of the hijackers entered the United States on legal visas, despite red flags that should have excluded several. At the time of the attacks, five had overstayed or otherwise violated the terms of their visas (Eldridge et al. 2004). Following 9/11, preventing future terrorist attacks became the highest national priority of the United States, and stopping entry by future would-be terrorists became a core pillar of that strategy. The attacks transformed border control from what had been essentially a public order issue into a national security issue. And it broadened the notion of border control from the historic focus on the southern border to concern with air and sea entries, and with the northern land border with Canada. The creation of DHS institutionalized the link between border security and terrorism. The department was created largely by merging three border control agencies—the Customs Service, the Immigration and Naturalization Service, and the Coast Guard—and border and immigration enforcement is by far the largest budget item for DHS, accounting for more than half of the agency's annual budget. (U.S. Department of Homeland Security 2011: 15)

In response to these two shocks, the United States has pursued for the first time in its history a serious, sustained campaign to gain control over the borders. The goal is to create a system in which the U.S. government will decide exactly who is allowed to come into the country and who is not, and will have the capacity to enforce those choices with a high level of success. For a large, open, democratic

---

A The use of apprehension data to measure attempted illegal entry has long been inadequate, but they are the only data that have been gathered consistently over time by the Border Patrol. Apprehensions count only those who are detected and arrested by Border Patrol agents, and do not include those who escape detection. The numbers thus underestimate attempted illegal entry. Further, apprehension data do not account for those who arrive in the United States legally and then overstay their visas. For a fuller discussion of measurement issues, see Alden and Roberts (2011).

country with a tradition of limited government, it ranks as one of the most ambitious government undertakings in American history.

HARDENING THE U.S. BORDERS

Foreigners can enter the United States legally in several ways. They can come temporarily as tourists or students or business travelers; they can come for longer periods of time to work on short-term visas, with the expectation that they will eventually return home; or they can immigrate permanently, either sponsored by a family member or on the basis of employment skills. The primary goal of border security (leaving aside drugs and other contraband) is to ensure that these legal channels are the only way to enter the United States.

The scale of that task in enormous. Last year, for instance, more than 8 million people applied for immigrant or non-immigrant visas to come to the United States, and just under 2 million were rejected. More than 16 million individuals were admitted without visas under the Visa Waiver Program. And more than 243 million legal entries were processed at the land borders with Canada and Mexico, a steady stream of cross-border traffic by people living, working, and doing business in the border regions. Illegal entries are far harder to track. There were 463,000 apprehensions made of individuals trying to cross illegally between the land border ports of entry. And an unknown number of individuals failed to leave when their visas expired, leaving them living illegally in the United States.

Over the past two decades, the U.S. government has systematically rolled out a series of measures aimed at reducing the flow of illegal immigrants. The first and most closely watched has been the expansion of a quasi-military presence at the U.S. land border with Mexico, and to a lesser extent with Canada. The Border Patrol, established in 1924, was for many years little more than a token presence between the land border ports of entry; today, it is the single largest law enforcement agency in the United States. Border Patrol agents have in recent years also been reinforced by the regular deployment of National Guard forces. Vehicle and pedestrian fencing has been constructed across nearly 700 miles of the border with Mexico; the former are metal barriers that block cars and trucks but do not stop walkers, while the latter are high steel barriers that can be breached only through ladders or tunneling. The border region is further monitored by electronic sensing devices and aerial drones that allow Border Patrol agents to respond quickly to breaches.

Determining the effectiveness of border enforcement is imprecise. Illegal immigration from Mexico has long been driven primarily by relative economic conditions in the two countries (Hanson and Spilimbergo 1996). As long as wages in the United States remain far higher than in Mexico and its other southern neighbors, there will continue to be many who will take the risk of trying to enter the United States illegally. But the data in recent years strongly suggest that enforcement has played a significant role in discouraging illegal entry across the southern border.

In the mid-1990s, for instance, the Border Patrol was making about 600,000 arrests annually in each of California and Texas, and about half that number in Arizona. Border crossing was much easier in the urban regions of California and Texas than in the harsh, unpopulated deserts of Arizona. Following the border buildup of the mid-1990s, however, that pattern changed. Apprehensions rose to more than 700,000 per year in Arizona even as they were falling sharply in California and Texas. There was no question that illegal migrants were responding to the tougher enforcement in those two states by seeking other, less defended routes. With a similar crackdown in Arizona over the past five years, apprehension numbers have fallen all along the border. The number of arrests last year was the lowest of any year since 1972. Through mid-2011, apprehensions had fallen even lower, to levels not seen since the 1960s. While the apprehension data are far from adequate as a measure of illegal crossing, the declining trend is unmistakable.

More difficult is assessing how much of the reduction in attempted crossings is due to enforcement and how much is the result of a weak U.S. economy with lower demand for immigrant workers. But again the numbers suggest that enforcement is playing a big part. Since 2006, the number of apprehensions has fallen by more than half. The decline coincided with the border buildup in the second term of the Bush administration, and predated the onset of the recession in 2008 (though the construction market, which is a magnet for illegal migrants, had begun to weaken sooner). The number of attempted entries has continued to fall every year. In comparison, the previous recessions in 2001–02, 1991–92 and 1981–82 had virtually no impact on illegal entries, producing only a small decline and a swift return to the pre-recession level of entries. While certainly the recent recession was deeper, and the recovery much slower, than previous postwar recessions, the figures suggest that enforcement has been a significant factor discouraging illegal entry.

Expanded land border enforcement has been matched by a similar effort in the air environment. Here the focus has been less on identifying potential illegal immigrants and more on identifying those with criminal records or ties to terrorist organizations. Entry into the United States from overseas now involves passing through an extraordinary, high-technology security gauntlet, nearly all of it constructed over the past decade. Visa applicants are required to give fingerprints and digital photographs, present themselves for interviews, and in some cases wait for lengthy security background screenings (Alden 2011). Those who do not require visas must still register their identities with the U.S. government in advance of travel. All passengers on incoming flights are screened against a terrorist watch list of roughly one million names. Upon arrival in the United States, all non-Americans must also provide digital fingerprints and photographs to border inspectors, both to verify identity and to check against archived fingerprints of suspected criminals or terrorists.[B] The U.S. government now has in its databases the fingerprint records of roughly 130 million individuals, as well as 142 million facial recognition images. The major hole remains the lack of a comprehensive system for tracking whether visitors to the United States overstay their visas, though the government increasingly has the capacity to do this by matching incoming passenger records with outgoing records, and is about to embark on a pilot project to exchange entry and exit data with Canada (Alden 2010a, Obama and Harper 2011).

Measuring success in these efforts is even more difficult than at the land borders. Since the purpose is to keep terrorists out of the United States, even a single mistake constitutes a major failure. Following the near-miss Christmas bombing of 2009, for instance, Congress stepped up calls for even tighter visa and border screening measures. The plotter, a young Nigerian man, had in fact been identified through passenger screening after he boarded the flight to Detroit, and Customs and Border Protection (CBP) officials were ready to pull him aside on his arrival in the United States, and would likely have sent him home. But that turned out to be too late, calling the efficacy of the entire system into question (White House 2010).

The Christmas bombing incident highlights one of the biggest problems in the current discussion of border security—the conflation of terrorism and illegal immigration. Since 9/11, border security has been considered as part of the larger counter-terrorism mission of DHS. To be effective, counterterrorism needs to be successful virtually all the time; even a single failure could be extremely costly in terms of lives lost. While Stephen Flynn has argued persuasively that the United States needs to develop resilience in responding to and recovering from terrorist attacks, the standard for successful deterrence will always be extremely high (Flynn 2007).

But border security for the purpose of dissuading illegal migration is an entirely different matter. Here, perfect security cannot be the goal. Even the Cold War border between the two Germanies—the most heavily fortified in modern history—was successfully breached a thousand or so times each year. There is simply no way for a large, open, and democratic country like the United States to construct and maintain perfect border defenses. It is hard to think of another issue where the public debate is so utterly at odds with what the government can realistically achieve (Ziglar and Alden 2011).

The administration and Congress have exacerbated this misperception by failing to put forward any serious proposals for a reasonable standard of enforcement (Whitley, Roberts, and Shea 2011; Alden and Roberts 2011). What percentage,

B The exception remains Canadian and Mexican crossers at the land border, primarily because the large volume of cross-border travel makes such intrusive inspection impossible as a routine matter. Individual travelers at the land borders are pulled aside for additional scrutiny at the discretion of border officers.

for instance, of illegal entries should the United States be able to prevent? While DHS does not currently measure the apprehension rate, the best guess is that between 40 and 60 percent of those who try to cross the southern land border illegally are arrested. Is that too low? Perhaps, but a comparison to crime statistics is illuminating. According to the FBI's Uniform Crime Reporting System, only the most serious criminals in the United States face a similar likelihood of apprehension. Sixty-four percent of murders, for instance, result in arrests and prosecution; the figures are 55 percent for aggravated assaults, and 45 percent for all violent crimes. But only 17 percent of property crimes and 13 percent of burglaries result in arrests and prosecution.[C]

It may be reasonable to set a higher goal for border apprehensions, so long as Congress is prepared to appropriate the necessary funds, though the current budget environment is one in which extra dollars are certain to be scarce. But no serious discussion of border enforcement is possible until reasonable targets can be set by political leaders.

SMUGGLER'S PARADISE

The purpose of border enforcement is not just to apprehend would-be border crossers, but to raise the costs for potential crossers and thus deter others from ever attempting illegal entry. Again, the evidence is sparse but it suggests that tougher enforcement is increasing the price for anyone wanting to enter the United States illegally. At the southern border, most of those attempting to enter illegally use smugglers and the costs of entry have grown significantly (Roberts et al. 2010).

But the rise in smuggling costs underscores a central problem that arises from trying to stem illegal immigration through enforcement measures alone: tougher enforcement increases the financial incentive to elude enforcement. The lesson is the same one that was learned during Prohibition and has yet to be learned in the 40-year war on drugs: any successful effort to outlaw a good that is in high demand invariably creates an organized crime problem, because the value of the prohibited good rises. Most of the violence in northern Mexico is a consequence of the U.S. demand for illegal drugs, not the smuggling of illegal migrants. But while U.S. private sector demand for immigrant labor is much weaker than it was before the financial crisis and the recession, it has not disappeared. Unless there are legal programs that allow some orderly way for immigrants to come and work in the United States, smugglers will continue to fill that demand illegally.

There has long been a debate over the relationship between legal work programs and illegal immigration. From 1942 to 1964, the United States permitted

C I am grateful to Bryan Roberts for assembling these figures and suggesting the relevance of the comparison to border apprehension rates.

several hundred thousand young Mexican men to come seasonally for work, most in the agricultural industry, under what was known as the Bracero Program. At its peak more than 400,000 agricultural workers came each year. In the absence of enforcement, the program did little to discourage illegal immigration; many farmers had the choice of hiring braceros or unauthorized workers, and one consequence was poor wage and working conditions for both. Those concerns led to the Bracero scheme being abolished in 1964 (Martin 2003). Whatever the problems with the Bracero Program, however, the number of illegal entries from Mexico began to rise immediately after it was ended and continued to increase steadily throughout the following decades.

The lack of any new mechanisms to improve legal work opportunities for low-skilled workers, especially from Mexico, is one of the most unfortunate consequences of the failure by Congress to pass comprehensive immigration reform. The original legislation proposed by Senators John McCain and Edward Kennedy in 2005 would have authorized as many as 400,000 guest workers annually, roughly the number that came at the height of the Bracero Program in the late 1950s. Coupled with improved enforcement at the border and the workplace, there are strong reasons to believe that such a program today would be far better managed than it was a half century ago, and would provide a genuine alternative to illegal migration, especially for seasonal workers. A further advantage is that the U.S. government could levy sizeable fees on those coming to work; individuals who are willing to pay upwards of $3,000 to a smuggler for the opportunity to enter the United States illegally would surely be willing to pay as much or more for the right to live and work here legally.

Instead, the administration and Congress appear determined to keep lining the pockets of the smugglers and other criminal organizations. Alongside increased border security, the major immigration initiative of the current Congress is an effort by House Judiciary Committee chairman Lamar Smith to mandate that all employers use an electronic verification system to ensure that they are hiring only legally authorized workers. Employer verification—like border security—will certainly help in discouraging illegal immigration, but it will also further enrich criminal enterprises engaged in producing increasingly sophisticated false documents to evade the system. While better employment verification is needed, unless it is coupled with a sensible legal work program for lower-skilled immigrants it will—like border enforcement—produce unintended consequences that diminish many of the benefits.

EFFECTS ON LEGAL TRAVEL AND IMMIGRATION

In its first strategic framework document, produced last year, the Department of Homeland Security stated: "Secure, well-managed borders must not only protect the United States against threats from abroad; they must also expedite the safe flow of lawful travel and commerce" (DHS 2010: 24). The facilitation side of the DHS mission, however, has consistently come a poor second to the enforcement mission. The United States continues to hurt itself through poorly targeted enforcement measures that discourage foreign students, keep out skilled immigrants, drive away tourists, and lead foreign investors to look for friendlier markets. These economic impacts of border enforcement have never been measured and aggregated in any precise way, but they are unquestionably large.

Take the tourist industry, for example, which is the largest U.S. service sector export, and accounts for nearly 9 percent of all exports. (Tourist dollars spent by foreigners in the United States are counted as an export in trade statistics.) In 2000, the United States welcomed 26 million foreign tourists; ten years later, in 2010, it welcomed exactly the same number—26 million. Yet in that decade the world tourist market grew by some 60 million passengers as growing middle classes in China, India, Brazil, and elsewhere began to travel abroad. Those additional travelers did not come to the United States. Over the past decade, the U.S. global share of long-haul travel has fallen from 17 per cent to 12.4 per cent. The U.S. travel industry estimated that if the United States were to regain that lost travel share, it would increase U.S. exports by $390 billion and create 1.3 million jobs (U.S. Travel Association 2011: 13).

It is difficult to know for certain whether it is border security measures or other unrelated factors that have dissuaded tourists from coming to the United States, but there are many reasons to believe border measures have played a significant role. The U.S. visa process is difficult, expensive, and often time-consuming for tourists and other travelers. A U.S. Travel Association survey of travelers from Brazil, China, and India found that large majorities were discouraged from visiting the United States by the visa process and security measures. Since those countries are the biggest sources of future travel growth, that is surely a damaging perception.

There have been other business costs as well. More detailed border inspections, even with the laudable efforts that have been made by CBP to streamline procedures for high-volume shippers and encourage enrollment in registered traveler programs like Nexus and Sentri, have slowed cross-border commerce (U.S. Chamber of Commerce and Canadian Chamber of Commerce 2009, and U.S. Chamber of Commerce 2011). Visa delays have discouraged foreign investors from the U.S. market, and may well have contributed to the declining U.S. share of foreign direct investment over the past decade (U.S. Commerce Department 2007). The United States has failed even to sign on the APEC Business Travel Card, a scheme designed to ease business travel in the fast-growing Asia-Pacific region.

The loss of tourist revenue and the discouragement of foreign investors and business travelers are certainly costly, especially in a weak economy with catastrophically high unemployment. But the more lasting consequence may be the loss of skilled immigrants. The United States has long been the most successful country in the world at recruiting and retaining highly talented immigrants—in sports, in entertainment, and most importantly in the scientific and technological fields that drive modern economies. Over the past decade, however, that advantage has shrunk significantly. The growth in foreign students slowed sharply, with many going to places like Australia and Canada, and even to long-closed Japan. Skilled workers are being lured by other countries that have overhauled their immigration laws and promise a smoother transition to a new life. And Chinese and Indians, the two largest groups of skilled migrants, are returning home in greater numbers to pursue job opportunities in their own fast-growing economies (Alden 2010b).

As with many of the other developments discussed in this article, it is hard to know for certain how much the U.S. effort to tighten its borders has been responsible for these trends. During this period, other countries have been waking up to the benefits that come from skilled immigration, and would likely have done more to lure talented migrants regardless of what the United States did. In addition, strong economic growth in China and India would surely have lured back many of their overseas students who might in the past have remained in the United States. But there is little question that U.S. policies have exacerbated these trends. At the very time much of the world has been opening itself to skilled immigration, the United States has been making it harder for these migrants to come here, and harder for them to stay.

THE FUTURE BORDER: FLEXIBLE AND SECURE

The United States will never again be a country with loosely guarded borders. The political coalition in favor of tough border control is strong and probably durable; the threats from terrorism or other transnational crime are severe enough to necessitate effective border measures; and the desire by many to migrate illegally to the United States will remain strong enough that deterrence through enforcement is essential. The challenge, therefore, is how to make border security compatible with a sensible immigration system that strengthens the U.S. economy rather than weakens it. That unfortunately still appears to be a long way off.

A more sensible direction for the future would involve three major elements. The first would be an honest, constructive political discussion on the goals of border security. The current debate remains infantile in the literal sense that it imagines that the United States can exist inside a perfect cocoon of border security. Every Government Accountability Office (GAO) report that notes, quite rightly, that the United States does not exercise firm control over each inch of its 7,500 miles of land borders is greeted with a political gasp of alarm, even from normally sober politicians like Senator Joe Lieberman (I-Conn.) (GAO 2010). The Obama administration and the heads of the relevant congressional committees should sit down together to set some sensible targets for border enforcement, agree on the resources needed to reach those targets, and relentlessly monitor progress towards those goals.

The second requirement flows from the first. Border enforcement does not exist in a vacuum. If the United States tomorrow were to end all legal immigration, border enforcement would need to be strengthened much more still just to prevent a surge in illegal immigration. Similarly, if the United States tomorrow were simply to abolish immigration quotas and open its doors to all comers, the need for enforcement (again leaving aside drugs and contraband) would disappear. It is obvious, though it is almost never portrayed that way in the public debate, that border security is closely connected to legal immigration levels. The program that would do the most to address the illegal immigration problem is a temporary worker program, primarily aimed at low-skilled Mexicans and Central Americans who make up the bulk of the illegal immigrant flow. There are a range of difficult issues to be resolved in designing and implementing such a program, but it would pay immediate benefits in reducing illegal migration.

The United States also needs a more flexible legal immigration system that is closely tied to the state of the economy; current U.S. quotas are unnecessarily rigid and unresponsive to economic conditions, in part because they require an act of Congress to change. The two major independent task-force reports of the past decade—one sponsored by the Migration Policy Institute and chaired by Lee Hamilton and Spencer Abraham, the other sponsored by the Council on Foreign Relations and chaired by Jeb Bush and Mack McLarty (I served as project director)—both recommended the formation of an independent government commission with defined and limited authority to adjust immigration levels in a timely fashion to respond to U.S. economic conditions (MPI 2006, CFR 2009).

There are certainly many—indeed the majority of the American public at the moment—who would argue against higher levels of immigration. That is perfectly reasonable. But the debate should be an honest one. Larger legal quotas, especially for less-skilled workers, would reduce the need for enforcement; smaller quotas would increase it. Instead, the discussion is a disingenuous one in which many in Congress insist that the border must first be "secured" before any serious consideration of immigration reform can be permitted. Legal immigration levels and border security are intimately tied to each other, and cannot be credibly separated in that fashion.

The third need is to reconsider our understanding of national security and border control. The close link in the public mind is largely a result of the specific circumstances of the 9/11 attacks, in which all the attackers entered the United States from overseas. The result has been an intense focus on policies designed to prevent similar future attacks, and border control has figured prominently. But if the attacks had been carried out by individuals who had lived many years in the United States—such as the perpetrators of the 2005 London subway bombing, who were all born or raised in the United Kingdom—the response would have been quite different. Immigration policy might still have figured prominently in the reaction, but the issue would have been—as it has largely been in Europe—the failure of integration rather than the failure of border control. Border control is a very limited counter-terrorism tool. While it can raise the hurdles for entry, there are many other ways to carry out terrorist attacks successfully. It is not coincidental that since 9/11 the majority of the terrorist conspiracies in the United States have involved U.S. citizens or permanent immigrants rather than recent arrivals. Terrorist groups have simply adapted to tougher border controls and recruited accordingly (Alden 2010c).

The more serious threat to U.S. national security is that ill-conceived or poorly implemented border controls will do lasting damage to the U.S. economy. America's military advantage stems largely from its wealth and superior technology, and both depend in no small measure on the U.S. ability to attract and retain the best and the brightest from across the globe. As Amy Chua (2007), the Yale law professor, has argued persuasively, the most successful empires in history have been those that opened their doors widely; turning inward is invariably associated with decline. A perfectly secure border would not bring perfect security to the United States; indeed the opposite is true.

REFERENCES

Alden, E. (2008) *The Closing of the American Border: Terrorism, Immigration and Security Since 9/11.* New York: Harper Collins.

——— (2010a) "Visas Overstays: Can They Be Eliminated?" Testimony before the Committee on Homeland Security, U.S. House of Representatives (25 March).

——— (2010b) "U.S. Losing Ground in Competitive Immigration." *World Politics Review* (27 July).

——— (2010c) "National Security and U.S. Immigration Policy." *St. John's Journal of International and Comparative Law* 1 (1): 19–30.

——— (2011) Testimony before the House Judiciary Committee, Subcommittee on Immigration Policy and Enforcement, Hearing on the Secure Visas Act, U.S. House of Representatives (11 May). Alden, E., and Roberts, B. (2011) "Are U.S. Borders Secure?" *Foreign Affairs* 90 (4): 19–26.

Chua, A. (2007) *Day of Empire: How Hyperpowers Rise to Global Dominance—and Why They Fall.* New York: Doubleday.

Council on Foreign Relations (2009) *U.S. Immigration Policy.* J. Bush and T. McLarty, co-chairs. Independent Task Force Report No. 63. Washington.

Durand, J.; Malone, N.; and Massey, D. (2003) *Beyond Smoke and Mirrors: Mexican Immigration in an Era of Economic Integration*. New York: Russell Sage.

Eldridge, T., et al. (2004) *9/11 and Terrorist Travel: Staff Report of the National Commission on Terrorist Attacks upon the United States*. Washington: National Commission on Terrorist Attacks.

Flynn, S. (2007) *The Edge of Disaster: Rebuilding a Resilient Nation*. New York: Random House.

Government Accountability Office (2010) *Border Security: Enhanced DHS Oversight and Assessment of Interagency Coordination Is Needed for the Northern Border*. GAO–11–97. Washington (December).

Hanson, G. H. (2007) "The Economic Logic of Illegal Immigration." Washington: Council on Foreign Relations Special Report. Washington.

Hanson, G. H., and Spilimbergo, A. (1996) "Illegal Immigration, Border Enforcement and Relative Wages: Evidence from Apprehensions at the U.S.-Mexico Border." NBER Working Paper No. 5592.

Martin, P. L. (2003) *Promise Unfulfilled: Unions, Immigration and Farm Workers*. Ithaca: Cornell University Press.

Migration Policy Institute (2005) *Immigration and America's Future: A New Chapter*. Report of the Independent Task Force on Immigration and America's Future. Abraham, S., and Hamilton, L. H., co-chairs. Washington: MPI.

Obama, B., and Harper, S. (2011) "A Declaration by the Prime Minister of Canada and the President of the United States." Ottawa (4 February). Available at www.bilateralist.com/2011/02/ 04/text-obama-harper-border-declaration.

Passel, J. S., and Cohn, D. (2011) *Unauthorized Immigration Population: National and State Trends, 2010*. Washington: Pew Hispanic Research Center.

Rasmussen Reports (2011) "Only 30% Say U.S.-Mexico Border Secure, 64% Say It's Not." (13 May).

Roberts, B.; Hanson, G.; Cornwell, D.; and Borger, S. (2010) "An Analysis of Migrant Smuggling Costs Along the Southwest Border." Department of Homeland Security, Office of Immigration Statistics Working Paper (November).

U.S. Chamber of Commerce (2011) *Steps to a 21st Century U.S.-Mexico Border*. Washington.

U.S. Chamber of Commerce and Canadian Chamber of Commerce (2009) *Finding the Balance: Shared Border of the Future*. Washington (July). Available at www.uschamber.com/reports/ finding-balance-shared-border-future.

U.S. Commerce Department (2007) "Visas and Foreign Direct Investment: Supporting U.S. Investment by Facilitating International Travel." Washington (November).

U.S. Department of Homeland Security (2010) "Quadrennial Homeland Security Review Report: A Strategic Framework for a Secure Homeland." Washington (February).

——— (2011) "Budget-in-Brief: Fiscal Year 2011." Washington: DHS.

U.S. Travel Association (2011) "Ready for Takeoff: A Plan to Create 1.3 Million U.S. Jobs by Welcoming Millions of International Travelers." Washington.

White House (2010) "Review Summary Regarding 12/25/2009 Attempted Terrorist Attack," Washington: Office of the Press Secretary (7 January).

Whitley, J., Roberts, B., and Shea, R. (2011) "Immigration and Border Control: How Data-Driven Management Could Enhance Success." Paper Presented at the Western Economic Association 86th Annual Conference, San Diego.

Ziglar, J., and Alden, E. (2011) "The Real Price of Sealing the Border." *Wall Street Journal* (8 April).

CHAPTER 9

ECONOMIC EFFICIENCY AND BUDGET CONCEPTS

By Ron Liggett

The idea of economic efficiency is a feature of resource allocation that economists highly regard. This type of efficient condition—sometimes referred to as Pareto optimality—can be viewed as an outcome based not merely on material goods, but also on the overall welfare of people.[A] Generally, an efficient outcome would make "people as well off as possible" while considering all factors relevant to their well-being.[1] Most obviously, improving one's welfare would include using resources optimally in the prevention of crime. So the focus in this section is to embrace the idea of efficiency, while also comprehending some of the basic challenges in determining the crime budget.

In Chapter One, I began with some general comments about the cyclical aspects of life, the economy, various business conditions, and criminal behavior. Likewise, in our Chapter 3 "Macro" discussion we analyzed cyclical conditions more closely. Let us briefly revisit the economic aspects of that discussion by looking more closely at the business cycle. We understand that peaks in the cycle signify economic expansion in the form of increased economic output, lower unemployment, and, most certainly, higher tax revenues. However, as the economy recedes into its trough and an economic downturn, we see these outcomes reversed, resulting in higher unemployment rates, decreased output, and lower tax revenues. A graph of the business cycle follows.

A "Pareto Optimal" was named after 19th century Italian economist Vilfredo Pareto, who was one of the first to address this concept.

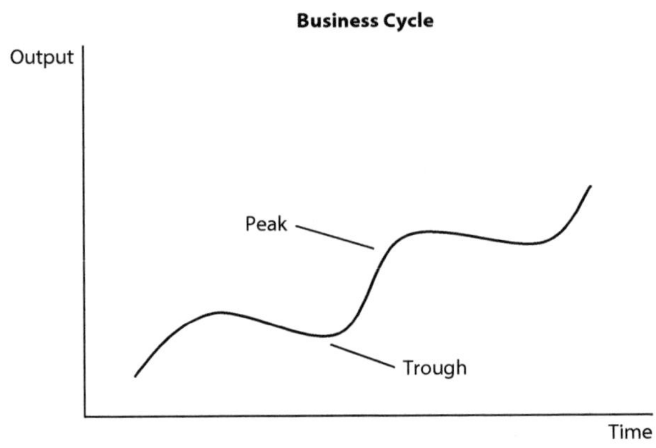

During cyclical downturns, there are multiple challenges likely occurring at all levels-federal, state, and local. First, there is the dilemma of finding the necessary funds to support the various public goods. Secondly, there are challenging decisions to be made within the budget in regards to allocating the precious dollars between specific departments. For this chapter we will begin with the expenditures side of the equation and take a look at a budgeting concept using marginal benefits (MB) and marginal costs (MC).

CRIME PREVENTION AS A PUBLIC GOOD

First, let us classify "crime prevention" as a **public good**. A public good is broadly defined as "any good where consumption by one person does not exclude consumption by another."[B] And when do we actually consume this public good known as crime prevention? Well, whether we are watching TV at home, eating out in a restaurant, or reading our economics textbook, we are in the process of "consuming" crime prevention. Accordingly, there is a level of safety and a deterrent effect in place due to our system of law enforcement. Of course one would hope that calls to the police for assistance are rare, and not needed at this exact moment, but the fact remains that Adam Smith was correct. Our current level of safety is due in part to the "the shelter of the civil magistrate." But in our appreciation of the public good known as crime prevention, we could also hypothesize about the state of affairs in our community if there were NO law enforcement of any kind. What would that be like? Such a situation—zero attempts at crime prevention and no law enforcement—would

B A more detailed analysis or description of public goods would include a discussion of rivalrous qualities along with the concept of excludability.

undoubtedly lead to an unpleasant existence while yielding a crime rate that we label the "laissez-faire crime rate."[C D]

BUDGET CONSIDERATIONS

In regards to a crime budget, we must ask, "How much is enough?" In the case of our most graphic crime, criminal homicide, the nationwide rate has fallen tremendously from the peaks in the 1980s and 90s and has averaged fewer than six deaths per 100,000 population for more than 15 years. From 2010 to 2015 the murder rate was less than five.[2] Overall, crime in the U.S. is near an all-time low with any significant spikes limited to a few specific cities. For example, between 2015 and 2016, nearly one-half of the increase in national murders was attributed to Chicago alone. While Chicago may be seen as a true 'outlier,' other cities, such as Baltimore, Houston, San Antonio and St. Louis, have also seen violent crime upturns in recent periods.[3 E]

Looking at the latter two, 2015 data showed San Antonio with a violent crime rate approximately 60% above the national average. For St. Louis, the homicide rate was at 59 per 100K population for 2015 when the national average was under five![4] What should that mean in terms of budgeting? Well, a higher budget and more resources seem to be necessary for both cities. Assume that funding does increase and the rate drops close to the national average, what then? If St. Louis homicides are measured at five homicides per 100K people, is that now acceptable?

As mentioned in the footnotes of Chapter One, the idea of an "acceptable" crime rate is one that we probe on occasion. But regardless of the acceptability of this notion, we, no doubt, do put a value on life, our property, and overall well-being. As an exercise along these lines, I have suggested to classes through the years that I have a policy in mind that would conceivably drop automobile fatalities to near zero. But their initial interest quickly fades when I provide the outline, as it calls for the following:

- Highway speed limits are capped at 30 mph.

C "Laissez-Faire Crime Rate" as used by Hellman and Alper in *Economics of Crime*. The likely outcome expected from this condition would be a significant increase in overall crime rates.

D Consider for example, the situation in Nuevo Laredo, Mexico, and other communities in that country where police chiefs have been murdered and, in some cases, entire police forces driven out by drug related violence. While the military attempts stop-gap measures, many of these situations remain ominous.

E Violent crimes are defined in the UCR Program as those offenses which involve force or threat of force. Per the FBI's Uniform Crime Reporting (UCR) Program, violent crime includes four offenses: murder and nonnegligent manslaughter, forcible rape, robbery, and aggravated assault.

- Off-highway speed limits are dropped to 20 mph.
- All cars are fitted with technology that would restrict them from exceeding the above limits.
- Occupants of the vehicle would wear helmets. (Okay, maybe this step could be waived.)
- And, for good measure, we would install roll bars in all vehicles and attach a thin layer of rubber around the outside (picture something like bumper cars).

Hypothetically, we have done it—fatalities near zero.[F] Yet students quickly reject the plan and, after some moaning about "driving too slow," they convert the discussion into one dealing with the economic issues. They consider the overall transportation and opportunity costs, a likely slowing of the economy, and the possibility of economic downturn. Does it mean that students, or other rational thinkers, are not concerned about automobile fatalities? My guess is that the answer is no; i.e., students, faculty, and others do care about such things. However, as is the case with many laws and certainly budgets, we put a value on things (including a life) and address our choices on a rational basis with economic tools available to guide us.

MARGINAL BENEFIT AND MARGINAL COST

In terms of spending, jurisdictions at the local and state levels (and federal as well) are forced to make difficult decisions in regards to funding a variety of public sector services and obligations, including crime prevention. Dollars must be collected via some form—taxes, fines, or fees, and then allocated accordingly. For local and state budgets, funding could also come from federal grants, etc.[G] Our focus here is on the allocation of the various funds as we employ a model that revolves around marginal benefits, marginal costs, and decisions at the margin.

Start with a most common economic principle and statement—"We make decisions at the margin." The statement supports the idea that the

F These are simple parameters; however, we will insert the condition of *ceteris paribus* to deter those who would muse over some rare or bizarre movement of the vehicle and its occupants.

G Transferring federal dollars to fund local law enforcement is sometimes met with mixed opinion. Aside from concerns over waste and inefficient use of the funding, there are constitutional considerations over the possibility of federalizing local crime, etc. The potential for creating what could be called a "nationalized" police force is disturbing to some.

incremental changes in the benefits and costs (as opposed to total benefits and costs) are considered the most pertinent in determining an appropriate allocation of resources. As referenced earlier, for our purposes, the relevant incremental changes are the marginal benefits and marginal costs, which are defined below.

Marginal Benefits—a change in Total Benefits divided by a change in some Quantity.

$$MB = \frac{\Delta TB}{\Delta Q}$$

Marginal Costs—a change in Total Costs divided by a change in some Quantity.

$$MC = \frac{\Delta TC}{\Delta Q}$$

In most cases, the cost side of the equation is readily determinable. For example, in the case of a police officer, we can easily ascertain relevant expenditures—salary and benefits, equipment, other economic capital, training costs, etc. Quantifying the benefit side is more challenging. This involves an attempt at determining how much better off society becomes when criminal acts are prevented. (See Chapter 2 by Mark Cohen, which provides some depth on this topic.)

Ultimately, it will be helpful to have some idea of the number of crimes being committed annually by criminals. In this area, there are many estimates, ranging from 180 per criminal on the high side, down to single digits. Truly the research and accompanying data vary significantly. However, we will avoid too much "fence straddling" on the topic and move forward with a couple of educated judgments. First data suggests that criminals do not commit crimes proportionately. That is, a small number of criminals likely commit a large number of the measured offenses. For example, a community that reports 100 criminal acts with 10 known offenders can be reasonably sure that each criminal did not commit exactly 10 offenses. Some criminals will be "busier" than others. The second observation is that research on crimes committed would seem to suggest a reliable estimate, on average, in the 8–12 range.[5]

So assuming that with some degree of satisfaction the costs and benefits can be quantified, a simple MB–MC analysis is presented in Table 1 on next page.

TABLE 1. COSTS AND BENEFITS OF CRIME PREVENTION—BUDGET ALLOCATION

(1)	(2)	(3)	(4)	(5)	(6)
Crime Prevention Units	Total Benefits	Marginal Benefits	Total Costs	Marginal Costs	Total Net Benefits
1	$ 250	$ 250	$ 75	$ 75	$ 175
2	475	225	150	75	325
3	675	200	225	75	450
4	850	175	300	75	550
5	1,000	150	375	75	625
6	1,125	125	450	75	675
7	1,225	100	525	75	700
8	1,300	75	600	75	700
9	1,350	50	675	75	675
10	1,375	25	750	75	625

A COUPLE OF ASSUMPTIONS IN REGARDS TO TABLE 1

1. "Crime Prevention Units" is an undefined concept.[6] Conceivably, it could consist of any number of expenditures; for example, a policeman, his patrol car, and perhaps expenses related to the jail. The most relevant proposition here is that the measurement is consistent; i.e., there is no difference in the composition of the first unit and the composition of the second.
2. For this example, we will simplify things and consider MC to be constant at $75,000. In reality the MC curve would be slightly U-shaped with a long upward slope reflecting increasing marginal costs over time.[H]
3. Total Net Benefits = Total Benefits – Total Costs

So let us take these and portray graphically the important components of MB and MC. Graph #1 is a more typical depiction of MB and MC. Graph #2 reflects the data from Table 1. Since we are holding MC constant, the MC line is horizontal in this graph. Once again, this is a simplifying assumption and does not reflect a typical MC curve. The MB curve slopes downward, reflecting a decrease in the MB provided by each additional unit. This negative slope and the accompanying relationship are known in economics as the **law of diminishing marginal returns.** The term describes, *ceteris paribus,* an empirical generalization

H Or as an engineering colleague noted, the general MC curve resembles a smoothly curved right-handed "check-mark" that slopes up and away from the origin.

about the resulting output provided by an increase in variable inputs.[7] That is, when all other inputs are held constant, an incremental increase of an input (in this case, more crime prevention units) will result in decreasing marginal output.

For example, consider a decision to assign police officers to a high school basketball game. Depending on the size of the crowd and assuming there is no harsh or bitter history between the teams, two officers might be sufficient. Would a third or fourth officer increase event safety? Likely they would; however, we would expect the marginal benefit of the third, fourth, fifth, sixth officer, etc., to decline accordingly. So in both this example and the data presented in Table 1, we would say that Total Benefits are increasing, but at a decreasing rate.

Graph 1. Typical MB and MC

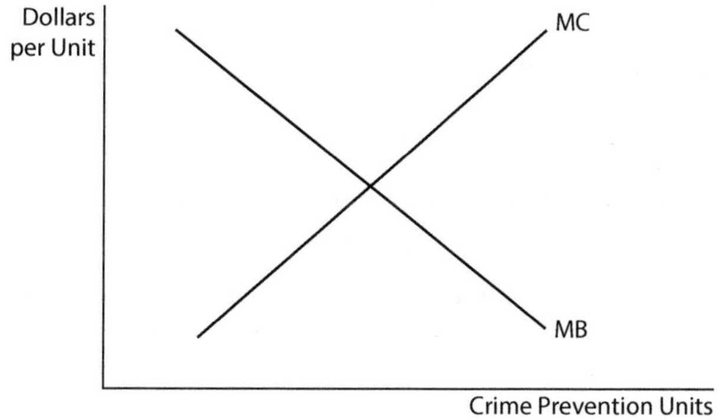

Graph 2. Table 1 Data

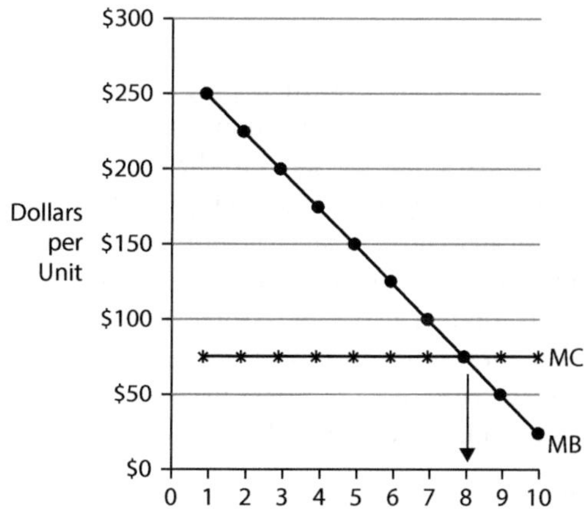

However, the key question remains: **What is the proper employment of crime prevention units and why?**

Graph #2 gives us the answer with the intersection of MB and MC at 8 units. Accordingly, **our overall goal is to employ crime prevention units up to the point where MB = MC.** This rule is analogous to the profit maximization formula, which suggests production of output up to the point where Marginal Revenue equals Marginal Cost (MR = MC). For Table 1, the 8th unit provides both MB and MC of $75,000. Aside from MB being equal to MC at this point, we can additionally determine that Total Net Benefit (TNB) is maximized as well. Graphically we can easily see the relationships in place. In the area to the left of the intersection, MB > MC. In the area to the right of the 8th unit, MB < MC.

A COUPLE OF RELEVANT QUESTIONS

> **Wouldn't we decrease crime further by employing the 9th unit?**
> Yes, most definitely. However, the marginal cost of $75K exceeds the MB of $25K and is therefore deemed to be inefficient.

Wouldn't we reduce costs by employing seven units rather than eight? (After all, costs would be less, and TNB would still be maximized.)

> While costs would be less, crime would actually be higher. Remember, the 8th unit is said to provide $75K of benefits—meaning reduced crime. The second part of the answer is simply to remember our goal is to employ up to the point where MB = MC.

AN INTANGIBLE SIDE TO THE MARGINAL COSTS OF CRIME

In regards to MC, there are three additional observations made from an intangible perspective that also suggest an upward-sloping curve. These include increasing opportunity costs, a restriction on freedoms, and the concept of a gifted or talented criminal.[I] The first point is related to the opportunity costs involved as jurisdictions make decisions regarding their budgets. Public sector expenditures are made to a variety of areas other than law enforcement, such as fire protection, roads and highways, parks, etc. As a crime problem worsens and more dollars need to be shifted into criminal justice, or to some other department, the decision to move dollars out of these other areas becomes more challenging. And, from an opportunity-cost perspective, these transfers become more expensive. Consider your own budget as a student. Assume a decrease on the income side of $20 per

I The concept of opportunity cost, freedoms, and a gifted criminal, as used for this topic, are synthesized from the works of other authors.

month. Where would you cut? Most likely not a difficult decision—perhaps we scratch the once-a-month movie night and the online charge for Xbox. (On second thought, maybe we'll keep the Xbox charge and scratch a couple of Starbucks trips instead.) Now what if the drop in income is $250 per month? The decisions just became harder, and the opportunity costs increased accordingly.

Early in the book we discussed at length the manner in which crime impacts our individual freedoms. Simply stated, an increase in unlawful or delinquent behavior results in a variety of changes, which impacts our liberty. Consider the steps we now go through at airports—clumsy pat-downs, intense searches, removal of shoes, greater limitations on what can be carried onto an airplane (please, no fingernail cutters), etc.—each of these imposes a type of restriction on various freedoms. As another example, increases in juvenile crime in specific cities sometimes result in calls to establish an age-restricted curfew—another restriction on freedoms.[J] Of course, this is <u>not</u> to say that there is zero merit to any of these policies, but rather an attempt to point out the impact of certain criminal behaviors and their overall costs.

A third point revolves around the concept that criminals are not created equal. That is, while some lawbreakers may be easily captured or discovered, there are others who present a bigger challenge for authorities. This may be due to the sophistication of the crime and/or the individual, or perhaps some other qualities or talents. Therefore, the corresponding cost to apprehend these individuals may become marginally higher. When hearing about a "sophisticated" criminal, one may conjure thoughts of the complex and princely "cat burglar" projected in various movies. However, a more realistic and recent matter would be the Bernie Madoff white-collar scenario where his Ponzi scheme escaped investigators for years—by some estimates as much as 40 years, or the almost 18-year hunt for the "Unabomber," to name two.[K]

ALLOCATING WITHIN THE BUDGET—THE EQUIMARGINAL PRINCIPLE AND ECONOMIC EFFICIENCY

Taking a deeper look into the budgetary process, we can apply the **equimarginal principle** to better explain the allocation between various facets or departments within an overall budget. This principle is defined as a condition where the last dollar spent on one facet of the budget provides the same benefit as the last dollar spent on another facet of the budget.[8]

J The removal of shoes, courtesy of failed British shoe bomber Richard Reid in 2001, is a classic example of the increased costs. Levitt and Dubner quantify this requirement in SuperFreakonomics.

K Per the Security and Exchange commission, a "Ponzi" scheme is defined an investment fraud that involves the payment of purported returns to existing investors from funds contributed by new investors. Ponzi scheme organizers often solicit new investors by promising to invest funds in opportunities claimed to generate high returns with little or no risk.

As an equation, the definition above, with two budget areas, would appear as follows:

$$\frac{MB1}{MC1} = \frac{MB2}{MC2}$$

Allocations could be made based on distinct crimes; i.e., Crime 1 and Crime 2, or, for example, in the case of a prison, the allotment might be made based on Equipment (e) and Personnel (p) as below:

$$\frac{MBe}{MCe} = \frac{MBp}{MCp}$$

GRAPHING THE EQUIMARGINAL PRINCIPLE

At any rate, the overall goal is an efficient allocation of both funds and resources. However, getting there represents a challenge as the point of efficiency inevitably shifts based on marginal changes in costs and benefits. So consider a hypothetical scenario where we distribute funds based on preventing two types of crimes as noted above—Crime 1 and Crime 2. This situation is presented in Graph #3. In this diagram we assume that the allocation of resources in the prevention of each of these crimes is analogous to methodology used for a simple Production Possibilities Curve (PPC).[L] Therefore, based on existing technology and resources, and in conjunction with a stated budget, the possibilities of preventing each crime are presented by the concave PPC curve. Deriving the slope of the PPC curve involves some understanding of the respective Costs for each type of crime.

For that part of the equation that deals with Benefits, we will use an Iso-Curve to display alternatives for production based on the benefits derived from preventing each crime. We will adapt and label this curve as an Iso-Benefit curve.[M] As part of the isoquant family, the iso-benefit curve will display characteristics similar to the indifference curve; these characteristics are enumerated on the following page.

L Some authors label this particular PPC as a Product Transformation Curve.

M This is an extension of the explanation provided by Hellman and Alper in *Economics of Crime*, p. 117.

Graph 3. Graphing the Equimarginal Principle

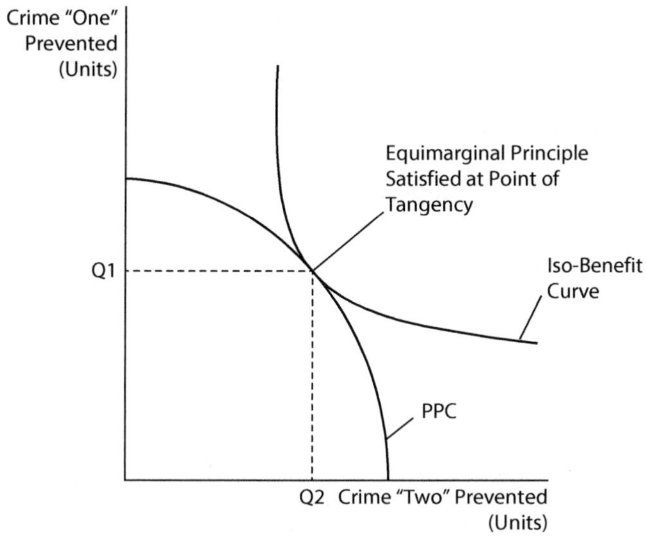

So what is being represented by each particular curve? Again, the PPC curve is plotting the quantities (or units) of each crime prevented based on a stated cost or expenditure. For example, assume we have a budget of $40,000. Holding resources and technology fixed, this budget and the accompanying resources and technology will prevent certain numbers of Crime 1 and Crime 2. The plotting of these numbers results in the PPC curve. The iso-benefit curve displays a specific amount of benefit we derive from preventing each crime. For example, the iso-benefit curve shown in Graph 3 might be based on Total Benefits of $50,000. Therefore, each point on the curve is presenting some combination of the two crimes prevented, which together, are providing $50,000 of total benefits.

ISO-BENEFIT (ISOQUANT) V. INDIFFERENCE CURVE

In comparing these two analytical tools, the four basic characteristics of each curve are essentially the same as noted below:

1. The curve will generally slope downward, denoting positive marginal benefits of each option.
2. The northeast curves indicate greater productivity, in that marginal benefits are increased.

3. The two curves cannot intersect.
4. The curve will generally be convex to the origin.

However, the measurements displayed are quite different. Where the indifference curve presents a "ranking" to assist with utility-maximization, the iso-benefit curve offers a display of production. That is, indifference curves offer ordinal measurement, and our iso-benefit curve will represent a cardinal type of measurement.

For Graph #3, we only display the iso-benefit curve, which is tangent to the PPC.[N] The slope of the curves at this point is noted below:

$$-\frac{MC2}{MC1} = -\frac{MB2}{MB1}$$

At the point of tangency between the PPC and the Iso-Benefit curve, we find that the equimarginal principle is satisfied. Mathematically, we could rewrite the above equation to convert back to the initial formula.

$$\frac{MB1}{MC1} = \frac{MB2}{MC2}$$

In summary, our simplified budget goal is to employ units of crime prevention up to the point where MB = MC. We can expand on this by using the equimarginal principle as we seek economic efficiency and a situation approaching Pareto Optimality.[O]

N As with an Indifference map, there would be additional Iso-Benefit curves lying northeast and southwest as part of a graphical presentation. However, we have included only the relevant curve, which is tangent to the PPC.

O Simply explained, a Pareto Optimal condition occurs, and our resources are allocated efficiently, when we cannot make a person better off without making another person worse off.

PRACTICE QUESTIONS

(Answers to #1 and #2 are found in the back of the text)

1. Fill in the table below and determine the most efficient number of crime prevention units based on MB = MC.

Crime Prevention Units	Total Benefits	Marginal Benefits	Total Costs	Marginal Costs	Total Net Benefits
1	30,000			8,000	
2		25,000		10,500	
3	75,000				44,000
4		15,000	46,000		
5	102,000		66,000		
6				22,000	19,000
7	110,000		116,000		

2. Use the equimarginal principle to determine the appropriate quantity of guards, surveillance equipment, and psychologists to employ based on the information below. As a hint—think about the equation for this scenario and remember MB/MC must be the same for all facets of the budget.

   The research staff of a local police department provides their chief with the following information concerning the benefits from employing various numbers of the following: Police, SWAT Equipment, Patrol Cars.

Marginal Benefits from Crime Prevention Services Provided			
Units	Police	SWAT Eqp	Patrol Cars
1	$70,000	$60,000	$64,000
2	60,000	45,000	56,000
3	50,000	30,000	48,000
4	40,000	15,000	40,000
5	30,000	12,000	32,000
6	20,000	10,000	24,000
7	10,000	5,000	16,000
8	5,000	2,500	8,000

The cost of each policeman is $10,000; the cost of each unit of SWAT equipment is $5,000; and the cost of each patrol car is $8,000. The budget is $118,000.

How many units of each should be employed?
Police ________
SWAT Equipment ______
Patrol Car(s) ______

3. What is the difference between the Iso-Benefit (Isoquant) curve and an Indifference curve?
4. Why does the typical MB curve slope downward?
5. What is a "laissez-faire" crime rate?

ENDNOTES

1. Browning, Edgar K. and Jacquelene Browning. (1989). *Microeconomic Theory and Applications*, 3rd Ed. Glenview, IL: Scott, Foresman and Company. p. 149.
2. https://ucr.fbi.gov/crime-in-the-u.s/2015/crime-in-the-u.s.-2015/tables/table-1. Accessed 2017 Sept 4.
3. https://www.brennancenter.org/sites/default/files/publications/Crime_2016_Preliminary_Analysis.pdf. Accessed 2017 Sept 4.
4. https://ucr.fbi.gov/crime-in-the-u.s/2015/crime-in-the-u.s.-2015/tables/table-8. Accessed 2017 Sept 4.
5. Freeman, Richard. (1996). "Why Do So Many Young American Men Commit Crimes and What Might We Do About It?" *The Journal of Economic Perspectives.* Vol 10. No 1 (Winter 1996) p. 28.
6. Sharp, Ansel M., Charles A. Register, and Paul W. Grimes. (2013). *Economics of Social Issues.* New York: McGraw-Hill.
7. Browning, Edgar K. and Mark A. Zupan. 1999. *Microeconomic Theory & Applications*, 6th Ed. Addison-Wesley. p. 149.
8. Sharp 132.

SECTION 3

CHAPTER 10

AN ECONOMIC DISCUSSION ABOUT ILLEGAL DRUGS AND THEIR MARKETS

"WHAT WERE ONCE VICES ARE NOW HABITS"

By Ron Liggett

"What Were Once Vices Are Now Habits" is the title of a 1974 album released by the rock-n-roll group known as The Doobie Brothers.[A] And, having personally spent a little time in the 1970's, the title seemed appropriate to include at the top of a chapter dealing with illegal drug markets. What could be more suitable in the discussion than vices, habits, and doobies? So while I am completely aware that most college students today have never listened to The Doobie Brothers' music, my instincts (and a bit of research) tell me that approximately 60% will have a firsthand idea what a "doobie" is. For the other 40% (or less), I can tell you that the doobie, a slang term for a marijuana cigarette, was a drug of choice in the 70s and most obviously remains popular in today's "organically" driven market.

In the few years since this book was first published the markets have made major adjustments and there has been a tidal wave of voting activity at the state level to legalize both the medicinal and recreation use of marijuana. Think about it: five years ago, recreational marijuana wasn't legal anywhere in the U.S! But today, there are eight states, along with Washington D.C., which have given the O.K. for recreation use and 28 states which have legalized its medical use for certain conditions.[1] With so many states having given a "green light" to the product, it is not surprising to see that legal pot sales hit $6.6 billion in 2016.[2] While the bulk of this is currently from the medicinal side, the sales number could triple by 2020 with the overall growth (including recreational use) in this industry being described as the "Green Rush." In fact, a California startup with the same name is one of several entities that is now "providing a legal weed-delivery service" for

A Not only did the "doobie" evolve into a drug of choice, it also undoubtedly influenced the name of this rock-n-roll band which is still performing more than 45 years after their start. And, for those so inclined, I might suggest "Another Park, Another Sunday" or "Black Water" from this particular album.

medicinal purposes.[3] (Will Amazon delivery be far behind?) Certainly, what were once vices ARE now habits in many settings.[B]

The markets are also adjusting in the hard core drug world where there is increasing competition from something inorganic and perilous—methamphetamine.[C]

> "The way investigators tell it, accused drug trafficker Javier Madrigal convinced a deputy who pulled him over a few weeks ago that the reddish, coagulated liquid in his truck's extra fuel tank was bad diesel from Mexico. The deputy had never seen anything like it and let Madrigal go. But as Madrigal barreled away, the supposed fuel that had splashed on the deputy's pants began to crystallize, according to court papers. The lawman had been played by the latest trick in the smugglers' handbook. The "bad diesel" was a liquefied batch of wildly popular methamphetamine, easily worth more than $1 million. And it was rolling away toward Houston, America's fourth-largest city."[4]

Who would have thought that we would see methamphetamine (meth) being explained as bad diesel fuel? When I read the paragraph above, I was nearly certain I had stumbled across part of a script from the critically acclaimed TV series *Breaking Bad*. The series chronicles the saga of Walter White, a fictional high school chemistry teacher who, after learning he has cancer, "breaks bad" to become the Southwest's major meth cook while partnering with one of his ex-students, Jesse Pinkman. And why would a respectable teacher make such a ruinous decision? For Mr. White, it is the hope of accumulating funds to leave behind for his family after the cancer has its way with his body. Undeniably he chooses a marketable product that, in today's real world, can bring a street price of more than $10,000 per pound.[D] But pricing and marketing this type of product presents quite a few challenges, as Walt and Jesse eventually find out.

> Walt: "Last time I checked, there was 16 ounces to a pound. What'd you do with the rest, smoke it?"
> Jesse: "Yo I been out there all night slangin' crystal. You think it's cake movin' a pound of meth one 'teenth at a time?"
> Walt: "So why you selling it in such small quantities? Why don't you just sell the whole pound at once?"

B It is quite important to note that Federal law has not followed the 'legalized' path of many states. In regards to how this divergence may play out, I would simply say, "stay tuned."

C Perilous may be an understatement. Vice cops tell horror stories of what meth does to the body. There are few "long-term" meth users—their body doesn't survive.

D Street price varies greatly depending mainly on purity; also on the region of the country in which it is sold. A price of $8,000 might be garnered on the lower end, or up to $50,000 on the high end.

Jesse: "To who? What do I look like? 'Scarface'?"
Walt: "This is unacceptable. I am breaking the law here. This return is too little for the risk. I thought you'd be ready for another pound today."
Jesse: "You may know a lot about chemistry man, but you don't know jack about slangin' dope."[5]

Walt and Jesse weave a fairly tangled web as fictional drug dealers; however, their antics do offer us a starting point for a look into the world of vices.[E] Realistically the economics of the drug world (and other vices) cannot be covered comprehensively in a few pages of text, so we will limit our discussion to an overview of economic theory as it pertains to the illegal narcotics trade. Specifically we will focus on the major street drugs, although there is a clear understanding that illicit drug activity stretches beyond marijuana, cocaine, crack, heroin, and meth.

In fact, while the legalization of marijuana has countless and interesting front page stories, and the meth market has been chronicled in a hit TV series, there is perhaps an even gloomier side to U.S. drug habits. According to the National Institute on Drug Abuse (NIDA), the country now finds itself facing a "public health crisis" due to opioid abuse and addiction.[F] More recently, in October 2017, President Donald Trump took this a step further by declaring, "This epidemic is a national health emergency."[6][G] Amazingly, statistics show that more than 90 Americans are dying each day due to an overdose on opioids.[7] The abuse has become more deadly due to the presence of fentanyl which is available legally and illegally in the black market.[H] This synthetic drug is estimated to be 50 times stronger than pure heroin (100 times stronger than morphine) and is blamed for a 73% increase in the opioid overdose death rate between 2014 and 2015.[8]

E Vice is our common term for behavior deemed as immoral or degrading, or simply a bad habit. It is taken from the Latin word *vitium*, meaning "defect or failing." Police who handle issues involving narcotics, prostitution, and gambling, etc., are called "Vice Cops." However, in some jurisdictions, the illegal drug trade is so substantial that a separate narcotics division exists.

F Per the NIDA, "opioids are a class of drugs that include the illegal drug heroin, synthetic opioids such as fentanyl, and pain relievers available legally by prescription, such as oxycodone, hydrocodone, codeine, morphine, and many others."

G Technically, such a declaration only lasts 90 days, but it can be renewed and should bring more funds and more public support into this battle which continues to plague the U.S.

H While fentanyl does have medicinal uses, the drug is truly dangerous and was blamed in the death of rock star Prince in 2016. Experts note that a dose that is medically helpful for one individual could, in fact, be deadly for another.

OPIOIDS AND THE WORKPLACE

Any type of chronic addiction has an economic effect in terms of impairing a portion of the labor supply. And, while all age groups have been hit by the opioid crisis, two 'older' segments in the population have been impacted particularly hard. The largest *increase* in opioid deaths is actually in adults aged 55–64. However, the 45–54 aged group has the highest overall rate for fatal overdoses.[9] It is apparent that sadly, the addiction to opioids has served to disrupt the prime earning period for these two age groups and has no doubt disrupted both individuals AND their families. From a macroeconomic perspective, Federal Reserve chairperson Janet Yellen has also referenced this problem in noting the negative impact these groups are having on the labor force participation rate.[10]

So, essentially what may begin as a legal opioid-type prescription for pain relief, can quickly turn into something direr when an addiction develops. If a disability situation follows, the economy is obviously impacted by both the social cost and the lost productivity that ensues.

There are many economic principles at work in every market, but a study of the illegal drug trade is particularly abundant with some standard economic applications. For example:

Willing Buyer–Willing Seller
Profits—Economic or Normal
Capital Flowing to Highest Use
The Concept of a Cartel
Price Elasticity as it Pertains to Addicts vs. the Social Users
Non-Price Determinants—Impact of Increased Enforcement
Price Elasticity of Supply
Legalize—Yes or No (If yes, then which drugs?)
Price Discrimination—New Users vs. Older (Experienced) Users

Let us start by addressing the first two items on the list. These two principles are foundationally important for an understanding of both participant behavior (buyers and sellers) and the enforcement issues faced by authorities. We will follow these with analysis of some of the other items on the list.

WILLING BUYER–WILLING SELLER

The first principle involves the concept of willing buyer–willing seller where participants are involved (at least perceptually) in what they see as a mutually beneficial exchange and utility-maximizing behavior. The buyer in this case could be an infrequent "social" user (termed "dabbler" in the work by Hellman and Alper) or, at the other end of the spectrum, an "addict" who is driven to consume

Demand Curve—Social Drug User (Elastic)

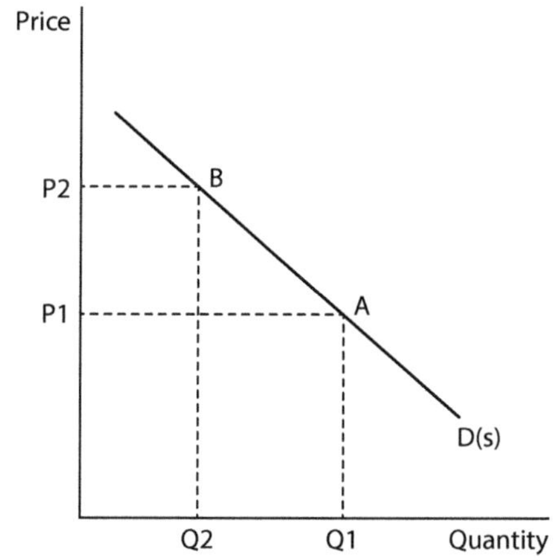

Graph 1

by physical dependence or other obsession.[I] Using simple Law of Demand analysis, we can see how this appears graphically and the differences that exist for each user in regards to the price elasticity of demand (See Graphs 1 and 2). For the social user, we see a more **elastic** relationship, while the addict faces an **inelastic** demand curve.[J] In presenting these graphs, we mathematically conclude the steeper slope of the addicts' inelastic curve. Additionally, if we assume some proportional relationship among the two axes we can postulate the idea that an inelastic curve will generally display a steep slope.

In the two graphs above, Point A denotes an initial equilibrium. Point B displays the price and equilibrium changes that occur from increased prohibition measures. (Note: the change from Q1 to Q2 is not necessarily proportional between the two graphs; i.e., we are not suggesting that percentage change in Quantity for the Social User will be substantially higher than for the addict.)

I Each individual in this discussion is motivated in some way to consume. So while we could debate whether or not the *addict* remains a *willing* buyer, the point to emphasize is that a market exists for him/her in which goods (or services in the case of prostitution) can be purchased. In essence, the consumers in this vice are still acting in their own self-interest.

J The concept of addictive behavior is frequently presented as the "textbook" example for a perfectly inelastic demand curve, which is vertical with an undefined slope.

Demand Curve—Addicted Drug User (Inelastic)

Graph 2

As a review, price elasticity of demand (∈ *d*), is defined as measurement of the percentage change in quantity demanded relative to the percentage change in price. With the corresponding inverse relationship between price and quantity demanded, as described with the law of demand, the elasticity measurement in this case will always be negative.[K]

Using absolute values, when the percentage change in demand divided by the percentage change in price is greater than one, the relationship is deemed elastic. When this relationship is less than one, we use the term inelastic. The basic formula is noted below, where Δ denotes "change."[L]

From the enforcement side, willing buyer–willing seller brings together two actors who are willing accomplices, so, in essence, there is no "victim" to report the violation to the authorities. In fact, an argument is frequently made that drug use is a victimless crime. Let us put that argument aside for the time being and simply note the added enforcement challenges that exist in this scenario. Police depend on victim reports and other communications to aid in apprehending criminals; the willing buyer–willing seller relationship deters or eliminates this

K The concept of Elasticity is widely used in many facets of economics and in several areas of this text where we are essentially measuring sensitivity to a change in a specific variable. As a non-price example, we will consider later the % Change in Crime based on some % Change in the Number of Police. (See Appendix)

L This is a simple elasticity measurement. In measuring price elasticities, we would typically use the mid-point formula, which for both denominators uses an average, i.e., (Q1 + Q2)/2.

chain of communiqué. The result, at least to some, is that law enforcement must therefore push the privacy envelope through various means such as undercover operations, "stings," and other tactics that may impact personal liberties.

ECONOMIC PROFITS

The second principle presents the idea that sellers in this market are driven by an urge for profits, not unlike any other businessperson. The costs faced by the seller may differ in some respects from those faced in legitimate entities, but they still represent expenses that need to be covered by revenues. As enforcement pressures increase, the costs faced by dealers/suppliers rise, and therefore the dynamic of the business model changes. In regards to profits, from an economic perspective we deal with two types—Normal and Economic. **Normal profits** result when revenues cover all explicit costs as well as the implicit costs, such as what an owner could have received from the next-best alternative employment of his resources. Simply stated, the owner is covering costs and is compensated for his time. **Economic profits** occur when there are earnings that are above and beyond any normal profits. These profits encourage growth and therefore generally result in an expanding industry. While it is likely impossible to determine exact profits in these illegal drug markets, we know from government reports that overall drug availability in the U.S. is increasing.[11] More specifically, abuse of the major illicit drugs (heroin, marijuana, and methamphetamine) appears to be increasing, most especially among the younger groups.[12] Accordingly, we would propose that economic profits are being earned to some degree at some level of the operating chain.[M]

MEXICAN DRUG FLOWS—ARE THEY REALLY CARTELS?

The dispute regarding movement across the southern border extends beyond human flows and human trafficking. According to the Department of Justice (DOJ), the greatest drug trafficking threat to the U.S. today is from drug organizations based in Mexico.[N] "They control most of the U.S. drug market and have established varied transportation routes, advanced communication capabilities, and strong affiliations with gangs in the U.S."[13] Additionally, they have set up activities in more than 230 U.S. cities. To obtain a better understanding of the impact of the drug flows coming north, please see the chart and maps located at the end of the book.

M An argument could be made that suppliers in the illegal trade are, to some degree, pursuing economic "rents" as opposed to "profits." For the time being, we will consider that debate to be a matter of semantics and one to be addressed at another time.

N Adding to this issue are reports of guns and weapons being shipped illegally <u>from</u> the U.S. <u>into</u> Mexico.

One of the most common terms used when discussing illegal drug markets is that of "drug cartel." In regards to suppliers from Mexico, we frequently hear reports that note involvement of the Sinaloa Cartel, Zeta Cartel, Gulf Cartel, Tijuana Cartel, and others. However, in a strict economic discussion, the organizations described in news reports are not actually functioning as cartels. Consider the textbook definition of a **cartel**—a group of independent producers and suppliers who coordinate pricing and output decisions in order to maximize profits.[O] Accordingly, the most defining component of such an organization is that of collusion where separate and distinct groups work together to fix prices. Based on the amount of violence currently experienced south of the border, we can be relatively sure that little collusion is taking place. Of course, in the U.S., such collusion is deemed illegal and private firms attempting to establish a cartel would be subject to antitrust laws, most likely as a violation of the Sherman Act.[14] Globally there is no restriction and collusive arrangements may occur with the most obvious example of a functioning cartel being the Organization of Petroleum Exporting Countries, or OPEC.[P]

As referenced in other chapters, violence across the border has been both constant and devastating, with various reports suggesting approximately 10,000 people killed in each of the last six years due to drug violence.[15] Additionally, as we noted, Mexico is the leading foreign supplier of both marijuana and meth and the country's role as a transshiper of Columbian cocaine is established as well. However, some reports suggest that fentanyl is now the "drug of choice" in this group. Where China was originally a main source of fentanyl, data now suggests that the Mexican drug groups have exploited the economics of the product by building their own labs.[16] In regards to shipping and product movement, not only is fentanyl more difficult to detect, but with the drug being exponentially stronger than heroin, the shipment quantities can be reduced. As stated earlier, markets adjust—even markets for the economic "bads."

Looking at the situation in Mexico, the individual drug groups definitely have the ability to mobilize production capabilities as their capital finds its highest return—in this case, fentanyl labs. But, the concept of collusion among these groups appears to still be one that is more foreign. So while the term might have made sense in Mexico in the 1970s when the individual groups were displaying some form of coordinated behavior, the current fragmentation[Q] of this organization has essentially ended any concept of a cartel—at least for now.[17]

O "Maximizing profits" is sometimes described as "earning monopoly profits."

P OPEC is composed of sovereign nations and therefore (most obviously) not subject to U.S. law.

Q The "fragmentation" began to occur in 1989 after the arrest of leading drug organizer Miguel Angel Felix Gallardo.

In regards to terminology, a more accurate, though less glamorous label for the groups listed earlier (Sinaloa, Zeta, Gulf, etc.) would be Drug Trafficking Organizations (DTOs), a term used in U.S. governmental circles. As defined by the Department of Justice (DOJ), a DTO refers to a complex organization with highly defined command-and-control structures that produces, transports, and/or distributes large quantities of one or more illicit drugs.[18]

AN ADDITIONAL LOOK AT PROFITS, INCREASED ENFORCEMENT, AND THE COST SIDE

Again, monitoring profits is challenging for the most part because so much of the drug trade is transacted in cash. However, when we assemble various data sources, observe lavish lifestyles by so-called drug lords, and the attempts to invest drug proceeds in a variety of ventures, the existence of economic profits becomes more obvious.[R] Accordingly, we will propose that economic profits at higher levels of the drug chain do exist, and therefore suggest that attempts by drug lords to expand their own market share will continue (e.g., trying to pass off meth as diesel fuel).

But do these profits trickle down to the lower levels of the distribution process? Likely not. In *Freakonomics*, Levitt and Dubner offer details to support this fact with a chapter entitled, "Why Do Drug Dealers Still Live with Their Moms?" In this chapter, they chronicle data obtained from Chicago street gangs by researcher Sudhir Venkatesh that clearly shows that lower-level drug distributors (primarily crack dealers in this study) were, in some cases, paid wages at or below minimum wage.[19] Such results seem to complement other studies that have found that dealers at lower levels frequently work part-time in the illegal trade, and must still continue in their legal occupations in order to cover basic living expenses.[20]

From the same study, Levitt et al. noted higher wages as one moved up the distribution chain. They specifically noted that "... a crack gang works pretty much like the standard capitalist enterprise: you have to be near the top of the pyramid to make a big wage," adding, "the gang's wages are about as skewed as wages in corporate America."[21]

High prices for the drugs are primarily triggered, of course, by the illegality of the product and the corresponding enforcement pressures from the authorities. Mix in the additional costs created by the potential for violence—on a daily basis—and one understands the inflated price in the market. However, evading

R Soccer clubs in Columbia have been tainted for years with charges that they are fronts for drug lords and are used for money laundering. Additionally, in June of 2012, a horse racing operation in Oklahoma was raided with charges that the Zetas drug group was funding and using the operation for laundering.

apprehension may mean more than just avoiding time behind bars. Researchers note that when law enforcement increases punishments, those who are able to avoid apprehension benefit from higher prices as the added revenues exceed the increase in unit costs brought on by more punishment.[22] Essentially, the culling of traffickers leaves behind greater wealth opportunities for the remaining suppliers.

CHALLENGES ON THE COST SIDE

Drug suppliers are part of an environment that is both fluid and dynamic from the cost side. And, as with a lawful business operation, rising input prices and other costs result in a leftward shift of the supply curve, and a reduction in consumption. Accordingly, for the supplier, there are significant challenges in the area of costs. Using simple Supply/Demand analysis, Graph #3 displays the impact of higher costs—whether explicit or implicit.

An obvious cost, and one not to be overlooked, is that those participating in unlawful acts are not able to use the court system or legitimate law enforcement measures in issues of contract enforcement. Therefore, the issues must be dealt with in another manner—typically with violence—that may require employment of additional resources, perhaps even mercenaries.[23]

In addition, carrying out the normal process of production, transportation, and distribution brings its own set of costs as the supplier is forced to seek paths of least resistance in regards to the shipping of product. This would suggest longer and slower product movement as suppliers opt for routes and processes that are not easily nor readily monitored by the government.[24] For drugs coming from Mexico, these so-called paths have included a variety of tunnels of varying sizes. Most of these tunnels are the result of a significant investment in man hours and additional capital outlays. For example, in 2006 authorities discovered a tunnel running from a warehouse in Tijuana, Mexico, to another warehouse in the Otay Mesa neighborhood of San Diego, California. The concrete tunnel ran a distance of 1,148 meters (picture 12 football fields!) and included lighting, electricity, and ventilation.[25][S] This tunnel was specifically identified due to its length; other shorter tunnels are discovered on a regular basis.[T]

S A couple of questions come to mind—"Did anyone notice the digging activity that removed approximately 90 dump truck loads of dirt?" I assume they didn't, so question two, "When digging a tunnel, what exactly is the pay scale for someone in authority to look the other way?" Operating costs seem to be everywhere.

T Once discovered, authorities must deal with the tunnels and close them down with concrete or by some other method. This can be expensive, perhaps costing $1 million or more.

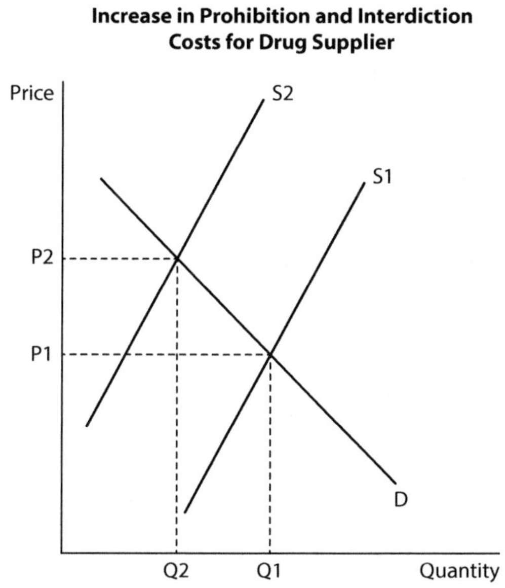

Graph #3

WHAT ABOUT A WALL?

No matter where one stands on the topic, the reality is that a structure would increase the costs incurred to cross and/or smuggle product across the border. Of course, as repeated frequently in this textbook, "markets adjust" and DTO's would certainly look for other options—much as they do now. Whether that means more tunnels or more tainted diesel fuel, it remains to be seen. A more detailed discussion of an enhanced border wall is found in Chapter 8.

Another cost example for distributors includes payoffs to law enforcement officials that are made to help facilitate border crossings. Consider the case of a U.S. Border Patrol agent (name has been withheld by authorities) now behind bars, who was paid to "shepherd" selected vehicles loaded with drugs across the border. According to prosecutors, the pay was lucrative, bringing $4,000 per car, $6,000 for a van, and a $10,000 retainer fee.[26]

Finally, we will close out our brief list of costs by referring again to interdiction and prosecution efforts. As authorities increase investment in these areas, more resources are required by drug suppliers to abate the efforts. Interestingly, Becker and other researchers have noted a difference in the amount of resources spent by traffickers to bring the drugs to market depending on the price elasticity of demand for the drugs.[27] The equation appears below where:

ΔR = Change in Resources Spent by Traffickers

ϵ = Price Elasticity of Demand

ΔC = The Increase in Costs from Interdiction and Prosecution Efforts

$$\Delta R = (1 + \epsilon)\Delta C$$

Therefore, when ϵ is elastic (and < -1), an increase in enforcement efforts will result in fewer resources expended by drug traffickers. In contrast, when ϵ is inelastic (and > -1), the increase in enforcement brings more resources from the traffickers as they attempt to get their product to specific buyers. Translation—there undoubtedly appears to be recognition of the increased profits accruing from consumers with an inelastic demand, i.e., addicts, etc.[28]

OUR DRUG POLICY TODAY AND TALKS OF LEGALIZATION

Frequently I begin lectures on the topic of drugs by asking, "What is prohibition?" The usual response involves some mention of alcohol prohibition. Of course we do use the term "Prohibition" as a simple reference to the period 1920–1933 when alcohol use in the U.S. was turned upside down, and the manufacture, sale, and transportation of the beverage became illegal. Today our basic policy regarding certain illicit drugs is also one of prohibition and so the comparison of this policy with the period of alcohol prohibition is common. Typically the inquiry begins like this, "Alcohol prohibition didn't work; why would we expect drug prohibition to work?" Good question.

The debate over drug legalization may be one of the most frequently discussed topics in the U.S.; however, we will not attempt to settle that argument in this section.[U] Certainly the lure of legalization is strong since it would theoretically allow for the collection of tax revenues while lowering enforcement, prosecution, and incarceration costs. We would still suggest however that many who propose to be in favor of legalizing drugs are actually more likely to support a decriminalization policy once they understand the specific difference. While legalizing drugs suggests a completely open and free market exchange, decriminalization can be defined as repealing criminal penalties against simple possession but retaining them against drug smuggling and selling.[V] Accordingly, there really are unique variances between the two positions.

U There are many, many outstanding debates, commentaries, and other op-eds on the topics. For example Milton Friedman and William Bennett both offered unique and scholarly discussions. Likewise, Gary Becker and Richard Posner have done the same.

V Essentially, you can grow it and use it, just don't sell it!

Understanding the market impact is not complicated and can be framed fairly clearly. In Graph #4 we see a hypothetical change from our current drug policy of prohibition with equilibrium of P1 Q1, to the other extreme—legalization—which displays equilibrium as P2 Q2. Two brief assumptions should be mentioned for this item. First, Graph #4 references "drugs" as a general term. Obviously there are differing thoughts regarding the legalization of marijuana vs. heroin or meth. Second, we assume a general or average slope for the demand curve rather than the inelastic measure of the addict. So the relevance of this graph is that it provides economic guidance regarding a policy of legalization and, in essence, helps answer the question, "What does economic theory tell us about moving from a policy of prohibition to one of legalization?" The quick answer is that, *ceteris paribus*, we would expect lower drug prices, an increase in equilibrium quantity, and accordingly, <u>more drug use</u>.

As noted in this graph, we assume that legalization will result in an increase in the Demand for drugs and therefore a rightward shift from D1 to D2. Students will sometimes argue that drug use by the so-called rebel user (who is drawn to drugs only by his/her rebellious nature) might decline. However, the assumption here is that this rebellious part of the market is likely small in number. The more prevailing argument is simply this—if drugs become legal, there will be more use in the aggregate.

The Supply side deserves a more careful examination. The rightward shift of the supply curve is easily explainable—no longer will suppliers get in trouble

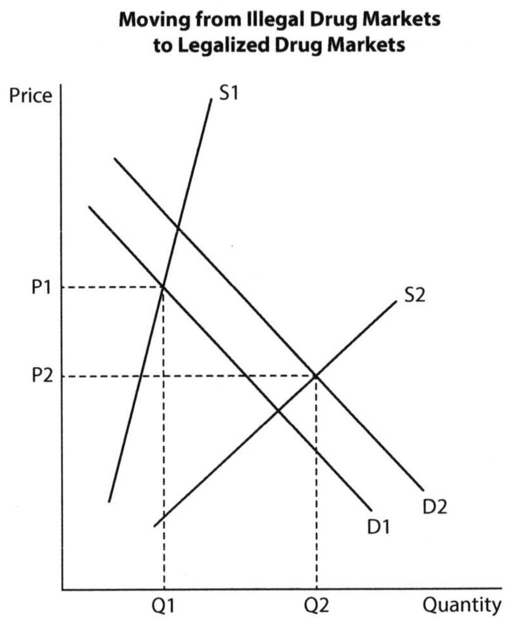

Graph #4

for providing what drug consumers want! This has been clearly borne out in states such as Colorado where one report noted that there are more marijuana dispensaries in the state than Starbucks, McDonalds, and 7-Elevens combined![29] Accordingly, we will have more firms willing to participate in such a market that legally brings together willing buyer and willing seller. However, we also rotate the supply curve to show a more elastic relationship in regards to the price elasticity of supply. The concept and formula behind price elasticity of supply parallels the calculation done on the demand side with price elasticity of demand. The relationship can be written as follows where we have simply replaced Quantity Demanded with Quantity Supplied:

$$\in (s) = \frac{\%\,\Delta\ in\ Quantity\ Supplied}{\%\,\Delta\ in\ Price} = \frac{Q2-Q1}{Q1} \bigg/ \frac{P2-P1}{P1}$$

In the initial S1 curve (prohibition) there is an additional cost issue that is completely unrelated to basic production of the good. This is the issue of criminal conduct that could place the supplier behind bars. Accordingly, this type of "cost" contributes to a more inelastic supply curve under a policy of prohibition. Legalization obviously removes the threat of incarceration. When this aspect is combined with other potential improvements in the business model—better travel and trade routes, access to the courts, etc.—then we can better understand the rightward shift and rotation of the supply curve.

COLLEGE STUDENTS AND VARIOUS DRUG HABITS

Many studies abound in this area. However, my own surveys over 15 years of approximately 1,800 college-age students suggest that about 60% have tried marijuana, and roughly 18% have used cocaine.[W] In regards to alcohol use, the number of students who state that they have been "drunk" averages out to approximately 80% of those responding.[X] One more item of interest is the age at which respondents either first used drugs or first drank. In both cases, the age of 16 is statistically significant—suggesting a strong relevance to the choice and availability of cohorts and potential cohorts during this developmental period. With the "revolution" in marijuana laws going forward, no doubt some of these responses could change.

WHAT ABOUT PRICE DISCRIMINATION?

The concept of price discrimination refers to situations where the same product may be sold at different prices to different buyers. A simple textbook example would be a movie theater charging lower prices to children, students, and senior citizens as compared to other customers. For price discrimination to occur, there are two basic requirements for the supplier: First, they need the ability to differentiate among buyers (know who is willing to pay what). Second, it is necessary to have some degree of market power.[Y] These two requirements are sufficient to provide a venue for price discrimination; however, for the seller to earn profits, they must also be able to prevent arbitrage, or resale of the product by their customers.

W Students in these surveys were from a junior-senior level course.

X Since the question regarding a drunken state is somewhat subjective, we processed the answer accordingly—if the respondent was not sure if they have ever been drunk then they likely have not been.

Y The essence of market power is the ability to control price through some mechanism, such as brand name, market saturation, or product differentiation (making your product special).

Referring back to our *Breaking Bad* characters Walt and Jesse, we find that they are able to produce an extremely superior quality of meth with high purity, nicknamed Crystal Blue Persuasion. By offering this type of high-quality product, they have achieved product differentiation and are able to charge a higher price. This does not necessarily mean that they will price discriminate, but it does suggest that they have some degree of market power with a superior product.

So can we assume that price discrimination exists in the world of drug trafficking? The answer is yes. Certainly the addict could be a target for higher prices due to their strong dependence.[Z] And, we have already noted that drug traffickers are more likely to introduce resources to protect their drug flows when the demand is inelastic. From another angle, we likely would expect discrimination when the seller is able to differentiate between a "new" user and an "old" (experienced) user. This is not to infer that an old user is necessarily an addict, but rather to point out that the supplier may deal with these two customers differently. Assuming that illegal drug dealers still have aversion to risk, we can postulate an increased willingness to work with buyers they are comfortable with.[30]

Logically, society would prefer less drug use and less crime. So a higher price for new users might result in a lower quantity demanded and less drug activity. A lower price for old (experienced) users could suggest lower rates of crimes.[31] However, the complexities in this area are significant, and it is just as likely that we see something closer to the opposite, where new users are introduced to a product with price discounting or sampling.

ECONOMIES OF SCALE, DRUG GANGS, AND MARKET POWER

Before leaving the discussion on illegal drug trade, let us theorize in a few areas. Illegal narcotic use in the U.S. is substantial. All the "usual suspects" remain—marijuana, crack, cocaine, and heroin. In addition, meth is quickly moving up as a drug of choice, even becoming a so-called party drug for some. Since reducing drug use and drug-related crime are clear goals for our society, the question remains, what is the best means of achieving these objectives? The two most apparent options are (1) a continuance of the "war on drugs" with enforcement and interdiction to reduce drug use and (2) an implementation of policy in the area of legalizing and/or decriminalizing, which, ideally, would remove some of the criminal elements in the market. (Again, we will defer discussions on the latter to Friedman, Bennett, et al.)

Z Thinking out loud... In regards to large purchases such as a home or car, a wise potential buyer will learn <u>not</u> to become emotionally attached when negotiating the transaction. The addict does not have this option since, by definition, he/she is attached—physically and emotionally.

AS A BUSINESS PRIMER

In the Schumpeter Blog of The Economist, the magazine offers an interesting look at the Breaking Bad TV series by analyzing some of the business principles as displayed by the stories' protagonist, Walter White. Specifically, they consider certain principles evident in the series which mirror the business activities we see in successful legitimate markets.

For example, the Harvard Business School noted that frequently, businesses run by "outsiders" were likely to have earnings which strongly outperform the S&P Index. At least part of the reasoning stems from the use of "fresh" ideas brought by these so-called outsiders. In Breaking Bad, Walter is the epitome of an outsider to the illegal drug trade and likewise brought newness to the market through his somewhat unique production method and his near obsession with the quality of his product. By obtaining large quantities of a necessary raw material, methylamine, and obsessing on the quality of his merchandise, Walter vastly distinguished himself from the traditional meth street dealers. Additionally, the large supply of methylamine he had obtained (by theft) likely contributed to robust economies of scale. With these elements and others combined, it is not surprising that Walter was able to obtain significant economic profits in a dangerous business.

As noted above, Walter was obsessed with the quality of his product. He was so obsessed in fact that he was willing, at times, to discard large quantities of his product if it did not meet his high standards. This discarding took place despite the fact that even Walter's low grade product was of a higher quality than the standard meth on the streets. Such behavior is not atypical among entrepreneurs who are so passionate about their product quality that they may, at times, fixate on this aspect, perhaps even to the detriment of their overall business model.

In the business world, the importance of industry associations and various alliances cannot be overstated. Here also Walter was on a course similar to that of the legal business sector by putting together his own alliances while partnering with others to further his "empire." And, while these alliances were certainly volatile at times (to say the least), they did contribute to the overall monetary and productive success of his venture.

Ultimately, some of the same issues discussed in earlier parts of the book relating to the fallacies of man contributed to Walter's downfall. He was after all, an entrepreneur, and in that role, the main character proved that the same greed and hubris which might disrupt a legitimate business activity can also play a role in the demise of an illegal business model.[1]

A MUSICAL IMPACT

As noted in other parts of the text—when we change a parameter, we shift a curve. This occurs in many economic relationships, but most clearly in regards to supply and demand. Accordingly, one of the most discernible displays of this economic principle occurred due to the music selection in the final Breaking Bad episode. As the show winds down to its final seconds and Walter White takes his last steps, the 1972 song "Baby Blue" from the now defunct group Badfinger plays in the background. Predictably, the demand for "Baby Blue" increased immediately after it aired. But the magnitude of the increase might have been surprising. By the end of Sunday night alone, the song would be downloaded 5,000 times with sales increasing by 3,000%! Additionally, in the 11 hours after the final episode, the song would log a 9,000% increase in global streams while reaching the Top 25 on iTunes top song list.[2]

$80 MILLION IN PROFITS IN ONE YEAR!

In the series, Walter accumulated $80 million in profits through his meth dealings. Fictional—yes. But, according to researchers in the field, the number correlates with the actual potential profits of the industry. The premised show price of $60 per gram is modest by some accounts. In real life, the drug price seems to vary significantly across the country, generally fluctuating between $50 and $150 per gram, which might make oil prices seem stable.[3] Yet, even with the "modest" price noted above, the use of approximately 400 gallons of methylamine in the cooking process, less a 35% distribution fee, likely would have put Walt "between $78 million and $96 million in profits," or, approximately $80 million.[4]

ENDNOTES

1. Schumpeter Blog. (2013 Sept 28). "Schumpeter Blog—The Breaking Bad School—The best show on television is also a first-rate primer on business." The Economist. <www.theeconomist.com>. Accessed 2013 Nov 30.
2. Hart, Tina. (2013 Oct 1). "Breaking Bad finale sees Baby Blue track sales soar 3,000%." <www.musicweek.com>. Accessed 2013 Dec 1.
3. Isidore, Chris. (2013 Sept 27). "Breaking Bad economy: How Walt made $80 million." CNN Money. <moneycnn.com>. Accessed 2013 Nov 30.
4. Isidore.

Monopoly Market
(Theorizing on Collusion by DTO's)

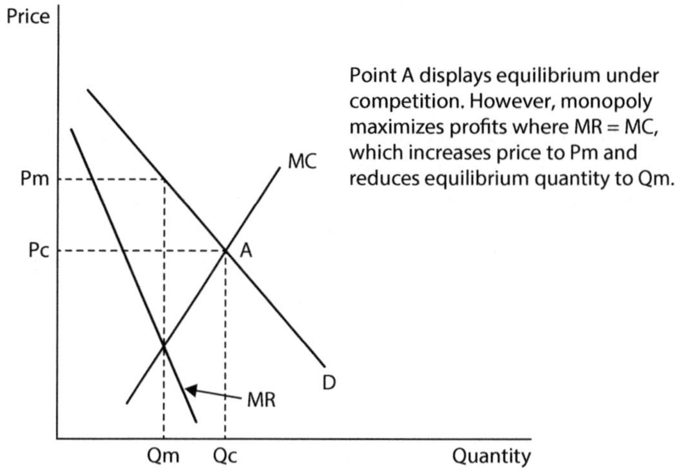

Graph #5

THEORIZING AND "THINKING OUT LOUD"

If we realistically assume that the only legalization possibility involves marijuana, we are still faced with a need for policy options on the more addictive drugs, and so the war on drugs will likely continue. However, we can use economic theory to hypothesize how the drug world might be altered if Mexican DTO's are able to regroup and coordinate their pursuits—in essence, collude. No doubt this is simply "thinking out loud," but a theoretical argument can be made that it could be to the public's advantage for such collusion to exist. As already noted, DOJ data clearly suggest that Mexican DTO's are the leading provider of illicit narcotics in the U.S. Therefore, if the small number of DTO's, which are functioning as an oligopoly, are able to coordinate on prices and supply issues, they would be able to realize greater profits—essentially monopoly profits—by producing <u>less output</u>.[AA] Society then benefits from the reduced output of drugs—in theory.[AB] For a better understanding, see Graph #5 and the following explanation.

AA An oligopoly is a market with few firms that, in the aggregate, contain a large market share. There are usually high barriers to entry into the market and some interdependence in the pricing of products.

AB A similar argument could be made for other so-called economic bads that are produced by organized crime activity, i.e., illegal gambling, prostitution, etc.

In a competitive market, we would assume an equilibrium point at the intersection of D and MC where the output result is Qc. However, monopoly power allows the firms to achieve profit maximization where MR = MC in the graph. This intersection determines the new equilibrium quantity Qm. Price, of course, is determined by the demand curve and increases accordingly to Pm. So again, society benefits from a lower production of what we observe as an economic "bad"—the illicit narcotics. Likewise, we would assume that the coordination of efforts means less violence, and therefore fewer negative externalities.

So why theorize on such a contingent topic? First, this is not advocating that we simply bring the DTO's to the negotiating table and ask them to "play nice" with the hope of making the world a better place. Rather, this is meant to extend our discussion of economic theory and help us gain a better understanding of the flexibility of economic analysis.

FINAL THOUGHTS

Will all due respect to those who advocate the legalization of drugs, we must realize the impact that this market and industry has on our economy. A 2007 study estimated the direct and indirect public costs attributable to crime, health, and lost productivity at $193 billion. Of this amount, the largest cost component was the last one, the estimated lost productivity, which totaled $120 billion and is composed of the following (the two largest items are noted in parentheses):

- Reduced labor participation ($49 billion)
- Incarceration ($48 billion)
- Premature mortality
- Being enrolled in drug treatment programs
- Hospitalization from illicit drug use [32]

Some may view these numbers as being a bit dated as this is a 10 year-old study with 10-year old data. However, billions are still billions, and, to be clear, the most relevant words in the first paragraph are probably the following—"LOST PRODUCTIVITY." Simply stated, the impact of unproductive resources from drug abuse is a profund one in our country, both socially and economically.

To conclude, the abuse of hard-core illicit drugs is not healthy for the individual or society. So regardless of the policy—legalization, decriminalization, war on drugs, etc.—fewer drugs and less drug use are the goals.

ENDNOTES

1. Rubin, Rita. (2016 Nov 16). "Many States Have Legalized Medical Marijuana, So Why Does DEA Still Say It Has No Therapeutic Use?" *Forbes*. https://www.forbes.com/sites/ritarubin/2016/11/16/many-states-have-legalized-medical-marijuana-so-why-does-dea-still-say-it-has-no-therapeutic-use/#49a2b7bf7ec2.

2. Smith, Aaron. (2017 May 26). "10 Things to Know About Legal Pot." *CNN Money*. http://money.cnn.com/2017/04/19/news/legal-marijuana-420/index.html.
3. Rega, Sam. (2017 Jan 1). "New Startup App Lets Dispensaries Legally Deliver Marijuana in 60 Minutes or Less." *Business Insider*. http://www.businessinsider.com/green-rush-legal-weed-delivery-2016-12.
4. Schiller, Dane (2012 Dec 10). *Houston Chronicle*. "Meth Flow into U.S. from Mexico Rising." <www.sfgate.com>. Accessed 2012 Dec 17.
5. *Breaking Bad*. (2008). "Crazy Handful of Nothin'." <www.imdb.com>. Memorable quotes. Accessed 2012 Dec 15.
6. Merica, Dan. (2017 Oct 26). "Trump Declares Opioid Epidemic a National Public Health Emergency." *CNN*. http://www.cnn.com/2017/10/26/politics/donald-trump-opioid-epidemic/index.html.
7. National Institute on Drug Abuse. Opioid Crisis. Revised June 2017. https://www.drugabuse.gov/drugs-abuse/opioids/opioid-crisis. Accessed 2017 Sept 2.
8. Brodwin, Erin. (2017 Feb 28). "Deaths From Opioid Overdoses Have Jumped—and One Age Group is Being Affected at Stark Rates." *Business Insider*. http://www.businessinsider.com/opioid-overdose-death-statistics-2017–2016. Accessed 2017 Sept 2.
9. Brodwin
10. Gray, Michael. (2017 July 23). "Yellen Links Opioid Crisis to Low Workforce Participation." *New York Post*. http://nypost.com/2017/07/23/yellen-links-opioid-crisis-to-low-workforce-participation/.
11. NDIC. (2011 Aug.) National Drug Intelligence Center. "National Drug Threat Assessment 2011." p. 2.
12. NDIC. 1.
13. NDIC. (2008 Dec.) National Drug Intelligence Center. "National Drug Threat Assessment 2009." <www.justice.gov/archive/ndic/pubs31/3179/dtos.htm>. Accessed 2012 Dec 18.
14. Meiners, Roger E., Al. H. Ringleb, and Frances L. Edwards. (2009). *The Legal Environment of Business*. 10th Ed. Mason, OH: South-Western Cengage. p. 512.
15. FoxNews. (2012 Nov 28). "Mexican Mayor Santos Gorrostieta Killed by Gunmen Was Defiant to the End." <www.latino.foxnews.com>. Accessed 2012 Nov 30.
16. Bromwich, Jonah Engel. (2016 June 2). "Prince Overdosed on Fentanyl. What is it?" *New York Times*. https://www.nytimes.com/2016/06/03/health/what-is-fentanyl.html.
17. Lacey, Marc. (2009 Sept 21). *New York Times*. "Drug Wars: When a 'Cartel' Really Isn't." <www.nytimes.com>. Accessed 2012 Dec 16.
18. DOJ National Drug Intelligence Center. 2010 Feb. "Drug Trafficking Organizations—National Drug Threat Assessment 2010." Welcome to the United States Department of Justice. Web. 1 Dec 2010. <http://www.justice.gov/ndic/pubs38/38661/dtos.htm#Top>.
19. Levitt, Steven D. and Stephen J. Dubner. (2005). *Freakonomics*. New York: HarperCollins. p. 103.

20. Knight-Ridder. (1990 July 11). "Average Drug Dealer Income: $24,000 a Year." <www.chicagotribune.com>. Accessed 2012 Dec 16.
21. Levitt
22. Becker, Gary S., Kevin M. Murphy, and Michael Grossman. (2006 Feb). *Journal of Political Economy*. "The Market for Illegal Goods: The Case of Drugs." Vol 114. No. 1. p. 44.
23. Levitt
24. Becker
25. Bohn, Kevin. (2006 Jan 26). *CNN News*. "Feds Smoke Out Largest Drug Tunnel Yet." <www.cnn.com>. Accessed 2012 Dec 16.
26. Canning, Andrea and Christian Ng. (2011 Sept 20). *ABC News*. "Jalied U.S. Border Agent Scary inside Look at Drug Cartels." <www.abcnews.go.com>. Accessed 2012 Dec 16.
27. Becker 42.
28. Becker
29. Hutmacher, Abby. (2015 Dec 25). "More Dispensaries in Colorado Than McDonalds & Starbucks, Combined." *Colorado Pot Guide*. https://www.coloradopotguide.com/colorado-marijuana-blog/2015/december/26/more-dispensaries-in-colorado-than-mcdonalds-starbucks-combined/. Accessed 2017 Sept 2.
30. Moore, Mark H. (1973 May). *The American Economic Review*. "Policies to Achieve Discrimination on the Effective Price of Heroin." Vol 63. No 2. p. 271.
31. Moore
32. NDIC 4.

CHAPTER 11

INTRODUCTION

By Ron Liggett

In the first edition of this text, we included a Cato study titled "The Budgetary Impact of Ending Drug Prohibition," which projected a few "what if" scenarios regarding drug legalizations. With the many recent changes in marijuana laws over a number of states, we may now be able to see some of the "what if's" playing out before us. Appropriately, with new information available, "The Effect of State Marijuana Legalizations," also a Cato publication, is included in the text.

To be clear, the analysis of local and state economies in this market is definitely in the infant stages, with the following pages limited to a gathering of information from four states: Colorado, Oregon, Washington, and Alaska. But, as noted in the previous chapter, since these four states first legalized recreation marijuana use, four additional states—California, Maine, Massachusetts, Nevada, and the District of Columbia—have also passed legislation to legalize. I would add that while "infant" stage is the appropriate term for the current analysis, things are moving fast! The addition of California to this list—with its size, population, climate, and resources—might be accurately labeled as a "game changer" in the industry.

In regards to drug use, some locales have swayed between legalization and decriminalization. Simply defined, the terms are as follows:

> **Legalization**—Allowing the use and sale of drugs under a regulated system, similar to alcohol and tobacco.
>
> **Decriminalization**—Repealing criminal penalties against simple possession but retaining them against drug distribution, smuggling, and selling.[1]

While some have used these terms interchangeably, in reality they are distinctly different, with legalization having more budgetary implications. Essentially, it eliminates most arrests and thereby reduces legal expense while also allowing for taxation, a potential windfall for which many states are hungry.

In regard to marijuana use, there are a number of questions and concerns that will still need to be observed over time. Crime rates, traffic accidents, test scores by students, even suicide rates—these are all issues deemed worthy for future analysis.[A] And, as with alcohol, the challenges of underage consumption are of great concern. Nonetheless, the following section seems to provide a good start in regards to dialogue in this area. The chapter includes a more detailed review of the legalization history, which might be of interest to some, and includes a plethora of graphs offering scrutiny of many other topics, including price.

Speaking of price, the cost to purchase recreational pot has been somewhat higher than what might have been projected in many circles. No doubt there are supply and demand issues in play. For example, on the supply side, high tax rates should be creating a leftward shift of the supply curve, leading to an increase in equilibrium price. There is also the fact that medical marijuana was already established in certain states; therefore, it's not as if the market in those locales is starting from scratch. Analysis would suggest that since those markets were, to some degree, legal, changes incurred from recreational pot may not be quite as pronounced in the early stages.

Let me close this introduction with one question and a couple of observations, all of which have economic consequences:

Question: What will be the federal government response to state legalization and when exactly will that response occur? To date, state and federal laws are seemingly at odds (not unlike sanctuary city issues in regard to illegal immigration) and therefore commerce regulations will, at some point, need to be addressed.

Observation 1: The notable expansion in what can be labeled the "craft" market. Similar to changes in the beer industry where small sector labels and brews are "in," the marijuana market has seen a comparable move with unique "grows" and product offerings attempting to grab market share.[2] Some feel that with the fast-paced changes in this industry, smaller firms may be able to more quickly adapt. Nonetheless, no firm can be protected from government intrusion forever. Just ask our Canadian neighbors to the north where 2018 legalization plans will likely reflect a healthy (or unhealthy, depending on your perspective) amount of government control.[3]

Observation 2: The potential of growth for firms in what is essentially still a "new" industry where initial public offerings (IPOs) will no doubt find their way to investors. And, while stock movements in this industry to-date have been mixed, the potential for growth is still intriguing for many. For example, projections see the annual industry sales tripling by 2020, with an estimate of

A While these topics will no doubt be analyzed, there's no suggestion here that these markets will ever retreat! The proverbial "genie is out of the bottle" and there will be no going back (e.g., There is no women's movement such as that which occurred leading up to alcohol prohibition in 1919).

$21.8 billion![B] That amount would be about 60 percent more revenue than what is currently generated in the National Football League![4]

ENDNOTES

1. Miron, Jeffrey A. and Katherine Waldock. "The Budgetary Impact of Ending Drug Prohibition," *Cato Journal*, vol. 32, no. 1. Copyright 2010 by Cato Institute.
2. Rough, Lisa. "The Rise of Craft Cannabis: Signs of a Maturing Industry," *Leafly*. Mar 29, 2017. https://www.leafly.com/news/industry/the-rise-of-craft-cannabis. Accessed 2017 Sept 10.
3. "Ontario Government's Marijuana Monopoly Could Weed out Craft Growers," *The Canadian Press*. Sept 9, 2017. http://www.cp24.com/news/ontario-government-s-marijuana-monopoly-could-weed-out-craft-growers-1.3582269. Accessed 2017 Sept 10.
4. Huddleston, Tom. "Legal Marijuana Sales Could Hit $6.7 Billion in 2016." *Fortune*. Feb 1, 2016. http://fortune.com/2016/02/01/marijuana-sales-legal/. Accessed 2017 Sept 10.

B With such potential for growth, perhaps one more question is warranted: When will "Big Tobacco" step into the picture, and what role will they play?

POLICY ANALYSIS

DOSE OF REALITY: THE EFFECT OF STATE MARIJUANA LEGALIZATIONS

By Angela Dills, Sietse Goffard, and Jeffrey Miron

SEPTEMBER 16, 2016 | NUMBER 799

EXECUTIVE SUMMARY

In November 2012 voters in the states of Colorado and Washington approved ballot initiatives that legalized marijuana for recreational use. Two years later, Alaska and Oregon followed suit. As many as 11 other states may consider similar measures in November 2016, through either ballot initiative or legislative action.

Supporters and opponents of such initiatives make numerous claims about state-level marijuana legalization. Advocates think legalization reduces crime, raises tax revenue, lowers criminal justice expenditures, improves public health, bolsters traffic safety, and stimulates the economy. Critics argue that legalization spurs marijuana and other drug or alcohol use, increases crime, diminishes traffic safety, harms public health, and lowers teen educational achievement. Systematic evaluation of these claims, however, has been largely absent.

This paper assesses recent marijuana legalizations and related policies in Colorado, Washington, Oregon, and Alaska.

Our conclusion is that state marijuana legalizations have had minimal effect on marijuana use and related outcomes. We cannot rule out small effects of legalization, and insufficient time has elapsed since the four initial legalizations to allow strong inference. On the basis of available data, however, we find little support for the stronger claims made by either opponents or advocates of legalization.

The absence of significant adverse consequences is especially striking given the sometimes dire predictions made by legalization opponents.

INTRODUCTION

In November 2012 the states of Colorado and Washington approved ballot initiatives that legalized marijuana for recreational use under state law. Two years later, Alaska and Oregon followed suit.[1] In November 2016 as many as 11 other states will likely consider similar measures, through either ballot initiative or state legislative action.[2]

Supporters and critics make numerous claims about the effects of state-level marijuana legalization. Advocates think that legalization reduces crime, raises revenue, lowers criminal justice expenditure, improves public health, improves traffic safety, and stimulates the economy.[3] Critics argue that legalization spurs marijuana and other drug or alcohol use, increases crime, diminishes traffic safety, harms public health, and lowers teen educational achievement.[4] Systematic evaluation of those claims after legalization, however, has been limited, particularly for Oregon and Alaska.[5]

This paper assesses the effect to date of marijuana legalization and related policies in Colorado, Washington, Oregon, and Alaska.

Each of those four legalizations occurred recently, and each rolled out gradually over several years. The data available for before and after comparisons are therefore limited, so our assessments of legalization's effect are tentative. Yet some post-legalization data are available, and considerable data exist regarding earlier marijuana policy changes—such as legalization for medical purposes—that plausibly have similar effects. Thus available information provides a useful if incomplete perspective on what other states should expect from legalization or related policies. Going forward, additional data may allow stronger conclusions.

Our analysis compares the pre- and post-policy-change paths of marijuana use, other drug or alcohol use, marijuana prices, crime, traffic accidents, teen educational outcomes, public health, tax revenues, criminal justice expenditures, and economic outcomes. These comparisons indicate whether the outcomes display obvious changes in trend around the time of changes in marijuana policy.

Our conclusion is that state-level marijuana legalizations to date have been associated with, at most, modest changes in marijuana use and related outcomes. Our estimates cannot rule out small changes, and related literature finds some effects from earlier marijuana policy changes such as medicalization. But the strong claims about legalization made by both opponents and supporters are not apparent in the data. The absence of significant adverse consequences is especially striking given the sometimes dire predictions made by legalization opponents.

The remainder of the paper proceeds as follows. The next section outlines the recent changes in marijuana policy in the four states of interest and discusses the timing of those changes. Subsequent sections examine the behavior of marijuana use and related outcomes before and after those policy changes. A final section summarizes and discusses implications for upcoming legalization debates.

HISTORY OF STATE-LEVEL MARIJUANA LEGALIZATIONS

Until 1913 marijuana was legal throughout the United States under both state and federal law.[6] Beginning with California in 1913 and Utah in 1914, however, states began outlawing marijuana, and by 1930, 30 states had adopted marijuana prohibition.[7] Those state-level prohibitions stemmed largely from anti-immigrant sentiment and in particular racial prejudice against Mexican migrant workers, who were often associated with use of the drug. Prohibition advocates attributed terrible crimes to marijuana and the Mexicans who smoked it, creating a stigma around marijuana and its purported "vices."[8] Meanwhile, film productions like *Reefer Madness* (1936) presented marijuana as "Public Enemy Number One" and suggested that its consumption could lead to insanity, death, and even homicidal tendencies.[9]

Starting in 1930, the Federal Bureau of Narcotics pushed states to adopt the Uniform State Narcotic Act and to enact their own measures to control marijuana distribution.[10] Following the model of the National Firearms Act, in 1937 Congress passed the Marijuana Tax Act, which effectively outlawed marijuana under federal law by imposing a prohibitive tax; even stricter federal laws followed thereafter.[11] The 1952 Boggs Act and 1956 Narcotics Control Act established mandatory sentences for drug-related violations; a first-time offense for marijuana possession carried a minimum sentence of 2 to 10 years in prison and a fine of up to $20,000.[12] Those mandatory sentences were mostly repealed in the early 1970s but reinstated by the Anti-Drug Abuse Act under President Ronald Reagan. The current controlling federal legislation is the Controlled Substances Act, which classifies marijuana as Schedule I. This category is for drugs that, according to the Drug Enforcement Administration (DEA), have "no currently accepted medical use and a high potential for abuse" as well as a risk of "potentially severe psychological or physical dependence."[13]

Despite this history of increasing federal action against marijuana (and other drugs), individual states have been backing away from marijuana prohibition since the 1970s. Beginning with Oregon 11 states[14] decriminalized possession or use of limited amounts of marijuana between 1973 and 1978.[15] A second wave of decriminalization began with Nevada in 2001; nine more states and the District of Columbia have since joined the list.[16] Fully 25 states and the District of Columbia have gone further by legalizing marijuana for medical purposes. In some states, these medical regimes approximate de facto legalization.

The most dramatic cases of undoing state prohibitions and departing from federal policy have occurred in the four states (Colorado, Washington, Oregon, and Alaska) that have legalized marijuana for recreational as well as medical purposes. We next examine these four states in detail.

COLORADO

In 1975 Colorado became one of the first states to decriminalize marijuana after a landmark report by the presidentially appointed Shafer Commission recommended lower penalties against marijuana use and suggested alternative methods to discourage heavy drug use. Decriminalization made possessing less than an ounce of marijuana a petty offense with a $100 fine.

In November 2000 Colorado legalized medical marijuana through a statewide ballot initiative. The proposal, known as Amendment 20 or the Medical Use of Marijuana Act, passed with 54 percent voter support. It authorized patients and their primary caregivers to possess up to two ounces of marijuana and up to six marijuana plants. Patients also needed a state-issued Medical Marijuana Registry Identification Card with a doctor's recommendation. State regulations limited caregivers to prescribing medical marijuana to no more than five patients each.

The number of licensed medical marijuana patients initially grew at a modest rate. Then, in 2009, after Colorado's Board of Health abandoned the caregiver-to-patient ratio rule, the medical marijuana industry took off.[17] That same year, in the so-called "Ogden Memo,"[18] the U.S. Department of Justice signaled it would shift resources away from state medical marijuana issues and refrain from targeting patients and caregivers.[19] Thus, although medical marijuana remained prohibited under federal law, the federal government would tend not to intervene in states where it was legal. Within months, medical marijuana dispensaries proliferated. Licensed patients rose from 4,800 in 2008 to 41,000 in 2009. More than 900 dispensaries operated by the end of 2009, according to law enforcement.[20]

In fall 2006 Colorado voters considered Amendment 44, a statewide ballot initiative to legalize the recreational possession of up to one ounce of marijuana by individuals aged 21 or older. Amendment 44 failed, with 58 percent of voters opposed.

In November 2012, however, Colorado voters passed Amendment 64 with 55 percent support, becoming one of the first two states to relegalize recreational marijuana. The ballot initiative authorized individuals aged 21 and older with valid government identification to grow up to six plants and to purchase, possess, and use up to one ounce of marijuana.[21] Colorado residents could now buy up to one ounce of marijuana in a single transaction, whereas out-of-state residents could purchase 0.25 ounces.[22]

In light of Amendment 64, Colorado's government passed new regulations and taxes to prepare for legalized recreational marijuana use. A ballot referendum dubbed Proposition AA that was passed in November 2013 imposed a 15 percent tax on sales of recreational marijuana from cultivators to retailers and a 10 percent tax on retail sales (in addition to the existing 2.9 percent state sales tax on all goods). Local governments in Colorado were permitted to impose additional taxes on retail marijuana.[23]

Following about a year of planning, Colorado's first retail marijuana businesses opened on January 1, 2014. Each business was required to pay licensing fees of several hundred dollars and adhere to other requirements.

WASHINGTON

In 1971 Washington's legislature began loosening its marijuana laws and decreed that possession of less than 40 grams would be charged as a misdemeanor. The state legalized medical marijuana in 1998 after a 1995 court case involving a terminal cancer patient being treated with marijuana brought extra attention to the issue and set the stage for a citizen-driven ballot initiative. In November 1998 state voters approved Initiative 692, known as the Washington State Medical Use of Marijuana Act, with 59 percent in favor. Use, possession, sale, and cultivation of marijuana became legal under state law for patients with certain medical conditions that had been verified by a licensed medical professional. Initiative 692 also imposed dosage limits on the drug's use. By 2009 an estimated 35,500 Washingtonians had prescriptions to buy medical marijuana legally.

In November 2012 Washington joined Colorado in legalizing recreational marijuana. Voters passed ballot Initiative 502 with 56 percent in support amid an 81 percent voter turnout at the polls. The proposal removed most state prohibitions on marijuana manufacture and commerce, permitted limited marijuana use for adults aged 21 and over, and established the need for a licensing and regulatory framework to govern the state's marijuana industry. Initiative 502 further imposed a 25 percent excise tax levied three times (on marijuana producers, processors, and retailers) and earmarked the revenue for research, education, healthcare, and substance-abuse prevention, among other purposes.[24]

Legal possession of marijuana took effect on December 6, 2012. A year and a half later, Washington's licensing board began accepting applications for recreational marijuana shops. After some backlog, the first four retail stores opened on July 8, 2014. As of June 2016, several hundred retail stores were open across the state.

OREGON

In October 1973 Oregon became the first state to decriminalize marijuana upon passage of the Oregon Decriminalization Bill. The bill eliminated criminal penalties for possession of up to an ounce of marijuana and downgraded the offense from a "crime" to a "violation" with a fine of $500 to $1,000.[25] State law continued to outlaw using marijuana in public, growing or selling marijuana, and driving under the influence. In 1997, state lawmakers attempted to recriminalize marijuana and restore jail sentences as punishment for possessing less than one ounce, and

Oregon's governor signed the bill. Activists gathered swiftly against the new law, however, and forced a referendum; the attempt to recriminalize ended up failing by a margin of 2 to 1.[26]

Oregon medicalized marijuana by ballot initiative in November 1998, with 55 percent support. The Oregon Medical Marijuana Act legalized cultivation, possession, and use of marijuana by prescription for patients with specific medical conditions.[27] A new organization was set up to register patients and caregivers. In 2004 voters turned down a ballot proposal to increase to 6 pounds the amount of marijuana a patient could legally possess. Six years later, voters also rejected an effort to permit medical marijuana dispensaries, but the state legislature legalized them in 2013.[28] As of July 2016, Oregon's medical marijuana program counted nearly 67,000 registered patients, the vast majority claiming to suffer severe pain, persistent muscle spasms, and nausea.[29]

Recreational marijuana suffered several defeats before eventual approval. In 1986 the Oregon Marijuana Legalization for Personal Use initiative failed with 74 percent of voters opposed.[30] In November 2012, a similar measure also failed, even as neighboring Washington passed its own legalization initiative. Oregon Ballot Measure 80 would have allowed personal marijuana cultivation and use without a license, plus unlimited possession for those over age 21. To oversee the new market, the measure would have established an industry-dominated board to regulate the sale of commercial marijuana. This proposal failed with more than 53 percent of the electorate voting against it.[31]

Full legalization in Oregon finally passed on November 4, 2014, when voters approved Measure 91, officially known as the Oregon Legalized Marijuana Initiative. This measure legalized recreational marijuana for individuals over age 21 and permitted possession of up to eight ounces of dried marijuana, along with four plants, with the Oregon Liquor Control Commission regulating sales of the drug. More than 56 percent of voters cast ballots in favor of the initiative, making Oregon the third state in the nation (along with Alaska) to legalize recreational marijuana.[32]

Oregon's legislature then adopted several laws to regulate the marijuana industry. Legislators passed a 17 percent state sales tax on marijuana retail sales and empowered local jurisdictions to charge their own additional 3 percent sales tax.[33] Later, the state legislature gave individual counties the option to ban marijuana sales if at least 55 percent of voters in those counties opposed Measure 91.[34]

Legal sales went into effect on October 1, 2015. As of June 2016, Oregon had 426 locations where consumers could legally purchase recreational marijuana.[35]

ALASKA

Alaska's debate over marijuana policy began with a 1972 court case. Irwin Ravin, an attorney, was pulled over for a broken taillight and found to be in possession of marijuana. Ravin refused to sign the traffic ticket while he was in possession of marijuana so that he could challenge the law. Ultimately, the Alaska Supreme Court deemed marijuana possession in the privacy of one's home to be constitutionally protected, and *Ravin* v. *State* established legal precedent in Alaska for years to come.[36]

Alaska's legislature decriminalized marijuana in 1975, two years after Oregon. Persons possessing less than one ounce in public—or any amount in one's own home—could be fined no more than $100, a fine eliminated in 1982. Marijuana opponents, however, mobilized later in the decade as law enforcement busted a number of large, illegal cultivation sites hidden in residences. A voter initiative in November 1990 proposed to ban possession and use of marijuana even in one's own home, punishable by 90 days of jail time and a $1,000 fine. The initiative passed with 54 percent support.[37]

In 1998 Alaska citizens spearheaded an initiative to legalize medical marijuana, and 69 percent of voters supported it. Registered patients consuming marijuana for health conditions certified by a doctor could possess up to one ounce of marijuana or up to six plants.[38]

Advocates then turned to recreational legalization. A ballot initiative in 2000 proposed legalizing use for anyone 18 years and older and regulating the drug "like an alcoholic beverage." The initiative failed, with 59 percent of voters opposed. Voters considered a similar ballot measure in 2004 but again rejected it.

A third ballot initiative on recreational marijuana legalization passed in November 2014 with 53 percent of voters in support. It permitted adults aged 21 and over to possess, use, and grow marijuana. It also legalized manufacture and sale. The law further created a Marijuana Control Board to regulate the industry and establish excise taxes.

State regulators had originally planned to start issuing applications to growers, processors, and stores in early to mid-2016. At the time of this writing, retail marijuana shops are not yet open. This delay, along with data limitations, makes it difficult to evaluate post-legalization outcomes in Alaska.

KEY DATES

To determine the effect of marijuana legalization and similar policies on marijuana use and related outcomes, we examine the trends in use and outcomes before and after key policy changes. We focus mostly on recreational marijuana legalizations, because earlier work has covered other modifications of marijuana policy such as medicalization.[39] The specific dates we consider, derived from the discussion above, are as follows:

COLORADO

- 2001, after legalization of medical marijuana
- 2009, after liberalization of the medical marijuana law
- 2012, after legalization of recreational marijuana
- 2014, after the first retail stores opened under state-level legalization

WASHINGTON

- 1998, after legalization of medical marijuana
- 2012, after legalization of recreational marijuana
- 2014, after the first retail stores opened under state-level legalization

OREGON

- 1998, after legalization of medical marijuana
- 2013, after the state legislature legalized medical marijuana dispensaries
- 2014, after legalization of recreational marijuana
- 2015, after the first retail stores opened under state-level legalization

ALASKA

- 1990, after voters recriminalized marijuana
- 1998, after legalization of medical marijuana
- 2014, after legalization of recreational marijuana

Our analysis examines whether the trends in marijuana use and related outcomes changed substantially after these dates. Observed changes do not necessarily implicate marijuana policy because other factors might have changed as well. Similarly, the absence of changes does not prove that policy changes had no effect; the abundance of potentially confounding variables makes it possible that, by coincidence, a policy change was approximately offset by some other factor operating in the opposite direction. Thus, our analysis focuses on the factual outcomes of marijuana legalization, rather than on causal inferences.

DRUG USE

Arguably the most important potential effect of marijuana legalization is on marijuana use or other drug or alcohol use. Opinions differ on whether increased use is problematic or desirable, but because other outcomes depend on use, a key step is to determine how much policy affects use. If such effects are small, then other effects of legalization are also likely to be small.

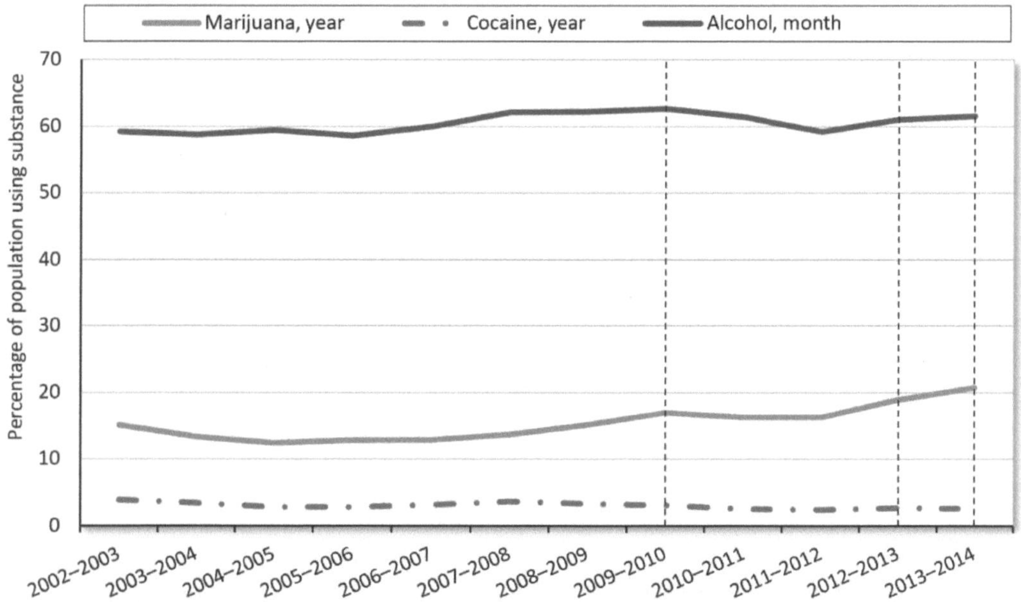

Figure 1. Colorado National Survey on Use and Health Results (all respondents, aged 12+)

Source: National Survey on Drug Use and Health, Substance Abuse and Mental Health Services Administration (SAMHSA), http://www.samhsa.gov/data/population-data-nsduh/reports?tab=33.

Figure 1 shows past-year use rates in Colorado for marijuana and cocaine, along with past-month use rates for alcohol.[40] The key fact is that marijuana use rates were increasing modestly for several years before 2009, when medical marijuana became readily available in dispensaries, and continued this upward trend through legalization in 2012. Post-legalization use rates deviate from this overall trend, but only to a minor degree. The data do not show dramatic changes in use rates corresponding to either the expansion of medical marijuana or legalization. Similarly, cocaine exhibits a mild downward trend over the time period but shows no obvious change after marijuana policy changes. Alcohol use shows a pattern similar to marijuana: a gradual upward trend but no obvious evidence of a response to marijuana policy.

Figure 2 graphs the same variables in Washington State. As in Colorado, marijuana, cocaine, and alcohol use proceed along preexisting trends after changes in marijuana policy.

Figure 3 presents analogous data for Oregon.[41] Legalization only took effect in 2015 (i.e., after the end of currently available substance use data), inhibiting any measurement of the effect of policy on data observed thus far. However, as in other legalizing states, past-year marijuana use has been rising since the mid-2000s.

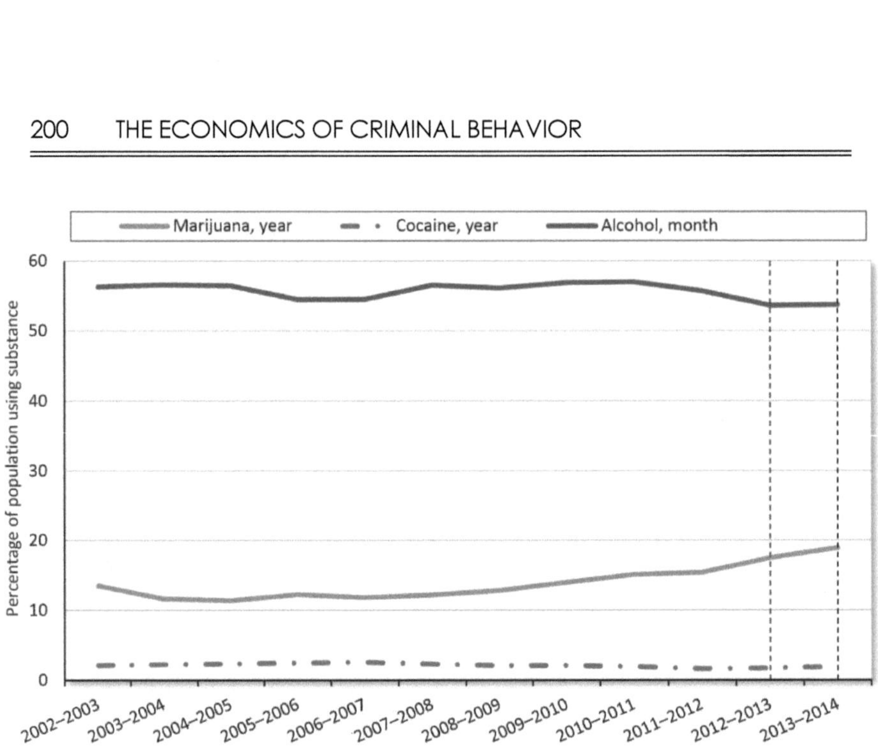

Figure 2. Washington State National Survey on Drug Use and Health Results (all respondents, aged 12+)

Source: National Survey on Drug Use and Health, Substance Abuse and Mental Health Services Administration (SAMHSA), http://www. samhsa.gov/data/population-data-nsduh/reports?tab=33.

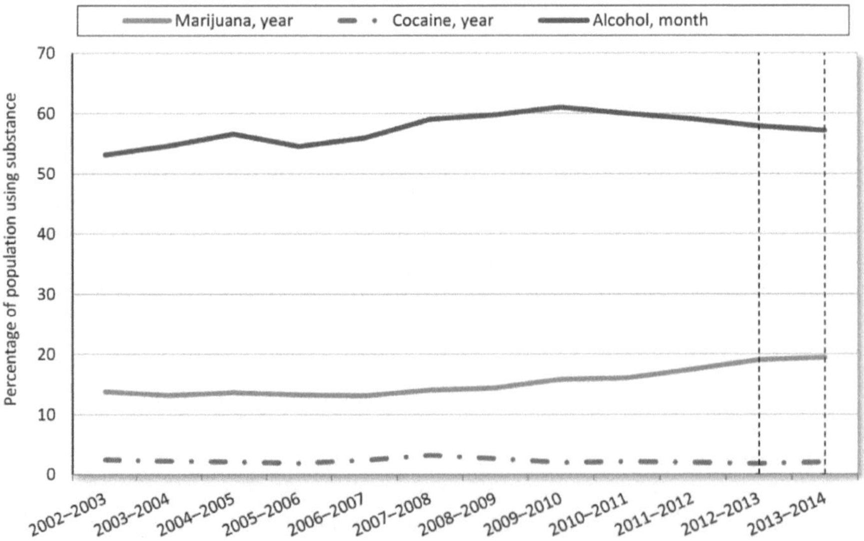

Figure 3. Oregon National Survey on Drug Use and Health Results (all respondents, aged 12+)

Source: National Survey on Drug Use and Health, Substance Abuse and Mental Health Services Administration (SAMHSA), http://www. samhsa.gov/data/population-data-nsduh/reports?tab=33.

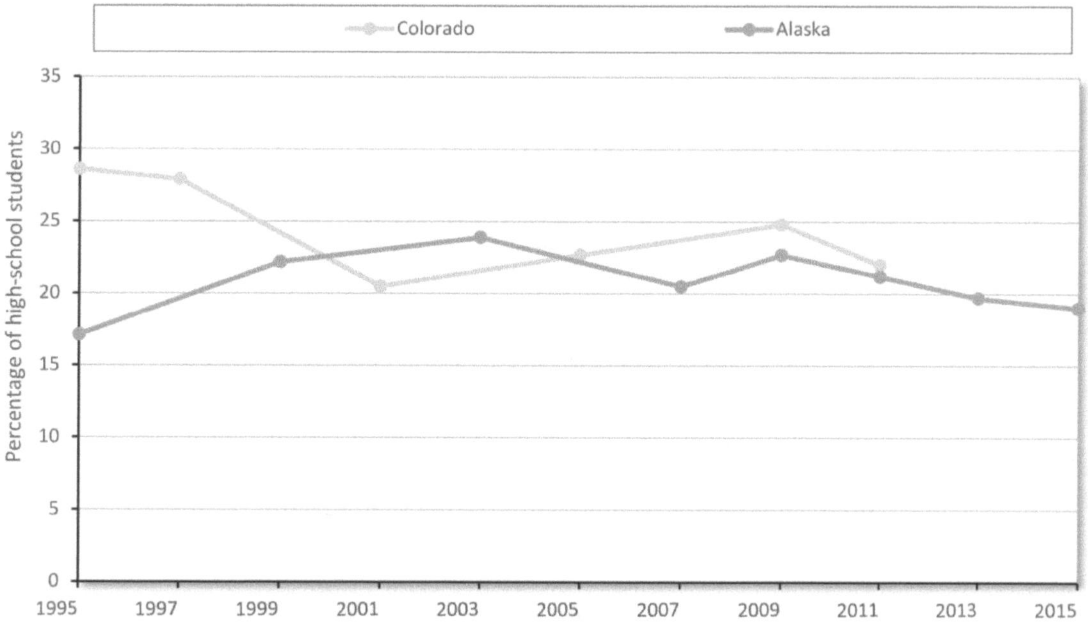

Figure 4. Youth Risk Behavior Survey Past Month Marijuana Use

Source: Youth Risk Behavior Survey, Centers for Disease Control and Prevention, http://www.cdc.gov/healthyyouth/data/yrbs/data.htm.

Figure 4 presents data on current (past-month) marijuana use by youth from the Youth Risk Behavior Survey, a survey of health behaviors conducted in middle schools and high schools. Data are unfortunately unavailable for Washington and Oregon. The limited available data for Colorado and Alaska show no obvious effect of legalization on youth marijuana use.

All those observed patterns in marijuana use might provide evidence for a cultural explanation behind legalization: as marijuana becomes more commonplace and less stigmatized, residents and legislators become less opposed to legalization. In essence, rising marijuana use may not be a consequence of legalization, but a cause of it.

Consistent with this possibility, Figure 5 plots, for all four legalizing states, data on perceptions of "great risk" from smoking marijuana monthly.[42] All four states exhibit a steady downward trend, indicating that fewer people associate monthly marijuana use with high risk. These downward trends predate legalization, consistent with the view that changing attitudes toward marijuana fostered both policy changes and increasing use rates. Interestingly, risk perceptions rose in Colorado in 2012–2013, immediately following legalization. This rise may have resulted from public safety and anti-legalization campaigns that cautioned residents about the dangers of marijuana use.

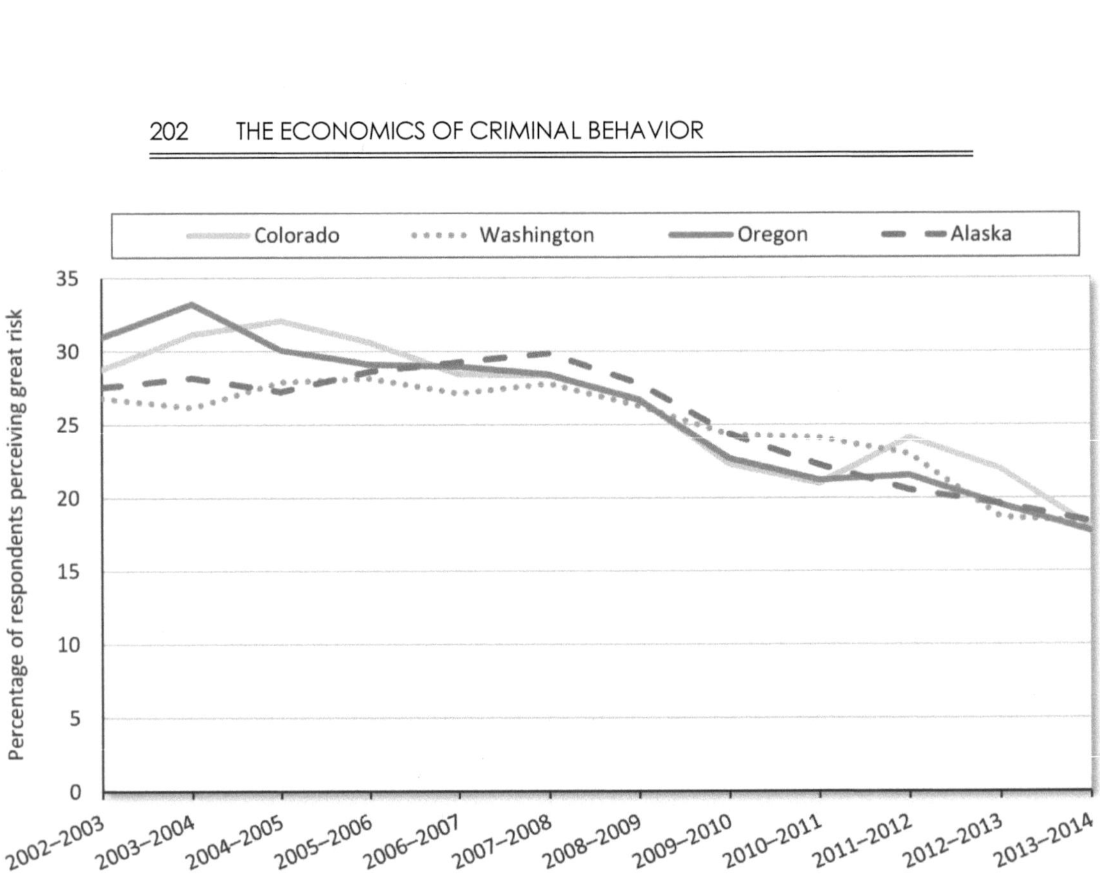

Figure 5. Perception of Risk

Source: National Survey on Drug Use and Health, Substance Abuse and Mental Health Services Administration (SAMHSA), http://www.samhsa.gov/data/population-data-nsduh/reports?tab=33.

Data on marijuana prices may also shed light on marijuana use. One hypothesis before legalization was that use might soar because prices would plunge. For example, Dale Gieringer, director of California's NORML (National Organization for Reform of Marijuana Laws) branch, testified in 2009 that in a "totally unregulated market, the price of marijuana would presumably drop as low as that of other legal herbs such as tea or tobacco—on the order of a few dollars per ounce—100 times lower than the current prevailing price of $300 per ounce."[43] A separate study by the Rand Corporation[44] estimated that marijuana prices in California would fall by 80 percent after legalization.[45] Using data from Price of Weed (priceofweed.com), which crowdsources real-time information from thousands of marijuana buyers in each state, we derive monthly average prices of marijuana in Colorado, Washington, and Oregon.[46] See Figures 6, 7, and 8.

In Colorado, monthly average prices were declining even before legalization and have remained fairly steady since. The cost of high-quality marijuana hovers around $230 per ounce while that of medium-quality marijuana remains around $190. The opening of shops in January 2015 seems to have had little effect. In Washington State, marijuana prices have been similarly steady and have

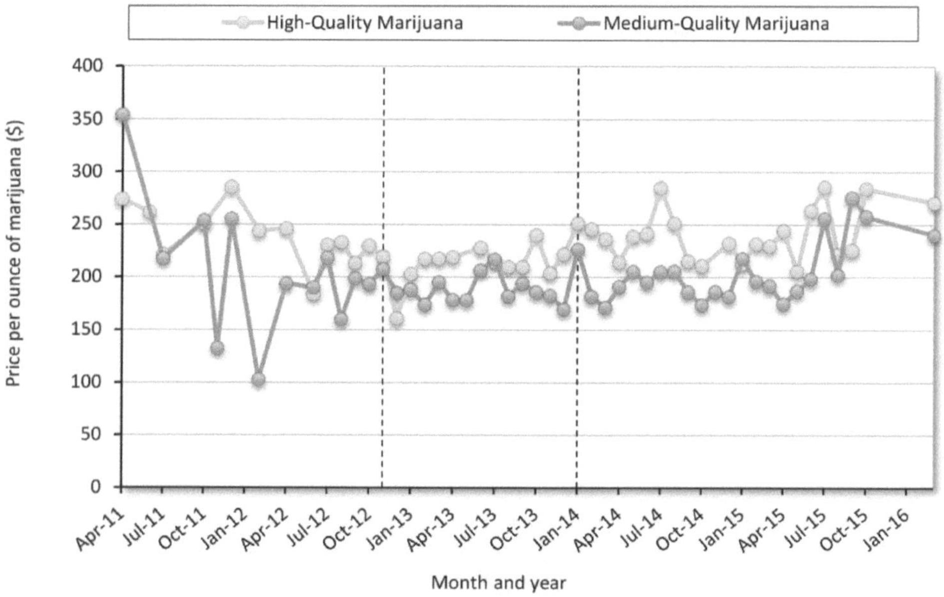

Figure 6. Colorado Marijuana Prices

Source: Priceofweed.com, http://www.priceofweed.com/prices/United-States/Colorado.html.

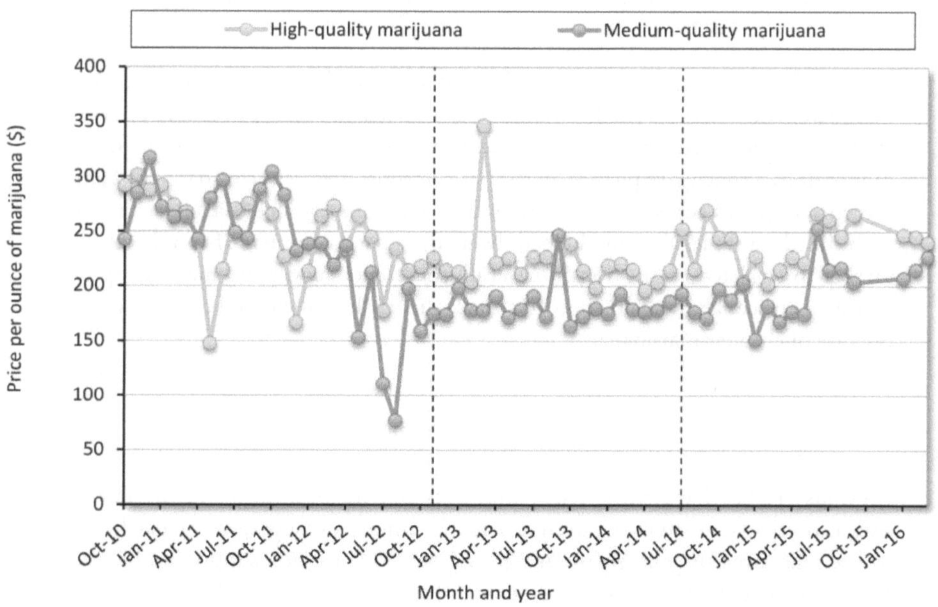

Figure 7. Washington Marijuana Prices

Source: Priceofweed.com, http://www.priceofweed.com/prices/United-States/Washington.html.

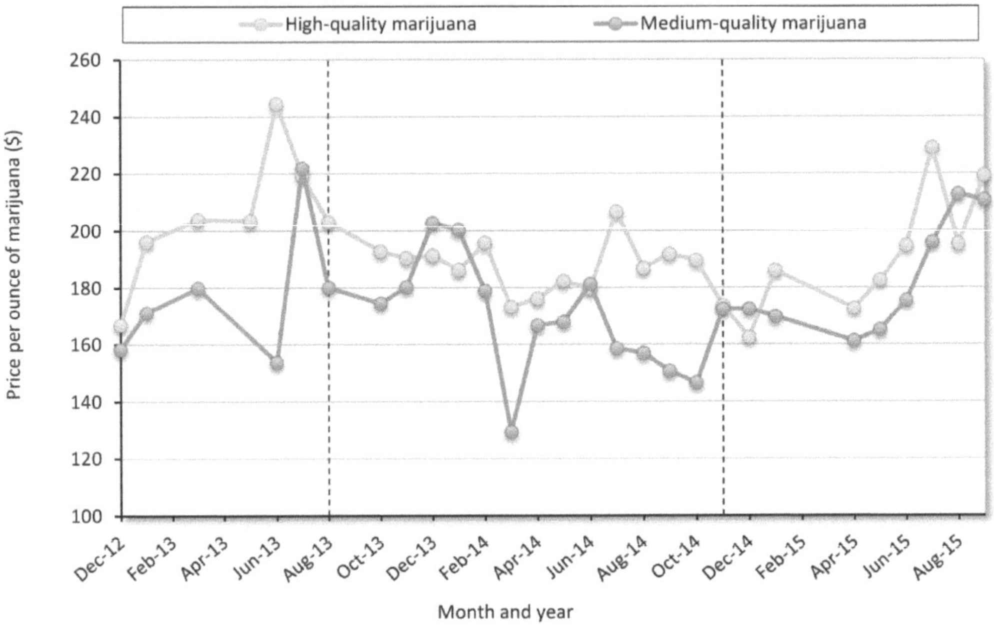

Figure 8. Oregon Marijuana Prices

Source: Priceofweed.com, http://www.priceofweed.com/prices/United-States/Oregon.html.

converged almost exactly to Colorado prices—roughly $230 for high-quality marijuana and $200 for medium-quality marijuana. Oregon prices show a rise after legalization, catching up to Colorado and Washington levels. Although we cannot draw a conclusive picture on the basis of consumer-reported data, the convergence of prices across states makes sense. This convergence is also consistent with the idea that legalization helped divert marijuana commerce from the black market to legalized retail shops.[47] Overall, these data suggest no major drop in marijuana prices after legalization and consequently less likelihood of soaring use because of cheaper marijuana.

HEALTH AND SUICIDES

Previous studies have suggested a link between medicalization of marijuana and a lower overall suicide rate, particularly among demographics most likely to use marijuana in general (males ages 20 to 39).[48] In fact, supporters believe that marijuana can be an effective treatment for bipolar disorder, depression, and other mood disorders—not to mention a safer alternative to alcohol. Moreover, the pain-relieving element of medical marijuana may help patients avoid more

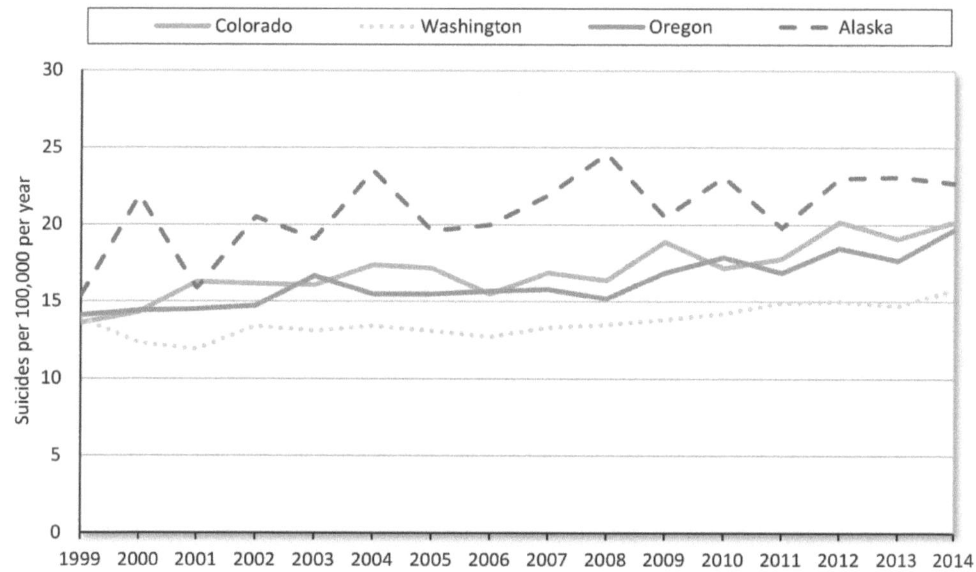

Figure 9. Annual Suicide Rates (per 100,000 people)

Source: Centers for Disease Control and Prevention, CDC Wonder Portal, http://wonder.cdc.gov/.

harmful prescription painkillers and tranquilizers.[49] Conversely, certain studies suggest excessive marijuana use may increase the risk of depression, schizophrenia, unhealthy drug abuse, and anxiety.[50] Some research also warns about long-lasting cognitive damage if marijuana is consumed regularly, especially at a young age.[51]

Figure 9 displays the overall yearly suicide rate per 100,000 people in each of the four legalizing states between 1999 and 2014.[52] Figure 10 presents the analogous suicide rate for males aged 20 through 39 years.[53] Suicide rates in all four states trend slightly upward during the 15-year-long period, but it is difficult to see any association between marijuana legalization and any changes in these trends. These findings contrast with many previous studies, so it is possible that any effects will take longer to appear. In addition, previous research has suggested a link between medical marijuana and a lower suicide rate; it is not obvious that recreational marijuana would lead to the same result, or that legalization of recreational marijuana after medical marijuana is already legalized would have much of an extra effect.[54]

Data on treatment center admissions provide a proxy for drug abuse and other health hazards associated with misuse. Figures 11 and 12 plot rates of annual admissions involving marijuana and alcohol to publicly funded treatment centers in Colorado[55] and King County, Washington (which encompasses Seattle).[56] Marijuana admissions in Colorado were fairly steady over the past decade but began falling in 2013 and 2014, just as legalization took effect. Alcohol admissions

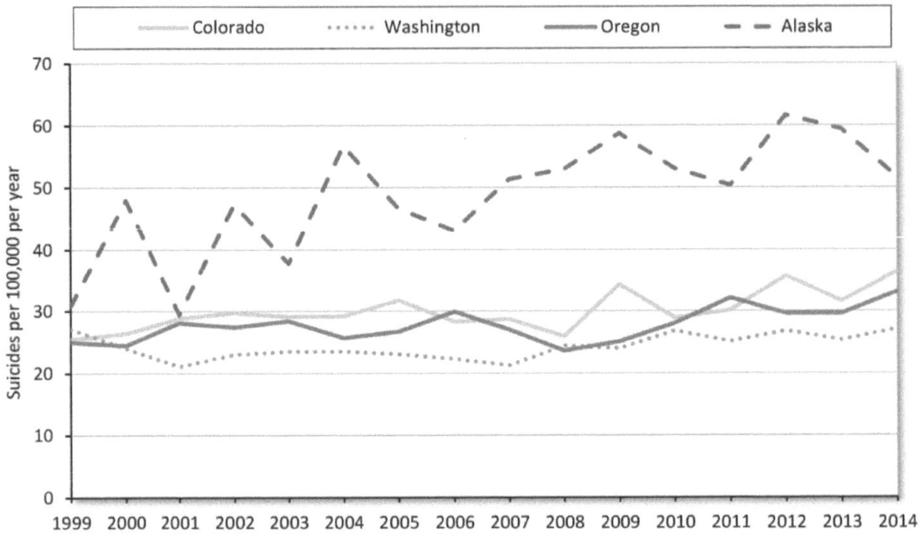

Figure 10. Suicide Rates for Males 20–39 Years Old

Source: Centers for Disease Control and Prevention, CDC Wonder Portal, http://wonder.cdc.gov/.

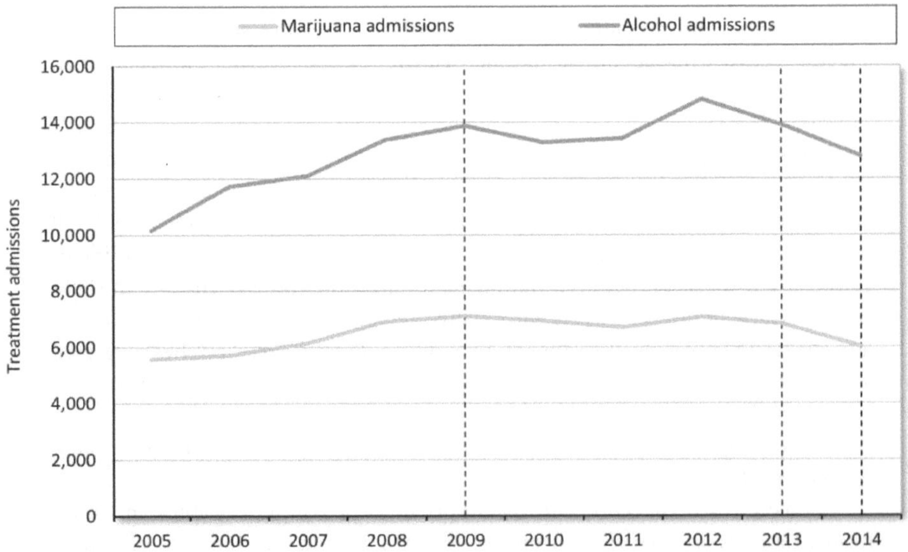

Figure 11. Colorado Treatment Admissions

Source: Rocky Mountain High Intensity Drug Trafficking Area (RMHIDTA) report, "The Legalization of Marijuana in Colorado: The Impact" (Vol. 3, September 2015), http://www.rmhidta.org/html/2015%20final%20legalization%20of%20marijuana%20in%20colorado%20the%20impact.pdf.

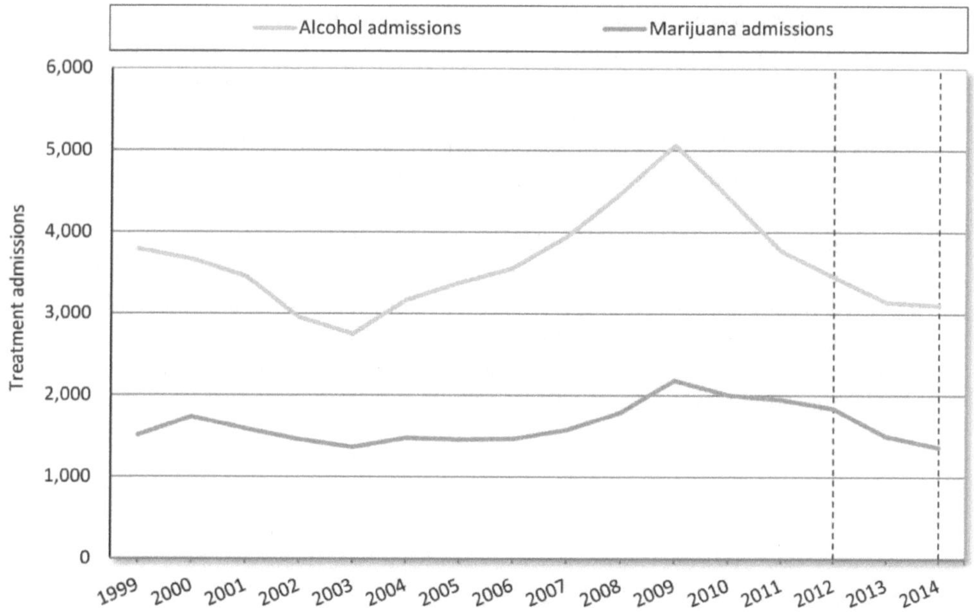

Figure 12. Treatment Admissions by Drug—King County, Washington

Source: University of Washington Alcohol and Drug Abuse Institute, http://adai.washington.edu/pubs/cewg/Drug%20Trends_2014_final.pdf.

began declining around the same time. In King County, admissions for marijuana and alcohol continued their downward trends after legalization. These patterns suggest that extreme growth in marijuana abuse has not materialized, as some critics had warned before legalization.

CRIME

In addition to substance use and health outcomes, legalization might affect crime. Opponents think these substances cause crime through psychopharmacological and other mechanisms, and they note that such substances have long been associated with crime, social deviancy, and other undesirable aspects of society.[57] Although those perspectives first emerged in the 1920s and 1930s, marijuana's perceived associations with crime and deviancy persist today.[58]

Before referendums in 2012, police chiefs, governors, policymakers, and concerned citizens spoke up against marijuana and its purported links to crime.[59] They also argued that expanding drug commerce could increase marijuana commerce in violent underground markets and that legalization would make it easy to smuggle the substance across borders where it remained prohibited, thus causing negative spillover effects.[60]

Proponents argue that legalization reduces crime by diverting marijuana production and sale from the black market to legal venues. This shift may be incomplete if high tax rates or significant regulation keeps some marijuana activity in gray or black markets, but this merely underscores that more legalization means less crime. At the same time, legalization may reduce the burden on law enforcement to patrol for drug offenses, thereby freeing budgets and manpower to address larger crimes. Legalization supporters also dispute the claim that marijuana increases neurological tendencies toward violence or aggression.[61]

Figure 13 presents monthly crime rates from Denver, Colorado, for all reported violent crimes and property crimes.[62] Both metrics remain essentially constant after 2012 and 2014; we do not observe substantial deviations from the illustrated cyclical crime pattern. Other cities in Colorado mirror those findings. Analogous monthly crime data for Fort Collins, for example, reveal no increase in violent or property crime.[63]

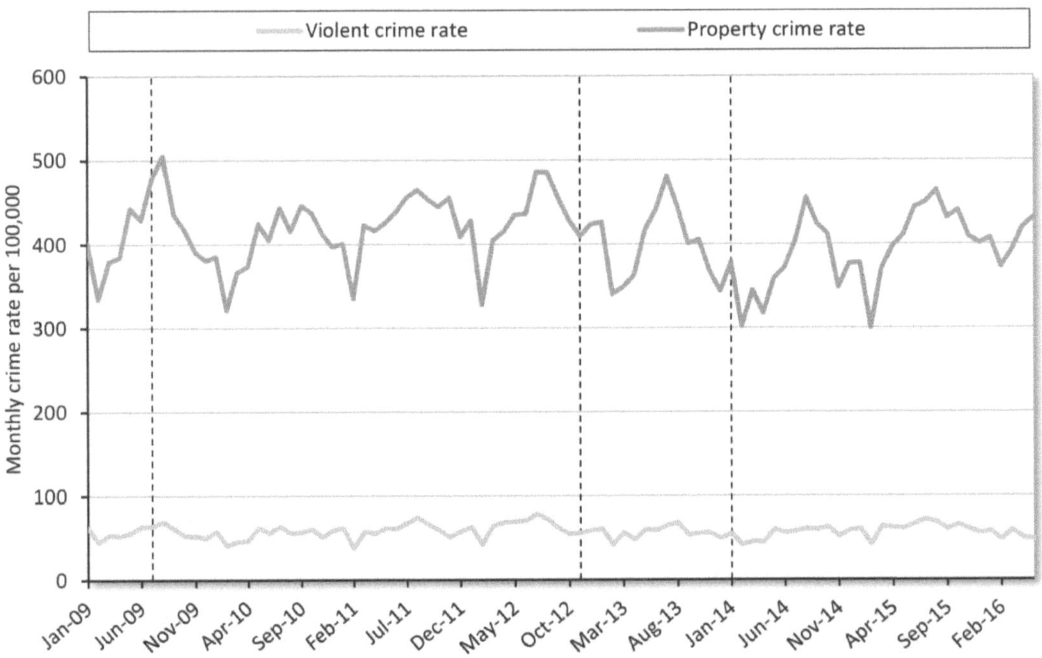

Figure 13. Denver Monthly Crime Rate (violent and property crime rates per 100,000 residents)

Source: Denver Police Department, Monthly Crime Reports, https://www.denvergov.org/content/denvergov/en/police-department/crime-information/crime-statistics-maps.html. Population data source: U.S. Census Bureau Estimates, http://www.census.gov/popest/data/intercensal/index.html.

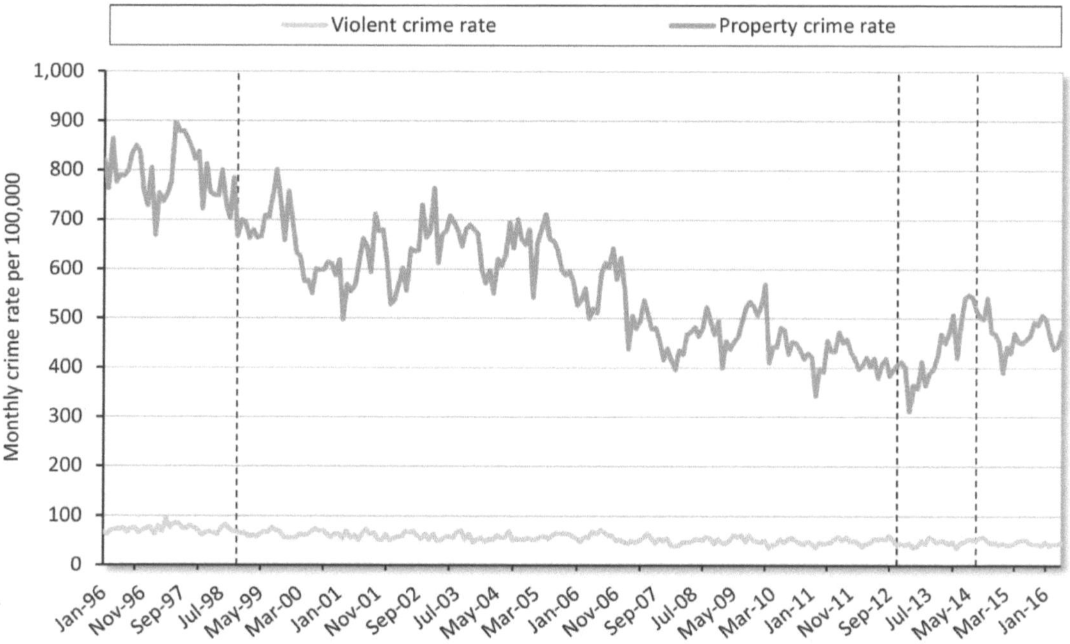

Figure 14. Seattle Monthly Crime Rate

Source: Seattle Police Department, Online Crime Dashboard, http://www.seattle.gov/seattle-police-department/crime-data/crime-dashboard. Population data source: U.S. Census Bureau Estimates. http://www.census.gov/popest/data/intercensal/index.html.

Figure 14 shows monthly violent and property crime rates as reported by the Seattle Police Department.[64] Both categories of crime declined steadily over the past 20 years, with no major deviations after marijuana liberalization. Property crime does appear to spike in 2013 and early 2014, and some commentators have posited that legalization drove this increase.[65] That connection is not convincing, however, since property crime starts to fall again after the opening of marijuana shops in mid-2014. All told, crime in Seattle has neither soared nor plummeted in the wake of legalization.[66]

Monthly violent and property crime remained steady after legalization in Portland, Oregon, as seen in Figure 15.[67] Portland provides an interesting case because of its border with Washington. Between 2012 and 2014, Portland (and the rest of Oregon) prohibited the recreational use of marijuana, while marijuana sales and consumption were fully legal in neighboring Washingtonian towns just to the north. This situation creates a natural experiment that allows us to look for spillover effects in Oregon. Figure 15 suggests that legalization in Washington and the opening of stores there did not produce rising crime rates across the border. Elsewhere in Oregon, we see no discernible changes in crime trends before and after legalization or medical marijuana liberalization.[68]

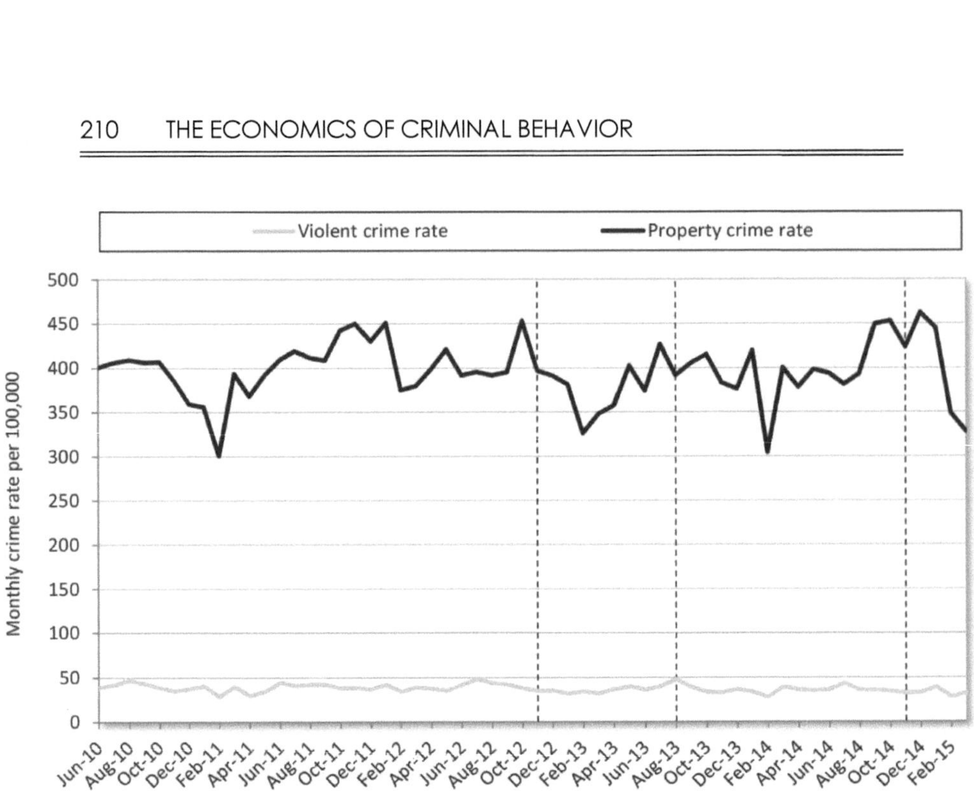

Figure 15. Portland Monthly Crime Rate

Source: Portland Police Bureau Neighborhood Statistics, http://www.portlandonline.com/police/crimestats/. Population data source: U.S. Census Bureau Estimates, http://www.census.gov/popest/data/intercensal/index.html.

ROAD SAFETY

We next evaluate how the incidence of traffic accidents may have changed in response to marijuana policy changes. Previous literature and political rhetoric suggest two contrasting hypotheses. One holds that legalization increases traffic accidents by spurring drug use and thereby driving under the influence. This hypothesis presumes that marijuana impairs driving ability.[69] The opposing theory argues legalization improves traffic safety because marijuana substitutes for alcohol, which some studies say impairs driving ability even more.[70] Moreover, some consumers may be able to drive better if marijuana serves to relieve their pain.

Rhetoric from experts and government officials has been equally divided. Kevin Sabet, a former senior White House drug policy adviser, warned that potential consequences of Colorado's legalization could include large increases in traffic accidents.[71] A recent Associated Press article noted that "fatal crashes involving marijuana doubled in Washington after legalization."[72] Yet Coloradan law enforcement agents are themselves unsure whether legal marijuana has led to an increase in accidents.[73] Research by Radley Balko, an opinion blogger for the *Washington Post* and an author on drug policy, claims that, overall, "highway fatalities in Colorado are at near-historic lows" in the wake of legalization.[74]

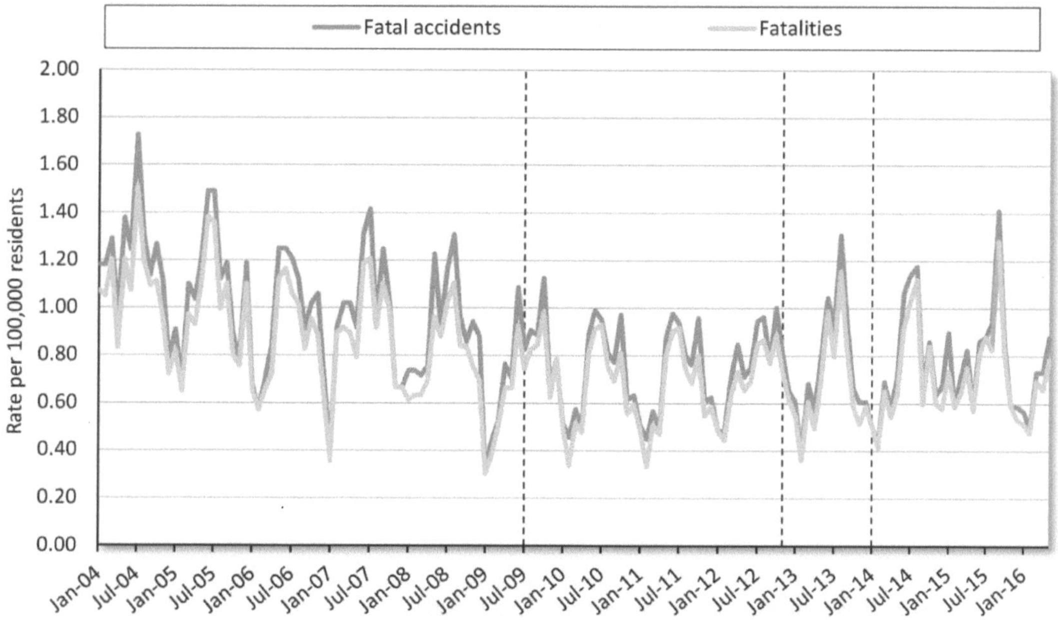

Figure 16. Colorado Car Crashes and Fatality Rate

Source: Colorado Department of Transportation, http://www.coloradodot.info/library/traffic/traffic-manuals-guidelines/safety-crash-data/fatal-crash-data-city-county/fatal-crashes-by-city-and-county/.

Figure 16 presents the monthly rate of fatal accidents and fatalities per 100,000 residents in Colorado.[75] No spike in fatal traffic accidents or fatalities followed the liberalization of medical marijuana in 2009.[76] Although fatality rates have reached slightly higher peaks in recent summers, no obvious jump occurs after either legalization in 2012 or the opening of stores in 2014.[77] Likewise, neither marijuana milestone in Washington State appears to have substantially affected the fatal crash or fatality rate, as illustrated in Figure 17.[78] In fact, more granular statistics reveal that the fatality rate for drug-related crashes was virtually unchanged after legalization.[79]

Figure 18 depicts the crash fatality rate in Oregon.[80] Although few post-legalization data were available at the time of publication, we observe no signs of deviations in trend after the opening of medical marijuana dispensaries in 2013. We can also test for possible spillover effects from neighboring Washington. Legalization there in 2012 and the opening of marijuana shops in 2014 do not seem to materially affect road fatalities in Oregon in either direction.

Finally, Figure 19 presents annual data on crash fatality rates in Alaska; these show no discernible increase after legalization and may even decline slightly.

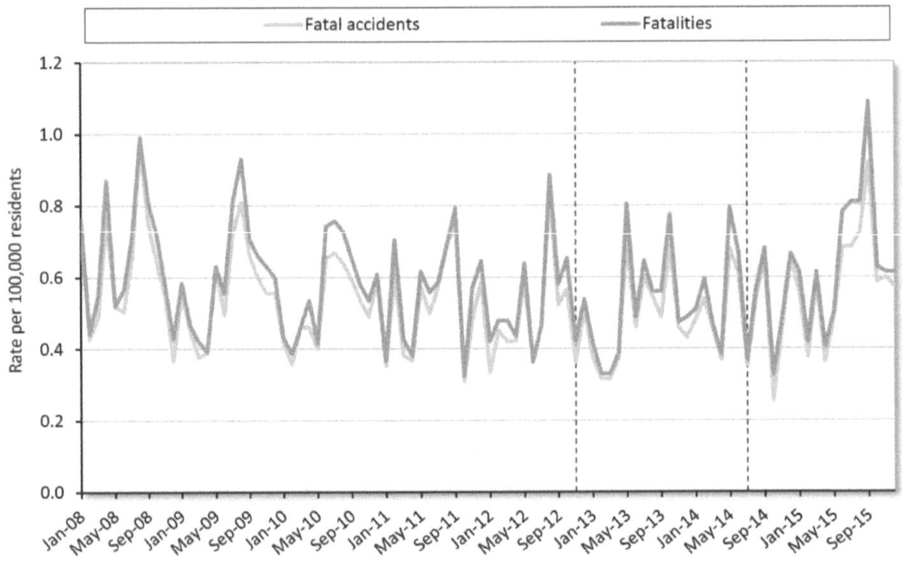

Figure 17. Washington Car Crashes and Fatality Rate

Source: Washington Traffic Safety Commission, Quarterly Target Zero Reports, http://wtsc.wa.gov/research-data/quarterly-target-zero-data/.

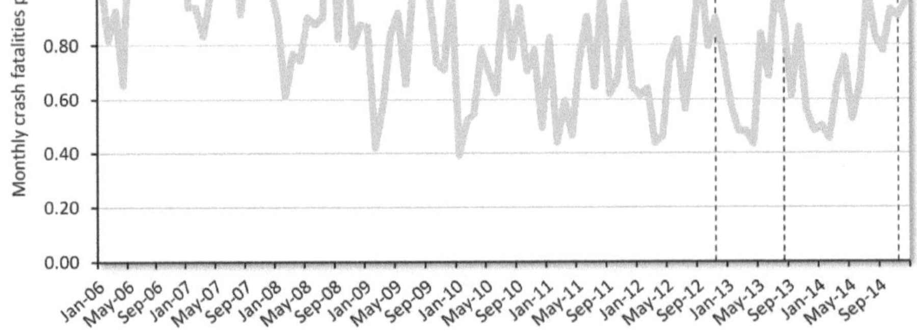

Figure 18. Oregon Car Crash Fatality Rate

Source: Oregon Department of Transportation, online Crash Summary Reports and in-person data request. Special thanks to Theresa Heyn and Coleen O'Hogan, http://www.oregon.gov/ODOT/TD/TDATA/pages/car/car_publications.aspx.

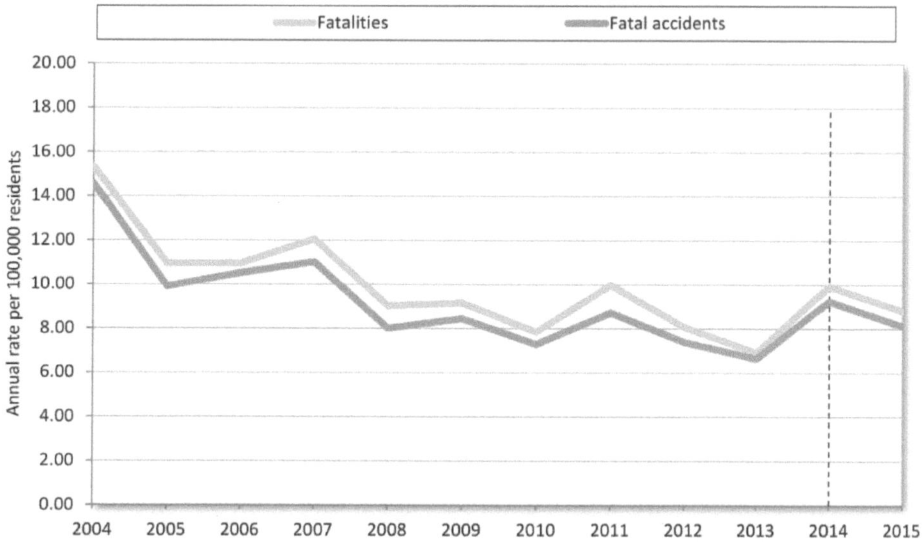

Figure 19. Alaska Car Crashes and Fatalities

Source: Alaska Highway Safety Office, http://www.dot.state.ak.us/stwdplng/hwysafety/fars.shtml.

YOUTH OUTCOMES

Much of the concern surrounding marijuana legalization relates to its possible effect on youths. Many observers, for example, fear that expanded legal access—even if officially limited to adults age 21 and over—might increase use by teenagers, with negative effects on intelligence, educational outcomes, or other youth behaviors.[81, 82]

Figure 20 displays the total number of school suspensions and drug-related suspensions in Colorado public high schools during each academic year.[83] Total suspensions trend downward over time, with a slight bump after 2014, but that bump was not one driven by drug-related causes. Drug-related suspensions appear to rise after medical marijuana commercialization in 2009 but stay level after full legalization and the opening of retail shops. Figure 21 shows public high school expulsions, both overall and drug-related. It reveals a parallel bump in drug-related expulsions right after marijuana liberalization in 2009, but expulsions drop steeply thereafter. In fact, by 2014, expulsions drop back to their previous levels.

We also consider potential effects on academic performance. Standardized test scores measuring the reading proficiency of 8th and 10th graders in Washington State show no indication of significant positive or negative changes caused by legalization, as illustrated in Figure 22.[84] Although some studies have found that frequent marijuana use impedes teen cognitive development, our results do not suggest a major change in use, thereby implying no major changes in testing performance.

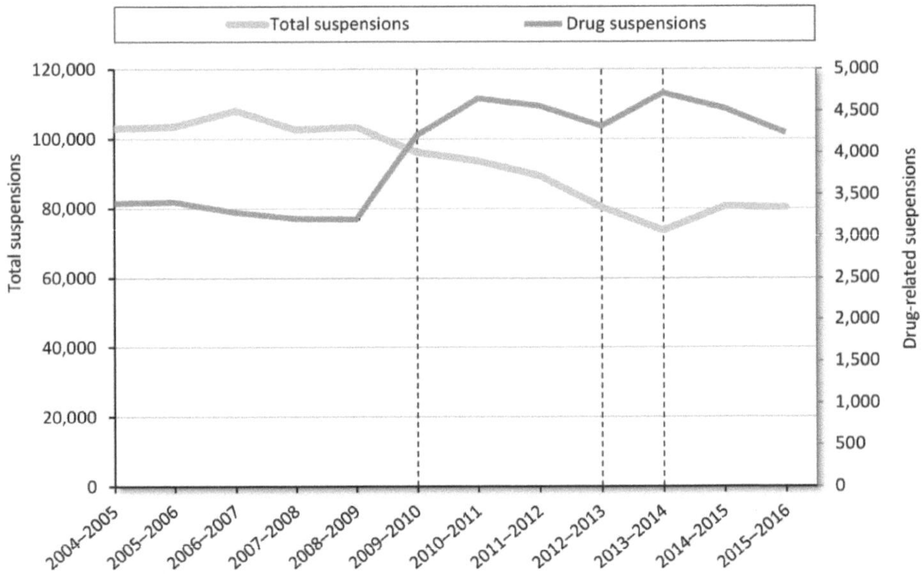

Figure 20. School Suspensions—Colorado

Source: Colorado Department of Education, 10-Year Trend Data, http://www.cde.state.co.us/cdereval/suspend-expelcurrent.

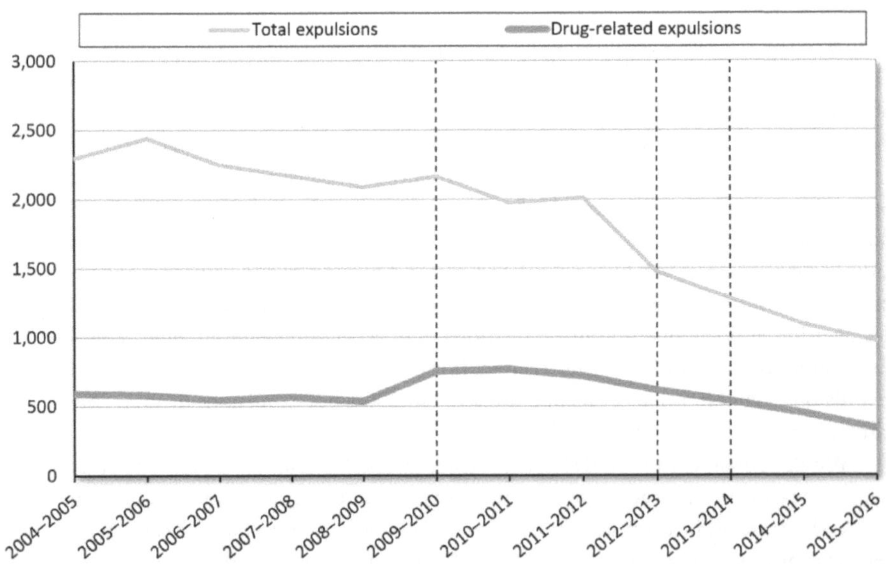

Figure 21. School Expulsions—Colorado

Source: Colorado Department of Education, http://www.cde.state.co.us/cdereval/suspend-expelcurrent.

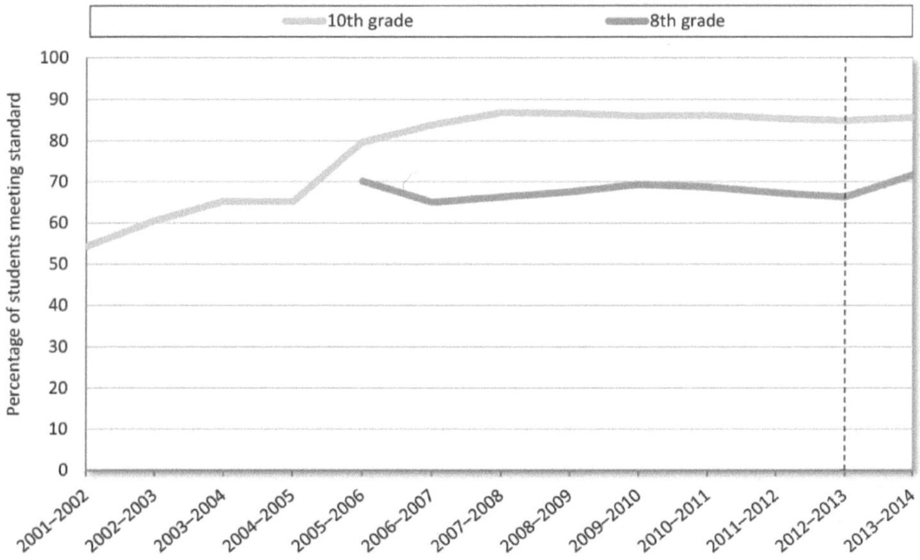

Figure 22. Washington Standardized Test Scores

Source: Washington State Office of the Superintendent of Public Instruction, http://reportcard.ospi.k12.wa.us/.

ECONOMIC OUTCOMES

Changing economic and demographic outcomes are unlikely to be significant effects of marijuana legalization, simply because marijuana is a small part of the overall economy. Nevertheless, we consider this outcome for completeness. Before legalization, many advocates thought that legalization could drive a robust influx of residents, particularly young individuals enticed to move across state lines to take advantage of loose marijuana laws. More recently, various news articles say housing prices in Colorado (particularly around Denver) are soaring at growth rates far above the national average, perhaps as a consequence of marijuana legalization. One analyst went so far as to say that marijuana has essentially "kick-started the recovery of the industrial market in Denver" and led to record-high rent levels.[85]

Figure 23 sheds doubt on these extreme claims by presenting the Case-Shiller Home Price Index for Denver, Seattle, and Portland, along with the national average.[86] Data show that home prices in all three cities have been rising steadily since mid-2011, with no apparent booms after marijuana policy changes. Housing prices in Denver did rise at a robust rate after January 2014, when marijuana shops opened, but this increase was in step with the national average.

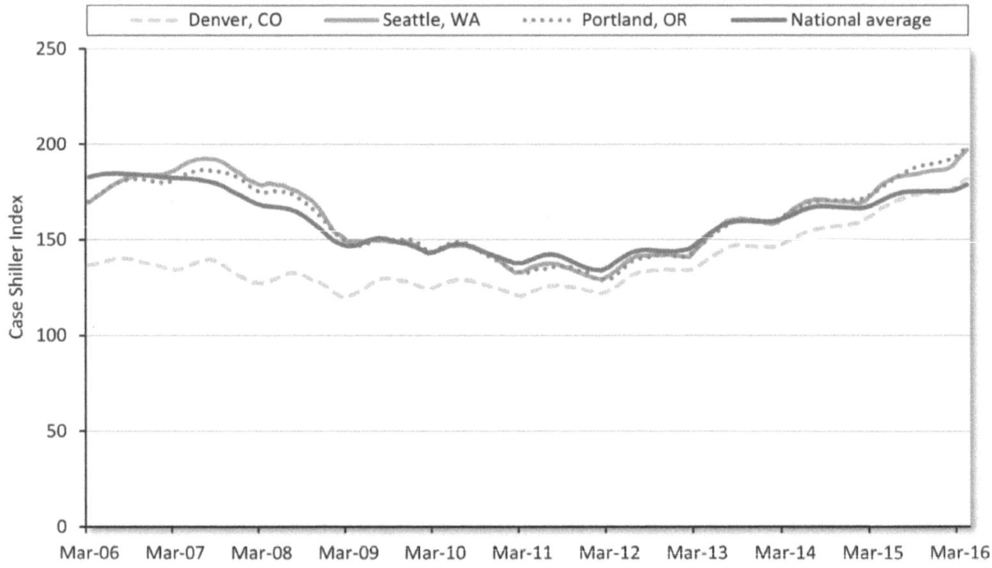

Figure 23. Case Shiller Home Price Index

Source: S&P Core Logic Case-Shiller Home Price Indices, http://us.spindices.com/index-family/real-estate/sp-corelogic-case-shiller.

Furthermore, marijuana legalization in all four legalizing states had, at most, a trivial effect on population growth.[87] Whereas some people may have moved across states for marijuana purposes, any resulting growth in population has been small and unlikely to cause noticeable increases in housing prices or total economic output.

Advocates also argue that legalization boosts economic activity by creating jobs in the marijuana sector, including "marijuana tourism" and other support industries, thereby boosting economic output.[88] Marijuana production and commerce do employ many thousands of people, and Colorado data provide some hint of a measurable effect on employment. As Figure 24 indicates, the seasonally adjusted unemployment rate began to fall more dramatically after the start of 2014, which coincides with the opening of marijuana stores.[89] These gains, however, have yet to be seen in Washington, Oregon, and Alaska. One hypothesis may be that Colorado, as the first state to open retail shops, benefitted from a "first mover advantage." If more states legalize, any employment gains will become spread out more broadly, and marijuana tourism may diminish.

Data from the Bureau of Economic Analysis show little evidence of significant gross domestic product (GDP) increases after legalization in any state.[90] Although it is hard to disentangle marijuana-related economic activity from broader economic trends, the surges in economic output predicted by some proponents have not yet materialized. Similarly, no clear changes have occurred in GDP per capita.

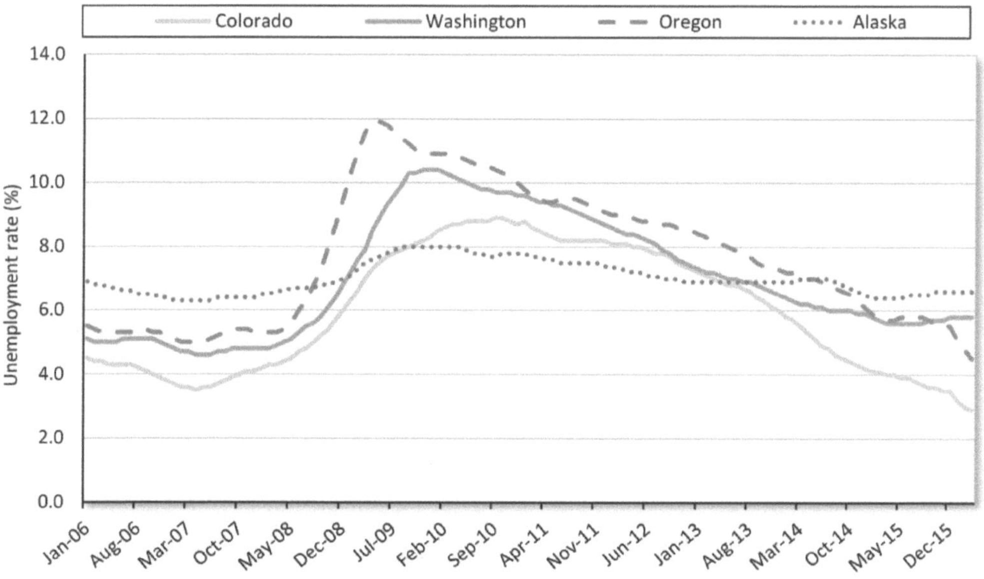

Figure 24. Unemployment Rates

Source: Bureau of Labor Statistics, Local Area Unemployment Statistics, http://www.bls.gov/lau/. Note: Rates are seasonally adjusted.

One area where legal marijuana has reaped unexpectedly large benefits is state tax revenue. Colorado, Washington, and Oregon all impose significant excise taxes on recreational marijuana, along with standard state sales taxes, other local taxes, and licensing fees. As seen in Figure 25, Colorado collects well over $10 million per month from recreational marijuana alone.[91] In 2015 the state generated a total of $135 million in recreational marijuana revenue, $35 million of which was earmarked for school construction projects. These figures are above some pre-legalization forecasts, although revenue growth was disappointingly sluggish during the first few months of sales.[92] A similar story has unfolded in Washington, as illustrated in Figure 26, where recreational marijuana generated approximately $70 million in tax revenue in the first year of sales[93]—double the original revenue forecast.[94] Oregon only began taxing recreational marijuana in January 2016, so data are still preliminary; however, state officials report revenues of $14.9 million so far, well above the initial estimate of $2.0 million to $3.0 million for the entire calendar year.[95] The tax revenues in these states may decline.

Limited post-legalization data prevent us from ruling out small changes in marijuana use or other outcomes. As additional post-legalization data become available, expanding this analysis will continue to inform the debate. The data so far provide little support for the strong claims about legalization made by either opponents or supporters.

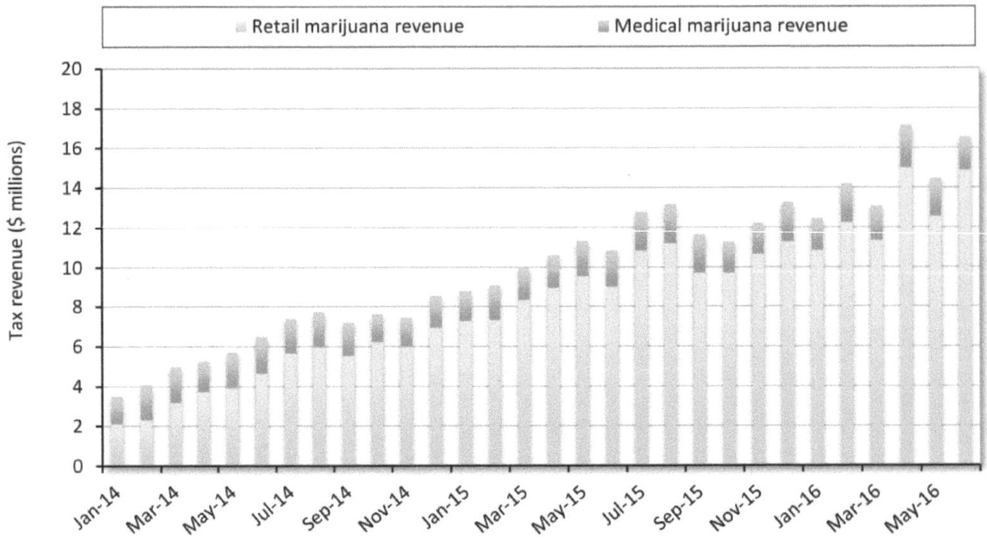

Figure 25. Marijuana Tax Revenues—Colorado (all values are nominal)

Source: Colorado Department of Revenue, https://www.colorado.gov/pacific/revenue/colorado-marijuana-tax-data.

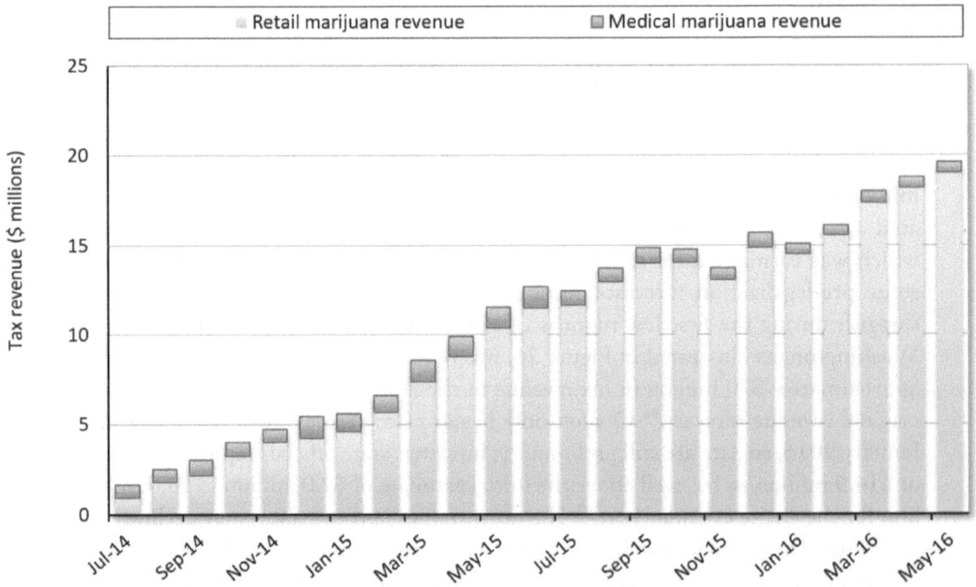

Figure 26. Marijuana Tax Revenues—Washington (all values are nominal)

Source: Washington State Department of Revenue, http://dor.wa.gov/Content/AboutUs/StatisticsAndReports/stats_MMJTaxes.aspx; Initiative 502 Data, http://www.502data.com/.

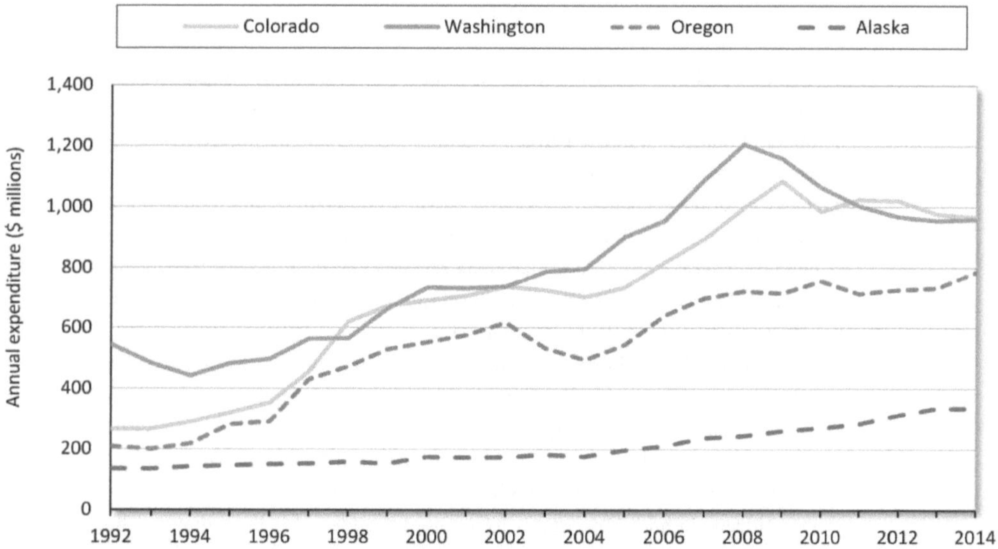

Figure 27. State Correctional Expenditures (all values are nominal)

Source: United States Census Bureau, American FactFinder Database, http://factfinder.census.gov/.

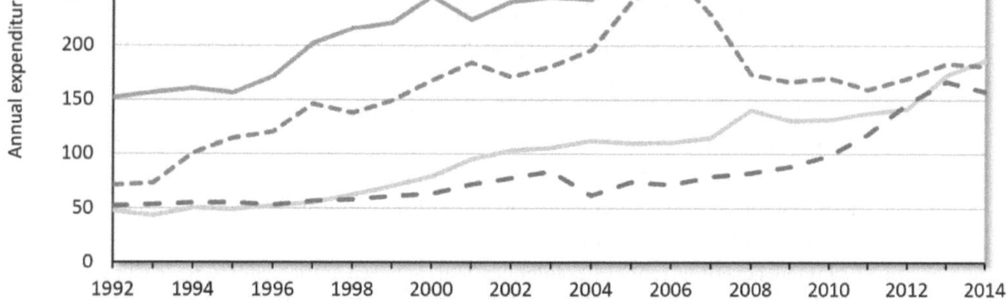

Figure 28. State Police Protection Expenditures (all values are nominal)

Source: United States Census Bureau, American FactFinder Database, http://factfinder.census.gov/.

NOTES

1. In November 2014, the District of Columbia voted overwhelmingly in favor of Initiative 71, which legalized the use, possession, and cultivation of limited amounts of marijuana in the privacy of one's home. It also permitted adults age 21 and over to "gift"—or transfer—up to two ounces of marijuana provided no payment or other exchange of goods or services occurred. Selling marijuana or consuming it in public, however, remain criminal violations. In addition, because of ongoing federal prohibition, marijuana remains illegal on federal land, which makes up 30 percent of the District. Therefore, we do not examine data for D.C. For more, see http://mpdc.dc.gov/marijuana.
2. In June 2016, the California secretary of state announced that a ballot referendum on marijuana legalization would occur in November, after a state campaign amassed enough signatures to put the question to a vote. Other likely candidates include Arizona, Florida, Maine, Massachusetts, Michigan, Missouri, Nevada, New York, Rhode Island, and Vermont. Organizations and private citizens in additional states have raised the idea of ballot initiatives but have not yet garnered the requisite signatures to hold a vote. See Jackie Salo, "Marijuana Legalization 2016: Which States Will Consider Cannabis This Year," *International Business Times*, December 30, 2015, http://www.ibtimes.com/marijuana-legalization-2016-which-states-will-consider-cannabis-year-2245024.
3. Ethan Nadelmann, for example, has asserted that legalization is a "smart" move that will help end mass incarceration and undermine illicit criminal organizations. See Nadelmann, "Marijuana Legalization: Not If, But When," *HuffingtonPost.com*, November 3, 2010, http://www.huffingtonpost.com/ethannadelmann/marijuana-legalization-no_b_778222.html.

   Former New Mexico governor and current Libertarian Party presidential candidate Gary Johnson has also advocated marijuana legalization, predicting that the measure will lead to less overall substance abuse because individuals addicted to alcohol or other substances will find marijuana a safer alternative. See Kelsey Osterman, "Gary Johnson: Legalizing Marijuana Will Lead to Lower Overall Substance Abuse," *RedAlertPolitics.com*, April 24, 2013, http://redalertpo litics.com/2013/04/24/gary-johnson-legalizing-marijuana-will-lead-to-less-overall-substance-abuse/.

   Denver Police Chief Robert White argues that violent crime dropped almost 9 percent in 2012. See Sadie Gurman, "Denver's Top Law Enforcement Officials Disagree: Is Crime Up or Down?" *Denver Post*, January 22, 2014, http://www.denverpost.com/2014/01/22/denvers-top-law-enforcement-officers-disagree-is-crime-up-or-down/.
4. Colorado governor John Hickenlooper (D) opposed initial efforts to legalize marijuana because he thought the policy would, among other things, increase the number of children using drugs. See Matt Ferner, "Gov. John Hickenlooper Opposes Legal Weed," *HuffingtonPost.com*, September 12, 2012, http://www.huffingtonpost.com/2012/09/12/gov-john-hickenlooper-opp_n_1879248.html.

Former U.S. attorney general Edwin Meese III, who is now the Heritage Foundation's Ronald Reagan Distinguished Fellow Emeritus, and Charles Stimson have argued that violent crime surges when marijuana is legally abundant and that the economic burden of legalization far outstrips the gain. See Meese and Stimson, "The Case against Legalizing Marijuana in California," Heritage Foundation, October 3, 2010, http://www.heritage.org/research/commentary/2010/10/the-case-against-legalizing-marijuana-in-california.

Kevin Sabet, a former senior White House drug policy adviser in the Obama administration, has called Colorado's marijuana legalization a mistake, warning that potential consequences may include high addiction rates, spikes in traffic accidents, and reductions in IQ. See Sabet, "Colorado Will Show Why Legalizing Marijuana Is a Mistake," *Washington Times*, January 17, 2014, http://www.washingtontimes.com/news/2014/jan/17/sabet-marijuana-legalizations-worst-enemy/.

The former director of the Drug Enforcement Administration, John Walters, claims that "what we [see] in Colorado has the markings of a drug use epidemic." He argues that there is now a thriving black market in marijuana in Colorado and that more research on marijuana's societal effects needs to be completed before legalization should be considered. See Walters, "The Devastation That's Really Happening in Colorado," *Weekly Standard*, July 10, 2014, http://www.weeklystandard.com/the-devastation-thats-really-happening-in-colorado/article/796308.

John Walsh, the U.S. attorney for Colorado, defended the targeted prosecution of medical marijuana dispensaries located near schools by citing figures from the Colorado Department of Education showing dramatic increases in drug-related school suspensions, expulsions, and law enforcement referrals between 2008 and 2011. See John Ingold, "U.S. Attorney John Walsh Justifies Federal Crackdown on Medical-Marijuana Shops," *Denver Post*, January 20, 2012, http://www.denverpost.com/2012/01/19/u-s-attorney-john-walsh-justifies-federal-crackdown-on-medical-marijuana-shops-2/.

Denver District Attorney Mitch Morrissey points to the 9 percent rise in felony cases submitted to his office during the 2008–11 period, after Colorado's marijuana laws had been partially liberalized, as evidence of marijuana's social effects. See Sadie Gurman, "Denver's Top Law Enforcement Officials Disagree: Is Crime Up or Down?" *Denver Post*, January 22, 2014, http://www.denver-post.com/2014/01/22/denvers-top-law-enforcement-officers-disagree-is-crime-up-or-down/.

Other recent news stories that report criticisms of marijuana liberalization include Jack Healy, "After 5 Months of Legal Sale, Colorado Sees the Downside of a Legal High," *New York Times*, May 31, 2014, http://www.nytimes.com/2014/06/01/us/after-5-months-of-sales-colorado-sees-the-downside-of-a-legal-high.html, and Josh Voorhees, "Going to Pot, *Slate.com*, May 21, 2014, http://www.slate.com/articles/news_and_politics/politics/2014/05/colorado_s_pot_experiment_the_unintended_consequences_of_marijuana_legalization.html.

Also, White House policy research indicates that marijuana is the drug most often linked to crime. See Rob Hotakainen, "Marijuana Is Drug Most Often Linked to Crime," McClatchy News Service, May 23, 2013, http://www.mc-clatchydc.com/news/politics-government/article24749413.html.

5. MacCoun et al. (2009) review the decriminalization literature from the first wave of decriminalizations in the 1970s, noting a lack of response. See MacCoun et al., "Do Citizens Know Whether Their State Has Decriminalized Marijuana? Assessing the Perceptual Component of Deterrence Theory." *Review of Law and Economics* 5 (2009): 347–71. Analysis of the recent U.S. state legalizations is more limited.

   Some noteworthy studies include Jeffrey Miron, "Marijuana Policy in Colorado," Cato Institute Working Paper no. 24, 2014; Andrew A. Monte et al., "The Implications of Marijuana Legalization in Colorado," *Journal of the American Medical Association* 313, no. 3 (2015): 241–42; Stacy Salomonsen-Sautel et al., "Trends in Fatal Motor Vehicle Crashes Before and After Marijuana Commercialization in Colorado," *Drug and Alcohol Dependence* 140 (2014): 137–44, which found a statistically significant uptick in drivers involved in a fatal motor vehicle crash after commercialization of medical marijuana in Colorado; Beau Kilmer et al., "Altered State?: Assessing How Marijuana Legalization in California Could Influence Marijuana Consumption and Public Budgets," Occasional Paper, Rand Drug Policy Research Center, Santa Monica, CA, 2010; Angela Hawken et al., "Quasi-Legal Cannabis in Colorado and Washington: Local and National Implications," *Addiction* 108, no. 5 (2013): 837–38; and Howard S. Kim et al., "Marijuana Tourism and Emergency Department Visits in Colorado," *New England Journal of Medicine*, 374 (2016): 797–98.

   For an analysis of whether Colorado has implemented its legalization in a manner consistent with the law, see John Hudak, "Colorado's Rollout of Legal Marijuana Is Succeeding," Governance Studies Series, Brookings Institution, Washing-ton, D.C., July 31, 2014, http://www.brookings.edu/~/media/research/files/papers/2014/07/colorado-marijuana-legalization-succeeding/cepmmjcov2.pdf. International evidence from Portugal (Glenn Greenwald, "Drug Decriminalization in Portugal," Cato Institute White Paper, 2009, http://object.cato.org/sites/cato.org/files/pubs/pdf/greenwald_whitepaper.pdf), the Netherlands (Robert J. MacCoun, "What can we learn from the Dutch cannabis coffeeshop system," *Addiction* 2011: 1–12 and Ali Palali and Jan C. van Ours, "Distance to Cannabis Shops and Age of Onset of Cannabis Use," *Health Economics* 24, 11 (2015): 1482–1501, parts of Australia (Jenny Williams and Anne Line Bretteville-Jensen, "Does Liberalizing Cannabis Laws Increase Cannabis Use?" *Journal of Health Economics* 36 (2014): 20–32) and parts of London (Nils Braakman and Simon Jones, "Cannabis Depenalization, Drug Consumption and Crime–Evidence from the 2004 Cannabis Declassification in the UK," *Social Science and Medicine* 115(2014): 29–37) suggest little to no effects of these laws on drug use. Jérôme Adda et al., "Crime and the Depenalization of Cannabis Possession: Evidence from a Policing Experiment," *Journal of Political*

Economy, 122, no. 5 (2014): 1130–1201 consider depenalization in a London borough, finding declines in crime caused by the police shifting enforcement to non-drug crime.

6. Opium, cocaine, coca leaves, and other derivatives of coca and opium had been essentially outlawed in 1914 by the Harrison Narcotic Act. See C. E. Terry, "The Harrison Anti-Narcotic Act," *American Journal of Public Health* 5, no. 6 (1915): 518, http://www.ncbi.nlm.nih.gov/pmc/articles/PMC 1286619/?page=1.
7. "When and Why Was Marijuana Outlawed," Schaffer Library of Drug Policy, http://druglibrary.org/schaffer/library/mj_outlawed.htm.
8. Ibid.
9. Mathieu Deflem, ed., *Popular Culture, Crime, and Social Control*, vol. 14, *Sociology of Crime, Law and Deviance* (Bingley, UK: Emerald Group Publishing, 2010), p. 13, https://goo.gl/ioAoVY.
10. Kathleen Ferraiolo, "From Killer Weed to Popular Medicine: The Evolution of Drug Control Policy, 1937–2000," *The Journal of Policy History* 19 (2007): 147–79, https://muse.jhu.edu/article/217587.
11. David Musto, "Opium, Cocaine and Marijuana in American History," *Scientific American* 20–27 (July 1991), http://www.ncbi.nlm.nih.gov/pubmed/1882226.
12. United Nations Office on Drugs and Crime, "Traffic in Narcotics, Barbiturates and Amphetamines in the United States," https://www.unodc.org/unodc/en/data-and-analysis/bulletin/bulletin_1956-01-01_3_page005.html.
13. "Drug Schedules," U.S. Drug Enforcement Administration, https://www.dea.gov/druginfo/ds.shtml.
14. The 11 states were Oregon (1973), Alaska (1975), California (1975), Colorado (1975), Maine (1975), Minnesota (1976), Ohio (1976), Mississippi (1977), New York (1977), North Carolina (1977), and Nevada (1978). See Rosalie Pacula et al., "Marijuana Decriminalization: What Does It Mean for the United States?" (National Bureau of Economic Research Working Paper no. 9690, NBER and RAND Corporation, Cambridge, MA, January 2004), http://www.rand.org/content/dam/rand/pubs/working_papers/2004/RAND_WR126.pdf.
15. Not all states followed such a straightforward path towards marijuana liberalization. Alaska, for example, decriminalized marijuana use and possession in one's home in 1975. In 1990, however, a voter initiative recriminalized possession and use of marijuana. See the section on Alaska for more details.
16. "States That Have Decriminalized," National Organization for the Reform of Marijuana Laws, http://norml.org/aboutmarijuana/item/states-that-have-decriminalized.
17. "The Legalization of Marijuana in Colorado: The Impact. A Preliminary Report," *Rocky Mountain HIDTA* 1 (August 2013): 3, http://www.rm hidta.org/html/final%20legalization%20of%20mj%20in%20colorado%20the%20impact.pdf.
18. David Ogden, the deputy attorney general at the time, issued a memorandum stating it would be unwise to "focus federal resources ... on individuals whose actions are in clear and unambiguous compliance with existing state law providing

for the medical use of marijuana." See "Memorandum for Selected United State Attorneys on Investigations and Prosecutions in States Authorizing the Medical Use of Marijuana," U.S. Department of Justice, October 19, 2009. https://www.justice.gov/opa/blog/memorandum-selected-united-state-attorneys-investigations-and-prosecutions-states.

19. The Ogden Memorandum did not permanently resolve confusion about the role of federal law in state marijuana policy. In 2011, the Department of Justice issued another memo entitled the "Cole Memo" which somewhat backpedaled on the Ogden Memo's position; it cautioned that "the Ogden Memorandum was never intended to shield such activities from federal enforcement action and prosecution, even where those activities purport to comply with state law." It was not until 2013 when those in the marijuana industry received a clear answer. A third memo unambiguously outlined the eight scenarios in which federal authorities would enforce marijuana laws in states where the substance was legal. Beyond those eight priorities, the federal government would leave marijuana law enforcement to local authorities. For more, see "Guidance Regarding the Ogden Memo in Jurisdictions Seeking to Authorize Marijuana for Medical Use," U.S. Department of Justice, June 29, 2011, https://www.justice.gov/sites/default/files/oip/legacy/2014/07/23/dag-guidance-2011-for-medical-marijuana-use.pdf. See also "Guidance Regarding Marijuana Enforcement," U.S. Department of Justice, August 29, 2013, https://www.justice.gov/iso/opa/resources/3052013829132756857467.pdf.
20. "The Legalization of Marijuana in Colorado: The Impact. A Preliminary Report," *Rocky Mountain HIDTA* 1 (August 2013): 4, http://www.rm hidta.org/html/final%20legalization%20of%20mj%20in%20colorado%20the%20impact.pdf.
21. "Amendment 64: Use and Regulation of Marijuana," City of Fort Collins, Colorado, http://www.fcgov.com/mmj/pdf/amendment64.pdf.
22. Ibid.
23. Numerous counties, including Denver County and others, have enacted local taxes on top of state taxes. In Denver, retail marijuana products are subject to a local sales tax of 3.65 percent in addition to a special marijuana tax of 3.5 percent. See "City and County of Denver, Colorado: Tax Guide, Topic No. 95," City of Denver (revised April 2015), https://www.denvergov.org/Portals/571/documents/TaxGuide/Marijuana-Medical_and_Retail.pdf.
24. This system of three separate taxes was eventually replaced by a single, 37 percent excise tax levied at the retail point of sale in July 2015. See "FAQs on Taxes," Washington State Liquor and Cannabis Board, http://www.liq.wa.gov/mj2015/faqs-on-taxes. See also Rachel La Corte, "Washington State Pot Law Overhaul: Marijuana Tax Reset at 37 Percent," Associated Press, *The Cannabist*, July 1, 2015, http://www.thecannabist.co/2015/07/01/washing-ton-state-pot-law-overhaul-marijuana-tax-reset-at-37-percent/37238/.
25. "State by State Laws: Oregon," National Organization for the Reform of Marijuana Laws, 2006, http://norml.org/laws/item/oregon-penalties-2.

26. See "Oregon Legislature Ends 24 Years of Marijuana Decriminalization," National Organization for the Reform of Marijuana Laws, news release, July 3, 1997, http://norml.org/news/1997/07/03/oregon-legislature-ends-24-years-of-marijuana-decrimnalization/. See also "State by State Laws: Oregon," National Organization for the Reform of Marijuana Laws, 2006.
27. "Medical Marijuana Rules and Statutes: Oregon Medical Marijuana Act," Oregon Health Authority, June 2016, http://public.health.oregon.gov/DiseasesConditions/ChronicDisease/MedicalMarijuanaProgram/Pages/legal.aspx#ors.
28. "Oregon Medical Marijuana Allowance Measure 33 (2004)," *Ballotpedia*, https://ballotpedia.org/Oregon_Medical_Marijuana_Allowance_Measure_33_(2004).
29. "Oregon Medical Marijuana Program Statistics," Oregon Health Authority, July 2016, https://public.health.oregon.gov/diseasesconditions/chronicdisease/medicalmarijuanaprogram/pages/data.aspx.
30. "Oregon Marijuana Legalization for Personal Use, Ballot Measure 5 (1986)," *Ballotpedia*, https://ballotpedia.org/Oregon_Marijuana_Legalization_for_Personal_Use,_Ballot_Measure_5_(1986).
31. "Oregon Cannabis Tax Act Initiative, Measure 80 (2012)," *Ballotpedia*, https://ballotpedia.org/Oregon_Cannabis_Tax_Act_Initiative,_Measure_80_(2012).
32. "Measure 91," Oregon Liquor Control Commission, https://www.oregon.gov/olcc/marijuana/Documents/Measure91.pdf.
33. Several counties in Oregon have enacted their own local taxes.
34. As of June 2016, 87 municipalities and 19 counties in Oregon had prohibited recreational marijuana businesses or producers in their jurisdiction. See "Record of Cities/Counties Prohibiting Licensed Recreational Marijuana Facilities," Oregon Liquor Control Commission, https://www.oregon.gov/olcc/marijuana/Documents/Cities_Counties_RMJ OptOut.pdf.
35. "Medical Marijuana Dispensary Directory," Oregon Health Authority http://www.oregon.gov/oha/mmj/Pages/directory.aspx.
36. *Ravin v. State*, 537 F.2d 494 (Alaska 1975).
37. "Alaska Marijuana Criminalization Initiative, Measure 2 (1990)," *Ballotpedia*, https://ballotpedia.org/Alaska_Marijuana_Criminalization_Initiative_Measure_2_(1990).
38. "Ballot Measure 8: Bill Allowing Medical Use of Marijuana," Alaska Division of Elections, http://www.elections.alaska.gov/doc/oep/1998/98bal8.htm.
39. Recent work includes the following: D. Mark Anderson et al., "Medical Marijuana Laws and Suicides by Gender and Age," *American Journal of Public Health* 104, no. 1 (December 2014): 2369–76; D. Mark Anderson et al., "Medical Marijuana Laws and Teen Marijuana Use," *American Law and Economic Review* 17, no. 2 (2015): 495–528; Choo, Esther K et al., "The Impact of State Medical Marijuana Legislation on Adolescent Marijuana Use," *Journal of Adolescent Health*, forthcoming.

    Yu-Wei Luke Chu, "Do Medical Marijuana Laws Increase Hard-Drug Use?" *Journal of Law and Economics* 58, no. 2 (May 2015): 481–517; Gorman, Dennis M. and J. Charles Huber, Jr. "Do Medical Cannabis Laws Encourage Cannabis

Use?" *The International Journal of Drug Policy*, 18, no. 3 (Ma7 2007): 160–67; S. Harper et al., "Do Medical Marijuana Laws Increase Marijuana Use? Replication Study and Extension," *Annals of Epidemiology* 22(2012): 207–212; Sarah D. Lynne-Landsman et al., "Effects of State Medical Marijuana Laws on Adolescent Marijuana Use," *American Journal of Public Health*, 103(2013): 1500–1506; Karen O'Keefe and Mitch Earleywine, "Marijuana Use by Young People: The Impact of State Medical Marijuana Laws," manuscript, Marijuana Policy Project (2011) and Hefei Wen et al., "The Effect of Medical Marijuana Laws on Marijuana, Alcohol, and Hard Drug Use," NBER Working Paper no. 20085, National Bureau of Economic Research, Cambridge, MA, 2014, which found that medical marijuana laws led to a relatively small increase in marijuana use by adults over age 21 and did nothing to change use of hard drugs.

Rosalie Liccardo Pacula et al., "Assessing the Effects of Medical Marijuana Laws on Marijuana and Alcohol Use: The Devil Is in the Details," NBER Working Paper no. 19302, National Bureau of Economic Research, Cambridge, MA, 2015, found that legalizing home cultivation and medical marijuana dispensaries were associated with higher marijuana use, while other aspects of medical marijuana liberalization were not.

Choo et al., "The Impact of State Medical Marijuana Legislation on Adolescent Marijuana Use," *Journal of Adolescent Health* 55, no. 2 (2014): 160–66, found no statistically significant differences in adolescent marijuana use after state-level medical marijuana legalization.

40. Data are reported as two-year averages. Data are from "National Survey on Drug Use and Health 2002–2014," Center for Behavioral Health Statistics and Quality, Substance Abuse and Mental Health Services Administration, http://www.icpsr.umich.edu/icpsrweb/content/SAMHDA/help/nsduh-estimates.html.
41. No post-legalization data were available for Alaska.
42. State-level data from "National Survey on Drug Use and Health, 2002–2014," Center for Behavioral Health Statistics and Quality.
43. Dale H. Gieringer, director, California NORML, "Testimony on the Legalization of Marijuana," Testimony before the California Assembly Committee on Public Safety, October 28, 2009, http://norml.org/pdf_files/AssPubSafety_Legalization.pdf.
44. Rand Corporation, "Legalizing Marijuana in California Would Sharply Lower the Price of the Drug," news release, July 7, 2007, http://www.rand.org/news/press/2010/07/07.html.
45. These analyses consider legalization at both the federal and state levels which would allow additional avenues for lower prices such as economies of scale, although also additional avenues for higher prices because of federal taxation and advertising.
46. The website Price of Weed allows anyone to submit anonymous data about the price, quantity, and quality of marijuana he or she purchases, as well as where the marijuana was purchased. Founded in 2010, the website has logged hundreds of thousands of entries across the country, and many analysts and journalists look to

it as a source of marijuana price data. It has obvious limitations: the data are not a random sample; the consumer reports do not distinguish between marijuana bought through legal means and through the black market; self-reported data may not be accurate; and the data are probably from a self-selecting crowd of marijuana enthusiasts. Nevertheless, Price of Weed provides large samples of real-time data. To reduce the impact of inaccurate submissions, the website automatically removes the bottom and top 5 percent of outliers when calculating its average prices. We were not able to calculate meaningful marijuana price averages from Alaska because of a relatively low number of entries from that state.

47. One further trend we observe in all three states is a widening price gap between high-quality and medium-quality marijuana. Among other things, this gap may be the result of fewer information asymmetries in the marijuana market. On the black market, it can be hard to know the true quality of a product. Marijuana trade is complex, with hundreds of different strains and varieties. Yet in the black market, consumers often have a difficult time differentiating between them and may end up paying similarly high prices for medium- and high-quality marijuana. In all three states, the gap between the prices rose after legalization, suggesting that consumers have had an easier time distinguishing between different qualities and strains of marijuana.
48. Anderson, Rees, and Sabia, "Medical Marijuana Laws and Suicides by Gender and Age."
49. D. Mark Anderson et al., "High on Life?: Medical Marijuana and Suicide," Cato Institute Research Briefs in Economic Policy, no. 17, January 2015, http://www.southerncannabis.org/wp-content/uploads/2015/01/marijuana-suicide-study.pdf.

    David Powell et al., "Do Medical Marijuana Laws Reduce Addictions and Deaths Related to Pain Killers?" NBER Working Paper no. 21345, National Bureau of Economic Research, Cam-bridge, MA, July 2015.
50. See, for example, Zammit et al., "Self-reported Cannabis Use as a Risk Factor for Schizophrenia in Swedish Conscripts of 1969," *British Medical Journal* 325 (2002); Henquet et al., "Prospective Cohort Study of Cannabis Use, Predisposition for Psychosis, and Psychotic Symptoms in Young People," *British Medical Journal* (December 2004); Gold-berg, "Studies Link Psychosis, Teenage Marijuana Use," *Boston Globe*, January 26, 2006; Shulman, "Marijuana Linked to Heart Disease and Depression," *U.S. News*, May 14, 2008.

    See also Jan C. van Ours et al., "Cannabis Use and Suicidal Ideation," *Journal of Health Economics* 32, no. 3 (2013): 524–37; Jan C. van Ours and Jenny Williams, "The Effects of Cannabis Use on Physical and Mental Health," *Journal of Health Economics* 31, no. 4 (July 2012): 564–77; Jan C. van Ours and Jenny Williams, "Cannabis Use and Mental Health Problems," *Journal of Applied Econometrics* 26, no. 7 (November 2011): 1137–56; and Jenny Williams and Christopher L. Skeels, "The Impact of Cannabis Use on Health," *De Economist* 154, no. 4 (December 2006): 517–46.
51. National Institute on Drug Abuse, "What Are Marijuana's Long-Term Impacts on the Brain?" Research Report Series, March 2016, https://www.drugabuse

.gov/publications/research-reports/marijuana/how-does-marijuana-use-affect-your-brain-body. Kelly and Rasul evaluate the depenalization of marijuana in a London borough and find large increases in hospital admissions related to hard drug use, particularly among younger men. See Elaine Kelly and Imran Rasul, "Policing Cannabis and Drug Related Hospital Admissions: Evidence from Administrative Records," *Journal of Public Economics* 112 (April 2014): 89–114.

52. "Detailed Mortality Statistics," Centers for Disease Control and Prevention, WONDER Online Databases, http://wonder.cdc.gov/.
53. Ibid.
54. The link between medical marijuana and lower suicide rates may stem partly from the fact that medical marijuana can substitute for other, more dangerous painkillers and opiates. Research by Anne Case and Angus Deaton found suicides and drug poisonings led to a marked increase in mortality rates of middle-aged white non-Hispanic men and women in the United States between 1999 and 2013. Other studies have linked opioid and painkiller overdoses to a recent surge in self-inflicted drug-related deaths and suicides. Medical marijuana, as a less risky pain reliever, may thus help lessen the rate of drug deaths and suicides. For more, see Case and Deaton, "Rising Morbidity and Mortality in Midlife among White Non-Hispanic Americans in the 21st Century," *National Academy of Sciences* 112, no. 49 (November 2015), http://www.pnas.org/content/112/49/15078.
55. Kevin Wong and Chelsey Clarke, *The Legalization of Marijuana in Colorado: The Impact* Vol. 3 (Denver: Rocky Mountain High Intensity Drug Trafficking Area, September 2015), http://www.rmhidta.org/html/2015%20final%20legalization%20of%20marijuana%20in%20colorado %20the%20impact.pdf.
56. Caleb Banta-Green et al., "Drug Abuse Trends in the Seattle-King Country Area: 2014," Report, University of Washington Alcohol and Drug Abuse Institute, Seattle, June 17, 2015, http://adai.washington.edu/pubs/cewg/Drug%20Trends_2014_final.pdf.
57. David Musto, "Opium, Cocaine and Marijuana in American History," *Scientific American*, no. 1 (July 1991): 40–47, http://www.ncbi.nlm.nih.gov/pubmed/1882226.
58. U.S. Drug Enforcement Administration, "The Dangers and Consequences of Marijuana Abuse," U.S. Department of Justice, Washington, May 2014, p. 24, https://www.dea.gov/docs/dangers-consequences-marijuana-abuse.pdf.
59. For example, Sheriff David Weaver of Douglas County, Colorado, warned in 2012, "Expect more crime, more kids using marijuana, and pot for sale everywhere." See Matt Ferner, "If Legalizing Marijuana Was Supposed to Cause More Crime, It's Not Doing a Very Good Job," *The Huffington Post*, July 17, 2014, http://www.huffingtonpost.com/2014/07/17/marijuana-crime-denver_n_5595742.html.
60. Jeffrey Miron, "Marijuana Policy in Colorado," Cato Institute Working Paper, October 23, 2014, http://object.cato.org/sites/cato.org/files/pubs/pdf/working-paper-24_2.pdf.

61. "Marijuana Is Safer Than Alcohol: It's Time to Treat It That Way," Marijuana Policy Project, Washington, https://www.mpp.org/marijuana-is-safer/. See also Peter Hoaken and Sherry Stewart, "Drugs of Abuse and the Elicitation of Human Aggressive Behavior," *Addictive Behaviors* 28: (2003): 1533–54, http://www.ukcia.org/research/AgressiveBehavior.pdf.
62. Denver Police Department, Uniform Crime Reporting Program, "Monthly Citywide Data—National Incident-Based Reporting System," http://www.denvergov.org/police/PoliceDepartment/CrimeInformation/CrimeStatisticsMaps/tabid/441370/Default.aspx.
63. Fort Collins crime data yield similar factual conclusions, showing no consistent rise in crime following either the November 2012 legalization or the January 2014 opening of stores.
64. "Crime Dashboard," Seattle Police Department, http://www.seattle.gov/seattle-police-department/crime-data/crime-dashboard.
65. Sierra Rayne, "Seattle's Post-Marijuana Legalization Crime Wave," *American Thinker*, November 13, 2015, http://www.americanthinker.com/blog/2015/11/seattles_postmarijuana_legalization_crime_wave.html.
66. Elsewhere in Washington State, this conclusion seems equally robust. Tacoma, a large city in northeastern Washington where stores have opened, has generally seen stable crime trends before and after legalization. Total monthly offenses, violent crime, and property crime have shown no significant deviation from their recent trends. See Kellie Lapczynski, "Tacoma Monthly Crime Data," Washington Association of Sheriffs and Police Chiefs, 2015, p377–78, http://www.waspc.org/assets/CJIS/crime%20in%20washington%20 2015.small.pdf.
67. "City of Portland—Neighborhood Crime Statistics," Portland Police Bureau, http://www.portlandonline.com/police/crimestats/.
68. In Salem, Oregon, violent crime, property crime, and drug offenses show no significant jumps post-legalization. Although Salem is farther from the border with Washington, there are no indications of major spillover effects between 2012 and 2014. See Linda Weber, "Monthly Crime Statistics," Salem Police Department, 2015, http://www.cityof salem.net/Departments/Police/HowDoI2/Pages/CrimeStatistics.aspx. Alaska is not covered in this section because reliable recent crime data for major Alaskan cities were unavailable at the time of writing.
69. For a review of this issues, see Rune Elvik, "Risk of Road Accident Associated with the Use of Drugs: A Systematic Review and Meta-Analysis of Evidence from Epidemiological Studies," *Accident Analysis and Prevention* 60 (2013): 254–67, doi:10.1016/j.aap.2012.06.017, http://www.ncbi.nlm.nih.gov/pubmed/22785089.
70. Academic studies examining this issue have suggested a possible substitution effect. A 2015 report by the Governors Highway Safety Organization cited one study revealing that marijuana-positive fatalities rose by 4 percent after legalization in Colorado. However, another study from the same report discovered no change in total traffic fatalities in California after its decriminalization of the drug

in 2011. See also Andrew Sewell et al., "The Effect of Cannabis Compared with Alcohol on Driving," *American Journal on Addictions* 18, no. 3 (2009): 185–93, http://www.ncbi.nlm.nih.gov/pmc/articles/PMC2722956/.

71. Kevin A. Sabet, "Colorado Will Show Why Legalizing Marijuana Is a Mistake," *Washington Times*, January 17, 2014, http://www.washington times.com/news/2014/jan/17/sabet-marijuana-legalizations-worst-enemy/.
72. Associated Press, "Fatal Crashes Involving Marijuana Doubled in Washington after Legalization," *The Oregonian*, August 20, 2015, http://www.oregonlive.com/marijuana/index.ssf/2015/08/fatal_crashes_involving_mariju.html.
73. Noelle Phillips and Elizabeth Hernandez, "Colorado Still Not Sure Whether Legal Marijuana Made Roads Less Safe," *Denver Post*, December 29, 2015, http://www.denverpost.com/2015/12/29/colorado-still-not-sure-whether-legal-marijuana-made-roads-less-safe/.
74. Radley Balko, "Since Marijuana Legalization, Highway Fatalities in Colorado Are at Near-Historic Lows," *Washington Post*, August 5, 2014, https://www.washingtonpost.com/news/the-watch/wp/2014/08/05/since-marijuana-legalization-highway-fatalities-in-colorado-are-at-near-historic-lows/.
75. These data include any kinds of crashes on all types of roads, as recorded by each state's department of transportation. See Colorado Department of Transportation's "Fatal Accident Statistics by City and County," http://www.coloradodot.info/library/traffic/traffic-manuals-guidelines/safety-crash-data/fatal-crash-data-city-county/fatal-crashes-by-city-and-county.
76. Annual crash data from the National Highway Traffic Safety Administration (NHTSA) confirm these findings. Our analysis uses state-level traffic accident data from individual state transportation departments because their data are mostly reported monthly and have a shorter reporting time lag than NHTSA data. For NHTSA data, see "State Traffic Safety Information," NHTSA, http://www-nrd.nhtsa.dot.gov/departments/nrd-30/ncsa/STSI/8_CO/2014/8_CO_2014.htm.
77. We additionally analyzed fatality rates for accidents involving alcohol impairment. Similarly, this time series shows no clear signs of significant swings after marijuana policy changes, suggesting that any substitution effect associated with marijuana has been small compared to overall drunk driving.
78. Washington Traffic Safety Commission, 2015, http://wtsc.wa.gov/research-data/crash-data/.
79. Washington State police routinely test drivers involved in car crashes for traces of various substances. The official legalization of marijuana use at the end of 2012 appears to have had at most a negligible effect on crash fatalities. The Washington Traffic Safety Commission recorded a total of 62 marijuana-related crash fatalities in 2013, compared to 61 in 2012. There does seem to be a temporary increase in fatalities caused by marijuana-related crashes around the same time as the establishment of Washington's first marijuana shops. Nevertheless, any sort of spike seems to have been temporary. In the first six months following the opening of stores, 46 crash fatalities were tied to using marijuana while driving; over the following six months, that number dropped to 32.

80. Monthly data on fatal crashes themselves were not available. Monthly 2015 data were also not available at the time of writing.
81. For instance, Meier et al. analyze a large sample of individuals tracked from birth to age 38 and find that those who smoked marijuana most heavily prior to age 18 lost an average of eight IQ points, a highly significant drop. See Madeline Meier et al., "Persistent Cannabis Users Show Neuropsychological Decline from Childhood to Midlife," *Proceedings of the National Academy of Sciences* 109, no. 40 (2012): E2657–E2664, http://www.ncbi.nlm.nih.gov/pubmed/22927402.

    However, other studies have found results that rebut Meier et al. Mokrysz et al. examine an even larger sample of adolescents and, after controlling for many potentially confounding variables, discover no significant correlation between teen marijuana use and IQ change. See Claire Mokrysz et al., "Are IQ and Educational Outcomes in Teenagers Related to Their Cannabis Use? A Prospective Cohort Study," *Journal of Psychopharmacology* 30, no. 2 (2016): 159–68, http://jop.sagepub.com/con tent/30/2/159.
82. Cobb-Clark et al. show that much of relationship between marijuana use and educational outcomes is likely due to selection, although there is possibly some causal effect in reducing university entrance scores. See Deborah A. Cobb-Clark et al., "'High'-School: The Relationship between Early Marijuana Use and Educational Outcomes," *Economic Record* 91, no. 293 (June 2015): 247–66.

    Evidence in McCaffrey et al. supports this selection explanation of the association between marijuana use and educational outcomes. See Daniel F. McCaffrey et al., "Marijuana Use and High School Dropout: The Influence of Unobservables," *Health Economics* 19, no. 11 (November 2010): 1281–99.

    Roebuck et al. suggest that chronic marijuana use, not more casual use, likely drives any relationship between marijuana use and school attendance. See M. Christopher Roebuck et al., "Adolescent Marijuana Use and School Attendance," *Economics of Education Review* 23, no. 2 (2004), 133–41.

    Marie and Zölitz estimate grade improvements are likely due to improved cognitive functioning among students whose nationalities prohibited them from consuming marijuana. See Olivier Marie and Ulf Zölitz, "'High' Achievers? Cannabis Access and Academic Performance," CESifo Working Paper Series no. 5304, Center for Economic Studies and Ifo Institute, Munich, 2015.

    Van Ours and Williams review the literature concluding that cannabis may reduce educational outcomes, particularly with early onset of use. See Jan van Ours and Jenny Williams, "Cannabis Use and Its Effects on Health, Education and Labor Market Success," *Journal of Economic* Surveys, 29, no. 5 (December 2015): 993–1010.

    For additional evidence on likely negative effects of early onset of use see also Paolo Rungo et al., "Parental Education, child's grade repetition, and the modifier effect of cannabis use," *Applied Economics Letters* 22(3)(2015): 199–203; Jan C. van Ours and Jenny Williams, "Why Parents Worry: Initiation into Cannabis Use by Youth and Their Educational Attainment," *Journal of Health Economics* 28, no. 1 (2009): 132–42; and Pinka Chatterji, "Illicit Drug Use and Educational Attainment," *Health Economics* 15, no. 5 (2006): 489–511.

83. "Suspension/Expulsion Statistics," Colorado Department of Education, 2015, http://www.cde.state.co.us/cdereval/suspend-expelcurrent.
84. "Washington State Report Card, 2013–14 Results," Washington State Office of the Superintendent of Public Instruction, http://reportcard.ospi.k12.wa.us/summary.aspx?groupLevel=District&schoolId=1&reportLevel=State&year=2013–14&yrs=2013–14.
85. Sarah Berger, "Colorado's Marijuana Industry Has a Big Impact on Denver Real Estate: Report," *International Business Times*, October 20, 2015, http://www.ibtimes.com/colorados-marijuana-industry-has-big-impact-denver-real-estate-report-2149623.
86. "S&P/Case-Schiller Denver Home Price Index," S&P Dow Jones Indices, http://us.spindices. com/indices/real-estate/sp-case-shiller-co-denver-home-price-index/.
87. U.S. Department of Commerce, Bureau of Economic Analysis, http://www.bea.gov/iTable/iTable.cfm?reqid=70&step=1&isuri=1&acrdn=1#reqid=70&step=30&isuri=1&7022=36&7023=0&7024=non-indust3000&7027=1&7001=336&7028=-&7031=0&7040=-083=levels&7029=36&7090=70.
88. As an example, Oregon state legislator Ann Lininger wrote an op-ed predicting a "jobs boom" in southern Oregon after marijuana legalization. See Lininger, "Marijuana: Will Legalization Create an Economic Boom?" *The Huffington Post*. October 1, 2015. http://www.huffingtonpost.com/annlininger/marijuana-will-legalizati_b_8224712.html.
89. "Local Area Unemployment Statistics," Bureau of Labor Statistics, http://www.bls.gov/lau/.
90. U.S. Department of Commerce, Bureau of Economic Analysis, http://www.bea.gov/iTable/iTablecfm?reqid=70&step=1&isuri=1&acrdn=1#reqid=70&step=10&isuri=1&7003=200&7035=-.
91. Colorado Department of Revenue, "Colorado Marijuana Tax Data," Colorado Official State Web Portal, https://www.colorado.gov/pacific/revenue/colorado-marijuana-tax-data.
92. Tom Robleski, "Up in Smoke: Colorado Pot Biz Not the Tax Windfall Many Predicted," January 2015, http://www.silive.com/opinion/columns/index.ssf/2015/01/up_in_smoke_colorado_pot_biz_n.html.
93. Washington State Department of Revenue, "Marijuana Tax Tables," http://dor.wa.gov/Content/AboutUs/StatisticsAndReports/stats_MMJTaxes.aspx and http://www.502data.com/.
94. "Washington Rakes in Revenue from Marijuana Taxes," RT (Russia Today television channel), July 13, 2015, https://www.rt.com/usa/273409-washington-state-pot-taxes/.
95. Oregon Department of Revenue, "Marijuana Tax Program Update," Joint Interim Committee on Marijuana Legalization, May 23, 2016, https://olis.leg.state.or.us/liz/2015I1/Downloads/CommitteeMeetingDocument/90434.

RELATED PUBLICATIONS FROM THE CATO INSTITUTE

High on Life? Medical Marijuana Laws and Suicide by D. Mark Anderson, Daniel I. Rees, and Joseph J. Sabia, Cato Institute Research Briefs in Economic Policy no. 17 (January 7, 2015)

Designer Drugs: A New, Futile Front in the War on Illegal Drugs by Ted Galen Carpenter, Cato Institute Policy Analysis no. 774 (May 27, 2015)

Marijuana Policy in Colorado by Jeffrey Miron, Cato Institute Working Paper no. 24 (October 23, 2014)

Medical Marijuana Laws and Teen Marijuana Use by D. Mark Anderson, Daniel I. Rees, and Joseph J. Sabia, Cato Institute Research Briefs in Economic Policy no. 11 (October 1, 2014)

On the Limits of Federal Supremacy: When States Relax (or Abandon) Marijuana Bans by Robert A. Mikos, Cato Institute Policy Analysis no. 714 (December 12, 2012)

The Budgetary Impact of Ending Drug Prohibition by Jeffrey Miron and Katherine Waldock, Cato Institute White Paper (September 27, 2010)

Drug Decriminalization in Portugal: Lessons for Creating Fair and Successful Drug Policies by Glenn Greenwald, Cato Institute White Paper (April 2, 2009)

Treating Doctors as Drug Dealers: The DEA's War on Prescription Painkillers by Robert T. Libby, Cato Institute Policy Analysis no. 545 (June 6, 2005)

CATO INSTITUTE POLICY ANALYSIS SERIES

798. **Terrorism and Immigration: A Risk Analysis** by Alex Nowrasteh (September 13, 2016)

797. **Five Myths about Economic Inequality in America** by Michael Tanner (September 7, 2016)

796. **Freedom of Speech under Assault on Campus** by Daniel Jacobson (August 30, 2016)

795. **25 Years of Reforms in Ex-Communist Countries Fast and Extensive Reforms Led to Higher Growth and More Political Freedom** by Oleh Havrylysyn, Xiaofan Meng, and Marian L. Tupy (July 12, 2016)

794. **Options for Federal Privatization and Reform Lessons from Abroad** by Chris Edwards (June 28, 2016)

CHAPTER 12

WHITE COLLAR CRIME—A DEFINITION

By Ron Liggett

"But because fraud is man's peculiar vice,
More it displeases God; and so stand lowest
The fraudulent, and greater dole assails them."
—From Dante's Inferno, Canto 11[1]

If we take the words of Dante as written, it would seem that a gloomy fate awaits the fraudulent, as they are described as the "lowest." Yet we know for certain that the literary warnings from the 14th-century poet were not heeded during the Middle Ages, nor in contemporary times. Accordingly, fraudulent behavior continues with a number of notable white collar and corporate crime cases in the last 15–20 years. Enron, Tyco, Global Crossing, Adelphia, and WorldCom are just a few of the large corporations that appear on this very visible list. On an individual basis, Bernie Madoff and his Ponzi-type investment scheme stand alone to some as the epitome of an out-of-control white collar felon. Additionally, the amount of white collar acts impacting small business throughout the U.S.—and the globe—also appears to be endless. But, before we examine any specific situations, let us reach some consensus on what we mean when we label certain crimes as "white collar."

Edwin Sutherland in a 1939 presentation to the American Sociological Society urged the group to "expand the boundaries of the study of crime to include the criminal acts of respectable individuals in the course of their occupations." He chose the label "white collar crimes" to describe these certain behaviors and this term has become an important part of criminal studies and lexicon.[2] Most obviously, he wanted these men punished, but in reality, it would be many years before white collar crime would be seriously addressed as objectionable behavior, i.e., criminal.

However, even with widespread acceptance of the white collar label, social scientists continually attempted through the years to exact a clearer definition and appropriate use of the term. Reaching an agreement on this definition was somewhat challenging. Perhaps Sutherland's initial phraseology contributed to the problem, but there was also a definite reluctance to pursue some of these individuals—many who were leaders of corporations and commerce.

Listed below, in no particular chronology, are various definitions for white collar crime:

> **First**—An illegal act or series of illegal acts committed by nonphysical means and by concealment or guile, to obtain money or property, to avoid the payment or loss of money or property, or to obtain business or personal advantage.[3]
>
> **Second**—A phrase connoting a variety of frauds, schemes, corruptions, and commercial offenses committed by business persons, con artists, and public officials. The term was originally intended as a classification of offenders but has expanded to include a broad range of non-violent offenses that have cheating and dishonesty as their central element.[4]
>
> **And Finally (the "Old Definition")**—An act defined approximately as a crime committed by a person of respectability and high social status in the course of his occupation.[5]

FOCUSING ON SUTHERLAND

Each of these descriptions has merit. But of particular interest is the last one offered by Sutherland. In this "Old Definition," the focus seemed to be more on the individual rather than the crime itself by specifying a "person of respectability" and of "high social status." Was the initial focus truly meant for these select groups? Some scholars suggest that, no, it was not the original intention to limit the definition. However, the relevance of such high positions is still apparent in the following analysis of his comments.

> It is clear however, that for Sutherland the offender characteristics of respectability and high social status had little relevance as causal factors in explaining criminal behavior. The significance of an offender's respectability of high social status lies primarily in the refutation of existing theories that look to the causes of crime in poverty and social disorganization. For Sutherland, the fact that an offender is respectable, or of high social status, or employed is no more important in explaining crime than is poverty or unemployment in explaining the crimes of others.
>
> This is not to suggest, however, that these factors have no relevance in understanding crime. One's respectability, occupational position, or

> access to wealth and power leads to and creates opportunity structures for crime that can be unique in and of themselves, or that may have corollaries to or spinoffs from what are often called common crimes.
>
> [...] First, as Sutherland so clearly pointed out in his research, the avenues available to the white-collar offender through the civil and administrative remedies allow such offenders to escape the traditional stigma of the criminal sanction, even though the harm of their actions is often as great or greater than the offenses normally trapped by the machinations of the criminal law.[6] [emphasis added]

Two noteworthy comments should be made in regards to the last paragraph—one contradictory and one affirming. First, in regards to "escaping stigma," it would seem that through prosecutorial attitudes, public opinion, and the flow of electronic information, there is no escape today. Names like Bernie Madoff, Dennis Kozlowski, Ken Lay, and others, appear, to many, as disgraced in the public arena. Likewise, long-term sentences exceeding 20 years given to Bernie Ebbers and Jeff Skilling, in addition to financial fines, certainly suggest no "escape."[A] (The extended sentence issued to Bernie Madoff will be discussed separately.) More specifically, Ebbers, who was convicted in the fraud which led to the bankruptcy of WorldCom, was sentenced to 25 years in prison while paying $5.5 million in cash and forfeiting approximately $40 million in other assets.[7] Skilling, convicted as part of the Enron debacle, was originally sentenced to 24 years (later reduced to 14) and likewise ordered to hand over approximately $40 million in assets.[8]

Second, we can affirm the point that these acts cause significant harm. The economic damages and financial ruin we have seen in recent years to both individuals and corporations cannot be minimized. Further, on a macro scale, when we analyze and study sources of the financial crisis and Great Recession of 2008 and the major role of the "housing bubble," we can see some semblance of white collar crime. For example, the falsification of loan documents by lenders and brokers allowed non-qualified borrowers access to mortgages they would never be able to afford. The impact of these types of offenses, with a flawed consumer base in the sub-prime market, faulty government policy, and some helter-skelter in mortgage securitization, contributed greatly to a devastating financial situation.

In regards to Sutherland, his abhorrence for this type of behavior was borne out of the backlash in the 1930's against the business elite.[B] And to say that he was

A It is worth noting, in both WorldCom and Enron, other individuals and former employees were also convicted and sentenced for a variety of white collar crimes.

B One could argue that Sutherland's pursuit in this area was more in line with a 'crusade' to see some of these business 'barons' punished. This is not meant to question his goal, just an observation.

passionate in his pursuits to see this behavior punished is likely an understatement. For years, the type of activity which today is clearly labeled as criminal was generally ignored or met with minor punishment at best. Using a term the scholar had come across in his readings—"criminaloid"[C]—he stated very firmly his true thoughts on these particular criminal behaviors in a harsh indictment: "...these white-collar criminaloids...are by far the most dangerous to society of any type of criminals from the point of view of effects on private property and social institutions."[9] Again, a rather harsh indictment which is likely not fitting in all cases.

ILLEGAL INSIDER TRADING AND CIVIL V. CRIMINAL

While we have not yet addressed the topic of illegal **insider trading** in our text, this type of behavior is often categorized as a white collar crime. Generally defined as the use of non-public material information in the buying or selling of a security, such behavior may not always fit neatly into the common elements approach mentioned in this chapter. And, while convictions are not uncommon, prosecution of this type of crime can be difficult with the outright proving of such behavior being deemed "ambiguous at best."[D] Additionally, "insider trading cases can be confusing for jurors who have little knowledge of the complex dealings of Wall Street."[10] As with most white collar crimes, the penalties in this area may vary from only a fine—a civil penalty—to the more serious criminal penalty of both fines and prison. Nonetheless, there are many individuals who have received harsh punishment with long-term sentences for this type of illegal stock trading. But what really determines whether the punishment is deemed civil versus criminal?

The following from Walt Pavlo, a former white collar criminal who now does extensive writing and consulting in this field is noteworthy:

> Raj Rajaratnam was sentenced to 11 years in prison as a result of trading on inside, confidential information related to publicly traded companies (namely Goldman Sachs). His profits were said to be over $80 million and his firm, Galleon Group, has since closed. William Marovitz, husband of then Playboy CEO Christie Hefner, traded on Playboy stock between 2004 and 2009 based on "pillow talk" inside information that allowed him to realize gains of over $100,000

C The use of the word criminaloid was meant to describe "people who commit acts that are not necessarily illicit but nevertheless undermine societal well-being." (See Soltes reference in endnotes).

D "Ambiguous at best" was a phrase used frequently by an investment advisor in noting how difficult it is when trying to determine the exact reasoning behind a specific trade, i.e., did one actually use "inside information" to trade? And, where exactly did the information accrue from?

> trading on Playboy stock. For his infraction, Marovitz paid a fine without admitting wrongdoing. While Marovitz and Hefner have since divorced, he was never in jeopardy of spending a night in federal prison. So why is one person jailed and the other fined for essentially the same crime? It depends on a number of factors.
>
> I reached out to Jordan Thomas, Labaton Sucharow partner and Chair of the Whistleblower Representation Practice and also a former Assistant Director and Assistant Chief Litigation Counsel in the Division of Enforcement at the SEC, for his perspectives. Thomas told me that in his experience the triggers for criminal insider trading charges were based on three primary factors:
>
> 1) Significance of wrongdoing (amount of money involved, the number of people affected by the trade and the duration of the activity)
>
> 2) Corroboration of others to prove a criminal case and provide evidence of wrongdoing (need someone to flip or have someone on tape)
>
> 3) Recidivists of any securities violations (always looking to clean up Wall Street)[11]

Obviously, the cases mentioned here have material differences in the estimate of profits, $80 million vs. $100K. However, it is likely relevant to again note the comment from above in regards to white collar cases as sometimes being "ambiguous at best."

A MORE CONTEMPORARY DEFINITION OF WHITE COLLAR CRIME

Having alluded to the variety of white collar meanings, we will attempt to simplify and subscribe to a seemingly uncomplicated Common Element Approach. In the aggregate, the following elements adequately present the characteristics we find most relevant for a definition of white collar crime:

- Committed in the course of one's occupation.
- Act is intentionally committed.
- Goal = money, property, power, prestige.
- Involves violation of trust (typically at a job).
- No physical force.[12]

With the Common Element Approach (CEA), we are not necessarily distinguishing between crimes committed by upper management and those committed by non-management, although some studies do address differences in those two categories of offenders. And while economic analysis would still use the rational approach of Becker to explain this type of behavior—i.e., if expected utility outweighs expected disadvantages, the offense will be committed—it is interesting to note other behavioral influences as well.

For example, a sociological theory of this crime "postulates that managers who commit economic offenses live in a social setting, i.e., culture, in which a very high value is placed on material success and individual wealth."[13] In lay terms the researchers are talking about "keeping up with the Joneses" or, in economic jargon, conspicuous consumption, a term first used by industrial economist Thorstein Veblen in 1899. A simple definition for this type of consumption would be the purchase of goods and services simply because of the prestige those items may provide. For Veblen, such purchases would include designer clothes, mansions, and other socially visible items.[14, E]

To summarize, certainly what is suggested here is to again apply the term to a higher-income individual or person of status. Additionally, it is also a certainty that at least some theorists propose "that strong striving for wealth and enjoyment in some way contributes to economic crimes committed by managers."[15 F]

WHITE COLLAR CRIME IN EUROPE—A PSYCHOLOGICAL PERSPECTIVE

Briefly we will note that the existence of white collar crime is certainly not limited to the U.S. and Capitalism alone; the idea of conspicuous consumption lives abroad as well. It has been reported that 42.5% of larger companies across Europe have experienced some type of economic crime, most prominently embezzlement and breach of trust.[16] From a psychological perspective, European studies note three key characteristics of participants in these offenses—high hedonism, low integrity, and high conscientiousness. What does each of these mean? The study defined hedonism, *ceteris paribus*, as placing a high value on material wealth and individual success. Integrity was determined through measurement of an offender's irresponsibility, their disregard for the rules, and their willingness to participate in high risk-taking. Conscientiousness was determined by measurement of personality traits that considered attributes such as "striving for competence, order, fulfillment of duties, achievement," among others.[17]

E According to Veblen, the idea of a socially visible good for the male industrialist even included the so-called trophy spouse. Colander, *Economics*, 8th Ed.

F In today's world, the idea of conspicuous consumption most definitely has application at lower income levels, as well. It is unlikely that Veblen could have anticipated the "bling" culture or the idea of high school dropouts craving $300 Gucci shoes and gold-plated teeth.

WHITE COLLAR IN OTHER PLACES

The *Legal Environment of Business*, by Meiners et al., offers a few thoughts in regards to white collar crime in other parts of the globe.

> Senior executives in the United States, such as the heads of Enron and WorldCom, were given long prison terms for activities that get lumped under the title white-collar crime. These cases get attention and raise concerns about bad behavior at the top of the corporate chain.
>
> There is good reason to suspect that law enforcement in the United States is tougher than it is elsewhere. In Korea, Japan, and most European nations, close ties between government and business cause many illegal financial activities to be overlooked or treated mildly. A slap on the wrist has been the usual "punishment." That may be changing as international capital markets demand greater accountability. Investors do not like being duped.
>
> Breaking with the tradition of ignoring white-collar crime in Korea, the long-time chairman of Hyundai Motor Company was found guilty of embezzlement and fraud. In Japan, where punishment of executives has been rare and government has kept such matters secret, the head of a successful internet company, Livedoor, was given a prison term for stock fraud. In Germany, the prominent Siemens Company has undergone a long criminal probe involving huge bribes paid around the world to get business. All countries have laws against white-collar crime; enforcement is another matter.[18]

WHITE COLLAR CRIMES—HOW DEMOCRATIC AND HOW VISIBLE?

To further our understanding of this topic, there are two observations proposed by Edelhertz in 1970 that are worth analyzing; note that these are not meant to conflict with any previous statements. First, his idea that white collar crime is democratic would still appear to be true. He proposed that crimes could be committed up the ladder by a bank executive or down the chain through a bank teller. In the public sector, it could be a high-ranking government official with some type of conflict of interest who goes astray. Or, at a lower level, a poor beneficiary of a poverty-program might enroll fictional workers into the plan and appropriate their funds. In today's technological world, the possibility of any of these has likely increased. Needless to say, there are many opportunities.

Second, Edelhertz labeled white collar crime as "low visibility" with a "high impact factor."[19] As we fast-forward to the present, it is safe to say that the low visibility characterization of 1970 is no longer valid. Each individual listed earlier in this section (and countless others) have been paraded across the national screens, with their criminal deeds noted in great detail. Accordingly, it would appear that the day of low visibility no longer exists and with more visibility comes higher costs. In fact, there are some who have questioned whether the penalties today are too harsh, when compared to 30 years ago.[20]

As for "high impact," that factor remains part of today's equation. For example, the white collar corruption which occurred at Enron essentially brought down the seventh-largest company in the country. This corporate failure was extraordinarily painful with 20,000 Enron employees directly affected, and indirectly, thousands more.[21]

A SLIGHTLY DIFFERENT VIEW

Finally, and somewhat surprisingly, the suggestion that white collar criminals are both sophisticated and "calculating" in their criminal behaviors might not always be correct. In a recently published book, Professor Eugene Soltes challenges the idea that these criminal executives are consistently applying cost-benefit analysis. With interesting scrutiny, Soltes examines numerous cases involving white collar behaviors and his book notes the following:

> "...The usual explanations fail to tell the whole story of why many seemingly successful people go over the line. White collar criminals are not merely driven by excessive greed or hubris, nor do they usually carefully calculate costs and benefits before breaking the law. Instead... most of the executives who committed crimes made decisions the way we all do—on the basis of their intuitions and gut feelings. The trouble is that those gut feelings are often poorly suited for the modern business world where leaders are increasingly distanced from the consequences of their decisions and the individuals they impact."[22]

In analyzing a behavior which is deemed to have gone "over the line," many on the outside might conclude that they'd never cross such a line by declaring, "I would never do that!" or, "This certainly could not happen to me." However, in reality, few individuals are presented with the type of "line" many of these executives have faced. Accordingly, it is difficult to determine what course of action one would actually take when confronted with these situations.

I cited comments from Walt Pavlo earlier in the chapter. Once convicted of fraudulent behavior as an employee of MCI (which later became part of WorldCom), Pavlo served nearly four years in prison and paid substantial fines for his crime. Having served his "time" and bore his punishment, he now spends time writing, consulting, and speaking to various groups, including college students, on the behaviors which led to his confinement.[G] His knowledgeable perspective is also very genuine. In dutifully examining and describing some of these behaviors—including his own—he offers a brief, but profound statement which likely fits some of the financial miscues referenced in this chapter.

In speaking of an individual who finds himself involved in white collar activity, Pavlo notes how the behavior (and situation) expands: "You dig your hole deeper and deeper and deeper."[23] In looking back, Skilling, Ebbers, Madoff, and many others might agree with the observation.

Finally, while speaking to a classroom of college students, Pavlo echoes similar concerns regarding the 'invincibility' alluded to by Soltes. He carefully asserts, "It isn't that far from the person sitting in the chair in the front row that I'm speaking to that they could be in the experience that I experienced."[24] For anyone in earshot of his remarks, these words ring with wisdom and hopefully help to direct some to a better path.

OTHER TERMS

There are a number of terms that are applicable in the world of white collar crime, so-called corporate crime, and also, to some extent, in the world of organized crime. Listed below are several that are useful in the study of this topic.

Bribery—An offer of or the taking of money, goods, services, or other items of value in order to influence official actions or decisions.

Counterfeiting—The copying of a genuine item without authorization, especially when it is passed off for the genuine item. This applies to the illegal copying of currency, most of which happens outside the U.S., in addition to copying designer clothes and other products.

Computer and Internet Fraud—Unauthorized use of or access to financial accounts, in addition to unauthorized use of computers, computer files, or any sabotage of computers.

Economic Espionage—The theft or misappropriation of valuable business information from a person or business, including trade secrets.

Embezzlement—The taking of money or other valuable property for their own use by a person of trust who has control over said property.

G Pavlo contributes to Forbes.com with a blog on white collar crime. He has also established a speaker's bureau on this subject entitled, 500 Pearl Street Speakers.

Fraud—Intentionally misrepresenting a material fact so that the person relying on the miscommunication suffers loss.

Insider Trading—The buying or selling of the securities of a firm based on information not yet available to the public with the intention of achieving a profit.

Money Laundering—The transfer of money obtained illegally through legitimate accounts or people so that the original source of the funds cannot be determined.

ENDNOTES

1. Alighieri, Dante. (1308–1321). "The Divine Comedy: Inferno." Canto XI.
2. Schlegel, Kip and David Weisburd. (1992). "White-Collar Crime: The Parallax View." *White-Collar Crime Reconsidered.* Northeastern University Press. p. 3.
3. Edelhertz, Herbert. (1970 May). "The Nature, Impact and Prosecution of White-Collar Crime." National Institute of Law Enforcement and Criminal Justice, Law Enforcement Assistance Administration. U.S. Department of Justice. Washington D.C.
4. Gifis, Steven H. (1984). *Law Dictionary*. New York: Barrons, p. 516.
5. Sutherland, Edwin H. (1939 Dec 29). "White-Collar Crime Violates Trust and Therefore Creates Distrust." Presentation to Joint Meeting of the American Sociological Society and the American Economic Association. As presented in *White-Collar and Corporate Crime* by Gilbert Geis. (2011). Santa Barbara, CA: Greenwood, p. 3.
6. Schlegel p. 5.
7. Johnson, Carrie. (2005 July 14). "Ebbers Gets 25-Year Sentence in Worldcom Fraud." *Washington Post.* http://www.washingtonpost.com/wp-dyn/content/article/2005/07/13/AR2005071300516.html.
8. Fuchs, Erin. (2013 May 8). "Deal Reached: Former Enron CEO Jeff Skilling Could Get Out of 10 Years Early." *Business Insider.* http://www.businessinsider.com/jeffrey-skilling-plea-deal-2013-5.
9. Soltes, Eugene. (2016). *Why They Do It—Inside the Mind of the White Collar Criminal,* p. 19. Public Affairs Publishing. New York, NY.
10. Pavlo, Walter. (2011 May 11). "Raj Rajaratnam Guilty—Why Things Didn't Go His Way." *Forbes.* https://www.forbes.com/sites/walterpavlo/2011/05/11/raj-rajaratnam-guilty-why-things-didnt-go-his-way/#495a1ef618bd
11. Pavlo, Walter. (2013 Oct 24). "Insider Trading: Civil Or Criminal Crime?" *Forbes.* https://www.forbes.com/sites/walterpavlo/2013/10/24/insider-trading-civil-or-criminal/#1e0e1abd6564
12. Hellman, Daryl A. and Neil O. Alper. (2006). *Economics of Crime: Theory and Practice.* Boston: Pearson Custom Publishing, p. 135.
13. Hellman p. 135.

14. Blickle, Gerhard, Alexander Schlegel, Pantaleon Fassbender, and Uwe Klein. (2006). "Some Personality Correlates of Business White-Collar Crime." *Applied Psychology: An International Review*. 2006, 55 (2), p. 222.
15. Colander, David C. (2010). *Economics*, 8th Ed. McGraw-Hill, p. 242.
16. Blickle p. 221.
17. Blickle p. 224.
18. Meiners, Roger E., Al. H. Ringleb, and Frances L. Edwards. (2009). *The Legal Environment of Business*. 10th Ed. Mason, OH: South-Western Cengage, p. 116.
19. Edelhertz
20. Soltes p. 42.
21. Geis, Gilbert. (2011). *White-Collar and Corporate Crime*. Santa Barbara, CA: Greenwood, p. 235.
22. Soltes Front Cover.
23. Pavlo, Walt. Speech to University of Mississippi students. https://www.youtube.com/watch?v=sPUuHn5_L1g. Accessed 2017 Sept 5.
24. Pavlo

BERNIE MADOFF—A WHITE COLLAR CRIME CASE STUDY

By Ron Liggett

Bernie Madoff was arrested December 11, 2008 for securities fraud; however, his Ponzi investment scheme may have gone on for as long as 40 years.[1] A Ponzi scheme is an investment scam that promises high rates of returns to investors, usually with little risk. In reality, the "old" investors essentially receive funds that are being deposited by the unknowing "new" investors. Ponzi schemes can appear to work deceptively well in prosperous times and perhaps if the economy had not deteriorated so severely in 2008, the con might have continued for an even longer period.

In reality, the investment hoax likely should have been discovered years before. There were multiple SEC investigations as well as testimony from an analyst who noted that Madoff's "reported investment returns were mathematically impossible." Madoff himself stated that had SEC examiners asked the right questions in a 2003 investigation, they would have caught him. But they didn't, and the fraud continued. "Like most criminals—people who break securities laws don't expect to get caught," and certainly Madoff fit this category.[2]

The white collar crime case of Bernard Madoff, a once-prominent investment advisor, is most notable for a variety of reasons. First, the size of the scam alone, as it is estimated that investors were defrauded of $65 billion! Second, many of those defrauded in this case were at the highest social levels and included celebrities such as Larry King and Steven Spielberg, major Jewish and charitable groups, and other large investment organizations. Additionally, it should be noted that, in fact, it was his sons who initiated the original indictments by reporting the frauds to their attorney. The SEC had seemingly overlooked Madoff's long-running scheme.[3]

The statement that follows was delivered by Madoff as part of his plea arrangement. For those unfamiliar with the case, he presents some explanation of the acts he was involved in, and therefore provides some depth to the swindle. The plea and apology had little impact, however, and Madoff received the maximum sentence of 150 years.[A] Translation—he will undoubtedly die in prison.

In the case of white collar crimes, it is interesting to note the length of sentencing in these high-profile cases. From an economic analysis, there is a preference to use fines as the form of punishment, particularly for non-violent criminals. Specifically, Becker notes that "social welfare is increased if fines are used whenever feasible."[4] Therefore, fines minimize resource allocation, maximize social welfare, and alleviate taxpayers having to "pick up the tab" for prison costs. However, it would be difficult to place the Madoff case into the "fines only" category. While both fines and restitution were imposed, and personal assets were confiscated, the financial damage imposed on victims of his deception was so colossal that monetary damages alone were not sufficient.

Text of the actual statement made by Bernie Madoff in U.S. District Court follows. The statement is helpful to provide a working knowledge of what is truly one of the most prominent white collar crime cases in our nation's history.

A The 150-year sentence issued to Madoff actually pales in comparison to the 845 years given to white collar criminal Sholam Weiss (www.forbes.com), although the outcome will likely be the same. That is, unless Mr. Weiss is somehow related to the Star Wars Jedi Yoda, he too will die in prison.

TEXT OF BERNARD MADOFF'S COURT STATEMENT[5]

MARCH 12, 2009

Your Honor, for many years up until my arrest on December 11, 2008, I operated a Ponzi scheme through the investment advisory side of my business, Bernard L. Madoff Securities LLC, which was located here in Manhattan, New York at 885 Third Avenue. I am actually grateful for this first opportunity to publicly speak about my crimes, for which I am so deeply sorry and ashamed. As I engaged in my fraud, I knew what I was doing was wrong, indeed criminal. When I began the Ponzi scheme I believed it would end shortly and I would be able to extricate myself and my clients from the scheme. However, this proved difficult, and ultimately impossible, and as the years went by I realized that my arrest and this day would inevitably come. I am painfully aware that I have deeply hurt many, many people, including the members of my family, my closest friends, business associates and the thousands of clients who gave me their money. I cannot adequately express how sorry I am for what I have done. I am here today to accept responsibility for my crimes by pleading guilty and, with this plea allocution, explain the means by which I carried out and concealed my fraud.

The essence of my scheme was that I represented to clients and prospective clients who wished to open investment advisory and individual trading accounts with me that I would invest their money in shares of common stock, options and other securities of large well-known corporations, and upon request, would return to them their profits and principal. Those representations were false because for many years up and until I was arrested on December 11, 2008, I never invested those funds in the securities, as I had promised. Instead, those funds were deposited in a bank account at Chase Manhattan Bank. When clients wished to receive the profits they believed they had earned with me or to redeem their principal, I used the money in the Chase Manhattan bank account that belonged to them or other clients to pay the requested funds. The victims of my scheme included individuals, charitable organizations, trusts, pension funds and hedge funds. Among other means, I obtained their funds through interstate wire transfers they sent from financial institutions located outside New York State to the bank account of my investment advisory business, located here in Manhattan, New York, and through mailings delivered by the United States Postal Service and private interstate carriers to my firm here in Manhattan.

I want to emphasize today that while my investment advisory business—the vehicle of my wrongdoing—was part of my firm Bernard L. Madoff Securities, the other businesses my firm engaged in, proprietary trading and market making, were legitimate, profitable and successful in all respects. Those businesses were managed by my brother and two sons.

To the best of my recollection, my fraud began in the early 1990s. At that time, the country was in a recession and this posed a problem for investments in the securities markets. Nevertheless, I had received investment commitments from certain institutional clients and understood that those clients, like all professional investors, expected to see their investments outperform the market. While I never promised a specific rate of return to any client, I felt compelled to satisfy my clients' expectations, at any cost. I therefore claimed that I employed an investment strategy I had developed, called a "split-strike conversion strategy," to falsely give the appearance to clients that I had achieved the results I believed they expected.

Through the split-strike conversion strategy, I promised to clients and prospective clients that client funds would be invested in a basket of common stocks within the Standard & Poor's 100 Index, a collection of the 100 largest publicly traded companies in terms of their market capitalization. I promised that I would select a basket of stocks that would closely mimic the price movements of the Standard & Poor's 100 Index. I promised that I would opportunistically time these purchases and would be out of the market intermittently, investing client funds during these periods in United States Government-issued securities such as United States Treasury bills. In addition, I promised that as part of the split-strike conversion strategy, I would hedge the investments I made in the basket of common stocks by using client funds to buy and sell option contracts related to those stocks, thereby limiting potential client losses caused by unpredictable changes in stock prices. In fact, I never made the investments I promised clients, who believed they were invested with me in the split-strike conversion strategy.

To conceal my fraud, I misrepresented to clients, employees and others, that I purchased securities for clients in overseas markets. Indeed, when the United States Securities and Exchange Commission asked me to testify as part of an investigation they were conducting about my investment advisory business, I knowingly gave false testimony under oath to the staff of the SEC on May 19, 2006, that I executed trades of common stock on behalf of my investment advisory clients and that I purchased and sold the equities that were part of my investment strategy in European markets. In that session with the SEC, which took place here in Manhattan, New York, I also knowingly gave false testimony under oath that I had executed options contracts on behalf of my investment advisory clients and that my firm had custody of the assets managed on behalf of my investment advisory clients.

To further cover up the fact that I had not executed trades on behalf of my investment advisory clients, I knowingly caused false trading confirmations and client account statements that reflected the bogus transactions and positions to be created and sent to clients purportedly involved in the split-strike conversion strategy, as well as other individual clients I defrauded who believed they had invested in securities through me. The clients receiving trade confirmations and account statements had no way of knowing by reviewing these documents that I had never engaged in the transactions represented on the statements and confirmations. I knew those false confirmations and account statements would be and were sent to clients through the U.S. mails from my office here in Manhattan.

Another way that I concealed my fraud was through the filing of false and misleading certified audit reports and financial statements with the SEC. I knew that these audit reports and financial statements were false and that they would also be sent to clients. These reports, which were prepared here in the Southern District of New York, among other things, falsely reflected my firm's liabilities as a result of my intentional failure to purchase securities on behalf of my advisory clients.

Similarly, when I recently caused my firm in 2006 to register as an investment advisor with the SEC, I subsequently filed with the SEC a document called a Form ADV Uniform Application for Investment Adviser Registration. On this form, I intentionally and falsely certified under penalty of perjury that Bernard L. Madoff Investment and Securities had custody of my advisory clients' securities. That was not true and I knew it when I completed and filed the form with the SEC, which I did from my office on the 17th floor of 885 Third Avenue, here in Manhattan.

In more recent years, I used yet another method to conceal my fraud. I wired money between the United States and the United Kingdom to make it appear as though there were actual securities transactions executed on behalf of my investment advisory clients. Specifically, I had money transferred from the U.S. bank account of my investment advisory business to the London bank account of Madoff Securities International Ltd., a United Kingdom corporation that was an affiliate of my business in New York. Madoff Securities International Ltd. was principally engaged in proprietary trading and was a legitimate, honestly run and operated business.

Nevertheless, to support my false claim that I purchased and sold securities for my investment advisory clients in European markets, I caused money from the bank account of my fraudulent advisory business, located here in Manhattan, to be wire transferred to the London bank account of Madoff Securities International Limited.

There were also times in recent years when I had money, which had originated in the New York Chase Manhattan bank account of my investment advisory business, transferred from the London bank account of Madoff Securities International Ltd. to the Bank of New York operating bank account of my firm's legitimate proprietary and market making business. That Bank of New York account was located in New York. I did this as a way of ensuring that the expenses associated with the operation of the fraudulent investment advisory business would not be paid from the operations of the legitimate proprietary trading and market making businesses.

In connection with the purported trades, I caused the fraudulent investment advisory side of my business to charge the investment advisory clients $0.04 per share as a commission. At times in the last few years, these commissions were transferred from Chase Manhattan bank account of the fraudulent investment advisory side of my firm to the account at the Bank of New York, which was the operating account for the legitimate side of Bernard L. Madoff Investment Securities—the proprietary trading and market making side of my firm. I did this to ensure that the expenses associated with the operation of my fraudulent investment advisory business would not be paid from the operations of the legitimate proprietary trading and market making businesses. It is my belief that the salaries and bonuses of the personnel involved in the operation of the legitimate side of Bernard L. Madoff Investment Securities were funded by the operations of the firm's successful proprietary trading and market making businesses.

Your Honor, I hope I have conveyed with some particularity in my own words, the crimes I committed and the means by which I committed them. Thank you.

ENDNOTES

1. Geis, Gilbert. (2011). *White-Collar and Corporate Crime.* Santa Barbara, CA: Greenwood,. pp. 274–275.
2. Investment News. (2012 July 29). "Editorial: Heavier SEC Fines Unlikely to Dent Fraud." <www.investmentnews.com>. Accessed 2012 Dec 3.
3. Geis.
4. Becker, Gary. (1976). *The Economic Approach to Human Behavior.* Chicago: University of Chicago Press, p. 63.
5. <http://www.justice.gov/usao/nys/madoff/madoffhearing031209.pdf>.

CHAPTER 13

CAPITAL PUNISHMENT—AN INTRODUCTION

By Ron Liggett

On a recent trip to San Diego to meet with my publisher, I was fortunate to book a hotel with an amazing view of the Pacific Ocean overlooking Scripps Park. While working on my laptop, I not only had the ocean as a backdrop, but also a clear view of myriad activity in the scenic park below. Tourists, locals, scuba divers and snorkelers, as well as families of all shapes, sizes, and nationalities were there to take in the picturesque ocean landscape, beaches, sea lions, and the beauty of the Pacific.

However, there was another observation to be made. With all the healthy activity in clear view, there were also individuals who had visibly fallen on difficult times. From the 3rd floor I observed one particular gentleman sort through a public garbage can. He pulled out what looked to be a large discarded Starbucks coffee cup, slowly checked the contents, and drank what was left of the beverage. When the drink was empty, he slowly went along his way. It was a poignant moment to be sure.

Certainly, in our day-to-day existence we may observe behaviors which illicit strong feelings and emotions. Whether we are observing something of a social nature, such as that in the previous paragraph, or something with criminal content, some issues may be difficult to discuss objectively as they appeal to our humanity. In the economics of crime, the topic of capital punishment is undoubtedly one of those poignant issues.

So, what do we make of legal policy that allows the taking of a life for certain dreadful and criminal acts? Most assuredly, there are other options we could choose rather than extinguishing a life. Is not a lifetime prison sentence adequate punishment for the worst of our offenders? The arguments surrounding this subject are many and varied, and, for some, there is no justification for the execution of anyone, including an individual convicted of a capital crime.[A] However, in

A A capital crime or offense is one deemed so serious that it may be punishable by death. While capital crimes may vary from state-to-state, they generally include first degree murder, murder with special circumstances, treason at the federal level, and other violent acts.

order to facilitate a discussion and a comparison between capital punishment and the alternative—namely being sentenced to 'life in prison'—we can use economic observations and briefly consider four questions.

1. Is there a moral justification for Capital Punishment and can we truly proclaim that executing a prisoner is not akin to murder?
2. Is there a deterrent effect from Capital Punishment?
3. Can we justify Capital Punishment from a 'cost' standpoint?
4. Can we be sure that no innocent individual is executed via a mistake in the justice system?

While these questions are individually challenging, answers do exist. To be sure, one can find data (or reasoning) to support both sides of these arguments. However, from observing more recent legislative and judicial activity at the state level, one might presume that the answer to these questions is a negative one as the number of executions falls.[1] Technically, 31 states still allow capital punishment, but this number too is slowly declining as a trend against the death penalty grows.[2]

Nonetheless, from an analytical perspective, one can also assert the following:

> First, by definition, capital punishment does not equate to murder.[B] The fact that one does not approve of capital punishment does not make it unlawful, or murder.
>
> Second, although some studies have found otherwise, research does exist which asserts that capital punishment is a deterrent to certain types of crime.[3]
>
> Third, while a long-held consensus suggests that capital punishment is ALWAYS more expensive, there <u>is</u> data which substantiates that life imprisonment can have a higher cost. When considerations are given to issues such as the explicit and implicit long-term costs, inflation, medical care, and the additional criminal acts frequently committed behind bars, the cost outlook can change.[C] So, while there is no doubt that the legal costs to prosecute a death penalty case are extremely high, the real question is this: "Can we <u>justify</u> capital punishment from a cost standpoint?"[D]

B Murder is defined as the unlawful and premeditated taking of a human life.

C Be forewarned, almost any suggestion that life imprisonment is more costly is likely to illicit a few guffaws from those opposed to the death penalty. As the saying goes, sometimes "perception becomes reality."

D It is worth noting that the biggest cost from a death penalty case—overwhelmingly—comes from legal fees and attorney costs. Arguably this is done to be sure that the prosecutors truly have the correct criminal.

Finally, the most important question (in the view of this author) is the last one. To state the obvious, in regards to question four, there is simply NO margin for error. And, while improved scientific methods exist in the analysis of evidence, the possibility of human error remains and is difficult to quantify. Additionally, we know that wrongful convictions have occurred in a variety of criminal cases. So, should this concern eliminate the death penalty as a means of punishment? Some states have indeed answered this question in the affirmative. However, no matter what position one takes, we know that the deeply problematic nature of this issue demands the highest level of scrutiny in the prosecution of these cases.

While there is certainly much more to be stated on this controversial topic, the remainder of the chapter is turned over to the thoughts and writings of two esteemed professors, the late Gary Becker and Judge Richard Posner. In addition to their decades of academic contributions, these two brilliant minds also made extensive contributions in the blogosphere via a series of discussions on a variety of issues. Having access to their scholarly debates is enriching and most assuredly serves to expand one's frame of reference on the topic.

ENDNOTES

1. Von Drehle, David. (2015 June 8). "The Death of the Death Penalty." *Time*. (http://time.com/deathpenalty/. Accessed 2017 Nov 22.
2. http://www.ncsl.org/research/civil-and-criminal-justice/death-penalty.aspx. Accessed 2017 Sept 6.
3. Dezhbakhsh, H., Rubin, P. and Shepherd, J.M. (2003) Does Capital Punishment Have a Deterrent Effect? New Evidence from Postmoratorium Panel Data. American Law and Economics Review, 5, 344–376. http://dx.doi.org/10.1093/aler/ahg021.

CAPITAL PUNISHMENT

By Gary S. Becker and Richard A. Posner

DECEMBER 18, 25, 2005

THE ECONOMICS OF CAPITAL PUNISHMENT—POSNER

The recent execution by the state of California of the multiple murderer Stanley "Tookie" Williams has brought renewed controversy to the practice of capital punishment, which has been abolished in about a third of the states and in most of the nations that the United States considers its peers; the European Union will not admit to membership a nation that retains capital punishment.

From an economic standpoint, the principal considerations in evaluating the issue of retaining capital punishment are the incremental deterrent effect of executing murderers, the rate of false positives (that is, execution of the innocent), the cost of capital punishment relative to life imprisonment without parole (the usual alternative nowadays), the utility that retributivists and the friends and family members of the murderer's victim (or in Williams's case, victims) derive from execution, and the disutility that fervent opponents of capital punishment, along with relatives and friends of the defendant, experience. The utility comparison seems a standoff, and I will ignore it, although the fact that almost two-thirds of the U.S. population supports the death penalty is some, albeit weak (because it does not measure intensity of preference), evidence bearing on the comparison.

Early empirical analysis by Isaac Ehrlich found a substantial incremental deterrent effect of capital punishment, a finding that coincides with the common sense of the situation: it is exceedingly rare for a defendant who has a choice to prefer being executed to being imprisoned for life. Ehrlich's work was criticized by some economists, but more recent work by economists Hashem Dezhbakhsh,

Paul Rubin, and Joanna Shepherd provides strong support for Ehrlich's thesis; these authors found, in a careful econometric analysis, that one execution deters eighteen murders. Although this ratio may seem implausible given that the probability of being executed for committing a murder is less than 1 percent (most executions are in southern states—fifty of the fifty-nine in 2004—which that year had a total of almost seven thousand murders), the probability is misleading because only a subset of murderers are eligible for execution. Moreover, even a 1 percent or one-half of 1 percent probability of death is hardly trivial; most people would pay a substantial amount of money to eliminate such a probability

As for the risk of executing an innocent person, this is exceedingly slight, especially when a distinction is made between legal and factual innocence. Some murderers are executed by mistake in the sense that they might have a good legal defense to being sentenced to death, such as having been prevented from offering evidence in mitigation of their crime, such as evidence of having grown up in terrible circumstances that made it difficult for them to resist the temptations of a life of crime. But they are not innocent of murder. The number of people who are executed for a murder they did not commit appears to be vanishingly small.

It is so small, however, in part because of the enormous protraction of capital litigation. The average amount of time that a defendant spends on death row before being executed is about ten years. If the defendant is innocent, the error is highly likely to be discovered within that period. It would be different if execution followed the appeal of the defendant's sentence by a week. But the delay in execution not only reduces the deterrent effect of execution (though probably only slightly) but also makes capital punishment quite costly, since there is a substantial imprisonment cost on top of the heavy litigation costs of capital cases, with their endless rounds of appellate and postconviction proceedings.

Although it may seem heartless to say so, the concern with mistaken execution seems exaggerated. The number of people executed in all of 2004 was, as I noted, only fifty-nine. (The annual number has not exceeded ninety-eight since 1951.) Suppose that were it not for the enormous delays in execution, the number would have been sixty, and the additional person executed would have been factually innocent. The number of Americans who die each year in accidents exceeds one hundred thousand; many of these deaths are more painful than death by lethal injection, though they are not as humiliating and usually they are not anticipated, which adds a particular dread to execution. Moreover, for what appears to be a psychological reason (the "availability heuristic"), the death of a single, identified person tends to have greater salience than the death of a much larger number of anonymous persons. As Stalin is reported to have quipped, a single death is a tragedy, a million deaths is a statistic.

But that's psychology; there is an economic argument for speeding up the imposition of the death penalty on convicted murderers eligible for the penalty; the gain in deterrence and reduction in cost are likely to exceed the increase in the very slight probability of executing a factually innocent person. What is more, by allocating more resources to the litigation of capital cases, the error rate could be kept at its present very low level even though delay in execution was reduced.

However, even with the existing, excessive, delay, the recent evidence concerning the deterrent effect of capital punishment provides strong support for resisting the abolition movement.

A final consideration returns me to the case of "Tookie" Williams. The major argument made for clemency was that he had reformed in prison and, more important, had become an influential critic of the type of gang violence in which he had engaged. Should the argument have prevailed? On the one hand, if murderers know that by "reforming" on death row they will have a good shot at clemency, the deterrent effect of the death penalty will be reduced. On the other hand, the type of advocacy in which Williams engaged probably had some social value, and the more likely the advocacy is to earn clemency, the more such advocacy there will be; clemency is the currency in which such activities are compensated and therefore encouraged. Presumably grants of clemency on such a basis should be rare, since there probably are rapidly diminishing social returns to death-row advocacy, along with diminished deterrence as a result of fewer executions. For the more murderers under sentence of death there are who publicly denounce murder and other criminality, the less credibility the denunciations have.

MORE ON CAPITAL PUNISHMENT—BECKER

Posner has a good discussion of the various issues related to capital punishment. I will concentrate my comments on deterrence, which is really the crucial issue in the acrimonious debate over capital punishment. I support the use of capital punishment for persons convicted of murder because, and only because, I believe it deters murders. If I did not believe that, I would be opposed because revenge and the other possible motives that are mentioned and discussed by Posner, should not be a basis for public policy.

As Posner indicates, serious empirical research on capital punishment began with Isaac Ehrlich's pioneering paper. Subsequent studies have sometimes found much weaker effects than he found, while others, including a recent one cited by Posner, found a much larger effect than even that found by Ehrlich. The available data are quite limited, however, so one should not base any conclusions solely on the econometric evidence, although I believe that the preponderance of evidence does indicate that capital punishment deters.

Of course, public policy on punishments cannot wait until the evidence is perfect. Even with the limited quantitative evidence available, there are good reasons to believe that capital punishment deters murders. Most people, and murderers in particular, fear death, especially when it follows swiftly and with considerable certainty following the commission of a murder. As Posner indicates, the deterrent effect of capital punishment would be greater if the delays in its implementation were much shortened, and if this punishment was more certain to be used in the appropriate cases. But I agree with Posner that capital punishment has an important deterrent effect even with the way the present system actually operates.

Opponents of capital punishment frequently proclaim that the state has no moral right to take the life of anyone, even a most reprehensible murderer. Yet that is absolutely the wrong conclusion for anyone who believes that capital punishment deters. To show why, suppose that for each murderer executed (instead of say receiving life imprisonment), the number of murders is reduced by three—which is a much lower number than Ehrlich's estimate of the deterrent effect. This implies that for each murderer not given capital punishment, three generally innocent victims would die. This argument means that the government would indirectly be "taking" many lives if it did not use capital punishment. The lives so taken are usually much more worthwhile than those of the murderers who would be spared execution. For this reason, the state has a "moral" obligation to use capital punishment if such punishment significantly reduces the number of murders and saves lives of innocent victims.

Saving three other lives for every person executed seems like a very attractive trade-off. Even two lives saved per execution seem like a persuasive benefit-cost ratio for capital punishment. But let us go further and suppose only one life was saved for each murderer executed. Wouldn't the trade-off still be desirable if the life saved is much better than the life taken, which would usually be the case? As the deterrent effect of capital punishment is made smaller, at some point even I would shift to the anti-capital punishment camp. But given the difference between victims and murderers, the deterrent effect would have to be considerably less than one person saved per murderer executed before I would shift positions, although account should also be taken of the considerable expense involved in using capital punishment.

Of course, one wants to be sure that the number of persons wrongly executed for murder is a very small fraction of the total number executed. Posner argues convincingly that the safeguards built into the American system are considerable. They do not prevent any innocent persons from being executed, but they certainly make the risk very low. Capital punishment cannot be used if the goal is never to erroneously execute anyone, but then its deterrent effect is lost completely.

European governments are adamantly opposed to capital punishment, and some Europeans consider the American use of this punishment to be barbaric. But Europeans have generally been "soft" on most crimes during the past half-century. For a long time they could be smug because their crime rates were well below American rates. But during the past twenty years European crime has increased sharply while American rates have fallen—in part because American apprehension and conviction rates have increased considerably. Now some European countries have higher per capita property crime rates than the United States does, although violent crimes are still considerably more common in the United States. At the same time that America was reducing crime greatly in part by greater use of punishments, many European intellectuals continued to argue that not just capital punishments, but punishments in general, do not deter.

To repeat, the capital punishment debate comes down in essentials to a debate over deterrence. I can understand that some people are skeptical about the evidence, although I believe they are wrong both on the evidence and on the common sense of the issue. It is very unpleasant to take someone's life, even a murderer's life, but sometimes highly unpleasant actions are necessary to deter even worse behavior that takes the lives of innocent victims.

FURTHER COMMENTS ON CAPITAL PUNISHMENT—BECKER

Our discussion last week on capital punishment generated a lot of comments that are worth discussing in more detail. Since capital punishment is so controversial, we decided to continue the same subject this week.

First, let me correct a misunderstanding in some of the comments. I never claimed the evidence is anywhere near conclusive that capital punishment has an important deterrent effect. I stated that the evidence from quantitative studies is decidedly mixed, yet I concluded that "the preponderance of evidence does indicate that capital punishment deters." Although the weight of the positive evidence should not be overstated, the frequently stated claim that some other studies prove that capital punishment does not deter is clearly false.

My belief in its deterrent effect is partly based on these limited quantitative studies, but also because I believe that most people have a powerful fear of death. David Hume said in discussing suicide that "no man ever threw away life, while it was worth living. For such is our natural horror of death..." Schopenhauer added also in discussing suicide "...as soon as the terrors of life reach a point at which they outweigh the terrors of death, a man will put an end to his life. But the terrors of death offer considerable resistance..."

Nevertheless, the main point of my comment last week was not to try to prove that capital punishment deters murders, but rather to argue against the view that it is "immoral" for the state to take lives through capital punishment even if we assume that the deterrent effect on murders is sizeable. Indeed, I believe that deterrence can be the only reasonable basis for capital punishment. Revenge, retribution, and other arguments sometimes made to justify capital punishment are too subject to government abuse, and have been abused.

Some readers interpreted my views as implying that a major goal of government policy should in general be to save lives. That is not my belief. I am against governments interfering, for example, with the rights of people to overeat even when that causes obesity, disease, and possibly early death because overeaters are primarily "harming" themselves. In my view, people should have the right to do that.

Murder, on the other hand, involves taking the lives of others, and any reasonable discussion has to distinguish such behavior from individuals taking actions that affect only their own lives. In economists' language, murder involves the most severe negative externalities. If we assume for the sake of this discussion that there are two fewer murders for each murderer executed, the state would reduce two of these severe externalities for each murderer that it executes. This issue of the effect of capital punishment on innocent victims has to be confronted by even those most opposed to its use. And I frankly do not see how any reasonable and relevant philosophy could oppose the use of capital punishment under the assumptions of this example.

Admittedly, the argument gets less clear-cut as the number of lives saved per execution falls from two to lower values, say, for example, to one life saved per execution. In this case, I compared the qualities of the life saved and the life taken, to the dismay of some readers. In particular, I wrote that "wouldn't the trade-off still be desirable if the life saved is much better than the life taken, which would usually be the case?" I do not see how to avoid making such a comparison. Consider a person with a long criminal record who holds up and kills a victim who led a decent life and left several children and a spouse behind.

Suppose it would be possible to save the life of an innocent victim by executing such a criminal. To me it is obvious that saving the lives of such a victim has to count for more than taking the life of such a criminal. To be sure, not all cases are so clear-cut, but I am just trying to establish the principle that a comparison of the qualities of individual lives has to be part of any reasonable social policy.

This argument helps explain why capital punishment should only be used for some murders, and not for theft, robbery, and other lesser crimes. For then the trade-off is between taking lives and reducing property theft, and the case in favor of milder punishments is strong. However, severe assaults, including some gruesome rapes, may approach in severity some murders, and might conceivably at times call for capital punishment, although I do not support its use in these cases.

A powerful argument for reserving capital punishment for murders is related to what is called marginal deterrence in the crime and punishment literature. If say perpetrators of assaults were punished with execution, an assaulter would have an incentive to kill the victims in order to reduce the likelihood that he would be discovered. That is a major reason more generally why the severity of punishments should be matched to the severity of crimes. One complication is that capital punishment may make a murderer fight harder to avoid being captured, which could lead to more deaths. That argument has to be weighed in judging the case for capital punishment. While marginal deterrence is important, I believe the resistance of murderers to being captured, possibly at the expense of their own lives, is really indirect evidence that criminals do fear capital punishment.

Some readers asked whether I also favor public executions of convicted murderers, mangling of their bodies, and other methods used in some countries still, and in most countries in the past? I do not because they seem unnecessarily abusive of convicted murderers without any compensating gains. However, I admit I would reconsider this position if it were demonstrated that such added punishments have a large effect in reducing the number of murders. For those who find such a position "barbaric," I would ask how many innocent victims are they willing to tolerate before they might take a more positive position on these additional punishments?

Of course I am worried about the risk of executing innocent persons for murders committed by others. In any policy toward crime, including capital punishment, one has to compare errors of wrongful conviction with errors of failing to convict guilty persons. My support for capital punishment would weaken greatly if the rate of killing innocent persons were as large as that claimed by many. However, I believe along with Posner that the appeal process offers enormous protection not against wrongful conviction but against wrongful execution. And this process has been strengthened enormously with the development of DNA identification. However, lengthy appeals delay the execution of guilty murderers, and that can only lower the deterrent effect of capital punishment.

So to summarize once again my position on this controversial question, I favor capital punishment because and only because I believe it has "sizeable" deterrent effects. I would join the anti-capital punishment side if this view turns out to be wrong, if it were proven that many innocent persons are wrongly executed, or if it is administered in such a racially biased manner as to wrongly convict many black persons, and to be little used against white murderers. But I do not believe that the available evidence strongly supports any of these arguments against the use of capital punishment.

FURTHER COMMENTS ON CAPITAL PUNISHMENT—POSNER

Becker has presented in his post today a compelling restatement of the economic case for capital punishment. I have a few minor disagreements and qualifications, and I will first mention them and then respond to some of the very large number of comments that my last week's posting elicited.

I do not consider revenge an impermissible ground for capital punishment. Revenge has very deep roots in the human psyche. As I have long argued, basing the argument on work by evolutionary psychologists such as Robert Trivers, the threat of revenge must have played an essential role in maintaining order in the "ancestral environment." That is a term that evolutionary biologists use to describe the prehistoric era in which human beings evolved to approximately their current biological state. In that era there were no laws, police, etc., so the indignation that would incite a person to revenge himself upon an aggressor must have had substantial survival value and become "hard wired" in our brains. The wiring remains, and explains some of the indignation that people feel, especially but not only the friends and family members of murder victims, toward the murderer. It seems plausible to me (here modifying what I said in my original posting) that the net increment in utility that they derive from the execution (versus life imprisonment) of the murderer exceeds the net increment in disutility that the murderer derives from being executed rather than imprisoned for life. The strong support for capital punishment in public opinion polls provides limited support for this conjecture.

I do not favor public executions; nor dismemberment or other horrific modes of execution. The incremental deterrent effect might well be nontrivial, but would be outweighed by public revulsion. There is also the danger of brutalization. As Friedrich Nietzsche pointed out, making people squeamish is one of the projects of modernity, and may explain the banning of blood sports as well as the movement away from public and gruesome executions. The idea is that if people become unaccustomed to bloody sights they will be less likely to employ violence in their relations with other people. Still another objection to public and gruesome executions is that they offer murderers an opportunity to die as heroes by showing fortitude.

I agree that marginal deterrence is important and that it generally argues for reserving the heaviest sentences for the most serious crimes. But there are two important qualifications. First, a very heavy sentence may be necessary to deter a minor crime because the likelihood of apprehension is very low The expected punishment cost of crime is, as a first approximation (ignoring attitude toward risk), the punishment if imposed multiplied by the probability of imposition, so if the probability is very low a compensating increase in punishment is indicated. This does not impair marginal deterrence as long as the crimes are not close substitutes: a heavy fine for litterers will not increase the robbery rate, whereas capital punishment for robbers would increase the murder rate (of robbers' victims)—were it not for my second qualification. Even if murder and robbery were both capital crimes, there would be marginal deterrence because the police would search much harder for a robber who murdered his victim; the more extensive search would compensate, in part anyway, for the loss of the information that the victim could have given the police to identify the robber. Moreover, capital punishment is merely a ceiling; even if robbery were a capital crime, judges and juries would be much less likely to impose the death sentence on a robber who had not killed his victim than on one who had.

Marginal-deterrence theory provides, however, a compelling reason to execute prisoners sentenced to life without parole who murder in prison; the threat of a sentence of imprisonment can have no deterrent effect on them.

Becker mentions the possibility of racial discrimination in execution. Studies done some years ago—I do not know whether they would be descriptive of current practice—revealed the following pattern: murderers of black people were less likely to be executed than murderers of white people. Since blacks were more likely to murder other blacks than to murder whites, this meant that blacks were less rather than more likely to be executed than whites, relative to the respective murder rates of the two races. (Blacks commit murders at a much higher rate than whites.) The explanation offered was that judges and juries tended to set a lower value on black victims of murder than on white ones. From this some observers inferred that capital punishment discriminates against blacks. The inference is incorrect. The proper inference is that murderers of blacks are underpunished.

I turn now to the comments on my posting. A long comment by "ohwilleke" makes a number of interesting points, but they do not support his opposition to capital punishment. He notes first of all that many factors influence the murder rate besides the probability of execution. That is true, but it does not, as he suggests, make it "insanely difficult to make any econometric estimate" that is not "meaningless." Econometrics, which is to say the set of statistical methods used by economists to try to tease out causal factors, enables the particular factor of interest, in this case the probability of execution, to be isolated. The methods are not entirely reliable, which is why neither Becker nor I claim that economists have proved that capital punishment deters; we merely claim that there is significant evidence that it does. I note how many commenters remark correctly that murder rates are higher in the South, even though that is where most executions occur, than in other regions. But that is not an argument that executions do not deter. The higher the background rate of murder, the more severe one expects punishments to be. A high murder rate implies a high expected benefit from murder and so the expected cost of punishment has to be jacked up to offset that greater benefit.

Ohwilleke's comment claims that the "error rate" in capital punishment is 10 percent. This is incorrect. Not a single person among the 119 that he contends were erroneously sentenced to death was executed. That is a zero error rate.

One commenter asks whether capital punishment "really deter[s] the type of person who actually does the murdering?" Of course if someone in a state that has capital punishment commits the kind of murder that puts him at risk of such punishment, the threat of capital punishment has not deterred. This is the usual situation with criminal punishment. People who commit crimes are people for whom the expected cost of punishment, combined with the other costs of crime, is less than the expected benefit of the crime. The purpose of punishing these people is not to deter them—by committing the crime in the face of threatened punishment they have shown themselves to be undeterrable—but to deter people who, were it not for the expected punishment cost, would commit the crime because its other costs were lower than its expected benefit.

Finally, several comments usefully point out that capital punishment has a secondary deterrent effect: it induces murderers to plead guilty and receive a life sentence.

CHAPTER 14

AN INTRODUCTION TO "UNDERSTANDING WHY CRIME FELL IN THE 1990s"

By Ron Liggett

Over the last 50 years we've watched the U. S. crime rate rise and then dramatically fall. Numerous researchers, scholars, and think tanks have attempted to explain the reduction in crime by addressing a common array of topics. Naturally, there is a variety of thought and differing conclusions on what is a challenging and subjective discussion.

As the concluding chapter in this text, the following paper from Steven Levitt addresses the significant decrease in crime which occurred during the 1990s. Many students may be familiar with Levitt from his popular *Freakonomics* book series, co-authored with Stephen Dubner. For this chapter, one might consider a "by the numbers" approach with a three-six-four format. What do the numbers mean? To begin, Levitt presents *three* significant "features" of the crime reduction. These set the stage for a discussion of six variables which, while being very relevant to any econ of crime discussion, are considered by Levitt as *not* statistically significant in the crime drop. Lastly, the author examines the *four* variables he feels *were* statistically significant in explaining the reduction in crime.

While there are those who may disagree with some of Levitt's conclusions, the article nonetheless offers a rather robust analysis via the ten total variables discussed. And, while you will notice that a few of these variables have been addressed in other areas of the book—macro economic performance and broken windows to name two—this chapter also introduces new subject matter and their relationship to changing crime rates. For example, there is a discussion of gun issues, offering arguments on both the increased opportunities to carry and the restrictions of gun control. Additionally, a more detailed look at incarceration is presented as part of the chapter. Finally, Levitt puts forth his thoughts on how the crime rate may have been impacted by legalized abortion—a position which, at times, has been met with some controversy.

DISAGREEMENT—ONE EXAMPLE

As noted, there are many theories regarding the decrease in crime during the 1990s, and the continuing smaller decline we have seen in the period since 2000. One area where there has been disagreement in regards to a Levitt conclusion is in the area of incarceration. I won't consider it a spoiler alert to share in advance that Levitt feels increased incarceration rates were significantly important in crime reduction during the 90s. However, some researchers who disagree cite the economic principle of diminishing returns, among other reasons.[A] [B] The suggestion being that as we imprison more criminals we begin to incarcerate offenders who may be guilty of lesser crimes, thereby offering "fewer crime control benefits."[1]

From an economic perspective, I would likely concur with both views, to a certain extent. There is no doubt that imprisonment is an extremely costly means of crime prevention, one that uses copious amounts of resources and frequently places individuals in a chaotic environment. Accordingly, to say that other means of punishment should be considered first gets no dispute on this end. For example, the argument in favor of fines over incarceration, when appropriate, is strongly supported by economists, and for good reason.[C] Unfortunately, there *are* times when the prison choice *is* appropriate. Therefore, while diminishing returns certainly play a role in many economic scenarios, it must be concluded that offenders are imprisoned for crimes which they have committed. So, whether they are the first individual apprehended, or the 100th, their chronological sequence is irrelevant.[D] As the cliché states, "beauty is in the eyes of the beholder," and sometimes even with empirical study (and regression analysis), the social sciences offer a different set of eyes. Accordingly, there are moments when "we agree to disagree."

A "CAPSTONE" CHAPTER?

Many collegiate programs conclude their degree plans with a capstone course, which allows students to apply what they have learned in a particular field of study. Similarly, one might consider this section as a type of capstone chapter for our book. Again, while explaining his reasoning for the changing crime rates, Levitt expounds on a variety of issues while also introducing a few new topics.

A The law of diminishing marginal returns is described in Chapter 9.

B Other negative thoughts regarding imprisonment from the various think tanks include the prison "experience," the proportion of minorities behind bars, and high recidivism rates.

C Obviously there are criminal statutes that guide sentencing.

D In reality, the question may not be in the 'number' of prisoners, but rather the behavior behind the punishment. This thought may be similar to our Chapter 6 discussion on NBA fouls, and when should a 'foul' be called.

Taken as a whole, this chapter offers a broad summary of the economics of crime, and, therefore, should present an opportunity for vibrant discussions in an economics of crime class.

ENDNOTE

1. Roeder, Oliver and Lauren-Brooke Eisen and Julia Bowling. "What Caused the Crime Decline?" Brennan Center for Justice at New York University School of Law, 2015. p. 17.

UNDERSTANDING WHY CRIME FELL IN THE 1990s

By Steven D. Levitt

FOUR FACTORS THAT EXPLAIN THE DECLINE AND SIX THAT DO NOT

Crime fell sharply in the United States in the 1990s, in all categories of crime and all parts of the nation. Homicide rates plunged 43 percent from the peak in 1991 to 2001, reaching the lowest levels in 35 years. The Federal Bureau of Investigation's (FBI) violent and property crime indexes fell 34 and 29 percent, respectively, over that same period. These declines occurred essentially without warning: leading experts were predicting an explosion in crime in the early and mid-1990s, precisely the point when crime rates began to plunge.

Although experts failed to anticipate the decline, there has been no shortage of hypotheses to explain the drop in crime after the fact. Table 1 presents a tally of a Lexis-Nexis search of the most frequently cited reasons for the crime decline in articles in major newspapers over the period 1991–2001. The single most frequent explanation given is the innovative policing strategies put into place. The crime decline is also frequently attributed to increased imprisonment, changes in the market for crack cocaine, the aging of the population, tougher gun control laws, the strong economy and increases in the number of police.

In this paper, I attempt to sort out why crime declined in the 1990s. I begin with a review of the facts. I then analyze the leading explanations for why crime fell, looking at possible determinants that changed in some substantial way in the 1990s. Most of the supposed explanations listed in Table 1 actually played little direct role in the crime decline, including the strong economy of the 1990s, changing demographics, better policing strategies, gun control laws, concealed weapons laws and increased use of the death penalty. Four factors, however, can account for virtually all of the observed decline in crime: increases in the number

Steven D. Levitt, "Understanding Why Crime Fell in the 1990s: Four Factors that Explain the Decline and Six that Do Not," *Journal of Economic Perspectives*, vol. 18, no. 1, pp. 163-190.

TABLE 1. MEDIA EXPLANATIONS FOR THE DECLINE IN CRIME IN THE 1990S, RANKED BY FREQUENCY OF MENTION

Explanation	Number of mentions
Innovative policing strategies	52
Increased reliance on prisons	47
Changes in crack/other drug markets	33
Aging of the population	32
Tougher gun control laws	32
Strong economy	28
Increased number of police	26
All other explanations	34

Notes: Based on a Lexis-Nexis search of articles written about the national decline in crime in leading newspapers over the period 1991–2001. Newspapers included in the tabulation are the *New York Times, Washington Post, USA Today, Houston Chronicle, San Francisco Chronicle, Chicago Sun Times, Boston Globe, Atlanta Journal Constitution, Minneapolis Star Tribune and San Diego Union-Tribune.* These are the ten largest circulation newspapers that are included in Lexis-Nexis.

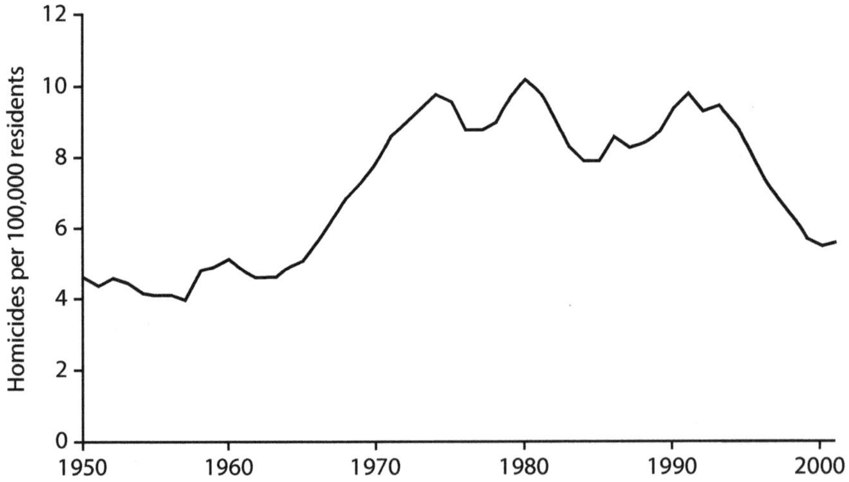

Figure 1. Homicide Rate, 1950–2001

of police, the rising prison population, the waning crack epidemic and the legalization of abortion.[A] Thus, I conclude that the decline in crime does not really pose a puzzle, but rather, is readily explained by the available theories. The real puzzle that stands unanswered, I argue, is why crime rates did not start falling earlier. In the final section, I offer some tentative observations about what crime trends might be expected in the next decade.

DEFINING FEATURES OF THE DECLINE IN CRIME IN THE 1990S

Several different aspects of the decline in crime are particularly noteworthy: its size, breadth and persistence across categories of crime; its universality across geographic and demographic groups; and its unexpectedness. I consider these characteristics in turn.

THE MAGNITUDE OF THE DECLINE

The most remarkable feature of the crime decline in the United States was its sheer magnitude. Figure 1 presents time series data for homicides from 1950 to 2001. Homicide is the most accurately measured and most serious crime and thus provides a useful benchmark. Homicide rates were relatively steady at about 4–5 per 100,000 population from 1950 through the mid-1960s, at which point they started rising to a peak of 10.2 per 100,000 population in 1980. From 1980 to 1991, the homicide rate fluctuated between 8–10 per 100,000 population. After that, the homicide trend began a large, steady decline. Between 1991 and 2000, homicide rates per capita fell from 9.8 to 5.5 per 100,000, a drop of 44 percent. Since that time, homicide rates have been steady.

The same pattern observed for homicide is present for every major crime category and in both of the commonly used measures of crime in the United States: the FBI's Uniform Crime Reports (UCR), covering crimes reported to the police, and the National Crime Victimization Survey (NCVS), a large, nationally representative phone survey of Americans. Table 2 reports the percentage decline between 1991 and 2001. For purposes of comparison, the percentage change in crime rates over the period 1973–1991 is also shown (1973 is the first year of availability for NCVS). For the period 1991–2001, crimes reported to the police fell between 24 and 46 percent across the various crime categories. The

A Reyes (2002) offers an additional intriguing explanation for the decline in crime: the reduction in levels of lead in the blood due to the elimination of leaded gasoline and lead-based paints. Because of the highly speculative nature of the Reyes conjecture at the present time, I do not discuss this hypothesis at greater length, although it is clearly an area worthy of continued future research.

TABLE 2. NATIONAL TRENDS IN SPECIFIC CATEGORIES OF CRIME

Crime category and data source	Percentage change in crime category, 1973–1991	Percentage change in crime category, 1991–2001
Crimes reported to the police from UCR		
Violent crime	+82.9	−33.6
Homicide	+5.4	−42.9
Rape	+73.4	−24.8
Robbery	+50.0	−45.8
Aggravated assault	+118.1	−26.7
Property crime	+38.2	−28.8
Burglary	+3.0	−40.9
Larceny	+56.7	−23.2
Motor vehicle theft	+49.8	−34.6
Criminal victimizations from NCVS		
Violent crime	+1.6	−50.1
Rape	−20.0	−45.0
Robbery	−15.5	−53.3
Aggravated assault	−3.9	−56.9
Simple assault	+10.7	−47.0
Property crime	−32.0	−52.8
Burglary	−41.3	−55.6
Theft	−46.5	−51.6
Motor vehicle theft	+16.2	−58.6

Notes: All values in the table are percentage changes in crime rates. Entries in the top panel of the table are based on Uniform Crime Report data collected by the Federal Bureau of Investigation. These changes are defined in terms of victimization rates per capita. Entries in the bottom panel are from the National Crime Victimization Survey. For violent crime, the reported values are percentage changes in crime per person age 12 and older. For property crime, the percentage changes are per household. The calculations in the table correct for the redesign of NCVS that occurred in 1993. Uniform Crime Report data from recent years is available online at http://www.fbi.gov. NCVS data is available from http://www.ojp.usdoj.gov/bjs.

TABLE 3. PERCENTAGE CHANGES IN CRIME RATES FOR DIFFERENT POPULATION GROUPS, 1991–2001

	Homicide	Violent Crime	Property Crime
Entire United States	−42.9	−33.6	−28.8
Region			
Northeast	−50.0	−42.9	−41.5
South	−44.6	−27.3	−25.6
Midwest	−32.1	−31.5	−23.3
West	−42.7	−38.1	−32.0
Urban/rural			
Within MSAs	−45.0	−36.7	−31.7
Cities outside MSAs	−31.4	−18.4	−18.1
Rural	−35.0	−2.9	−11.0
City size			
>250,000	−49.2	−43.2	−36.1
50,000–250,000	−41.4	−37.5	−31.9
<50,000	−34.9	−22.7	−23.2

Source: FBI Uniform Crime Reports.
Notes: Entries in the table are the percentage changes in per capita crime reports between the years 1991 and 2001 according to the FBI Uniform Crime Reports.

reduction in criminal victimizations in NCVS is even greater, ranging from 45 to 58 percent.[B]

The decline in crime has also been remarkable in its steady persistence. Homicide rates fell in nine of the ten years in the decade of the 1990s, with the only exception being a minor upward blip in 1992. In the previous three decades, homicide had never fallen for more than three consecutive years. Robbery, burglary and larceny each fell every year between 1991 and 2000. Prior to 1991, robbery rates had fallen in only eight of the preceding 30 years.

The drop in U.S. crime appears to be unusual among countries of the world, although definitional and reporting differences across countries, as well as the poor quality of crime statistics in most countries other than the United States, make such international comparisons difficult. Barclay, Tavares and Siddique (2001)

B The congruence between the UCR and NCVS data for the 1990s is heartening, given that the aggregate trends in these two data sources have failed to track closely one another historically, as evidenced in the first column of the table. Between 1973 and 1991, the UCR data suggest sharply rising crime in most categories, whereas the victimization data finds declines in crime for more than half of the categories. Boggess and Bound (1997) argue that a partial explanation for the different patterns is that the two data sets measure somewhat different crimes; for example, NCVS crimes tend to be less serious, even within a crime category.

TABLE 4. HOMICIDE TRENDS IN LARGE U.S. CITIES

City	Year that homicide peaked	Peak homicide rate (per 100,000)	2001 homicide rate (per 100,000)	Percentage decline in homicide, peak to 2001
New York City	1990	30.7	8.1	−73.6
San Diego	1991	14.7	4.0	−72.8
Austin	1985	12.8	3.9	−69.5
San Jose	1985	7.8	2.4	−69.2
Seattle	1994	12.8	4.4	−65.6
Jacksonville	1990	27.6	9.9	−64.1
Houston	1991	36.5	13.4	−63.3
San Antonio	1992	22.5	8.5	−62.2
Dallas	1991	48.6	19.7	−59.5
Denver	1992	19.3	7.9	−59.1
Honolulu	1986	5.6	2.3	−58.9
San Francisco	1993	17.5	7.7	−56.0
Boston	1990	24.9	11.0	−55.8
Washington, D.C.	1991	80.6	40.6	−49.6
Los Angeles	1993	30.5	15.6	−48.9
Columbus	1991	21.6	11.4	−47.2
Philadelphia	1990	31.7	20.4	−35.6
Detroit	1987	62.8	41.3	−34.2
Chicago	1992	33.1	22.9	−30.8
Phoenix	1994	21.5	15.3	−28.8
Indianapolis	1991	19.4	14.0	−27.8
Memphis	1993	32.0	24.1	−24.7
Las Vegas	1991	15.7	11.9	−24.2
Baltimore	1993	48.2	38.7	−19.7
Milwaukee	1991	25.6	21.1	−17.6

Notes: All cities with population greater than 500,000 in 1991 are included in the table. The peak year for homicide is defined in homicides per 100,000 residents. For San Francisco, 2001 homicide rates are not available, and the 2000 homicide rates are used instead.

provide one of the most careful cross-country comparisons of crime trends. That analysis reports that homicide rates fell 4 percent on average in European Union (EU) member states between 1995 and 1999, a period over which U.S. homicide rates fell 28 percent. Violent crime rose 11 percent on average in EU countries over that same time period, compared to 20 percent drops in U.S. violent crime. Burglary and motor vehicle theft fell 14 percent and rose 7 percent, respectively, in the EU, while falling 19 and 22 percent in the United States.

THE UNIVERSALITY OF THE DROP IN CRIME

The drop of crime in the 1990s affected all geographic areas and demographic groups. Table 3 presents the percentage decline in homicide, violent crime and property crime from 1991–2001 by region, urban/rural and city size. In each of these subgroups and for all crime categories, the trend has been downward. Crime declines in the Northeast outpaced the rest of the country, whereas the Midwest was a laggard. The greatest percentage improvements in crime occurred within metropolitan statistical areas (MSAs) and especially among large cities with populations over 250,000. Rural areas, particularly on violent and property crime, saw much smaller declines in both absolute terms and percentage terms. For instance, the homicide rate per 100,000 residents in large cities fell 12.9 per 100,000 (from 26.2 to 13.3). The decline in homicide rates for cities with populations less than 50,000 was only 1.5 (from 4.3 to 2.8).

Table 4 shows changes in homicide for the 25 most populous cities as of 1991. The first column lists the peak year for homicide by city. In almost three-fourths of the cities, the peak occurred between 1990 and 1993. The next two columns present the homicide rate per 100,000 residents in the peak year and in 2001. The final column is the percentage reduction in homicide from the peak year to 2001. The cities are ordered by the percentage decline in homicide they experienced. New York City, which has garnered enormous attention for its success in fighting crime, leads the list with a 73.6 percent reduction in homicide. A number of other cities (San Diego, Austin, San Jose, Seattle) that have received far fewer accolades, however, nearly match the New York City experience. Even the cities near the bottom of the list have experienced homicide reductions of roughly 20 percent. The universality of these gains argues against idiosyncratic local factors as the primary source of the reduction.

In demographic terms, breakdowns of crime offending rates by race, gender and age are not directly available, because in many cases offender characteristics are unknown. In those cases where an arrest is made, however, information is gathered by the FBI in the Uniform Crime Reports. Across every crime category and every breakdown by race, gender and age, substantial declines in arrest rates have occurred.

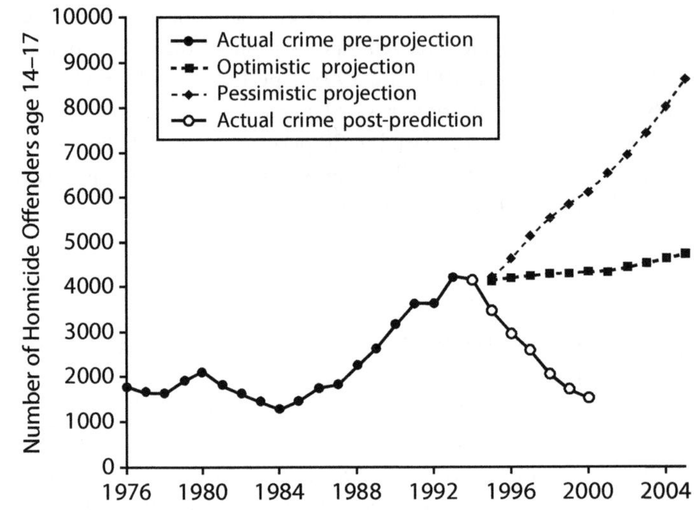

Figure 2. Expert Forecast Made by James Alan Fox in 1995 vs. Actual Teen Homicide Offenders

THE UNEXPECTEDNESS OF THE DROP IN CRIME

Having just lived through an enormous reduction in crime, it is hard to reconstruct just how unexpected such a decline really was. Even after the fall had begun, some of the world's most prominent criminologists dismissed the decline as a transitory blip that would quickly be reversed.

For example, in 1995 the U.S. Attorney General commissioned a report on crime trends from Northeastern professor James Alan Fox, one of the most widely quoted criminologists in the popular press. Figure 2 reproduces and extends one of the figures from that report. The line in Figure 2 up until 1994 reflects the observed number of homicides by 14–17 year olds. The two dotted lines represent Fox's (1996) optimistic and pessimistic future projections. In the optimistic case, youth homicides were projected to rise by about 15 percent. In the pessimistic scenario, youth homicide was going to more than double over the next decade, prompting Fox to say in a 1996 *Scientific American* article, "the next crime wave will get so bad that it will make 1995 look like the good old days." The dashed line shows what actually happened: juvenile homicide rates fell by more than 50 percent in the ensuing six years.[C]

C Two years after his initial report, in spite of sharply declining juvenile crime rates in the intervening years, Fox (1997) continued to project large increases in juvenile homicide over the next decade. No further reports were commissioned.

Fox was not alone in predicting that the 1990s would be a dire decade with respect to crime. James Q. Wilson (1995, p. 507) wrote, 'Just beyond the horizon, there lurks a cloud that the winds will soon bring over us. The population will start getting younger again.... Get ready." In a symposium on crime published in *Journal of Economic Perspectives* in 1996, John DiIulio (1996, p. 8) wrote, "It is not inconceivable that the demographic surge of the next 10 years will bring with it young male criminals who make the... Bloods and Crips look tame by comparison." Even President Clinton got into the act, stating: 'We've got about six years to turn this juvenile crime thing around, or our country is going to be living with chaos" (Allpolitics, 1997). In short, the crime decline was so unanticipated that it was widely dismissed as temporary or illusory long after it had begun.

SIX FACTORS THAT PLAYED LITTLE OR NO ROLE IN THE CRIME DECLINE

The list of explanations offered as to why crime has fallen is a lengthy one. Here, I begin with six commonly suggested and plausible theories that in practice do not appear important in explaining the decline of crime rates.

1) THE STRONG ECONOMY OF THE 1990S

The decade of the 1990s saw sustained economic growth. Real GDP per capita grew by almost 30 percent between 1991 and 2001. The annual unemployment rate fell from 6.8 in 1991 to 4.8 percent in 2001. If macroeconomic performance is an important determinant of crime rates, then the economy could explain falling crime.

In economic models of crime such as Becker (1968), improvements in legitimate labor market opportunities make crime relatively less attractive. This prediction is likely to be more relevant for crimes involving direct financial motivation such as burglary, robbery and auto theft, but less important for homicide, assaults and rape. On the other hand, to the extent that activities that are associated with increased levels of either offending or victimization are normal goods—like alcohol consumption, frequenting nightclubs and owning a car—the link between economic activity and crime is theoretically ambiguous.

Empirical estimates of the impact of macroeconomic variables on crime have been generally consistent across studies: Freeman (1995) surveys earlier research, and more recent studies include Machin and Meghir (2000), Gould, Weinberg and Mustard (1997), Donohue and Levitt (2001) and Raphael and Winter-Ebmer (2001). Controlling for other factors, almost all of these studies report a statistically significant but substantively small relationship between unemployment rates and property crime. A typical estimate would be that a one percentage point increase in the unemployment rate is associated with a one percent increase in property crime. Violent crime, however, does not vary systematically with the unemployment rate. Studies that have used other measures of macroeconomic performance like wages of low-income workers come to similar conclusions (Machin and Meghir, 2000; Gould, Weinberg and Mustard, 1997).[D] Based on these estimates, the observed 2 percentage point decline in the U.S unemployment rate between 1991 and 2001 can explain an estimated 2 percent decline in property crime (out of an observed drop of almost 30 percent), but no change in violent crime or homicide. The sharp increases in crime in the 1960s—a decade of strong economic growth—further corroborate the weak link between macroeconomics and crime.

If the economy has a major impact on crime, the likely channel is not through the direct effect estimated in the studies noted above, but rather, indirectly through state and local government budgets. Two of the factors that I identify as most important in reducing crime are increased spending on police and prisons. To the extent that these budget items are affected by macroeconomic performance, one would expect to observe a stronger link between the economy and crime than is found in the studies above, which control for criminal justice variables when estimating the link between economic variables and crime.

2) CHANGING DEMOGRAPHICS

The aging of the baby boomers represents a profound demographic shift. The elderly have extremely low rates of both offending and criminal victimization. In 2001, people over the age of 65 had per capita arrest rates approximately one-fiftieth the level of 15–19 year olds. Perkins (1997), using NCVS data, reports that those over the age of 65 experience victimization rates for serious violent crime that are less than one-tenth of those of teenagers. Given that the share of the elderly population increased during the 1990s, a purely demographically driven decline in crime might be expected.

Two other concurrent demographic changes, however, counterbalance the crime-related benefits of an aging population. First, between 1990 and 2000, the black population rose from 12.1 percent to 12.9 percent. For reasons that are only partly understood (Sampson and Lauritsen, 1997), blacks have elevated victimization and offending rates relative to other Americans, particularly for homicide, where the differences across races are almost an order of magnitude.[E]

D The studies cited in this paragraph use U.S. data, except for one study that focuses on the United Kingdom. Cross-county estimates also fail to show a consistent relationship between GDP per capita and crime, although high levels of income inequality are correlated with high crime, as in Soares (1999).

E The growth in the Hispanic population was even greater (from 9.0 percent to 12.5 percent of the population between 1990 and 2000). For the most part, however, Hispanic offending and victimization rates are only slightly above those of whites.

Second, in spite of the overall aging of the population, the echo of the baby boom is leading to a temporary increase in the number of teenagers and young adults. Between 1995 and 2010, the number of 15–24 year olds is projected to increase by roughly 20 percent, and the share of the population between the ages of 15 and 24 will increase from 13.7 percent to 14.6 percent. (In comparison, 15–24 year-olds represented 18.7 percent of the population in 1980.) This age group has a greatly elevated involvement in crime. Indeed, many of the dire predictions for increased crime rates in the 1990s were based in part on the increasing number of adolescents.

Overall, these various demographic shifts probably had a slight ameliorating effect on crime. The estimates of Levitt (1999), using an Oaxaca-decomposition approach, suggest that overall changes in the age distribution may have reduced homicide and violent crime by a few percent and property crime by as much as 5–6 percent. Changes in racial composition largely offset the age-distribution benefits for homicide and reduce the estimate somewhat for violent crime, but the property crime benefit largely remains. Thus, demographic shifts may account for a little more than one-sixth of the observed decline in property crime in the 1990s, but are not an important factor in the drop in violent crime.

3) BETTER POLICING STRATEGIES

An enormous amount of media attention has focused on the policing strategies instituted in New York City under the leadership of Police Commissioner William Bratton and Mayor Rudy Guiliani. Their crime-fighting approach involved increased enforcement of nuisance activities like aggressive panhandling and better use of technology in identifying crime "hot spots." Other changes in policing strategy such as "community policing," in which the police attempt to work more closely as allies with communities rather than simply responding to emergency calls, were widely adopted in many other cities in the 1990s. In Boston, an innovative multiagency collaboration targeted gang violence (Kennedy, Piehl and Braga, 1996).

There have been very few rigorous academic studies of the impact of policing strategies. A number of early quasi-randomized studies, discussed in Wilson (1985), provided little evidence that community policing strategies lowered crime. Indeed, it is often difficult to identify which police departments have adopted particular practices, when the adoptions occurred and why. In the 1990s, federal funds were available to police departments that implemented community policing initiatives, leading many departments to advertise themselves as doing community policing, whether or not they actually changed policing practices. Due to such difficulties, no compelling cross-city comparisons of policing practices have been performed.

Since New York City is held up as the clear innovator in policing practices, and since it enjoyed the greatest crime declines of any large city, an analysis of that city's experience represents a logical starting point.[F] In my opinion, there are reasons for skepticism regarding the claim that New York City's policing strategy is the key to its decline in crime. First, the drop in crime in New York began in 1990. Crime declines of roughly 10 percent across a wide range of offenses occurred in 1991 and 1992. Guiliani, however, did not take office until 1993, at which point Bratton was moved from the New York City Transit Police, where he had been using the same approaches, and appointed police commissioner. With the exception of homicide, which does decline sharply in 1993, the trend in crime shows no obvious break after Bratton is appointed. Second, the change in policing strategies was accompanied by enormous growth in the size of the police force. Between 1991 and 2001, the New York City police force grew 45 percent—an increase three times greater than the national average. I argue later in this paper that increases in the number of police are effective in reducing crime. By my estimates, the unusually large expansion of the police force in New York City would be expected to reduce crime there by 18 percent more than the national average, even without any change in policing strategy. If one adds 18 percent to New York City's crime homicide experience in Table 2 (changing the decline from 73.6 percent to 55.6 percent), New York City is about average among large cities. Third, given that few other cities in Table 2 instituted New York City-type policing approaches, and certainly none with the enthusiasm of New York City itself, it is difficult to attribute the widespread declines in crime to policing strategy. Even Los Angeles and Washington, D.C., two cities notorious for the problems they have experienced with their police forces (Los Angeles Police Commission, 1996; Thompson, 1997), achieved declines in crime on par with New York City once the growth in the size of New York City's police force is accounted for. Fourth, New York City has had abortion rates among the highest of anywhere in the nation since abortion was legalized there in 1970, three years before the Supreme Court decision in *Roe v. Wade* (410 U.S. 113 [1973]) made abortion legal nationwide. If one believes my arguments later in this paper that a link exists between rates of abortion and later rates of crime, this connection provides further evidence against the argument that there is an unexplained crime decline in New York City that can be attributed to policing strategy.

Thus, while the impact of policing strategies on crime is an issue on which reasonable people might disagree given the lack of hard evidence, my reading of the limited data that are available leads me to the conclusion that the impact of

F In a recent working paper, Corman and Mocan (2002) analyze the New York City case using monthly time-series data. They find that aggressive policing tactics (as proxied by the number of misdemeanor arrests) are negatively associated with robbery and motor vehicle thefts, but do not have a statistically significant impact on other crimes. One difficulty with the Corman and Mocan approach, however, is that they are not able to include reliable controls for the extent of the crack epidemic, which was steadily waning at the same time that aggressive policing tactics were put into place.

policing strategies on New York City crime are exaggerated, and that the impact on national crime is likely to be minor.

4) GUN CONTROL LAWS

There are more than 200 million firearms in private hands in the United States—more than the number of adults (Cook and Ludwig, 1996). Almost two-thirds of homicides in the United States involve a firearm, a fraction far greater than other industrialized countries. Combining those two facts, one might conjecture that easy access to guns in the U.S. may be part of the explanation for our unusually high homicide rates. Indeed, the most careful study on the subject finds that higher rates of handgun ownership, which represent about one-third of all firearms, may be a causal factor in violent crime rates (Duggan, 2001).

There is, however, little or no evidence that changes in gun control laws in the 1990s can account for falling crime. For example, the Brady Handgun Violence Prevention Act of 1993 instituted stricter requirements for background checks before a gun is sold. However, Ludwig and Cook (2000) report no difference in homicide trends after the passage of the Brady Act in states affected by the law and states that already had policies in place that were at least as stringent as those in the Brady Act. Given the realities of an active black market in guns (Cook, Molliconi and Cole, 1995), the apparent ineffectiveness of gun control laws should not come as a great surprise to economists. Even in the late 1980s, prior to the Brady Act, only about one-fifth of prisoners reported obtaining their guns through licensed gun dealers (Wright and Rossi, 1994).

Gun buy-back programs are another form of public policy instituted in the 1990s that is largely ineffective in reducing crime. First, the guns that are typically surrendered in gun buy-backs are those guns that are least likely to be used in criminal activities. The guns turned in will be, by definition, those for which the owners derive little value from the possession of the guns. In contrast, those who are using guns in crimes are unlikely to participate in such programs. Second, because replacement guns are relatively easily obtained, the decline in the number of guns on the street may be smaller than the number of guns that are turned in. Third, the likelihood that any particular gun will be used in a crime in a given year is low. In 1999, approximately 6,500 homicides were committed with handguns. There are approximately 65 million handguns in the United States. Thus, if a different handgun were used in each homicide, the likelihood that a particular handgun would be used to kill an individual in a particular year is one in 10,000. The typical gun buy-back program yields fewer than 1,000 guns. Thus, it is not surprising that research evaluations have consistently failed to document any link between gun buy-back programs and reductions in gun violence (Callahan, Rivera and Koepsell, 1994; Kennedy, Piehl and Braga, 1996; Rosenfeld, 1996; Reuter and Mouzos, 2003).

More stringent gun-control policies such as bans on handgun acquisition passed in Washington, D.C., in 1976 and the ban on handgun ownership in Chicago in 1982 do not seem to have reduced crime, either. While initial research suggested a beneficial impact of the D.C. gun ban (Loftin, McDowall, Weirsema and Cottey, 1991), when the city of Baltimore is used as a control group, rather than the affluent Washington suburbs, the apparent benefits of the gun ban disappear (Britt, Kleck and Bordua, 1996). Although no careful analysis of Chicago's gun ban has been carried out, the fact that Chicago has been a laggard in the nationwide homicide decline argues against any large impact of the law. From a theoretical perspective, policies that raise the costs of using guns in the commission of actual crimes, as opposed to targeting ownership, would appear to be a more effective approach to reducing gun crime (for instance, Kessler and Levitt, 1999). The most prominent of these programs, Project Exile, which provides prison sentence enhancements for gun offenders, however, has been convincingly demonstrated to be ineffective by Raphael and Ludwig (2003), apparently in part because of the small scale on which it was carried out.

5) LAWS ALLOWING THE CARRYING OF CONCEALED WEAPONS

The highly publicized work of Lott and Mustard (1997) claimed enormous reductions in violent crime due to concealed weapons laws. The theory behind this claim is straightforward: armed victims raise the costs faced by a potential offender.

The empirical work in support of this hypothesis, however, has proven to be fragile along a number of dimensions (Black and Nagin, 1998; Ludwig, 1998; Duggan, 2001; Ayres and Donohue, 2003). First, allowing concealed weapons should have the greatest impact on crimes that involve face-to-face contact and occur outside the home where the law might affect gun carrying. Robbery is the crime category that most clearly fits this description, yet Ayres and Donohue (2003) demonstrate that empirically the passage of these laws is, if anything, positively related to the robbery rate. More generally, Duggan (2001) finds that for crimes that appear to decline with the law change, the declines in crime actually predate the passage of the laws, arguing against a causal impact of the law. Finally, when the original Lott and Mustard (1997) data set is extended forward in time to encompass a large number of additional law enactments, the results disappear (Ayres and Donohue, 2003). Ultimately, there appears to be little basis for believing that concealed weapons laws have had an appreciable impact on crime.

6) INCREASED USE OF CAPITAL PUNISHMENT

In the 1980s, a total of 117 prisoners were put to death in the United States. That number more than quadrupled to 478 in the 1990s. The debate over the effectiveness of the death penalty as a deterrent has been ongoing for three decades.

Ehrlich (1975, 1977) presented early evidence arguing in favor of a deterrent effect. A number of critics demonstrated the sensitivity of the Ehrlich findings to seemingly minor changes in specification (Forst, Filatov and Klein, 1978; Passell and Taylor, 1977; Leamer, 1983; Cameron, 1994). A series of more recent studies that incorporate data from the 1990s, however, have tended to once again find a deterrent effect (Dezhbakhah, Rubin and Shepherd, 2002; Mocan and Gittings, 2003).

Largely lost in this debate, however, are two important facts (Katz, Levitt and Shustorovich, 2003). First, given the rarity with which executions are carried out in this country and the long delays in doing so, a rational criminal should not be deterred by the threat of execution. Despite increases in capital punishment in recent years, the likelihood of being executed conditional on committing murder is still less than 1 in 200. Even among those on death row, the annual execution rate is only 2 percent, or twice the death rate from accidents and violence among all American men. Among the subsample of individuals engaged in illegal activities, the death rates are likely to be much higher. Levitt and Venkatesh (2000) report a death rate of 7 percent annually for street-level drug sellers in the gang they analyze. Kennedy, Piehl and Braga (1996) estimate violent death rates to be 1–2 percent annually among all gang members in Boston. It is hard to believe the fear of execution would be a driving force in a rational criminal's calculus in modern America. Second, even taking as given very large empirical estimates of the deterrent impact of the death penalty—such as Ehrlich's (1975) classic estimate of seven murders deterred per execution or Mocan and Gittings (2003) estimate of six murders deterred per execution—the observed increase in the death penalty from 14 executions in 1991 to 66 in 2001 would eliminate between 300 and 400 homicides, for a reduction of 1.5 percent in the homicide rate, or less than one-twenty-fifth of the observed decline in the homicide rate over this time period. Moreover, any deterrent effect from such executions cannot explain the decline in other crimes. Given the way the death penalty is currently practiced in the United States, it is extremely unlikely that it exerts significant influence on crime rates.

FOUR FACTORS THAT EXPLAIN THE DECLINE IN CRIME

Having argued that many common explanations for the decline in crime are unlikely to hold the true answers, I now turn to four factors that did, in my reading of the evidence, play a critical role in the crime reduction of the 1990s: the increasing number of police, the skyrocketing number of prisoners, the ebbing of the crack epidemic and legalization of abortion in the 1970s.

1) INCREASES IN THE NUMBER OF POLICE

Police are the first line of defense against crime. More than $60 billion is spent each year on policing. Studies on the connection between the number of police and crime in the 1970s and 1980s, as surveyed by Cameron (1988), tended to find an insignificant or negative correlation, because these studies typically failed to account for the endogeneity problem. The political response to rising crime is to hire more police, so the number of police affect the amount of crime, but the amount of crime also affects the number of police. A number of recent studies have addressed this endogeneity problem with a wide variety of identification strategies and reached the conclusion that more police are associated with reductions in crime.

Marvell and Moody (1996), using a "Granger-causality" approach on panel data for U.S. states and large U.S. cities demonstrate that increases in the number of police are associated with reductions in crime in the future. They estimate elasticities of crime with respect to the number of police of approximately −0.30. Corman and Mocan (2000) use high-frequency time-series data to reduce the endogeneity problem. They argue that the government response to rising crime occurs only with a lag of a number of months, so that endogeneity will be less important when analyzing monthly data than annual data. Using time-series data for New York City, Corman and Mocan find elasticities ranging from −0.29 to −1.385 across crime categories, with a median value of −0.452. Levitt (1997) uses the timing of mayoral and gubernatorial elections as an instrument for police hiring. Politicians disproportionately increase the size of the police force in advance of elections, but elections are unlikely to impact crime directly, making elections a plausible instrumental variable. Using this identification strategy, elasticity estimates range between −0.05 and −1.98 across crime categories, with a median value of −0.79 (although see McCrary, 2002, which points out that correctly computed standard errors make those point estimates statistically insignificant). Levitt (2002) finds much more precisely estimated elasticities of −0.43 to −0.50 when using changes in the number of firefighters as an instrument for changes in the number of police. Firefighters are a logical instrument for police because spending on these two types of protective services tend to be similarly affected by local budgets and preferences, but firefighters are unlikely to exert any direct influence on crime rates.

The number of police officers per capita, which is tracked by the FBI and reported annually in the Uniform Crime Reports, increased by 50,000–60,000 officers, or roughly 14 percent, in the 1990s. Although this increase was greater than in previous decades, it was smaller than might have been expected given the 1994 omnibus crime bill, which, by itself, had promised an extra 100,000 new police officers on the streets. Using an elasticity of crime with respect to the number of police of −0.40, the increase in police between 1991 and 2001 can account for a crime reduction of 5–6 percent across the board. The increase in police can thus explain somewhere between one-fifth and one-tenth of the overall decline in crime.

Whether this investment in police has been a cost-effective approach to reducing crime is a different question. As noted above, annual expenditures on police are approximately $60 billion, so the cost of the 14 percent increase in police (assuming marginal cost is equal to average cost, which is likely to be a reasonable approximation) is $8.4 billion a year. The benefits of crime reduction are more difficult to quantify. The most commonly used estimates of the cost of crime to victims (for example, Miller, Cohen and Rossman, 1993) places the costs of crime at roughly $500 billion annually in the early 1990s. Given the sharp declines in crime, today's estimates would likely be substantially lower—perhaps $400 billion in current dollars. If the increase in police reduced crime by 5–6 percent, then the corresponding benefit of crime reduction is $20–25 billion, well above the estimated cost. Thus, at least to a crude first approximation, the investment in police appears to have been attractive from a cost-benefit perspective.

2) THE RISING PRISON POPULATION

The 1990s was a period of enormous growth in the number of people behind bars, as demonstrated in Figure 3. After many decades of relatively stable imprisonment rates, the prison population began to expand in the mid-1970s. By 2000, more than two million individuals were incarcerated at any point in time, roughly four times the number locked up in 1972. Of that prison population growth, more than half took place in the 1990s. The increase in prisoners can be attributed to a number of factors, the most important of which were the sharp rise in incarceration for drug-related offenses, increased parole revocation and longer sentences for those convicted of crimes (Kuziemko and Levitt, 2003).

The theory linking increased imprisonment to reduced crime works through two channels. First, by locking up offenders, they are removed from the streets and unable to commit further crimes while incarcerated. This reduction in crime is known as the incapacitation effect. The other reason prisons reduce crime is deterrence—the increased threat of punishment induces forward-looking criminals not to commit crimes they otherwise would find attractive. Empirical estimates of the impact of incarceration on crime capture both of these effects.

The evidence linking increased punishment to lower crime rates is very strong. Typical estimates of elasticities of crime with respect to expected punishment range from −.10 to −.40, with estimates of the impact on violent crime generally larger than those for property crime (Marvell and Moody, 1994; Spelman, 1994; Levitt, 1996; Donohue and Siegelman, 1998). But most of these estimates are based on simple correlations. Given the clear endogeneity between crime and imprisonment (when crime is rising, the prison population will also rise if expected punishment per crime is held constant), one might suspect that such correlations estimates would understate the true impact of imprisonment on crime. Indeed,

TABLE 5. SUMMARIZING THE ESTIMATED CONTRIBUTION OF VARIOUS FACTORS TO THE DECLINE IN CRIME IN THE 1990S

	Percentage change in crime that this factor accounts for over the period 1991–2001:			
Factor	Homicide	Violent crime	Property crime	Certainty level of estimated impact
Strong economy	0	0	−2	High
Changing demographics	0	−2	−5	High
Better policing strategies	−1	−1	−1	Low
Gun control laws	0	0	0	Medium
Concealed weapons laws	0	0	0	High
Increased usage of capital punishment	−1.5	0	0	Medium
Increases in the number of police	−5.5	−5.5	−5.5	Medium
Increases in the prison population	−12	−12	−8	High
The decline of crack	−6	−3	0	Low
Legalized abortion	−10	−10	−10	Medium
Total of all factors considered	−36	−33.5	−31.5	
Actual change in UCR reported crime	−43	−34	−29	
Actual change in NCVS victimization	—	50	−53	

Notes: The estimated impacts reported in the table are based on the discussion presented throughout the text of this article. The last column of the table gives my appraisal of how speculative the estimates are for each of the factors considered.

TABLE 6. SUMMARIZING THE ESTIMATED CONTRIBUTION OF VARIOUS FACTORS TO THE DECLINE IN CRIME, 1973–1991

	Percentage change in crime that this factor accounts for over the period 1973–1991:		
Factor	Homicide	Violent crime	Property crime
Strong economy	0	0	2
Changing demographics	4	1	−6
Better policing strategies	0	0	0
Gun control laws	0	0	0
Concealed weapons laws	0	0	0
Increased usage of capital punishment	0	0	0
Increases in the number of police	−3	−3	−3
Increases in the prison population	−35	−35	−24
The rise of crack	16	8	0
Legalized abortion	−2	−2	−4
Total of all factors considered	−20	−31	−35
Actual change in UCR reported crime	5	83	38
Actual change in NCVS victimization	—	2	−32

Notes: The estimated impacts reported in the table are based on the same set of assumptions underlying Table 5, but applied to the observed changes in the factors indicated over the period 1973–1991.

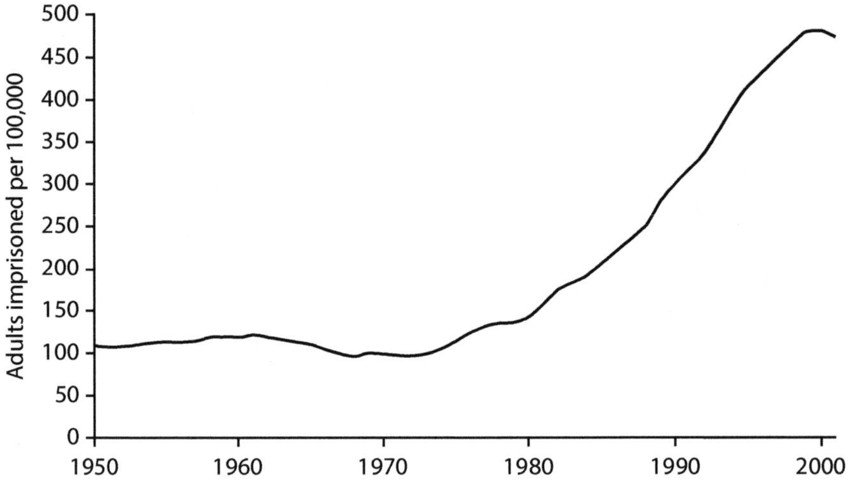

Figure 3. Adult Incarceration Rate, 1950–2001

Levitt (1996) obtains estimates at the high end of the range when using prison overcrowding litigation as an instrument for the size of the prison population. Court decisions in prison overcrowding lawsuits are a plausible instrument for the prison population because these decisions have a large impact on the growth rates in state prison inmates, but there is little reason to believe that such litigation affects crime rates, except through the impact on the number of people incarcerated. Surveys of prison inmates yield estimates of reductions in crimes due to incarceration that are consistent with the econometric studies (Dilulio and Piehl, 1991).

Using an estimate of the elasticity of crime with respect to punishment of –.30 for homicide and violent crime and –.20 for property crime, the increase in incarceration over the 1990s can account for a reduction in crime of approximately 12 percent for the first two categories and 8 percent for property crime, or about one-third of the observed decline in crime.[G]

G In the light of the estimates linking increased incarceration to lower crime, it is perhaps surprising that the rising prison population of the 1980s did not induce a commensurate decline in crime in that period. Among adults, crime rates were in fact steadily falling throughout the 1980s. These declines, however, were masked by sharply rising youth crime in the 1980s. These increases in juvenile crime appear to be due in part to the crack epidemic (discussed below), as well as to falling punishments in the juvenile justice system over this same time period (Levitt, 1998).

Annual expenditures on incarceration total roughly $50 billion annually. Combining this spending figure with the cost of crime to victims and elasticities noted above, expenditures on prisons appear to have benefits that outweigh the direct costs of housing prisoners, subject to three important caveats. First, a dollar spent on prisons yields an estimated crime reduction that is 20 percent less than a dollar spent on police, suggesting that on the margin, substitution toward increased police might be the efficient policy. Second, it seems quite plausible that substantial indirect costs are associated with the current scale of imprisonment, such as the adverse societal implications of imprisoning such a large fraction of young African American males. Finally, given the wide divergence in the frequency and severity of offending across criminals, sharply declining marginal benefits of incarceration are a possibility. In other words, the two-millionth criminal imprisoned is likely to impose a much smaller crime burden on society than the first prisoner. Although the elasticity of crime with respect to imprisonment builds in some declining marginal returns, the actual drop off may be much greater. We do not have good evidence on this point. These caveats suggest that further increases in imprisonment may be less attractive than the naive cost-benefit analysis would suggest.

3) THE RECEDING CRACK EPIDEMIC

Beginning in 1985, the market for crack cocaine grew rapidly. Crack cocaine is produced by heating a mix of powder cocaine and baking soda. The resulting precipitate takes the form of airy nuggets. Extremely small quantities of this compound, when smoked, produce an intense, short-lived high. The emergence of crack cocaine represented an important development both because it facilitated the sale of cocaine by the dose for a retail price of $5–$10 and because the extreme high associated with crack proved to be popular among consumers. Crack frequently sold in open-air markets with youth gangs controlling the retail distribution. The crack cocaine trade proved highly lucrative for gangs, leading to violence as rival gangs competed to sell the drug (Levitt and Venkatesh, 2000).

A number of authors have highlighted the extreme patterns in violence that strongly suggest an important role for crack (most notably, Blumstein and Rosenfeld, 1998; Cook and Laub, 1998). Figure 4, for instance, presents homicide rates by age and race for the period 1976–2000. Beginning in 1985, homicide rates for black males under the age of 25 began a steep ascent, more than tripling in less than a decade, before once again falling dramatically to levels slightly above those of the pre-crack era. In stark contrast, the homicide rates of older black males continued on a long-term secular decline. Young white males also experienced a short-run increase in homicide in the late 1980s, but both the base rates and the increases for whites are much lower. The concentration and timing of the homicide spike among the young black males, which coincides with the rise and fall of the crack market, is suggestive of crack cocaine playing a critical role.

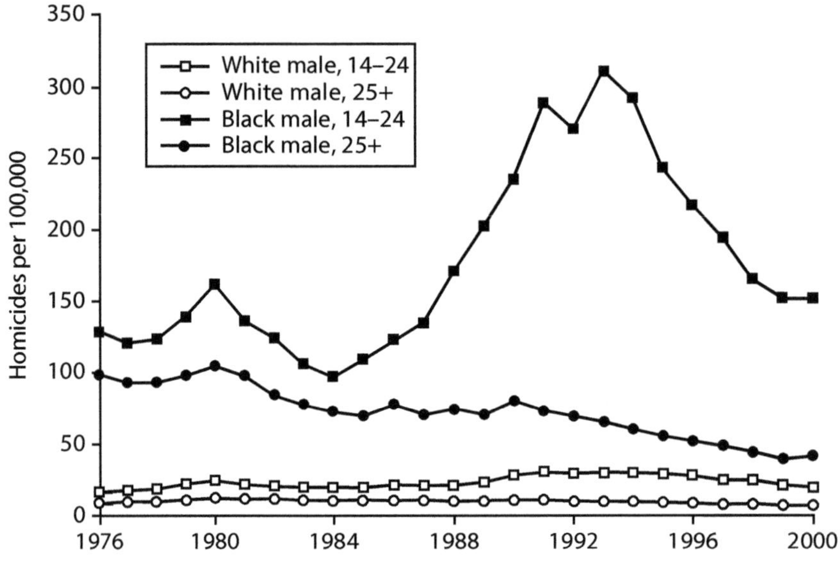

Figure 4. Homicide Offending Rates by Race and Age

Despite the seeming importance of crack in explaining the crime fluctuations since 1985, remarkably little quantitative research on the subject goes beyond pictures like Figure 4. Goldstein, Brownstein, Ryan and Bellucci (1997) carried out in-depth analysis of homicides in New York City in 1988. They classify over 25 percent of these homicides as crack-related. Almost all of these homicides involved crack distribution, rather than homicides induced by the psychopharmological effects of crack or the need of drug users to obtain money. The lack of clear indicators of the importance of crack markets across time and space has made it difficult to study the possible links to crime. I have not seen a study that links the ebbing of the crack epidemic to falling crime, and I am aware of only two studies that attempt to relate the rise of crack cocaine to increased crime. Cork (1999), using city-level data, finds that sharp increases in juvenile crack arrest rates happen coincident with or shortly in advance of similarly sharp increases in juvenile gun homicides. Grogger and Willis (2000) use cocaine-related emergency room visits and a survey of police chiefs in an attempt to identify when crack first enters a city. They then use differences-in-differences between the central city and the surrounding suburbs to identify the impact of crack. They conclude that crime rates in a broad range of categories are elevated about 10 percent in these central cities due to the arrival of crack, although their study is not particularly useful for calculating the contribution of the waning crack epidemic on crime in the 1990s.[H]

Although the research is limited, I nonetheless believe that crack has quite likely played an important role in the decline in homicide in the 1990s, at least for homicide. Figure 4 suggests an alternative strategy for estimating that number, which is probably inferior to Grogger and Willis (2000), but more relevant to the question at hand. Under the assumption that the spike in homicide by young black males is driven primarily by crack, then one can use older black males, young white males or even all people except young black males as potential control groups. Since crack was not wholly confined to young black males, one would expect that any of these estimates would likely represent a lower bound. Alternatively, one can calculate the differences-in-differences between young and old blacks and whites. As crack ebbed from 1991 to 2001, young black males experienced a homicide decline of 48 percent, compared with 30 percent for older black males, 42 percent for young white males and 30 percent for older white males. Depending on which control group one views as most reasonable, the estimated impact of crack on homicides committed by young black males ranges from 6 to 18 percent. Given that young black males commit about one-third of homicides, this translates into a reduction of 2–6 percent in overall homicides in the 1990s due to crack receding. Based on strong prior beliefs and the likelihood that these estimates represent lower bounds, I view the 6 percent number as plausible, which would mean that the decline of crack explains about 15 percent of the fall of homicide. With respect to crimes other than homicide, however, my priors suggest smaller impacts: perhaps 3 percent (10 percent of the observed decline) for violent crime and no impact on property crime.

4) THE LEGALIZATION OF ABORTION

The U.S. Supreme Court's *Roe v. Wade* decision in 1973 may seem like an unlikely source of the decline in crime in the 1990s, but a growing body of evidence suggests an important role for legalized abortion in explaining falling crime rates

---

H Although the Grogger and Willis (2000) identification strategy is clever and the best work to date on the subject, I remain skeptical of the estimates for a number of reasons. First, central cities and suburbs have very different baseline levels of crime, which makes the differences-in-differences approach more difficult to justify (although the authors do their best to address this issue in the paper). Second, the assumption that crack only influenced central cities and not suburbs is unlikely to be accurate. In percentage terms, homicide rates of suburban blacks increased as much as central city blacks during the time period when crack was emerging (the same is true for whites in suburbs and central cities). Thus, the identification in this method is coming primarily from differences in the racial composition of central cities and suburbs, rather than through differences between blacks in cities and suburbs, which would seem to be a more plausible source of variation under the assumption that crack is only in central cities.

two decades later. The underlying theory rests on two premises: 1) unwanted children are at greater risk for crime, and 2) legalized abortion leads to a reduction in the number of unwanted births.

With respect to the first premise, the negative impact of adverse home environments generally on eventual criminality, the evidence is quite clear (Loeber and Stouthamer-Loeber, 1986; Sampson and Laub, 1993). A number of studies have looked at cases of women living in jurisdictions in which governmental approval to have an abortion was required, who sought to have an abortion, but were denied the ability to do so (Dagg, 1991; David, Dytrych, Matejcek and Schuller, 1988). For example, Dagg (1991) reports that these women overwhelmingly kept their babies, rather than giving them up for adoption, but that they often resented the unwanted children. These children who were born because their mothers were denied an abortion were substantially more likely to be involved in crime, even when controlling for the income, age, education and health of the mother.

The evidence for the second premise that legalized abortion leads to a reduction in the number of unwanted births also appears compelling. Levine, Staiger, Kane and Zimmerman (1999) find that legalization of abortion is associated with roughly a 5 percent drop in birthrates. They estimated that the drop in births was roughly twice as great for teenage and nonwhite mothers as it was for the non-teen, white population. Consistent with this finding, the number of children put up for adoption fell dramatically after abortion became legal (Stolley, 1993). Also consistent is the decline in infanticide in the United States that is documented by Sorenson, Wiebe and Berk (2002) following the legalization of abortion. Indeed, other studies have documented improvements in a wide range of outcomes for those born at a time of legalized abortion, including reduced infant mortality, childhood poverty and growing up in a single-parent household (Gruber, Levine and Staiger, 1999), as well as lower rates of drug usage (Charles and Stephens, 2002).

Donohue and Levitt (2001) report a number of pieces of evidence consistent with a causal link between legalized abortion and crime, a hypothesis that to my knowledge was first articulated in Bouza (1990). The five states that allowed abortion in 1970 (three years before *Roe v. Wade*) experienced declines in crime rates earlier than the rest of the nation. States with high and low abortion rates in the 1970s experienced similar crime trends for decades until the first cohorts exposed to legalized abortion reached the high-crime ages around 1990. At that point, the high-abortion states saw dramatic declines in crime relative to the low-abortion states over the next decade. The magnitude of the differences in the crime decline between high- and low-abortion states was over 25 percent for homicide, violent crime and property crime. For instance, homicide fell 25.9 percent in high-abortion states between 1985 and 1997 compared to an *increase* of 4.1 percent in low-abortion states. Panel data estimates confirm the strong negative relationship between lagged abortion and crime. An analysis of arrest rates by age reveal that only arrests of those born after abortion legalization are affected by the law change.

A number of other studies confirm a link between abortion and crime.[I] Reyes (2002) reports somewhat smaller, but still substantial estimates of abortion on crime using U.S. data. Sen (2002) finds a link between abortion and crime in Canadian data that mirrors the U.S. experience. Pop-Eleches (2002) documents the effects of an unexpected abortion ban imposed in Romania in 1966. Extrapolating the conservative estimates of Donohue and Levitt (2001) to cover the period 1991–2000, legalized abortion is associated with a 10 percent reduction in homicide, violent crime and property crime rates, which would account for 25–30 percent of the observed crime decline in the 1990s.

SUMMARIZING THE EVIDENCE

The basic conclusions of the analysis for the 1990s are summarized in Table 5. Each row of the table corresponds to a possible explanatory factor discussed in the paper. The first three columns represent my estimates of the impact that factor has had on homicide, violent crime and property crime, respectively. The final column is my assessment of how speculative the estimates in the row are. The bottom three rows of the table present the estimated cumulative impact of the listed factors and the actual decline in crime according to police reports and victimization surveys. Note that the bottom three rows match up relatively closely, particularly for the reported crime data. The declines in victimization are larger than the predicted declines. For the most part, however, the decline in crime in the 1990s is not a mystery. The observed crime patterns can be reconciled in a straightforward manner with what we know about the factors that influence crime.[J]

I Only one published study, Joyce (2003), has challenged the hypothesis linking abortion and crime, arguing that the link between abortion and crime is not present for the period 1985–1990. In a reply to Joyce, however, Donohue and Levitt (2003) demonstrate that for the precise cohorts that Joyce finds no reduction in crime in 1985–1990, lifetime rates of criminality are indeed reduced. Joyce's results appears to be due to the fact that crack hit the high-abortion states, in particular New York and California, earlier and harder than other states.

J The western European experience lends further support to a causal role of these four factors in the U.S. crime reduction. Unlike the United States, Europe has experienced relatively small increases in police and prison populations. Nor was crack ever a major factor in Europe. Although legal rules regarding abortion vary widely across Europe, no western European country has an abortion rate close to the American rate. Given the absence of these catalysts for crime reduction, it is not surprising Europe has not matched the U.S. crime decline.

EXTENDING THE ANALYSIS TO THE PERIOD 1973–1991

The emphasis of this article is on explaining the decline in crime in the 1990s. It is also interesting, however, to explore the extent to which changes in the set of factors I analyze can explain the observed patterns of crime in earlier periods. The year 1973, when data from the NCVS first becomes available, serves as a logical time period in which to begin the analysis.

Table 6 summarizes the results of the analysis for the period 1973–1991. The structure of Table 6 parallels that of Table 5. The one factor that dominates all others in terms of predicted impact on crime in this earlier period is the growth in the prison population. Between 1973 and 1991, the incarceration rate more than tripled, rising from 96 to 313 inmates per 100,000 residents. By my estimates, that should have reduced violent crime and homicide by over 30 percent and property crime by more than 20 percent. Note that this predicted impact of incarceration is much larger than for the latter period.

The rise of crack cocaine served as a strong counterbalancing force to rising prison populations in this earlier period, especially for homicide. Between 1984 (roughly the date at which crack first appeared) and 1991, homicide rates of young black males nearly doubled. The growth in homicide was much smaller for other groups: 30, 40 and 7 percent increases for older black males, young white males and older white males, respectively. (Between 1973 and 1984, homicide trends across these groups were generally similar.) If homicide rates of black males had mirrored that of the rest of the population between 1984 and 1991, overall homicide rates would have been 16 percent lower in 1991, which I take as a best guess of the impact of crack over this time period. Following the same logic used earlier, the implied impact of crack on violent crime is half as large and the impact on property crime negligible.

The estimated impact of adding more police and legalized abortion is much smaller in the earlier decades than in the 1990s. Between 1973 and 1991, the number of police per capita grew only 7 percent (compared with 14 percent in the 1990s). By the year 1991, the proportion of the population at-risk for criminal activity that had been exposed to abortion *in utero* was still small. Abortion was legalized in most of the country in 1973, implying that abortion exposure was primarily limited to those 17 and under in 1991. Thus, while increased police and abortion exposure worked to reduce crime in the period 1973–1991, these factors played a much more limited role than was the case in the 1990s.

The factors that were unimportant in explaining crime changes in the 1990s generally also had little impact in the early period. The lone exception to this conclusion is the impact of demographic shifts, which served to increase homicide rates in the 1970s and 1980s slightly, but to reduce property crime. The differential impact of demographics on homicide and property crime is driven by two factors. First, between 1973 and 1991, there was a drop in the share of teenagers relative to young adults. Teenagers disproportionately engage in property crime, whereas young adults are at greater risk for homicide and violence. Second, increases in the fraction of the population that is black have a much larger impact on homicide than property crime since the racial gap in homicide rates is much greater than it is for property crime.

In summary, the factors I examine cumulatively predict crime declines between 1973 and 1991 of between 20 and 35 percent. Essentially all of this predicted reduction is attributable to increased incarceration; the other factors largely counterbalance one another. Comparing these predictions to the observed pattern in reported crime (as shown in Table 2 and also presented in the penultimate row of this table), the hypothesized crime declines failed to materialize. For all crime categories, crimes reported to the FBI actually increased between 1973–1991, in some cases sharply (reported violent crime rose 83 percent). Comparing the predictions to NCVS victimization trends, the numbers are much closer. Although a substantial gap between predicted violent crime and victimization remains, the magnitude of the gap is only one-third as large as for reported crime. For property crime, the predicted and actual victimization are nearly identical.

Thus, in contrast to the 1990s, the actual crime experience in the 1973–1991 period is not well explained by the set of factors analyzed in this paper. There appears to be a substantial unexplained rise in crime over the period 1973–1991. Because reported crime and victimization data show so little congruence prior to the 1990s, it is difficult to know the true magnitude of the residual.

CONCLUSIONS

Crime fell sharply and unexpectedly in the 1990s. Four factors appear to explain the drop in crime: increased incarceration, more police, the decline of crack and legalized abortion. Other factors often cited as important factors driving the decline do not appear to have played an important role: the strong economy, changing demographics, innovative policing strategies, gun laws and increased use of capital punishment. In stark contrast, the crime experience between 1973 and 1991 is not well explained by the factors identified in this paper. The real puzzle in my opinion, therefore, is not why crime fell in the 1990s, but why it did not start falling sooner.

An additional conclusion from this analysis is that the simplistic accounts of why crime fell offered by so-called experts to the media can be quite misleading. Of the eight reasons most frequently cited in newspapers, I conclude that only three of the factors are truly important. A fourth factor I consider important, legalized abortion, does not receive a single mention. To the extent that the allocation of resources for reducing crime is influenced by such pronouncements, the money may very well be misspent.

Does the analysis of this paper provide any guidance as to the likely fluctuations in crime rates over the next decade? Given the historical volatility in crime fluctuations and the failure of the factors examined to explain crime prior to the 1990s, the honest answer to that question may be "not much." Nonetheless, the past may shed some light on the future. Of the four factors that I believe to account for much of the recent crime decline, only rising numbers of police officers and legalized abortion are likely to be continuing contributors to future crime declines. Given that the number of police has been growing for four decades, it seems plausible that this trend will continue unless local government budget problems become extreme, contributing perhaps a 5 percent reduction in crime over the next decade. With respect to abortion, a substantial fraction of the criminally active population today was born prior to legalization. As that population continues to age and is replaced by new cohorts born after legalization, some ongoing reductions in crime might be expected, amounting to perhaps a 5–10 percent cumulative crime reduction over the period 2001–2010. Prison populations are unlikely to continue to grow unchecked and have stabilized in recent years. With many states facing difficult fiscal constraints, it would appear likely that prison populations may actually fall over the next decade, giving a slight impetus to crime. Crack-related violence appears to have reached a steady state, with little future crime reduction to be expected through that channel. I see little reason to believe that factors that were not influential on crime in the preceding three decades will be influential in the next ten years.

With respect to new threats looming on the horizon, one potential contributor to increased crime rates that does not appear to be adequately appreciated is the coming of age of so-called "crack babies," and more generally, those who spent their early childhood years in families and neighborhoods ravaged by crack. The evidence regarding the direct physiological impact of exposure to crack *in utero* suggests that adverse effects are short-lived, providing reason for optimism (Frank, Augstyn, Knight, Pell and Zuckerman, 2001). On the other hand, the home environment of such babies, or children raised in crack-afflicted areas more generally, may be quite difficult, inducing a criminogenic effect. Overall, however, it appears that continued crime declines over the next decade remain a realistic possibility, albeit on a scale that is likely to be much more moderate than in the recent past.

I would like to thank Brad De Long, John Donohue, VictorFuchs, Andrei Shleifer, Timothy Taylor and Michael Waldman for their comments and advice on this paper. This research was funded by the National Science Foundation.

Steven D. Levitt is the Alvin H. Baum Professor of Economics, University of Chicago, and Research Fellow, American Bar Foundation, both in Chicago, Illinois. This article was written while the author was a fellow during the 2002–2003 academic year at Center for Advanced Study in the Behavioral Sciences, Stanford University, Stanford, California.

REFERENCES

Allpolitics. 1997. "Clinton Unveils Flurry of Plans to Fight Crime." Available at http:// images.cnn.com/ALLPOLITICS/1997/02/19/clinton.crime/.

Ayres, Ian and John Donohue. 2003. "Shooting Down the 'More Guns, Less Crime' Hypothesis." *Stanford Law Review.* 55:4, pp. 1193–312.

Barclay, Gordon, Cynthia Tavares and Arsa-laan Siddique. 2001. "International Comparisons of Criminal Justice Statistics 1999." *Home Office Statistical Bulletin.* May, 6/01.

Becker, Gary. 1968. "Crime and Punishment: An Economic Approach." *Journal of Political Economy.* 76:2, pp. 169–217.

Bennett, William, John DiIulio and John Walters. 1996. Body Count. New York: Simon and Schuster.

Black, Dan and Daniel Nagin. 1998. "Do 'Right-to-Carry' Laws Deter Violent Crime?" *Journal of Legal Studies.* 27:1, pp. 209–19.

Blumstein, Alfred and Richard Rosenfeld. 1998. "Explaining Recent Trends in U.S. Homicide Rates." *Journal of Criminal Law and Criminology.* 88:4, pp. 1175–216.

Boggess, Scott and John Bound. 1997. "Did Criminal Activity Increase During the 1980s? Comparisons Across Data Sources." *Social Science Quarterly.* 78:3, pp. 725–39.

Bouza, Anthony V. 1990. *The Police Mystique: An Insider's Look at Cops, Crime, and the Criminal Justice System.* New York: Plenum Press.

Britt, Chester, Gary Kleck and David Bordua. 1996. "A Reassessment of the D.C. Gun Law: Some Cautionary Notes on the Use of Interrupted Time Series Designs for Policy Assessment." *Law and Society Review.* 30:2, pp. 361–80.

Callahan, Charles, Frederick Rivera and Thomas Koepsell. 1994. "Money For Guns: Evaluation of the Seattle Gun Buy-Back Program." *Public Health Reports.* 109:4, pp. 472–77.

Cameron, Samuel. 1988. "The Economics of Crime Deterrence: A Survey of Theory and Evidence." *Kyklos.* 41:2, pp. 301–23.

Cameron, Samuel. 1994. "A Review of the Econometric Evidence on the Effect of Capital Punishment." *Journal of Socio-Economics.* Spring/ Summer, 23, pp. 197–214.

Charles, Kerwin Cofi and Melvin Stephens Jr. 2002. "Abortion Legalization and Adolescent Substance Abuse." NBER Working Paper No. 9193.

Cook, Philip and John Laub. 1998. "The Unprecedented Epidemic in Youth Violence," in *Crime and Justice: An Annual Review of Research*. Michael Tonry, ed. Chicago: University of Chicago Press, pp. 26–64.

Cook, Philip and Jens Ludwig. 1996. *Guns in America: Results of a Comprehensive Survey of Gun Ownership and Use*. Washington: Police Foundation.

Cook, Philip, Stephanie Molliconi and Thomas Cole. 1995. "Regulating Gun Markets." *Journal of Criminal Law and Criminology*. 16:1, pp. 59–92.

Cork, Daniel. 1999. "Examining Space-Time Interaction in City-Level Homicide Data: Crack Markets and the Diffusion of Guns Among Youth." *Journal of (Quantitative Criminology*. 15:4, pp. 379–406.

Corman, Hope and H. Naci Mocan. 2000. "A Time-Series Analysis of Crime, Deterrence, and Drug Abuse in New York City." *American Economic Review*. June, 90, pp. 584–604.

Corman, Hope and H. Naci Mocan. 2002. "Carrots, Sticks, and Broken Windows." NBER Working Paper No. 9061.

Dagg, Paul K. 1991. "The Psychological Sequelae of Therapeutic Abortion—Denied and Completed." *American Journal of Psychiatry*. May, 148:5, pp. 578–85.

David, Henry, Zdenek Dytrych, Zdenek Matejcek and Vratislav Schuller. 1988. *Born Unwanted: Developmental Effects of Denied Abortion*. New York: Springer.

Dezhbakhsh, Hashem, Paul Rubin and Joanna Shepherd. 2002. "Does Capital Punishment Have a Deterrent Effect? New Evidence from Post-Moratorium Panel Data." Mimeo, Emory University.

Dilulio, John. 1996. "Help Wanted: Economists, Crime, and Public Policy." *Journal of Economic Perspectives*. Winter, 10, pp. 3–24.

Dilulio, John and Anne Piehl. 1991. "Does Prison Pay? The Stormy National Debate over the Cost-Effectiveness of Imprisonment." *Brookings Review*. Fall, pp. 28–35.

Donohue, John and Steven Levitt. 2001. "Legalized Abortion and Crime." *Quarterly Journal of Economics*. 116:2, pp. 379–420.

Donohue, John and Steven Levitt. 2003. "Further Evidence That Legalized Abortion Lowered Crime: A Reply to Joyce." *Journal of Human Resources*. Forthcoming.

Donohue, John and Peter Siegelman. 1998. "Allocating Resources among Prisons and Social Programs in the Battle against Crime." *Journal of Legal Studies*. 27:1, pp. 1–43.

Duggan, Mark. 2001. "More Guns, More Crime." *Journal of Political Economy*. 109:5, pp. 1086–114.

Ehrlich, Isaac. 1975. "The Deterrent Effect of Capital Punishment: A Question of Life and Death." *American Economic Review*. 65:3, pp. 397–417.

Ehrlich, Isaac. 1977. "Capital Punishment and Deterrence: Some Further Thoughts and Evidence." *Journal of Political Economy*. 85:4, pp. 741–88.

Forst, Brian, Victor Filatov and Lawrence Klein. 1978. "The Deterrent Effect of Capital Punishment: An Assessment of the Estimates," in *Deterrence and Incapacitation: Estimating the Effects of Criminal Sanctions on Crime Rates.* A. Blumstein, D. Nagin and J. Cohen, eds. Washington, D.C.: National Academy of Sciences, pp. 336–60.

Fox, James. 1996. "Trends in Juvenile Violence: A Report to the United States Attorney General on Current and Future Rates of Juvenile Offending." Washington, D.C.: Bureau of Justice Statistics.

Fox, James. 1997. "Trends in Juvenile Violence: An Update." Washington, D.C.: Bureau of Justice Statistics.

Frank, D. A., M. Augstyn, W. G. Knight, T. Pell and B. Zuckerman. 2001. "Growth, Development, and Behavior in Early Childhood Following Prenatal Cocaine Exposure: A Systematic Review." *Journal of the American Medical Association.* 285:12, pp. 1613–625.

Freeman, Richard. 1995. "The Labor Market," in *Crime.* James Q. Wilson and Joan Petersilia, eds. San Francisco: ICS Press, pp. 171–92.

Goldstein, Paul, Henry Brownstein, Patrick Ryan and Patricia Bellucci. 1997. "Crack and Homicide in New York City: A Case Study in the Epidemiology of Violence," in *Crack in America: Demon Drugs and Social Justice.* Craig Reinarman and Harry Levine, eds. Berkeley, Calif.: University of California Press, pp. 113–30.

Gould, Eric, Bruce Weinberg and David Mustard. 1997. "Crime Rates and Local Labor Market Opportunities in the United States: 1979–1991." Working paper.

Grogger, Jeff and Michael Willis. 2000. "The Emergence of Crack Cocaine and the Rise in Urban Crime Rates." *Review of Economics and Statistics.* November, 82, pp. 519–29.

Gruber, Jonathan, Phillip Levine and Douglas Staiger. 1999. "Abortion Legalization and Child Living Circumstances: Who is the 'Marginal Child'?" *Quarterly Journal of Economics.* 114:1, pp. 263–91.

Joyce, Ted. 2003. "Did Legalized Abortion Lower Crime?" *Journal of Human Resources.* Forthcoming.

Katz, Lawrence, Steven Levitt and Ellen Shustorovich. 2003. "Prison Conditions, Capital Punishment, and Deterrence." *American Law and Economics Review.* 5:2, pp. 318–43.

Kennedy, David, Anne Piehl and Anthony Braga. 1996. "Youth Violence in Boston: Gun Markets, Serious Youth Offenders, and a Use Reduction Strategy." *Law and Contemporary Problems.* 59:1, pp. 147–83.

Kessler, Daniel and Steven Levitt. 1999. "Using Sentence Enhancements to Distinguish between Deterrence and Incapacitation." *Journal of Law and Economics.* April, 42, pp. 343–63.

Kuziemko, Ilyana and Steven Levitt. 2003. "An Empirical Analysis of Imprisoning Drug Offenders." *Journal of Public Economics.* Forthcoming.

Leamer, Edward. 1983. "Let's Take the Con out of Econometrics." *American Economic Review*. March, 73:1, pp. 31–43.

Levine, Philip, Douglas Staiger, Thomas Kane and David Zimmerman. 1999. "Roe v. Wade and American Fertility." *American Journal of Public Health*. 89:2, pp. 199–203.

Levitt, Steven. 1996. "The Effect of Prison Population Size on Crime Rates: Evidence from Prison Overcrowding Litigation." (*Quarterly Journal of Economics*. 111:2, pp. 319–52.

Levitt, Steven. 1997. "Using Electoral Cycles in Police Hiring to Estimate the Effect of Police on Crime." *American Economic Review*. 87:3, pp. 270–90.

Levitt, Steven. 1998. 'Juvenile Crime and Punishment." *Journal of Political Economy*. December, 106, pp. 1156–185.

Levitt, Steven. 1999. "The Exaggerated Role of Changing Age Structure in Explaining Aggregate Crime Changes." *Criminology*. August, 37, pp. 537–99.

Levitt, Steven. 2002. "Using Electoral Cycles in Police Hiring to Estimate the Effect of Police on Crime: A Reply." *American Economic Review*. September, 92, pp. 1244–250.

Levitt, Steven and Sudhir Venkatesh. 2000. "An Economic Analysis of a Drug-Selling Gang's Finances." *Quarterly Journal of Economics*. August, 115, pp. 755–89.

Loeber, Rolf and Magda Stouthamer-Loeber. 1986. "Family Factors as Correlates and Predictors of Juvenile Conduct Problems and Delinquency," in *Crime and Justice, An Annual Review of Research, Volume 7*. Michael Tonry and Norval Morris, eds. Chicago: University of Chicago Press, pp. 29–150.

Loftin, Colin, David McDowall, Brian Wiersema and Talbert Cottey. 1991. "Effects of Restrictive Licensing of Handguns on Homicide and Suicide in the District of Columbia." *New England Journal of Medicine*. 325:23, pp. 1615–620.

Los Angeles Police Commission. 1996. "In the Course of Change: The Los Angeles Police Department Five Years after the Christopher Commission." Los Angeles Board of Police Commissioners, May 30.

Lott, John and David Mustard. 1997. "Right-to-Carry Concealed Guns and the Importance of Deterrence." *Journal of Legal Studies*. January, 26, pp. 1–68.

Ludwig, Jens. 1998. "Concealed Gun Carrying Laws and Violent Crime: Evidence from State Panel Data." *International Review of Law and Economics*. September, 18, pp. 239–54.

Ludwig, Jens and Philip Cook. 2000. "Homicide and Suicide Rates Associated with Implementation of the Brady Handgun Violence Prevention Act." *Journal of the American Medical Association*. 284:5, pp. 585–91.

Machin, Stephen and Costas Meghir. 2000. "Crime and Economic Incentives." Unpublished manuscript.

Marvell, Thomas and Carlisle Moody. 1994. "Prison Population Growth and Crime Reduction." *Journal of Quantitative Criminology.* 10:2, pp. 109–40.

Marvell, Thomas and Carlisle Moody. 1996. "Specification Problems, Police Levels, and Crime Rates." *Criminology.* November, 34, pp. 609–46.

McCrary, Justin. 2002. "Do Electoral Cycles in Police Hiring Really Help Us Estimate the Effect of Police on Crime? Comment." *American Economic Review.* September, 92, pp. 1236–243.

Miller, Ted, Mark Cohen and Shelli Rossman. 1993. "Victim Costs of Violent Crime and Resulting Injuries." *Health Affairs.* 12:4, pp. 186–97.

Mocan, Naci and R. Kaj Gittings. 2003. "Getting Off Death Row: Commuted Sentences and the Deterrent Effect of Capital Punishment." *Journal of Law and Economics.* October, Forthcoming.

Passell, Peter and John Taylor. 1977. "The Deterrent Effect of Capital Punishment: Another View." *American Economic Review.* 67:3, pp. 445–51.

Perkins, Craig. 1997. "Age Patterns of Victims of Serious Violent Crime." Department of Justice, Office of Justice Programs, Bureau of Justice Statistics Special Report, NCJ-162031.

Pop-Eleches, Christian. 2002. "The Impact of an Abortion Ban on Socio-Economic Outcomes of Children: Evidence from Romania." Unpublished paper, Columbia University.

Raphael, Stephen and Jens Ludwig. 2003. "Prison Sentence Enhancements: The Case of Project Exile," in *Evaluating Gun Policy: Effects on Crime and Violence.* Jens Ludwig and Philip Cook, eds. Washington, D.C.: Brookings Institution, chapter 7.

Raphael, Stephen and Rudolf Winter-Ebmer. 2001. "Identifying the Effect of Unemployment on Crime." *Journal of Law and Economics.* 44:1, pp. 259–84.

Reuter, Peter and Jenny Mouzos. 2003. "Australia: A Massive Buyback of Low-Risk Guns," in *Evaluating Gun Policy: Effects on Crime and Violence.* Jens Ludwig and Philip Cook, eds. Washington, D.C.: Brookings Institution, chapter 4.

Reyes, Jessica Wolpaw. 2002. "The Impact of Childhood Lead Exposure on Crime." Unpublished paper, Harvard Department of Economics.

Rosenfeld, Richard. 1996. "Gun Buy-Backs: Crime Control or Community Mobilization," in *Under Fire: Gun Buy-Backs, Exchanges and Amnesty Programs.* Martha R. Plotkin, ed. Washington, D.C.: Police Executive Research Forum, pp. 1–28.

Sampson, Robert and John Laub. 1993. *Crime in the Making: Pathways and Turning Points through Life.* Cambridge: Harvard University Press.

Sampson, Robert and Janet Lauritsen. 1997. "Racial and Ethnic Disparities in Crime and Criminal Justice in the United States," in *Crime and Justice: A*

Review of Research, Volume 21. M. Tonry, ed. Chicago: University of Chicago Press, pp. 311–74.

Scientific American. 1996. "Profile: James Alan Fox—Catching a Coming Crime Wave." June, pp. 40–41.

Sen, Anindya. 2002. "Does Increased Abortion Lead to Lower Crime? Evaluating the Relationship between Crime, Abortion, and Fertility." Unpublished paper, University of Waterloo Department of Economics.

Soares, Rodrigo. 1999. "Development, Crime, and Punishment: Accounting for the International Differences in Crime Rates." Unpublished paper, University of Chicago Department of Economics.

Sorenson, Susan, Douglas Wiebe and Richard Berk. 2002. "Legalized Abortion and the Homicide of Young Children: An Empirical Investigation." *Analyses of Social Issues and Public Policy*. 2:1, pp. 239–56.

Spelman, William. 1994. *Criminal Incapacitation*. New York: Plenum Press.

Stolley, K. S. 1993. "Statistics on Adoption in the United States." *The Future of Children: Adoption*. 3:1, pp. 26–42.

Thompson, Cheryl. 1997. "Detailing Failings of D.C. Police Department." *Washington Post*. April 9.

Wilson, James Q. 1985. *Thinking About Crime*. New York: Random House.

Wilson, James Q. 1995. "Crime and Public Policy," in *Crime*. James Q. Wilson and Joan Petersilia, eds. San Francisco: ICS Press, pp. 489–510.

Wright, James and Peter Rossi. 1994. *Armed and Considered Dangerous: A Survey of Felons and Their Firearms*. New York: Aldine de Gruyter.

APPENDIX 1

FATHER GUIDO AND A REVIEW OF PRINCIPLES

Father Guido Sarducci is a fictional character who was part of many Saturday Night Live skits during the 70's, 80's, and 90's. Made famous by comedian Don Novello, the chain-smoking priest with tinted eyeglasses still makes appearances in various settings including the occasional college campus. In fact, there is one particular skit which generally plays well to the college audience.

In this sketch, Father Guido satirically offers a college degree by teaching only what the typical college student remembers five years after they graduate. Per the comedic Priest, this takes all of <u>five minutes</u>! For example, to satisfy the requirements for Business, his advice is simple, "Buy something, and then sell it for more." To earn a credit in Economics, he asks the audience to repeat the following: "Supply and Demand."

We would like to think that Father Guido is mildly off-base in his theory, and that certainly "*our*" college students retain a little more information than his routine portrays. However, I wholeheartedly agree with the good "father" in his decision to include "supply and demand" on the retention list. Accordingly, I have added this short appendix covering various principles as a review for those students who may have been away from economics for a while or have yet to master Father Guido's curriculum.

"CHANGE A PARAMETER, SHIFT A CURVE"

"Change a parameter, shift a curve" is a phrase I heard frequently as an economics student, and one that is exceedingly appropriate in the understanding of most basic economic models including supply and demand. However, before we do any shifting, let us address some basic terminology and define three specific laws.

Variable – a value which changes with respect to another value. For supply and demand, we are talking about the relationship between price and quantity.

Parameter – a value which unites or ties together multiple variables. For supply and demand, these are the "non-price determinants," the items other than price which impact our demand for a good and/or our willingness to supply a good.

Ceteris paribus – a Latin term meaning "all other things held constant." It is used in most economic models to denote that all other parameters remain constant and are unchanged during a period of time.

Law of Demand – As price increases, the quantity demanded will decrease, with all other things being held constant, or *ceteris paribus*. Likewise, as price decreases, the quantity demanded will increase, *ceteris paribus*. (There is an Inverse relationship between P and Qd).

Law of Supply – As price increases, the quantity supplied will increase, *ceteris paribus*. Likewise, as price decreases, the quantity supplied will decrease, *ceteris paribus*. (There is a direct relationship between P and Qs).

Law of Product Equilibrium – In free enterprise, market forces will continuously work via self-interest to direct price and quantity towards that point where demand and supply intersect—the equilibrium point (Qd = Qs).[A]

A FEW GRAPHS

With Price on the vertical axis and Quantity on the horizontal axis, a demand curve will generally yield a downward slope, which displays the inverse relationship noted above. Under this same condition, the supply curve will generally display an upward slope. This confirms the positive relationship generally in place between price and quantity supplied.

Accordingly, the typical demand curve is shown in graph A-1:

A The point of equilibrium implies that the market is "at rest," and quantity demanded is equal to quantity supplied.

Graph A-1: Typical Demand Curve

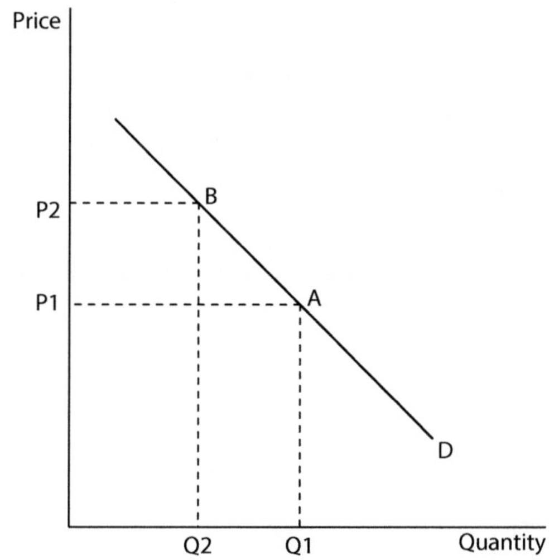

Any movement along this curve, such as movement from point A to point B is deemed to be a "Change in Quantity Demanded." For this graph, more specifically, a decrease in quantity demanded is shown.

A typical supply curve follows in graph A-2:

Graph A-2: Typical Supply Curve

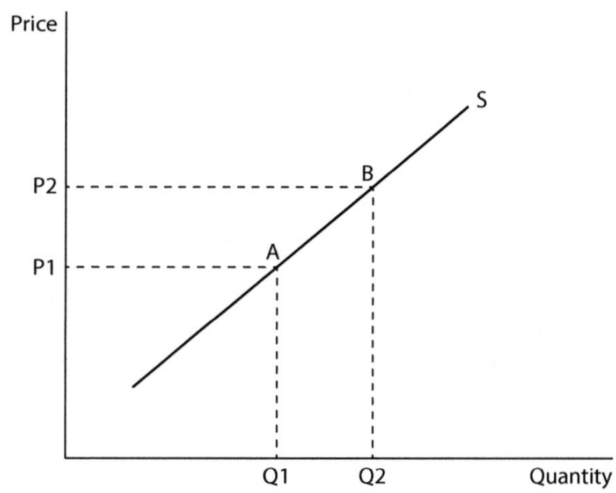

Any movement along this curve, such as movement from point A to point B is deemed to be a "Change in Quantity Supplied." More specifically, an increase in quantity supplied is shown here.

Each of these individual curves (supply and demand) is simply displaying a "willingness" to buy a good, or a "willingness" to sell a good. Putting both curves together in the same graph, we see the equilibrium point which occurs at the intersection of supply and demand in graph A-3.

Graph A-3: Supply / Demand with Equilibrium

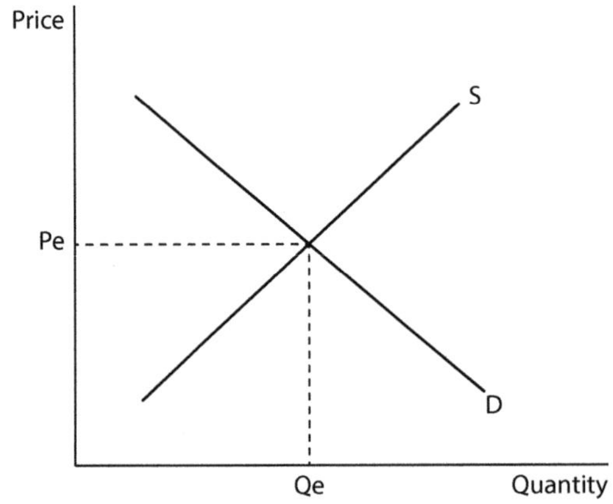

Up to this point, we have only been dealing with the variables of price and quantity, essentially studying what happens to quantity demanded (or supplied) when price changes under a condition of *ceteris paribus*. It is now time to bring parameters into the discussion.

DEMAND SHIFTS

On the demand side, there are several parameters which we frequently label as "non-price determinants." These are entities other than price that impact our overall demand for a good. The typical entries in this discussion would include:

- Taste or Preference[B]
- Income

B Of course our preference is for LESS crime, therefore we behave accordingly.

- Price of related goods[C]
- Expectations
- The number of buyers in a market

So under a condition of *ceteris paribus*, all of the non-price determinants (parameters) listed above will be held constant—they do not change in any way. However, when we allow any of these parameters to change, then we would expect to see the entire demand curve shift leftward (a decrease in demand), or rightward (an increase in demand) depending on the particular parameter movement.

Graph A-4: Increase in Demand

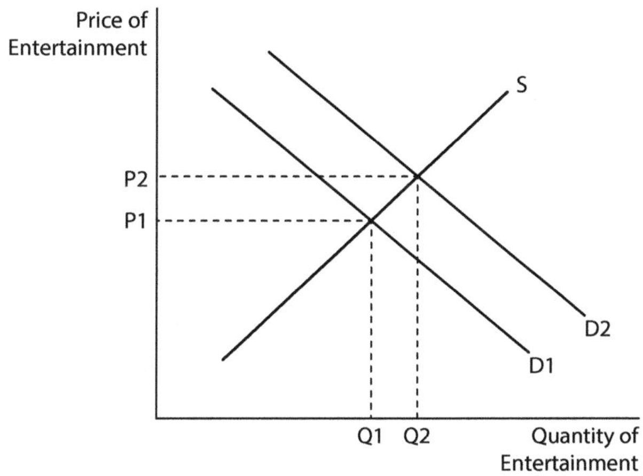

For example, in the market for entertainment (movies, concerts, sporting events, etc.), an increase in income would likely increase our consumption of those items and the demand curve would shift to the right as noted in graph A-4.[D] Equilibrium price has risen, and equilibrium quantity has increased.

C Goods may be complementary, such as bacon and eggs, or competing, such as Coke and Pepsi. For crime, a study of property insurance and security equipment would be appropriate. Some insurance companies may provide a price discount to customers who have security devices in place for their property.

D By definition, if an increase in income results in an increase in the demand for a good, that item is said to be a "normal good."

Certainly criminal activity could also be viewed as a parameter consumers must deal with, likely in the category of "tastes or preferences." For example, if there is an increase in robberies and burglaries in our entertainment district, we would expect that consumers might avoid this area. Therefore, we would expect a decrease in demand at these venues which is displayed by a leftward shift in the demand curve and shown in graph A-5. Equilibrium price would fall and equilibrium quantity would decrease as well.[E]

Graph A-5: Decrease in Demand

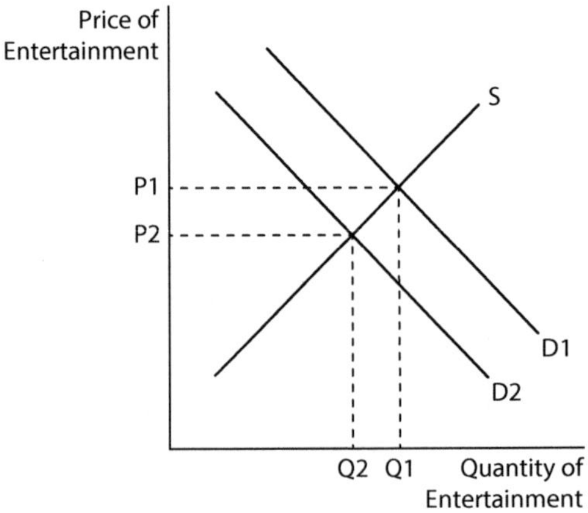

Each of the last two graphs are displaying a "change in demand." Please note that these movements are the result of a parameter change, not the result of change in price.

Students frequently get confused when discussing the following terminology:

E It is likely that the proprietors (the suppliers) in the area would then take steps on their end to lessen criminal activity. This could mean more security personnel, hiring off-duty police officers, perhaps more lighting in parking lots, etc. This increase in cost would ultimately result in a leftward shift of the supply curve.

Change in Quantity Demanded vs. Change in Demand

In reality, this is a simple concept.

A change in quantity demanded for a good describes a movement up or down a specific curve and occurs only with a change in price of that particular good. The curve does NOT shift. *Ceteris paribus* exists.

A change in demand implies that a parameter has changed, there is no *ceteris paribus* condition, and the entire curve has shifted.

SUPPLY SHIFTS

On the supply side, there are also parameters which we label as "non-price determinants." These are items other than price that impact our overall supply of a good. A sample list of these would include the following, with crime areas included for some:

- Price of inputs (labor, materials, security personnel, etc.)
- Government regulations[F]
- Taxes[G]
- Expectations (including expectations of criminal acts)
- Price of other goods
- Technology

Again, when all of these parameters remain unchanged, then the supply curve stays in place and a change in price would simply result in movement up or down the existing supply curve. However, if any of these parameters should change, then the entire supply curve would either shift leftward (a decrease), or rightward (an increase).

For example, in the market for breakfast cereal, what happens if the price of sugar (an input) decreases? As noted in graph A-6, the supply curve would shift to the right denoting an increase in supply. The price of producing the good has declined, and the market is able to produce more product at each level of price. Equilibrium price has fallen and equilibrium quantity has increased.

From a crime perspective, what happens to equilibrium prices in a department store when there is rash of shop lifting and employee theft, and the store must hire more security? As shown in graph A-7, we see a decrease in supply due to the higher costs and a corresponding increase in equilibrium price and decrease in equilibrium quantity.

F As noted in Chapter One, criminal activity yields more government regulations, and higher cost for business.

G Some cities have, at times, introduced a specific "crime tax," generally as part of the sales tax system.

Graph A-6: Increase in Supply

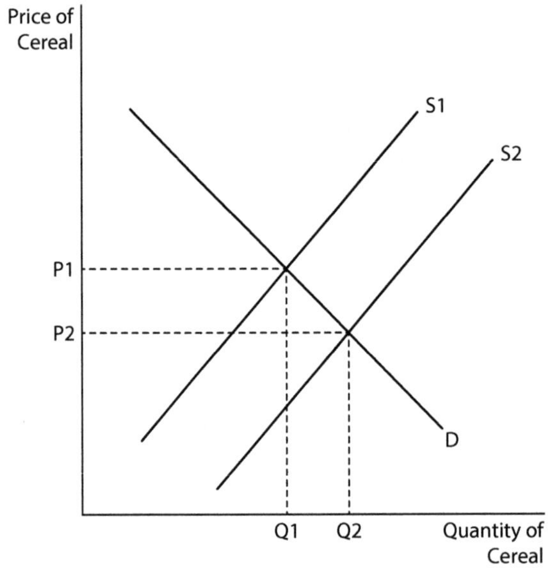

Graph A-7: Decrease in Supply

ELASTICITY

The concept of elasticity is used repeatedly in economic studies and simply involves measuring a variable's sensitivity, or responsiveness, to a change in another variable. For example, with price elasticity of demand, we measure the percentage change in quantity demanded as it relates to a percentage change in price. When price increases, we know that quantity demanded (Qd) decreases. Elasticity again measures responsiveness and quantifies the percentage change that has occurred.

A simple formula for price elasticity of demand follows:

$$\in (d) = \frac{\%\,\Delta\ in\ Quantity\ Demanded}{\%\,\Delta\ in\ Price} = \frac{Q2-Q1}{Q1} \Big/ \frac{P2-P1}{P1}$$

A more accurate assessment of elasticity would use what is known as the "mid-point" formula for each denominator. Accordingly, instead of Q1, the value would be the average of Q1 and Q2, or (Q1 + Q2) / 2. Likewise, rather than P1, we would use the average of P1 and P2, or (P1 + P2) / 2. For our purposes, a simple model will generally suffice, however keep the mid-point formula in mind to facilitate your understanding of elasticity.

The following is a list of common elasticity measurements which you may have studied previously:

Price Elasticity of Demand
Price Elasticity of Supply
Cross-Price Elasticity of Demand
Income Elasticity of Demand
Wealth Elasticity of Demand

Again, numerous uses for this measurement exist in basic economic models, but uses exist for crime studies as well. Consider a couple of examples. First, what is the impact of hiring additional police on the occurrence of property crimes? Using simple analysis, our formula would be as follows where Q = property crimes and P = the number of police:

$$\in (Police) = \frac{\%\,\Delta\ in\ Property\ Crimes}{\%\,\Delta\ in\ Police} = \frac{Q2-Q1}{Q1} \Big/ \frac{P2-P1}{P1}$$

Another application of elasticity measurement would be to determine the change in property values based on a corresponding increase in the crime rate. Of course, the conventional wisdom would be that an increase in crime rates would reduce property values in a given area. The simple formula for such a comparison would be as follows where V = property value, and C = the crime rate:

$$\in (Property\ Value) = \frac{\%\,\Delta\ in\ Property\ Value}{\%\,\Delta\ in\ Crime} = \frac{V2-V1}{V1} \Big/ \frac{C2-C1}{C1}$$

One final point, when using price elasticity of demand, we generally present our results by using absolute values. This simplifies our analysis of determining elastic vs. inelastic tendencies since the relationship between P and Q is generally negative. In this case the following terminology is used to describe the relationships on:

$\in < 1$, Inelastic
$\in > 1$, Elastic
$\in = 1$, Unitary

The terms above are most useful for price elasticities of demand and supply. However, in our study of crime-driven elasticities, determining the positive or negative relationship is relevant and absolute values will not be used. Accordingly, in both of the crime elasticity examples previously mentioned, we would expect to see negative relationships.

APPENDIX 2

DRUG MAPS

Internal Cocaine Movement, FY2008–FY2010

Source: U.S. Department of Justice. Copyright in the Public Domain.

COCAINE

Southern California and South Texas are the primary entry points for cocaine, much of which is transported toward heavily populated cities in the eastern United States. Atlanta, in particular, has emerged over the past several years as a key wholesale cocaine distribution hub. Significant quantities of cocaine smuggled into California transit the Pacific Region for Canada. Colombian and Dominican TCOs still use maritime and commercial air conveyances to smuggle cocaine into New York City and Miami for distribution in some East Coast locales, but cocaine smuggled across the Southwest Border is increasingly being distributed in these markets.

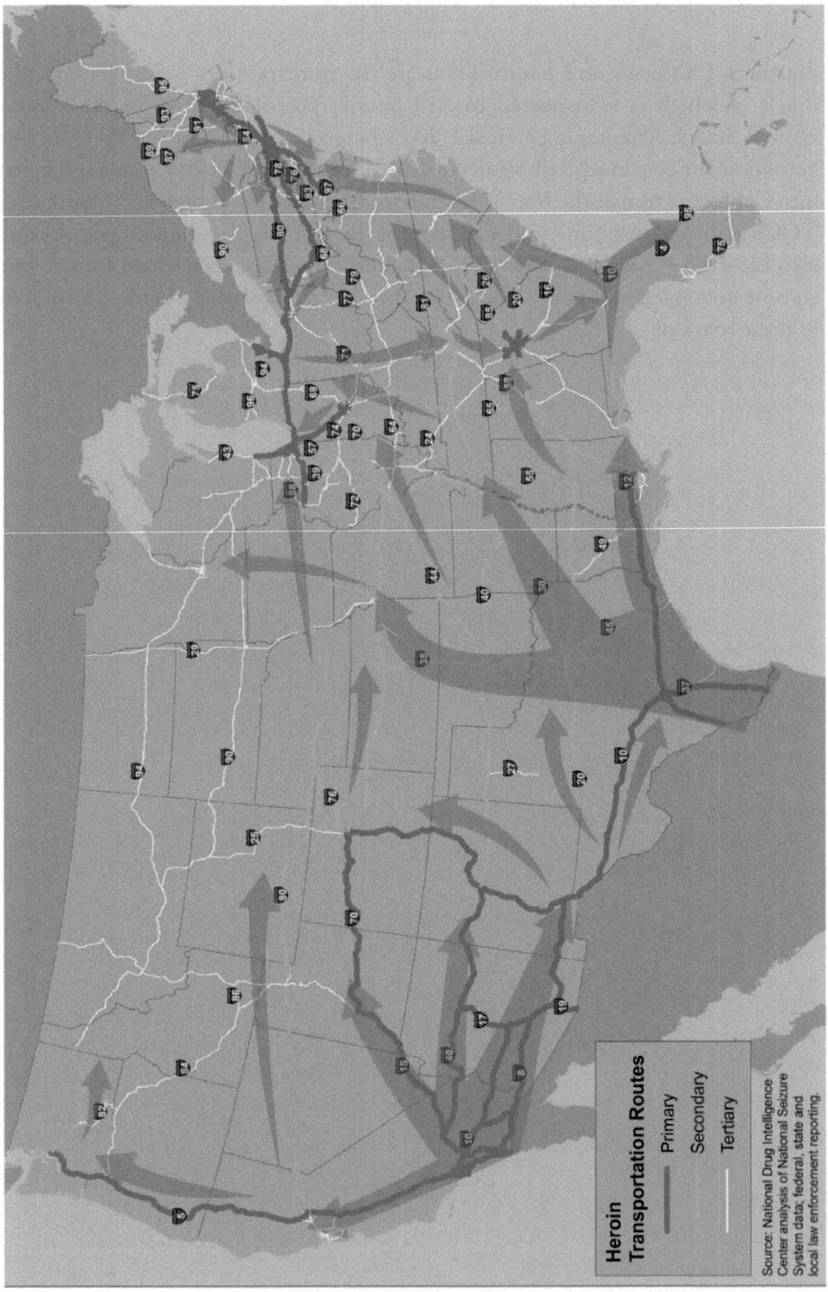

Internal Heroin Movement, FY2008–FY2010

Source: U.S. Department of Justice. Copyright in the Public Domain.

HEROIN

Mexican heroin enters the country primarily at crossing points in southern California, South Texas and, increasingly, Arizona. It is largely destined for western states, where it is preferred, but it is simultaneously being moved to eastern markets on a smaller but increasing scale. An increasing amount of South American heroin available in the United States is smuggled across the Southwest Border and subsequently shipped to East Coast markets, where it is sold along with South American heroin smuggled into Chicago, New York City, Miami, and other East Coast metropolitan areas by Colombian and Dominican TCOs.

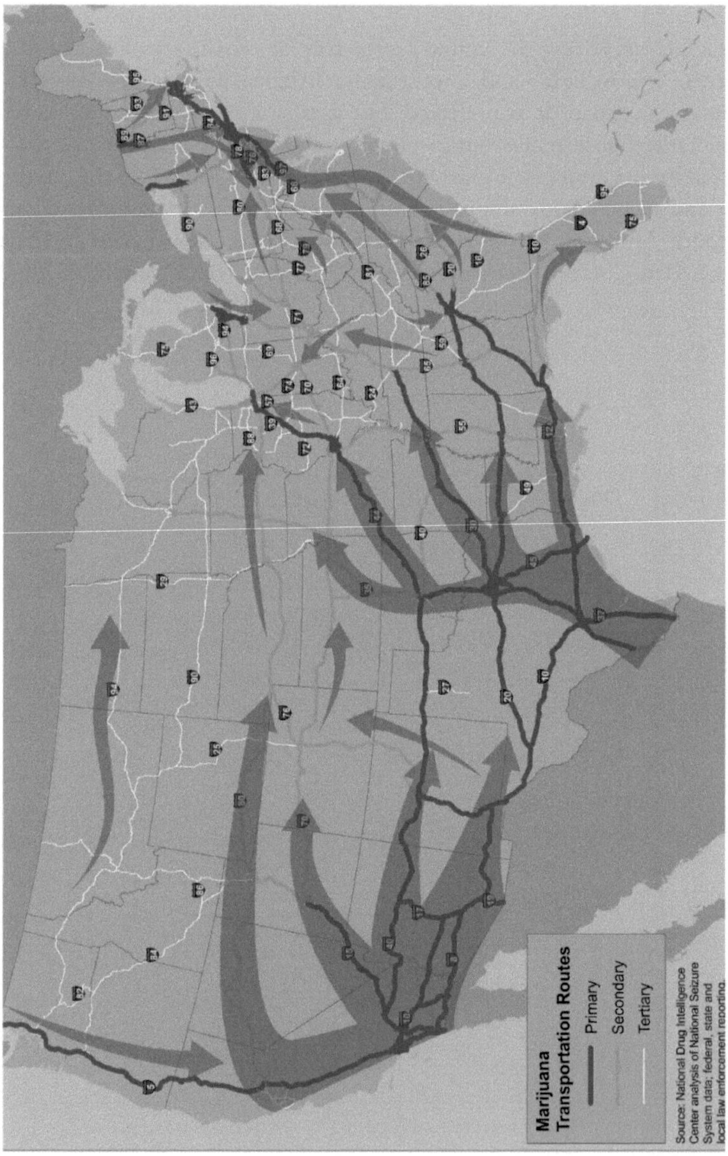

Internal Marijuana Movement, FY2008–FY2010

Source: U.S. Department of Justice. Copyright in the Public Domain.

MARIJUANA

Mexico-produced marijuana enters the country primarily in Arizona, California, and South Texas, while high-potency Canadian marijuana is usually smuggled through and between POEs in Washington, Michigan, New York, and Vermont. Both forms of marijuana are distributed nationally. Similarly, domestically produced marijuana is transported from grow sites to markets nationwide.

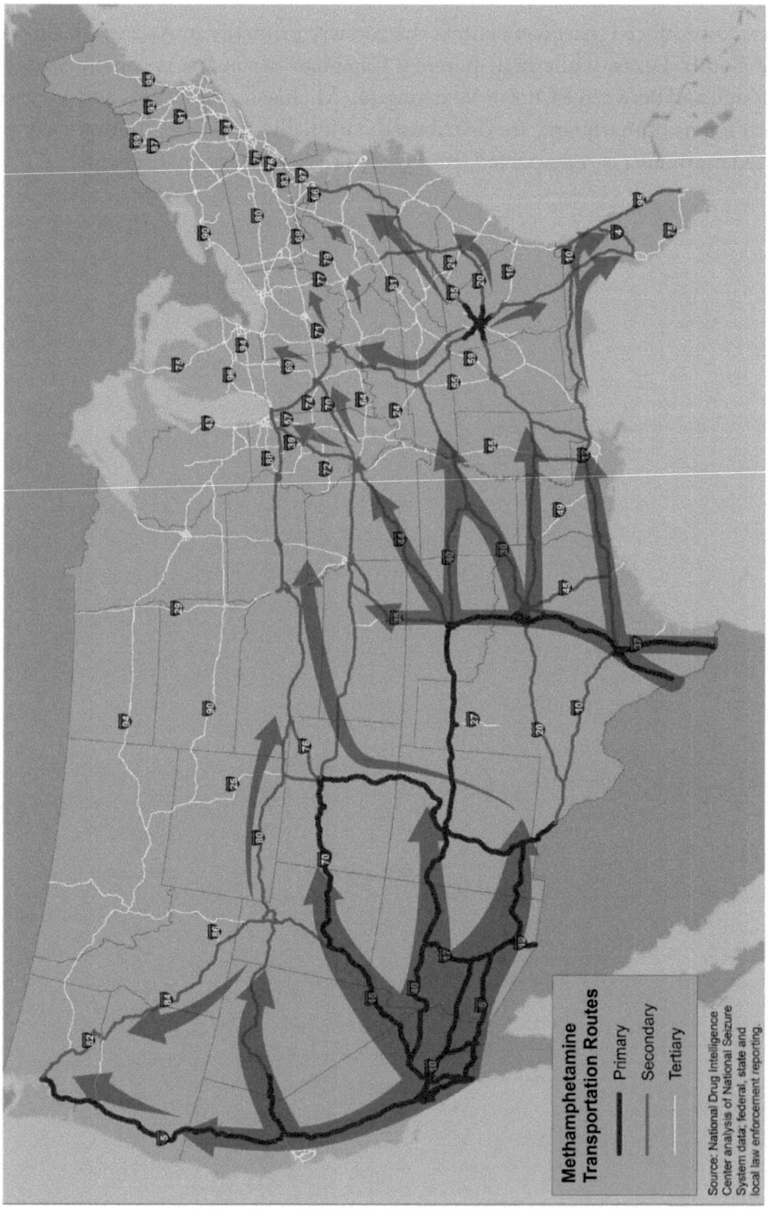

Internal Methamphetamine Movement, FY2008–FY2010

Source: U.S. Department of Justice. Copyright in the Public Domain.

METHAMPHETAMINE

Mexican traffickers supply drug markets in the western United States and, on a smaller but increasing scale, eastern drug markets with methamphetamine smuggled over the Southwest Border and with methamphetamine produced in California superlabs.[A] Methamphetamine crossing the Southwest Border is primarily smuggled through California and South Texas POEs. Methamphetamine produced in small domestic laboratory operations is usually consumed locally.

A Superlabs are laboratories capable of producing 10 or more pounds of methamphetamine in a single production cycle.

APPENDIX 3

CHAPTER 9 SOLUTIONS

QUESTION #1

Crime Prevention Units	Total Benefits	Marginal Benefits	Total Costs	Marginal Costs	Total Net Benefits
1	30,000	30,000	8,000	8,000	22,000
2	55,000	25,000	18,500	10,500	36,500
3	75,000	20,000	31,000	12,500	44,000
4	90,000	15,000	46,000	15,000	44,000
5	102,000	12,000	66,000	20,000	36,000
6	107,000	5,000	88,000	22,000	19,000
7	110,000	3,000	116,000	28,000	−6,000

The most efficient allocation would be to employ four (4) units of crime prevention since this is the level at which MB = MC.

QUESTION #2

Marginal Benefits from Crime Prevention Services Provided			
Units	Police	SWAT Eqp	Patrol Cars
1	$70,000	$60,000	$64,000
2	60,000	45,000	56,000
3	50,000	30,000	48,000
4	40,000	15,000	40,000
5	30,000	12,000	32,000
6	20,000	10,000	24,000
7	10,000	5,000	16,000
8	5,000	2,500	8,000

The cost of each policeman is $10,000; the cost of each unit of SWAT equipment is $5,000; and the cost of each patrol car is $8,000. The budget is $118,000.

The goal is to satisfy the equimarginal principle while also satisfying the budget requirement.

Solution: It is necessary to calculate MB/MC for each facet of the budget and for each unit.

For example, Police would show the following:
Unit 1 - $70K/$10K = 7
Unit 2 - $60K/$10K = 6
Unit 3 - $50K/$10K = 5
Etc...

SWAT Eqp
Unit 1 - $60K/$5K = 12
Unit 2 - $45K/$5K = 9
Unit 3 - $30K/$5K = 6
Etc...

Patrol Car
Unit 1 - $64K/$8K = 8
Unit 2 - $56K/$8K = 7
Unit 3 - $48K/$8K = 6
Etc...

Following this pattern we are able to determine that there are 3 combinations where the equimarginal principle is satisfied and MB = MC for all 3 expenditure categories. These are found where MB/MC = 2, 3, and 6.

(2) MB = MC with 6 police, 6 SWAT, 7 cars
(3) MB = MC with 5 police, 4 SWAT, 6 cars
(6) MB = MC with 2 police, 3 SWAT, 3 cars

While all of the above satisfy the equimarginal principle, only one combination fits the budget of $118,000.

Option (3)
5 Police × $10K = $50K
4 SWAT × $5K = $20K
6 Cars × $8K = $48K
Total Expenditure = $118K

Therefore:
How many units of each should be employed?
5 Police
4 SWAT
6 Patrol Cars

9 781516 512980

Printed by Libri Plureos GmbH in Hamburg,
Germany